*The*Election

A Voters' Guide
Edited by David McKie

FOURTH ESTATE · *London*

First published in Great Britain in 1992 by
Fourth Estate Limited
289 Westbourne Grove
London W11 2QA

SOURCES:

Many facts and figures in this book are based on Central Statistical Office publications, especially the Annual Abstract of Statistics, Social Trends, Economic Trends, and UK National Accounts (the Blue Book). Tables given here are often simplified versions of the full CSO tables which must be consulted for full details. Compilation of the section on the Government record has also relied heavily on Keesing's Contemporary Archives (Longman) and its successor for domestic events, Keesing's UK Record. (The fact that Keesing's has been divided since 1988 into two publications, one largely domestic and the other mainly concerned with events abroad, appears not yet to have penetrated some otherwise useful public libraries). Among books on the Thatcher years, Hugo Young's One of Us (Macmillan), Dennis Kavanagh's Thatcherism and British Politics (Oxford) and The Thatcher Effect, edited by Kavanagh and Anthony Seldon, The Thatcher Years by John Cole (BBC Books) and The Thatcher Decade, by Peter Riddell (Blackwell) have been especially useful, as have successive volumes of the Annual Register (Longman). British Political Facts 1900-1985 by David and Gareth Butler and the psephological works of the late F.W.S.Craig, especially British Electoral Facts and successive editions of Britain Votes, are indispensable, as is Robert Waller's guide to parliamentary constituencies, The Almanac of British Politics (Routledge). Grateful thanks also to the London Borough of Sutton, whose central library is a glorious rebuke to all who disparage local government. D.McK.

A catalogue record for this book is available from the British Library

ISBN 1-85702-041-3

Designed and produced by PDU, The Guardian, London.
Editor: Clive Graham-Ranger. **Picture research:** Michelle Emery. **Additional research** by Helen Martin, Chief Librarian, and the staff of The Guardian Library, London, Helen Birch, Sean O'Neill and Jo Swain.
Computer research on the marginal constituencies by Gordon McKie. With thanks for advice and guidance to Paul Brown, John Carvel, Malcolm Dean, James Erlichman, David Fairhall, John Gittings, Daniel John, Victor Keegan and Martin Linton.
Photographs by: Martin Argles, Stephen Berkauer, Howard Davies, Ted Ditchburn, EPA, Malcolm Gilson, Jorgensen, Don McPhee, Frank Martin, Press Association, REX Features, Kenneth Saunders, Denis Thorpe, Garry Weaser, E. Hamilton-West.

Printed in Great Britain by Cambridge University Press

*The*Election

CONTENTS

PREFACE

by David McKie

HAD Margaret Thatcher collected just four more votes in her leadership contest with Michael Heseltine in November 1990, enough to win on the first ballot, the coming general election might have looked very different. Then we would plainly have been offered more of the same: more of the cheerful certainty with which she applied her conclusions, disdainful of consensus; more of the radical fervour with which in 12 eventful years she had turned the world upside down, rewriting the language of politics in ways which opponents found themselves driven to follow.

But she lost: and the picture now is a little different. John Major wasted no time in signalling that Britain was under new management. Thatcher's flagship, the poll tax, was brutally scuttled. The line on Europe began to stress the positive: working with our partners was pleasure rather than pain. So perhaps there is not quite the sense there was that a fourth Conservative victory would set Thatcher's achievements in stone, even perhaps confirm that Britain had now become an ideological fiefdom.

Yet this is still in a sense a watershed election. Since 1979 the parties of opposition have been transformed. Neil Kinnock's Labour, ready to work with the market, forswearing nationalisation, embracing Europe, no longer committed to unilateral disarmament, bears startlingly little resemblance to the party he took over in 1983. The Liberals have gone after more than a century; so, virtually, has the SDP which lit up the sky in the early eighties. Now, under Paddy Ashdown, the Liberal Democrats, in their rigorous organisation and their market approach, still carry the stamp of the old Alliance. If after all these epic adjustments to the facts of electoral life these parties fail yet again to topple the Conservatives, if the Conservatives achieve what no party has managed for more than 150 years and win a fourth term, the sense may grow that Britain is moving towards a system like Japan's, where the changes which matter occur within the ruling party rather than through alternation.

Thatcher's long incumbency has left its mark. Past Guardian guides would balance a government's record against that of its predecessors. After more than a decade of Conservative supremacy, what Labour did in 1974-79 seems distant history. This guide attempts to record as many facts and figures as possible about events in the Conservative years, above all on the issues on which elections principally turn. The economy first, since most voters make their choice on the basis of how they feel about their own and their families' well-being and what they expect for the future; but also the NHS and public education, on which most British families, even after years of privatisation, inescapably depend; and Europe, the issue which in 1989-90 convulsed the Conservative party and finished Thatcher. The course of the coming Parliament ought to determine whether, as both Major and Kinnock in their different ways intend, we can steer a course which, while making us good Europeans, does not subordinate Britain's decision-making on economic and political issues to the mightier power of Brussels; or whether, as some believe and the Liberal Democrats hope, we are now irrevocably set on a road to an ultimate federal Europe. ●

FIGHTER TO THE BITTER END

by Hugo Young

This was Hugo Young's judgment on the Thatcher years in The Guardian on November 23 1991, immediately after she resigned

SHE died as she had lived, in battle. It was a quite extraordinary end, but it was in keeping with everything important that had gone before. There was a continuity, not only in the texture of these events but in the circumstances of her long life and swift demise. Just as her triumphs were often rooted in her zest for combat, her refusal to listen to advice and her unwillingness to admit that she could be wrong, so were these the sources of her last predicament. It was a shocking way to go. Having lost no vote either in the Commons or in the country, she was disposed of by the unaccountable will of fewer than 400 politicians. There has been nothing like it in the democratic era: no verdict apparently so perverse and unprovoked delivered by a governing party against a leader upon whom it had fawned and under whom it had grown fat for so many years. For the first time in her prime ministership she provoked, while not requesting it, the human sympathy reserved for a helpless creature at bay.

The symmetry between the life and the death was nonetheless compelling. She was a leader of lurid style and risky habits, especially in the field of personal relations. Aggressive to a fault, she spent years scorning not only consensual policies but the consensual demeanour. With nerveless indifference she was prepared to see the larger portion of her friends as well as enemies in high places depart the scene as a direct result of her behaviour. A kind of rough justice therefore now prevails, its chemistry precipitated by the most enduring victim of these gross habits, Geoffrey Howe. She who lived by fire and insult cannot wholly complain when the ultimate insult repays her.

These have, however, been years which will not be forgotten. The Callaghan era might never have happened, for all that history makes of it. This is less true of the periods to which Harold Wilson and Ted Heath attach their names, but what lingers from them is notoriety more than fame. The Thatcher era will be different, and nowhere more so than in the evidence it offers that personality can be the single most potent contributor to the pattern of events. For better or for worse, this will truly and for ever be called the Thatcher Era. She was a creature of her times. Although as a minister under Heath she showed an opportunist's capacity to find different times congenial enough, from the mid-seventies she rode the tide of liberal economics and anti-state politics with missionary aplomb. All reformers need circumstance to coincide with destiny. But character matters more. There were things that happened which would, I think, have happened quite differently without her.

The first was the Falklands war. It was a prime example of ignorance lending pellucid clarity to her judgment. Surrounded by ministers who knew what war was and dithered at its prospect, she understood what the soldiers wanted and shirked neither the military consequences nor the huge political risk. This quality of leadership was justly rewarded. She was, in fact, especially decisive in war. But for her it is also certain that American bombers would not have been allowed to bomb Libya from British bases in April 1986. Second, the conduct of economic policy in the early eighties owed almost everything to her moral fibre. It may have been a failed policy, but it was hers. She was committed to an economic theory and committed against caring about unemployment. When Lord Hailsham told her, in July 1981, that she would destroy the Conservative party as surely as Herbert Hoover led the Republicans to oblivion in 1932, she spat in his eye. Blood on the streets did not alarm her, any more than the hunger strikes of Irish republicans.

She worried not about the jobless masses but the looted shopkeepers: a priority which, nine years later, no longer seems odd. Third, and for similar reasons, the dethroning of trade union power would have taken a different course without her. She acted out with utmost seriousness the anti-union prejudice which most other Tories shared but which many of them had not dared to deploy. Public sector strife, culminating with the 1984 coal strike, was permitted to drag out as ministers watched with almost sadistic fascination. But without the gimlet eye of their leader upon them, their record suggests that they would have lost their nerve well before the desired "demonstration effect", which always mattered more than the money, was achieved.

With Thatcher's fourth irreplaceable mark, we reach more contentious territory: the region, in fact, where hubris and nemesis met, to ultimately catastrophic effect. Few qualified observers doubt that her stand against the European Community achieved a British advantage in the early days, which was unavailable by other means. By asking reasonable questions in a wholly unreasonable manner, she secured more of "our money" from Brussels. A decade's combative diplomacy made for a quite different British presence. Arguably, we counted for more in Europe, in a constructive as well as a critical role, in 1985 than in 1975.

But here came the first source of her trouble. The mark in Brussels became a kind of curse at home. Her elemental convictions about nationhood and sovereignty were not accompanied by sufficient sensitivity to the opposite feelings of significant colleagues. The issue became an emblem of the style as well as the content at the heart of her difficulties. It showed the falsity of this distinction. With this leader the style was the woman.

In modified form, this was also a key to her fifth uniquely personal policy, the poll tax. It is the only tax in the western world to have grown more out of character than reason. Reason, expressed by Nigel Lawson and the Treasury, said that it would be unjust, unworkable and insupportably expensive. Character, sticking blindly with a Thatcher commitment dating from 1974, insisted that it must go forward and enlisted another consistent trait of these years: the incautious support of enough meekly compliant ministers for the blame to be spread.

Policies alone, however, do not define the place she will take in the annals. The intangibles are perhaps more important and may ensure her name a longer life. Thatcherism embodies a style and a set of values that will take a long time to disappear from British politics. At the least, they may be the model of what to avoid: a memory studiously honoured in the breach.

More likely, they will endure as an example others cannot neglect. As a leader she developed abrasiveness into an art form. She despised, above all, consensus: the goal of most other leaders but not her. She inveighed against it with as much vigour in November 1990 as she did before she became Prime Minister. As a leader, also, she needed to know everything and often seemed to do so. There never has been a leader better briefed, with readier riposte, more scornfully deployed against her ignorant enemies.

This most formidable capacity was some kind of answer to those who charged her, accurately, with an insatiable desire to interfere in every minister's business. Hardly anything moved in Whitehall without her approval; but for hardly anything that happened did she fail to have a detailed justification.

As well as this ambiguous virtue, however, she had a plainer one. She did not want to be liked. The least likeable of all leaders, according to consistent opinion poll findings, she nonetheless won three elections. In this she was wholly admirable. She did not pander to the people. They often remarked on how much they hated her, even as they admitted to a grudging respect. This quality, often described as a flaw, did much for the moral calibre of our politics. No other leader in our time will be so easily willing to resist the desire to please.

She used this harshness to establish a more prominent British presence in the world. Of all the people bewildered by what has happened, none flounder in deeper astonishment than foreigners from all over. For most of them, Thatcher has given a passable imitation of the Britannia whom, during the Falklands crisis, she shamelessly sought to personify. Before her, a series of faceless men, usually in grey suits, trod the global stage pretending to an influence that depended on past glories some of them could almost remember. They rarely said or did anything worthy of report on an inside page of the New York Times.

In the Thatcher era, the image has been different. During the Reagan years, moreover, image proclaimed more than mere appearance. Through their shared ideology they formed a society for the mutual support of leaders determined to abolish the post-war consensus. Thatcher visited Washington often, was invariably feted and, if an election year loomed, notionally drafted for the presidency. She had a very special relationship with Reagan and, as the interlocutor with Gorbachev, a special role in the dialogues that led to the ending of the Cold War. When that ice age broke up, moreover, it was to the Thatcher model that many of the newly free countries consciously turned for guidance on the modalities of the free market. All this was due to her personal charisma.

Evangelism and showmanship captured the East, beginning in the Soviet Union shortly before the 1987 election. Some might say that the influence thereby attained was a little illusory. How could a weak country like Britain aspire to change the world, especially when Germany was becoming so manifestly the dominant power in Europe? But that only serves to reinforce the Thatcherite point: without her peculiar quality of conviction, proclaimed by her flamboyant personality, Britain would have continued to take its proper place as an increasingly obscure island off the shore of north-west Europe. It is a destination her successor will have the greatest difficulty in avoiding.

So this defiance of historic inevitability may not last long. There were signs of it waning well before she fell. Developments in both East and West were beginning to relegate Britain back into the second division. What the lady spoke for at home, on the other hand, could expect a longer shelf-life. It was here that her legacy had the best chance of surviving, if only because some of it has been seized by her opponents.

She spoke, as no one else did, for business Britain. Not just for big business but, rather more, for small. Detached from her party she could easily have been a latter-day Poujadist, expressing the economic but also the social philosophy of little England shopkeeping, the world from which she sprang. In entrepreneurship, in profit making, in market place success she saw the unalterable foundations of a successful society. She never deviated from this philosophy and never tired of reiterating its principles as a guide to human conduct. Doubted and even despised during the seventies, these at last became conventional wisdom in the eighties.

Nowhere was this more apparent than in the Labour party. Arguably, the new model Labour party was one of her most important creations. She often vowed not to leave politics until socialism had been scorched off the face of Britain. One more term, she thought, would finally disabuse the country as well as Labour that the politics of the Left had any future. A pseudo-socialist Labour party has outlived her, which she will deeply regret.

But the pseudery is significant. In Labour rhetoric, the virtues of private property and market economics have replaced ancient promises to dismantle the integument of the capitalist system. By departing, Thatcher may have removed Kinnock's favoured electoral target: but she leaves an Opposition more anxious to retain than remove a fair amount of what she has done. She also leaves an economy which, for all their railing, is stronger than it was. Maybe the most history will be able to say is that the Thatcher years decelerated British decline. Certainly the wondrous miracle, which many of her former colleagues saluted in their obituary tributes to her, takes its reality only from an assumption about where we might have been without the medicine she administered in the early eighties. Even so, if we grant that all political careers can be said to end in failure, with their grand promises never fully achieved, this career can nonetheless be deemed less of a failure than many.

There were failures, however. And of many candidates for consideration, two strike me as reaching close to the heart of the Thatcher experience. Just as there were positive events unattainable without her, so were there the negative: specific and peculiar to her person. The first concerned her attitude to government itself, and in particular the role of the state. She came into power determined to reduce it. Most Tory leaders have said as much, but she was the first who announced a conscious mission to abandon paternalist aspirations and get government, even benign government, off the people's backs.

This was conspicuously accomplished in only one department, that of state ownership. The privatising of productive business will never be reversed, and even the utilities are likely, under Labour, to remain outside the public sector. Selling council houses and cheap shares in gas switched a few million people from being clients of Labour, as the party of public ownership, to being clients of the capitalist party.

But elsewhere, Thatcher's relations with the state ended in confusion, futility and contradiction. One of her famous axioms was that no such thing as society existed: which postulated a dismantling of the collective institutions that propped society up. This did not happen. Her sentiment was widely regarded with ridicule and incomprehension, even among her own supporters. Society at large showed no inclination to assume its disintegrating role. Quite the opposite. Every test of public opinion showed that in her didactic task, of persuading people that the state could not be benign, she failed.

But her actions, also, countermanded her ambition. In the Thatcher years there were many ways in which the central state grew more not less powerful. In finance, in education, in health services, the edicts of the centre overrode those of the locality, as local government was substantially undermined. She was aware of this paradox. In schools and hospitals, a democracy. But in the end the gentlemen, and un-gentlewoman, in Whitehall knew best. We were told that this would be temporary. But a government of different temper will find a lot of new instruments in place, the tools of Thatcher's rage for action, conveniently ready for use.

Add to this the curtailments of civil liberties, notably concerning free expression, and the Thatcher era will go down as one in which state power increased. All Tory leaders have been vigilant in defence of the state's policing power. But a special edge was given this trait by this prime minister. Her own experience with terrorism, always an underrated aspect of her psyche, made her an unyielding proponent of media curbs which touched upon it. She was in favour of freedom as long as it could be paid for: a less reliable defender of the intangible liberties of man.

The second failure concerned, in the end, her view of what political leaders were meant to be and do. She had the vices of her virtues. This was what finally engulfed her.

She was strong, but put excessive weight on strength. She accumulated more personal power than any peacetime prime minister in history; and in that guise will interest the constitutional historians for many years. But she saw too little value in the art of compromise. Leadership, for her, was equated too often with the satisfaction of her will. How often, when challenged with being over-mighty, did she deride the notion of a leader who gave precedence to other virtues than strength. She was a conviction politician, but too often scorned the reasoned statement of different convictions, sometimes by her closest colleagues. Argument she relished, as long as she won, but persuasion she neglected. Give-and-take and the other techniques of sweet reason were alien to her nature. This made for abrasive and often decisive government, but it was fatally disabling for any kind of collective leadership.

For surprisingly many years, it wrought no lasting damage. The collective was willing to put up with its uncomradely supremo because, essentially, it was persuaded that she was going in the right direction: and in any case she kept on winning elections.

But at the end, over Europe, the one issue on which the Conservative party was prepared to concede that it is most seriously divided, the obedience of the collective beginning with Nigel Lawson and ending with Geoffrey Howe, and not forgetting the destruction wrought by Nicholas Ridley in between, collapsed.

Behind Thatcher's political method lay a vision of Britain but, perhaps more importantly, also a vision of herself. Although insecurity was never entirely missing from her make-up, it coexisted with even less confidence in the ability of anyone else to do what she was doing.

For many years she thought she was irreplaceable, a judgment which grew not out of simple vanity so much as an assessment of Britain's plight and what she could contribute to it. When the tumbrils began to roll, she still could not credit that this verdict was being revised. Nor could many other people.

But finally the system, which says that this is cabinet and not prime ministerial government, reacted. There was a point beyond which it declined to be flouted. This point was identified by an age-old reflex: the perception that an election was about to be lost and power surrendered to the other side. No fear exceeds that of politicians faced with the loss of office, not even fear of the avenging virago across the table. So in the end, in a drama whose outlandishness aptly reflected the years before, she went. ●

THE CHOICES IN THE WORLD AFTER THATCHER

by Michael White

L ANDING in Britain in the New Year of 1992 a visitor from Mars would have found the political parties in a state of relative quiescence. It was the product of over-exhaustion during the previous summer and autumn when their frenetic conduct had been consistent with the experienced inter-galactic observer's idea of a general election campaign among the Caucasian earthlings.

Once John Major had let it be known – during Labour's October conference – that he was not going to risk the November election which might end his premiership after less than a year, the attention of the political classes wavered, leaving ministers to focus on getting safely through the Maastricht summit on December 9-10. What Chancellor Lamont called the "green shoots" of economic revival seemed as fragile as ever and the November inflation figure showed a renewed rise, from 3.7 to 4.3 per cent. Owner-occupied housing repossessions, many in sensitive Tory marginals where upwardly mobile Thatcherites had bought their own homes and then lost their jobs, edged towards the 90,000 a year mark. Such economic indicators had persuaded some Conservatives that they dare not risk soldiering on to the spring of 1992 in case things got worse. Another such calculation was the prospect of Margaret Thatcher leading a split over Europe and what she had called "the conveyor belt to federalism."

In the circumstances government supporters, many of them supposed Euro-sceptics, reacted with more jubilation than the small print warranted when Mr Major emerged from two days of hard negotiations at Maastricht to claim "game, set and match" in his dealings with the EC 11. What he had achieved was an opt-out clause for Britain not to join a single European currency should one emerge in the late nineties, but he did so at the cost of allowing the 11 to impose a timetable for the necessary economic convergence, no later than 1999. The odds on it actually happening had shortened as a result of Maastricht, though few purported to notice immediately. As for the hated social policies, which Mr Major feared would impose fresh employment costs and labour regulations on his newly-liberated free market economy, the 11 would go their own way on that too, leaving Britain to offer inward investors a low wage and, some said, low skill economy on the edge of Europe.

It would take many months to see whether the underlying momentum of the Maastricht text would vindicate Whitehall's belief in the looser model for political co-operation and its free enterprise economic claims against what it perjoratively dubbed the corporatist and federalist continental model. Meanwhile Mr Major enjoyed a tactical political triumph, "a chief whip's triumph" as Opposition critics put it, good only in the short term. Maastricht had interrupted much agitated discussion of the great upheavals which had occurred on the domestic political scene since the election of 1987, though these might have seemed trivial in comparison with events in the wider world – events that saw Mikhail Gorbachev's Soviet Union crumble at spectacular speed as Christmas approached. Thatcher's Britain could plausibly claim to have played a useful role in these developments, albeit more modest than the Iron Lady usually claimed. In reality the four years had seen the country, like its banknotes, shrink still further.

In such rapidly changing circumstances it was obvious even before the abortive coup against Gorbachev in Moscow started its momentous chain reaction, that the post-Cold War order contained both danger and opportunity for order or disorder in equal measure. The Gulf crisis had brutally demonstrated it. So did the civil war in Yugoslavia and the looming chaos and hunger in Russia. Would the imminent British election explore such themes as the wider Europe, the global environmental threat or the role of a revitalised UN? The short answer was "no, of course not", though populist echoes like European immigration policy or the Queen's head on the currency would be exploited as appropriate. Its chief significance might be to make a gut-conservative electorate even more cautious with its vote.

More surprising to a visiting Martian who had also witnessed the 1987 contest might have been the sense that both major parties – to his credit Ashdown, the third party leader, pretended no such thing – were inviting the voters to accept that their opponents had not changed at all; that Thatcherism, blue in tooth and claw, still held sway in Major's Cabinet room; and, alternatively, that Kinnock's Labour party remained one in which the left-wing impulse to nationalise and unionise, to tax and control from the centre was as strong as its nuclear pacifism. The impulse looked like an amputated limb whose loss the central nervous system had not yet acknowledged.

In truth all three parties had changed a great deal. In a disciplined and orderly retreat from Clause Four socialism, Labour had finally done in its 1987-89 Policy Review what the German SPD did at Bad Godesberg in 1959 and abandoned "the commanding heights of the economy" to something vaguely but fashionably identified as the social market. Trailing by up to 27 per cent in the previous year's polls, the Tories had acted with even more ruthless despatch. They had struck down one of the most successful leaders they had ever had and hurled upon the funeral pyre her most conspicuously disastrous policy, the poll tax. They had also moved, belatedly, to address quality concerns in public education, the welfare state and transport and had adopted a less hectoring tone. For his part, Ashdown had pulled together the disparate elements of the ruptured Alliance, the seriousness of the SDP and some old-fashioned Liberal idealism to create a platoon capable of taking up to 20 per cent of the vote in some polls, thus sounding alarm bells among the Tories. Labour took comfort from Ashdown's push to the right in economic matters, but in a close election he would remain an important wild card, as would the resurgent Scots Nationalists and the Ulster Unionists. When the Tories lost their 18th consecutive byelection in November, the Lib-Dem victory in prosperous Kincardine and Deeside gave them more MPs in Scotland than Mr Major.

For the Government to disown the economic legacy of the Thatcher-Lawson high noon was a good deal more awkward than Labour's shifts. The recession which arrived in late 1990 proved deeper and longer than any of them had dared admit. Ministers had to find ways to convince the voters that the worst was over and that the underlying strength of the economy, wrought by the Thatcher Revolution, would enable it to bounce back. Labour needed to establish the heartfelt conviction that the recession ravaging the white-collar service industries of the south, as its predecessor in 1980-81 had ravaged the industrial North and Midlands, was as inevitable as the unregulated consumer-led boom which preceded it, and that events had now shown that for all the claims that had been made for it, there had been no economic miracle at all.

Just as Labour gave the Government little credit for taming union follies or nurturing would-be entrepreneurs, so ministers refused to acknowledge that Labour would not resort to high tax-ing, high spending policies in office: "15 pence on income tax" duly became the preposterous tabloid charge. In fact Kinnock and Smith's desire for respectability in the nation's boardrooms was such that they had abandoned macro-economic levers to an extent which alarmed many thoughtful supporters. Supply-side socialism (a rare sighting of the -ism word) would create a sta-ble framework in which business and industry could flourish, providing the necessary infrastruc-ture and skilled workforce. Whereas devaluation had always been a Labour instinct, British mem-bership of the European Exchange Rate Mechanism (ERM) was to be a discipline for managers and workers alike under Chancellor Smith as much as Chancellor Lamont. Labour remained a cheap money party, preferring lower interest rates and tighter credit management, but that was all. The implicit pessimism about what was possible had a distinctly post-modern ring, prompt-ing some to argue that the job might as well be left to proper Tories.

Love her or hate her, Thatcher had always been a great drama. With its lingering sense of national self-importance the British public had perversely enjoyed her international fame and tur-bulent certainties. Now that she had indicated a willingness to surrender to a peerage, politics were already duller. That seemed to fit the public mood, too. The pace of politicking might become more frenetic as if to make up for the loss. And if Labour's solid 40-42 per cent or so of the vote through most of 1991 proved unmovable, the re-emergence of dirty tricks and Sun "exclusives" would be a barometer of Conservative jumpiness. This would be the first election since 1974 in which the result was fundamentally in doubt.

But how to achieve the supposedly classless society – that was something else. Labour remained much more pro-active, willing to use the state's muscle, if not the Treasury's money, to bring improvements in health care, education and training, environmental protection and (flavour of the month) public transport, all for the benefit of – key word – the consumer.

Both opposition parties tried to talk of citizenship as a network of interests and obligations wider than the family-based individualism of Margaret ("there is no such thing as society") Thatcher. Even in her prime Thatcher had nursed contradictory impulses about the role of the state – whose power she proved very capable of deploying when it suited her. Yet despite the rhetoric of the Citizen's Charter, the Big Idea in Major's election plans, Clarke calmly Balkanised the school system into the hands of a fragile coalition dominated by parents and governors; and Waldegrave played Chairman Mao to the NHS, inflicting permanent managerial upheaval on the only surviving institution of the Attlee age which public affection had saved from destruction. Whenever the voters were worried about the NHS (and Labour's Robin Cook kept them perma-nently anxious) government popularity fell.

British Rail and British Coal enjoyed no such affection and were due to be privatised, though the policy no longer aroused much outrage either way. Profits and management salaries in the ex-state sector did. In the struggle to devise cost-effective mechanisms to improve the quality of life and public services, the Tory chairman, Chris Patten, seemed aware of the limits of market individualism and its nineties embodiment, the traffic jam. But his early enthusiasm for German "social solidarity" and other quasi-paternalistic language from the Christian Democrat lexicon was quickly squashed by the right. Yet, despite all the threats and speeches, by Christmas it was obvious that the Thatcher-Ridley-Tebbit threat to raise their banner against the Belgian Empire was a bluff Mr Major could safely call.

The public, ever agnostic, was content that Major had changed Thatcher's tone over Europe. The details they were prepared to take on trust, unless Labour could prove – as it tried too – that all the Prime Minister had done was keep his party together at the expense of rights for British employees and economic opportunites for British firms. In reality, though Mr Major could hardly admit it, the two front benches now differed chiefly over the pace and emphasis of European integration. Despite the sound and fury Europe too was part of the dull new consensus. All of which suggested that the election would, as usual, be fought in the nation's wallet, with the imperatives of television technology giving a still more presidential flavour to the campaigns of the party leaders.

Thatcher had learned the hard way the limits of presidential pretensions in the British system. But the Gulf war and the summit circuit had shown Major their advantages. Personalities would be important to this election on both sides for two very good reasons. First there was the absence of a great ideological divide. Second, and more important was the fact that each side thought its opponents' leader was vulnerable.

A predictable election agenda then? Perhaps. But deeper trends about the way Britain would be governed in the 21st century were at work, and neither electoral indifference nor thundering leaders in the quality press would deflect them for long. They were best exemplified by the evident reluctance of this reforming Conservative Government at Westminster to concede political power, "sovereignty" in the trite phrase, either up the line to the European Council or Commission, its Parliament, Court or Bank, or down the line to elected local authorities – long emasculated by this regime. Even if Labour's conversion to modernity was as skin deep as the Tories liked to claim when they were not claiming it was a reversion to Wilsonism, the party had thought longer and harder than the Conservative think tanks on constitutional reform and its package reflected serious concerns. The Liberal Democrats had always been in favour of sweeping changes of which they could hope to be beneficiaries and did so in the name of a spurious fairness.

Fairness might not be the issue, but if the type of legislative and executive functions now being envisaged to run post-Thatcherite Britain as well as the new Europe were more technocratic and less declaratory, then it seemed probable that a different type of public official might be needed and different types of arrangements for government. Some thoughtful Tories acknowledged that their ministers were at a disadvantage when negotiating in Brussels because the instinct to stitch up an ad hoc coalition around any given table came naturally to politicians schooled in the politics of proportional representation as it did not to first-past-the-post Anglo-Saxons. The logic which made Labour accept PR for its proposed Scottish Assembly still had a long way to run on both sides of election day if the campaign proved tight; electoral reform could yet be the decisive card to play.

It was all a far cry from the high Victorian politics of Trollope or the uncomplicated welfarism of Bevin or Bevan. But with their Cellnet phones and opinion pollsters, their continental holidays and their hard-won numeracy, so were the politicians of the nineties – and their electoral masters. ●

MAN OF JELLY OR GREAT GREY HOPE?

by Andrew Rawnsley

EVEN now people still ask the question. Who is John Major? Is the Conservative party's great grey hope a nice guy who accidentally came first? Or is he a rather cleverer, rather more ruthless man who has used his outward agreeableness to disguise an inward ambition which propelled him to the top at such astonishing speed? As he struggles to keep himself there, the real John Major may have to stand up. In an election it will no longer be enough to be not Margaret Thatcher, or not Neil Kinnock.

Major is untried in the field of electoral combat. He was heavily managed during the contest for the Tory party leadership, most of which took place behind closed doors rather than on television screens. During the last election campaign he was only a junior minister at the Department of Social Security, just a glint in Thatcher's eye.

Colleagues may testify to a steel girder up his backbone, but the outer shell is brittle. Like most politicians, he is insecure; unlike most, he lets it show. It reveals itself as a virtue in his engaging line in self-deprecation. "Well," he said, addressing his first Cabinet as Prime Minister, "who would have believed it?" It comes out in that slightly lost look he still conveys in public appearances, as if he had only agreed to try out the job for a bet. More perilously for a prime minister fighting an election, it also shows in a vulnerability verging on a paranoia about examination of his roots or criticism of himself. As Chancellor he spent the day before he presented his first Budget clambering around the attic searching for documents which would disprove a newspaper story that his father had not been a trapeze artist.

The Freudian School of political analysis would trace that insecurity back to his celebrated childhood, and it would not be entirely wrong. As a symbol of meritocratic upward mobility, the Brixton Boy to Downing Street story is a Tory adman's dream. But the Major childhood nightmare was his family's downward plunge from middle-class gentility to two rooms in a Coldharbour Lane tenement block as his father lost all his money and then his sight. The one subject that has ever inflamed him to public passion is inflation – "I loathe it" – because he blames it for Major Major's disastrous foray into the garden gnome business. He has been overheard saying of one Cabinet colleague with a taste for high public spending and conspicuous private consumption: "The trouble with that man is that he has simply no idea of what it is like to run out of money before the end of the week."

This makes it less surprising that somebody with such a colourful early life could turn out so famously grey. If your father had been a peripatetic circus acrobat, the most different thing you could do is run away and join a troupe of accountants. He has anchored the rest of his life in solid, uninspired things, like the bank manager's home in Huntingdon, and the habits of the compulsively cautious. Whether or not he really does tuck his shirt into his underpants, which only Norma can know, he looks as though he would.

The cricketers he admires most, like Cyril Washbrook who got a CBE in his first honours list, were batsmen who totted up runs gradually and without self-advertisement. The politicians he despises are Macmillan – a sham, and Disraeli – an adventurer. The taste for brown sauce and red jelly is a genuine expression of his lack of pretension. "When I am prime minister," he once told Jeffrey Archer, "I shall have jelly all the time."

That greyness is, though, only skin-deep. Like many people who rarely lose their temper, when he does it is ferocious and prolonged. The schoolboy who had to wear a secondhand blazer bought from the School Fund, and the young man who was failed as a bus conductor and drew the dole, learnt early lessons in humiliation. It was one of the reasons he dropped out of school; the other was "the unthinking obedience people wanted". There is a deep well of resentment about being "pushed around", which comes up as a loathing for bureaucrats in public services and Oxbridge snobs in his own party. "Being patronised sends me into orbit." It also helps explain why he has been so resistant to the efforts of the image-makers to put some colour into his public persona. "People think he has only one tie," Norma once said. "But he has six. They're just all the same."

The dislike of authority has always been combined with a desire, even a desperation, to be liked by everybody. He turned it into a skill by ingratiating himself with a series of powerful patrons who could further his career. Former colleagues at Standard Chartered bank remember him as a consummate "office politician". The winning of friends in high places and influencing people in unusual ones helped him to create a circle of admirers wide enough to range from Ken Livingstone to Margaret Thatcher, though she has now let her subscription to the Major fan club lapse. That skill lubricated his astonishing rise up the greasy pole. When, on a narrow-boat holiday in 1987, it first occurred to him that he might lead his party, he determined to allow as many colleagues as possible to believe he shared their views. Entirely nice guys don't even think about coming first, let alone plotting how to get there.

His favourite self-description is: "I am a practical politician." The brief and aborted attempt to project him as a philosopher-king was a flop. There are Majorettes, but it is unlikely there will ever be Majorism. In so much as it has been practised, it has been a mixture of pragmatism and plagiarism; giving Thatcherism a social conscience while trying to rob the Opposition of good ideas. His self-proclaimed guru is Iain Macleod, who died suddenly in 1970 after just a month as Ted Heath's Chancellor. He has adopted Macleod's credo of a Conservatism that is economically competitive, but socially compassionate, while classless. But Macleod is both a convenient and a vague icon, because his early death means it is difficult to tell what much of that would have amounted to in practice.

Citizen John's Charter was less a Big Idea and more his personality made policy. A compulsion for making the trains run on time is not confined to nature's Mussolinis, of whom he is not one. It is also the preoccupation of the sort of man he looks most like: the chap strap-hanging on the 7.15 from suburbia into Waterloo muttering that the train has been delayed "for a very considerable period of time".

There is not much sense of intellectual daring in clearing the roads of cones. He has "tremendous" private convictions, according to Norma, who is baffled that "he can't do it on television". Yet that struggle to articulate a bigger vision is not just because his rhetorical range is so small.

During his brief and unhappy time as Foreign secretary he told some of his civil servants that he preferred the Treasury because there you dealt with numbers, while at the Foreign Office you had to grapple with concepts.

Always playing for safety can be risky; being all things to all voters may, at the crunch, mean you are nothing to any of them. A prime minister, particularly leading his party into an election, has to be confident in conflict as well as conciliation. And as he prepares for that campaign, Mr Major of all people knows how ruthlessly Conservatives dispose of leaders who are perceived to have failed. Win, and they will crown him in ovations. Lose, and he could sink without trace as rapidly as he rose. ●

LAST CHANCE FOR THE
LARYNX OF FIRE

by Andrew Rawnsley

OF all the party leaders Neil Kinnock has the most experience of fighting elections, and losing them. He has been leader of the Opposition for a record-breaking eight years – each day of that gruelling haul etched into his once affable and ebullient face. The voters are intimately acquainted with every wrinkle and wart, a familiarity which has bred mixed feelings. No honest opponent questions the courage, will and resilience it has taken to rescue Labour from the edge of self-destruction and drag it back to the brink of power. His weaknesses are equally well advertised, as much by colleagues as by opponents. The dangerously short fuse. The perilously long sentences. The temptation, particularly whenever he is lured on to the personally treacherous terrain of economics, for too many words to chase too little meaning. It is a measure of his achievement – but also of his problem – that having made Labour fit to govern, the Labour leader will spend much of the coming campaign still being asked to prove that he is personally fit to lead a government.

Though his project has been to forge a new model Labour with added appeal to the middle-classes, its leader was fashioned from impeccably working-class Welsh stock: the son of a valley miner, forced out of the pit by injury, and a district nurse, who could probably have been a doctor if the opportunity had existed. Their only child is always at his most moving when speaking of himself as an offspring of the opportunities of the welfare state. "Why am I the first Kinnock in a thousand generations to go to university? Were all my predecessors thick?" That question has reverberated back in the repeated jibes about what he achieved at university in Cardiff, which was not much: a "pass" degree in industrial relations at the second attempt. Contemporaries always put it down to a failure of application, rather than intelligence. The young Kinnock was more interested in chasing rugby balls, the presidency of the Students' Union and Glenys. The stabs about his intelligence have been less sharp since the Conservatives elected themselves a leader who has difficulties adding up his number of O levels, but they still wound. Gathered with some members of his shadow team one night the mood turned a little morose. "Of course," said Kinnock, "you've all got bloody doctorates."

A more illuminating part of his educational record is the score he achieved for the Certificate of Education: a 'C' for theory, but an 'A' for practice. He has never been a theorist. Writing is the sort of thing Roy Hattersley does. Nor has Kinnock been a happy guest around the dinner tables of the nattering classes, preferring a Chinese takeaway and a video at home in Ealing with his family or close friends. His socialism is more felt than thought; his politics less from the head, more from the gut – particularly the sickening feeling that he might never walk over the threshold of Number 10.

He can suffer deep gloom, sometimes called Celtic. After the 1987 election defeat there was one low point, personally and in the polls, after which he thought about throwing it all in. But the 1987 campaign showed the flipside – his ability to kick-start himself with an emotional adrenalin that makes him a formidable operator on the stump. Though he has abandoned many of the convictions of his hero-mentors, Nye Bevan and Michael Foot, he retains their oratorical ability to command a crowd, particularly of the converted. He has no contemporary equal at the political walkabout. "Hiya kid, how are you?" he plunges in, slapping backs and pumping hands, playing the old politician's trick of greeting complete strangers as if they were long lost friends, yet playing it so well that you momentarily forget that it is a trick. The wiser Tories will recall that the Kinnock Factor can be a positive one. The Hugh Hudson-directed Larynx of Fire party political blockbuster drew votes to Labour at the last election – albeit far from enough.

Just as he has reconstructed his party, he has also had to reinvent himself, closing down parts of his character and beliefs, in the effort to demonstrate that he has both the brains and the bottom to occupy Number 10. The innately genial, impulsively jokey, freckle-faced favourite of the Left, a much-loved turn at the party conference revues, has been stifled in the search for grizzled gravitas. He has recast and power-dressed himself as the jut-jawed, cuff-shooting Prime Minister-in-waiting, as buttoned-down as his double-breasted suits. Labour's successive policy reviews have been accompanied by a series of personal acts of apostasy. The unilateralist gave up his CND card and took to wearing quasi-regimental ties. The back-bench rebel who voted against the Civil List is eager to boast of dining with Her Majesty at Windsor. The miner's son who turned down an invitation to address the Durham Miners' Gala is the host of £500-a-plate, fund-raising dinners in Mayfair.

On the other hand, Labour's wooing of the City has not taken him to many boardrooms. Uncomfortable there, others have been left to lead the Prawn Cocktail Offensive. It remains beyond his comprehension that some of his Labour colleagues can be on drinking terms with Tories. That showed in his undisguised and unwise glee at the fall of Thatcher. It may have been honest, but it came over as churlishly unstatesmanlike.

So long at the rough end of her reinforced handbag inevitably meant that he has learnt some lessons in leadership from her, some of them perhaps too well. There is a similar way of asking whether colleagues are "one of us?", and of regarding those who are not wholly for him in everything as utterly against him. The succession of Major has been a double-edged sword. The Labour leader finds it easier to joust with him on equal terms, something a son of the valleys found difficult against a long-serving woman prime minister. Yet Kinnock also finds that, having remade some of himself in her imperial image of resoluteness and endurance, he now faces a fresh Tory leader who plays the common man.

The Labour leader has tried to purge himself of the Prolix Tendency. It is not true that he does not work hard enough on his public performances. If anything, he tries too hard, insisting on drafting most speeches himself, rather than letting other hands make it lighter listening. His most hazardous terrain, and it will be no more so than during an election, is the radio and television interview. That is where he has so often been, in his own word, "kebabed" by his own verbosity.

If he does get the keys to Downing Street at his second attempt he will be the only 20th-century prime minister apart from Ramsay MacDonald to have had no previous ministerial experience.

There will be a steep learning curve for both man and country. If he fails, it is almost certain that he will never be given a third chance to take this test. ●

LABOUR'S SEARCH FOR A LASTING UNITY

By Patrick Wintour

JAMES Callaghan, Labour's last Prime Minister, signed off his memoirs Time And Chance by writing: "The Labour government of 1974 to 1979 had nothing to be ashamed of, and a great deal to be proud of." It was a lofty judgment that did not entirely accord with the assessment of the Labour rank and file. The 1979 election defeat and the Callaghan government's record, indeed, ushered in an era of vicious blood-letting even more recriminatory than the inquest that followed the downfall of the Wilson government in 1970. Labour MPs were accused by a resurgent Left, led by Tony Benn, of abandoning the party's programme and principles. Pictures of "The Guilty Men" were published in Tribune.

But the Left in Opposition did not just plan to recriminate, or redraft the party programme. No profit could be gained from repeating the experience of 1970-74 when the party in Opposition, under Benn's chairmanship of the home policy committee of the party's National Executive, devised a radical socialist programme only to see it ignored in government on Wilson's return to power in 1974. This time the principal goal had to be to ensure Labour ministers and MPs were made accountable to the rank and file.

A Holy Trinity of left-wing demands emerged – the reselection of MPs, a widening of the franchise for the selection of the leader and greater democratic control of the election manifesto. Some of these constitutional resolutions had been creaking their way through the party's democratic machinery before the Callaghan government fell. But the 1979 defeat, under the weight of the winter of discontent, made the demands unstoppable.

Explaining the Left's thinking, Chris Mullin, then a Tribune journalist, said: "All the pressure on you as an MP is to look up to the fount of power, the Prime Minister, and do what he would like you to do. The object of reselection and other mechanisms – however humble – was to make the MP look down at the base, to the people who put him there."

The narrow election of Michael Foot as party leader in preference to Denis Healey only confirmed the tide. Even if he had wished to stop the calls for constitutional change, Foot would have been powerless to do so. Reselection duly went through at conference in October 1980. Three months later the party's special conference agreed to extend the franchise for the election of the party leader to the unions and constituencies. By the vagaries of the block vote, as much as political judgment, the party agreed that the unions should be given the largest share of the vote (40 per cent) with MPs and the constituencies granted 30 per cent each. Only the proposal to bring control of the manifesto under the National Executive failed.

The reforms were no sooner written into the party constitution than they were put to the test. Tony Benn mounted a challenge to Denis Healey for the deputy leadership of the party in 1981.

The post has virtually no practical significance within the party, but Benn's challenge symbolised the battle between Left and Right that had been left unresolved by the election of the supposedly unifying figure of Michael Foot as leader in 1979. If Healey had lost there might have been a further haemorrhage of Labour defections to the SDP. Healey claimed his defeat would have meant the end of the 80-year-old Labour party. History does not often turn on a decimal point, but Healey scraped home by 50.426 per cent to 49.574 per cent in the electoral college.

The party had survived, but the six-month exercise in internal democracy had exacted a terrible price. A highly unpopular Conservative government had started 1981 over 13 points behind Labour. By the end of the year Labour's civil war had halved the party's standing in the polls, the SDP had been formed and many were gloomily comparing Labour's future to that of the Communist party in France.

As a result Foot's leadership came under increasing internal challenge between the winter of 1981 and the election in May 1983. But because such decisions now lay in the hands of the newly installed electoral college, no faction within the unions or the Shadow Cabinet had the means to force him to resign.

Deeply divided by the sending of the task force to the Falklands, Labour was unable to match the spirit of the South Atlantic. Foot, the inveterate peacemonger, hardly chimed with Britain's jingoistic mood. The party also suffered a self-inflicted by-election disaster in Bermondsey in February 1983 as Foot renounced the Labour candidate Peter Tatchell and then found he had no power to impose an alternative.

In the months to polling day in June, Labour consistently trailed the Tories by as much as 10 to 14 points. Labour's election campaign, conducted on the most radical manifesto since the war, was only distinguished by its sheer amateurism. Denis Healey, for instance, found himself on one exhausting campaign day visiting no fewer than three old people's homes in the West Midlands for fear that some pensioner might feel offended at being missed out. The bespectacled and bookish Foot was ill-suited to the TV studio, preferring the familiarity of oratory in front of the party faithful in a draughty hall. In interviews he always looked ill-at-ease and rarely said anything headline-grabbing.

The campaign, badly constructed at the outset, started to take in water as soon as it left the slipway. On the very first day of the campaign Healey asserted that the manifesto promise to carry through a non-nuclear defence policy in the lifetime of the next parliament only meant the party supported no first use of its nuclear weaponry. The following day Healey compounded the unilateralists' anger when he announced Polaris would only be abandoned in return for substantial concessions from the Russians. Foot tried to plug the hole a week later by saying the party would "move to a non-nuclear policy", but his work was blown apart when Callaghan, with all his authority as a former prime minister, denounced the policy in its entirety. Labour looked bound to lose anyway, but the defence row contributed to a loss of eight points during the campaign.

The statistics of Foot's defeat were funereal. The party lost more than a quarter of its 1979 vote; its share of the vote was the lowest ever won by the principal opposition party. The average vote for a Labour candidate was the lowest since 1900. Eccentrically, Tony Benn hailed the result as over eight and a half million votes for socialism, but Foot, in resignation, knew it was also 3 million fewer than in any post-war general election.

Michael Foot's chosen successor was Neil Kinnock. Young, confident and brimming with energy, the 41-year-old Welshman could not have been a sharper contrast to his predecessor. In his speech to the party conference in 1983, hours after easily defeating Roy Hattersley for the leadership, Kinnock made it his mission to ensure the party never repeated the trauma of the early eighties. It was a theme he was to restate again and again. "Unity is the price of victory," he said. "Not unity for the four weeks before the general election, not unity for four weeks before the European elections, but unity here and now and henceforth." He lectured the party: "Anyone who becomes tempted to go back to the old ways should always remember one thing. Think to yourself – June 9 1983 – never again will we experience that."

Eventually the lecture was to prove effective, because it contained a message that the bulk of the party membership wanted to hear. Many on the Left, including important figures on the National Executive, began to recant their Bennite past. The new alliance between the right and centre-left on the NEC – a realignment mirrored right across the party in humbler constituency General Committees – began to give Kinnock the majorities he needed if he was to enjoy decisive control of the party.

Left intellectuals such as Eric Hobsbawm accelerated the process further by arguing that "the delusion of the Left in the early eighties had been to think that organisation could replace politics". The Left had to accept the depth of social change within the working class if it was to understand, let alone defeat Thatcherism. Socialism had to be reinterpreted to accommodate the new emphases on consumerism, individualism and choice. But the process of readjustment was retarded by the deeply emotive responses engendered within the party by the miners' strike from March 1984 to March 1985 and, to a far lesser extent, by the Militant-led battle in Liverpool against the District Auditor.

Kinnock, his loyalty to the suffering miners strained to the limit by Arthur Scargill's leadership, still felt unable to condemn the union leadership's decision not to hold a ballot. Similarly, it took many months before he felt confident enough of his power base on the NEC to attack Militant. Throughout the year of the miners' strike – with unemployment fixed at 3m – Labour's poll standing stood obstinately about three to four points below the 40 points it would need to give it any hope of unseating the Tories. A string of indifferent by-election results did not help. Kinnock's own performances in the Commons failed to lift party morale.

But with the miners and Militant finally behind him, Kinnock turned to the effective relaunch of the party. Helped by the appointment in October 1985 of Peter Mandelson, a talented young TV producer, to the new post of Communications Director, Kinnock gave communications a wholly new prominence in the party.

In conjunction with Philip Gould, Mandelson and the Leader's Office agreed that there should be a shift away from grassroots opinion-forming to influencing electoral opinion through the mass media. The electorate's own response to Labour was also to be sampled and tested with a new thoroughness. Within two months of its formation, Labour's Shadow Communications Agency – a heterodox group of advertising people – had given the party a new corporate image, which was launched in April 1986 with the glossy Freedom and Fairness campaign. The image gained endorsement by the voters in April 1986 when Labour won the Fulham by-election with a 10 per cent swing against the Tories. By September 1986 Kinnock felt modestly optimistic that at his first attempt he could defeat a government ravaged by Westland. The party had enjoyed a poll lead for eight unbroken months.

A succession of individually trivial, but collectively momentous incidents marked Labour's subsequent decline. The October conference designed to highlight the party's unity instead emphasised defence, the issue on which the party was most divided. Its new economic campaign in October did little to diminish the party's reputation for economic incompetence. By November the Lawson boom was starting and unemployment was firmly predicted to fall below 3m by 1987. In December Kinnock completed the first of two unsuccessful visits to the US to sell the party's unilateralist stance. Its own domestic defence campaign, the Power to Defend Our Country, again raised the salience of defence. By the end of the month the Tories had suddenly gained an 8.5-point lead. The turn-around had been swift, but was to prove irreversible. With the loony left tag impossible to discard in London, Labour suffered the loss of Greenwich to the Alliance in February 1987. A further disastrous visit to the US by Kinnock in April, the botch of the party's next jobs package due to a silly row in the Commons tea room between John Prescott, the front bench Employment spokesman, and Callaghan, and further trouble over the loony left added to the chapter of accidents and blunders. Once again Labour was to go into an election facing a Tory lead of more than 10 points. It was to emerge the other side of polling day facing a 101-seat Tory majority.

Labour had run an effective, modern and televisual campaign. Kinnock had not failed his party and indeed suddenly became its best asset. It was the defeat without excuses.

Ironically, in the subsequent inquest the strongest call to stand firm and not pander to "the trendy, upwardly-mobile middle classes", came not from the Left, but from Roy Hattersley, the bastion of the Right. He argued: "I've not gone through the last six years – the defeat of '79 as well as the humiliation of '83 – to make the Labour party into a new sort of Social Democratic party."

His remarks underscored the huge job of party management facing Kinnock as he sought to keep the Left and Right happy while at the same time ensuring that the party absorbed the lessons of defeat. The two-year policy review provided the right framework. In an effort to prevent the usual inquest over past policy mistakes Kinnock stressed: "The question of whether the policies were right or wrong in 1987 is of course a matter of some interest. But the question of whether the policies will be right or wrong for 1991 will be the matter of the most profound importance. That is the dominant consideration of this review."

The extent to which the outcome of the review was predetermined by a small group, who had fixed views on which policies to abandon, remained a matter of controversy. Certainly there was genuine intellectual debate over the two years and much soul searching. But the Shadow Communications Agency also provided a context against which policies could be tested.

The outcome was an abandonment of many of the party's most sacred shibboleths. Out went penal taxation, unilateral nuclear disarmament, full restoration of trade union immunities, renationalisation of the utilities and hostility towards the EC. Soon after the launch of Meet The Challenge, Make The Change, polls showed a public overwhelmingly aware that Labour had changed and become less extreme. The negatives had been triumphantly and visibly ejected. But the same polls showed much less clarity about what the modern Labour party stood for. In the anxious months before the final drafts of the policy review were completed, Patricia Hewitt, one of the formidable brains behind the review, drew on a quotation from Bruce Babbitt about the US Democrats to set out Labour's dilemma: "The party has succeeded in scrubbing the graffiti of its past off the wall, but we still have not painted the mural of the future."

Kinnock's attempts to scrub out that old graffiti had been helped immeasurably by the decision of the Left in 1988 to mount a challenge to his leadership. At the time the challenge was the last thing Kinnock wanted. He was having trouble explaining, perhaps as much to himself as to the outside world, his tangled abandonment of unilateralism. The Tories were at their zenith and the policy review seemed stalled. In the event the Left's challenge simply demonstrated the extent to which they had misread the party's mood in the wake of the '87 defeat. Tony Benn, once the darling of the constituencies, was crushed by Kinnock. In the deputy leadership, the potentially more serious challenge to Hattersley mounted by Prescott foundered.

That gave Kinnock the open ground to launch the kind of policy review he wanted, as well as to push through gradual reforms in the structure of the party.

Fortuitously, the timing of the launch – May 1989 – could not have been better. The completion of Thatcher's decade in power came just as the shine was rubbing off the Tory economic miracle and divisions within the Tory party over Europe were surfacing. The June European elections, conducted by Labour as a referendum on Thatcher's domestic record, became the first national election in which Labour had triumphed in more than a decade. Labour took 40.1 per cent of the vote to the Tories' 34.7 per cent.

Enjoying unparalleled authority within his party, Kinnock used the November Shadow Cabinet elections for a reshuffle that brought his new generation – Gordon Brown and Tony Blair – to the fore. As the Tories faced a growing revolt over high interest rates and the poll tax, Labour in March 1990 won the Mid-Staffordshire by-election, the most dramatic example yet of the Tories' inability to hold safe seats. Kinnock kept the momentum going in April 1990 in yet another glossy launch in which the final touches in the rebuilding of Labour were completed with refinements, notably on union law and support for the Exchange Rate Mechanism.

But Kinnock was a victim of his own success. The Tories began to think his image-builders had made him electable. Even the growing Gulf crisis failed to turn to the Tories' advantage. The unprecedented poll leads for Labour through the summer of 1990 became too good. They led directly to the loss of one of Kinnock's greatest assets, Thatcher, and her replacement by Major, a homely, likeable consensualist.

It took Labour two months to work out the tone of its attack on the new Prime Minister, not least because he had so little history, identity or known views. The strategy eventually arrived at was to pin responsibility for the recession on him. The success or failure of that strategy, and the party's own reconstruction, will be demonstrated in this election. ●

ACTION MAN IN THE CENTRE GROUND

by Andrew Rawnsley

THE first thing that everybody knows about Paddy Ashdown is the last thing he likes to be reminded of. Action Man Ashdown, with the glamorously sinister past in the Special Boat Squadron, says he hates "that macho image". All the same, it has been a great help in grabbing the voters' attention, never that easy for the third party or its leader. The rugged, well-used looks, and the scrunchiness around the eyes as if he is always staring into the sun, make him look like the commando he once was; no handicap in the age of the presidential election campaign. Nor is an ability to kill silently a negligible skill in politics.

The Captain is engaged on that familiar mission which several predecessors have found impossible – to break the two-party grip on British politics. There will be no Thorpe-style hovercrafts or Steel-like battle buses this time. It will be an airborne mission, as the constitutional reformer's Rambo drops into the TV studios from a plane chartered by sympathetic Asian businessmen.

"I can't wait," he has told colleagues. If nothing else the Ashdown campaign will be energetic, if not hyperactive. This is a man who works out before breakfast, believes "lunch is for wimps", and calls himself "ninety percent vegetarian". This is also a man who enjoys a cigarette and a glass of whisky before bedtime.

A desire for power is not the only thing he shares with his two rival leaders. Like Major he was propelled into the leadership of his party, if not from nowhere, with a haste some envious colleagues thought indecently quick. Like Kinnock he has rescued his party from near-oblivion by stamping his own personality on it.

He calls his first two years as leader "the most frightening period of my life". He inherited the bloody baby of the shotgun marriage between the Liberals and the SDP; a party which could not even agree on its name and at the European elections in 1989 was humiliated into fourth place by the Greens. The leader, for all his fame as somebody who could speak fluent Mandarin and parley with Borneo head-hunters in their own tongue, struggled to find the language to make an impact on parliament or to impress the public.

Now, as his own act and his party's poll ratings have vastly improved, he goes into the election with arguably a better chance of breaking the mould than the Alliance ever had in 1983 or 1987. The same parliamentary colleagues who once eagerly rubbished him now lavish their leader with embarrassing praise. Lord Jenkins – the great grandee of the Liberal Democrats – offered both an accolade and an explanation for why the Captain had turned round his party. He had shown "grace under pressure" – high praise from a claret drinker about a man who makes his own primrose wine.

"A good war" during the Gulf conflict further sharpened his profile. Flying hour after hour of continuous television airtime, delivering enormous payloads of soundbites, he developed the knack of not sounding like a party leader and at the same time quietly promoting himself and his party. It was also the final break with any lingering memories of his time as the darling of the organic beards and peacenik sandals wing of the old Liberal party, most of whom – a little sadly – have either migrated or gone into hibernation as a result of his emphasis on a more managerial style.

The easy self-confidence he puts down to his public school days at rugger-and-tumble Bedford School. He was following father and grandfather, a family of merchant-adventurers in imperial India who could trace themselves back to the days of Clive's derring-do. Though christened Jeremy, an Irish accent picked up when his father made an unwise attempt to farm pigs in County Down earned him the nickname Paddy. The name stuck; the accent did not. Yet he is still instantly recognisable from a school report which praised him as a "an excellent leader" while lamenting his compulsion "to reorganise everything at a moment's notice".

He says: "I'm an enthusiast," while recognising that is also another way of saying he can be impetuous. There is a frenetic attraction to ideas or strategies. "Paddy!" his wife Jane has been known to interrupt one torrent of thoughts, "You don't really believe that, do you?"

The propensity to live dangerously is a habit he has never lost. Leaving the services to work for the Foreign Office at the British Mission to the UN in Geneva, he found life as a diplomat in Switzerland sybaritic, but too soporific. So he chucked it all in and returned to Britain to try and become an MP. "It was," he says, "deeply irresponsible." He suffered two, long, demoralising periods on the dole, gambling both career and family finances for Yeovil, an apparently hopeless seat. Until he won it in 1983.

As party leader he has also made some death-defying leaps. As Labour and the Tories have scrambled into the centre ground he has tried to outflank them both by out free-marketeering the Conservatives on some aspects of economic policy, and outbidding Labour on some aspects of social policy. He has also tried to seize the moral high ground – natural territory for somebody who enjoys climbing rocks for pleasure – with support for Hong Kong, attacks on King Car, to promises to put up income tax to pay for improvements to schools. "Let me tell you, frankly..." has become both a catchphrase and a motto. Who Dares may hold the balance of power.

This coming campaign will be as little as possible like that of the Alliance's two Davids. The one Paddy is more interested in policy than Steel, and carries less ego in his knapsack than Owen. If he has modelled himself on a previous leader, it is Jo Grimond – who also tried to march his party "towards the sound of gunfire" armed with ideas.

Like all his predecessors, this leader will spend much of his time being asked which of the other two parties he would prefer to work with. "I dislike each of the other parties equally", is the well-rehearsed answer, combined with the well-rehearsed demand that the price for Liberal Democrat support is proportional representation. While more temperamentally empathetic to the Labour leader, he evidently has more respect for the Tory leader. Policies aside, Kinnock would be his preferred companion at a dinner table, Major would be his preferred partner around a Cabinet table. A place there is likely to be another price of his support for either; assuming that he is in a position to make any demands with menaces after the election.

It is the voting system he is pledged to overthrow which will most decide whether the Captain who was once licensed to kill for his country is given the opportunity to pilot it. ●

UNHOLY ALLIANCE WITH A CASTING VOTE

by Patrick Wintour

IN November 1979, on the eve of his return from his stint in Brussels as President of the European Commission, Roy Jenkins gave the Dimbleby lecture and called for the strengthening of the radical centre and a party free from union domination. The lecture, entitled Home Thoughts from Abroad, began the process of the realignment of the centre-left of British politics. But dating the precise moment when it became inevitable that a new party was to be formed from within the Labour party is more hazardous, if only because the four founders often cite different reasons for breaking the mould of British politics.

One turning point came at Labour's special conference at Wembley in June 1980 at which delegates agreed to reject cruise missiles. The October party conference was another, when the party agreed to take Britain out of the European Community without a referendum. The defeat a month later of Denis Healey in the party leadership election by the unilateralist Michael Foot in November was yet another. At that point Shirley Williams announced she would not be a Labour candidate again, while David Owen refused to stand for the Shadow Cabinet. Bill Rodgers also protested by refusing a specific Shadow Cabinet portfolio. David Owen opened private discussions with Roy Jenkins about his plans.

Gradually, a mood developed among the Gang of Four that Labour could not become the vehicle of radical post-class politics the eighties needed. Tied to the unions, innately conservative, increasingly dominated by the Bennite Left Labour was irredeemable, they thought. Drafts of what was to be the Limehouse Declaration were beginning to be circulated. The point of no return came when Labour at its January 1981 special conference gave the unions a say in the election of the party leader. The day after, on the 25th, the Gang of Four released the Limehouse Declaration and announced the Council for Social Democracy, the embryo of the SDP. Two months later, on March 26, the SDP was formally launched and Owen and Rodgers resigned the Whip.

For many months the Liberal leadership had been closely watching this fracturing of the Labour party. The Liberal party, led since 1976 by David Steel, had enjoyed power for the first time since 1945 during the brief Lib-Lab Pact of 1977-78. At the 1979 election its number of MPs may have fallen from 13 to 11, but its total poll of over 4m was double its vote throughout the seventies. Should it seek to attract disillusioned Labour MPs to its own ranks or should it welcome a loose coalition with this new social democratic grouping? Steel never had any doubts. He thought that, at this stage, a separate SDP was appropriate. Months earlier he had persuaded Roy Jenkins in private not to join the Liberals, but to help launch a new party. That party would signal something new, capture disillusioned working-class, former Labour voters unattracted to Liberalism and give the electorate proof that political parties could work together in coalition.

The SDP's support may have sprung from no identifiable existing social movement, but its formation generated a revivalist atmosphere. A new swathe of previously apolitical voters were attracted to the SDP. They were overwhelmingly white-collar professionals committed to a set of beliefs including fairness, opposition to the old parties and an end to the old class politics.

Jenkins, fighting the first by-election for the SDP on July 16, captured 42 per cent of the vote in the rock-solid Labour seat of Warrington. "My first defeat in 30 years of British politics and it is by far the greatest victory I have ever participated in," he said after the count. By September's Liberal conference at Llandudno David Steel was able to say, without fear of ridicule: "I have the good fortune to be first Liberal leader for over half a century who is able to say to you at the end of our annual assembly: 'Go back to your constituencies and prepare for government.' " In November Shirley Williams returned to the Commons, seizing the north-west Tory seat of Crosby, destroying a Tory majority of 20,000. Support for the two centre parties had already leapt from the Liberal doldrums of 15 per cent in November 1980 to 32 per cent on the formation of the SDP in March 1981. Crosby took the centre parties to their high-water mark in the polls of 50 per cent in December 1981 (four-fifths of that support was credited to the SDP).

But from then on a gentle decline in the polls was to start. In one of the most hard-fought by-elections Jenkins only narrowly won the Glasgow Hillhead seat in March 1982 with a majority of 2,038. The band-wagon continued to roll, but the wheels were turning more slowly.

Relations between the Liberals and the SDP – the issue that was to haunt both parties for seven years – probably started the slow decline. Unattractive haggling between the parties on the allocation of seats for the next election even led to a brief breakdown in relations at Christmas. The SDP believed the Liberals had done too well. Owen, convinced that the SDP must be distinct, philosophically and administratively, became increasingly suspicious that Jenkins was the source of the trouble. Jenkins, he feared, saw the new party as "a transit camp to a full merger with the Liberals". Owen quibbled about the allocation of seats, the presence of too many SDP leaders at the Liberal Assembly and the sheer amateurism of Steel's party. In the election for the SDP's first leader in June 1982, the unstated issue became the future relationship with the Liberals. Jenkins, the advocate of closer ties and the most senior politician in the party, emerged the victor with 26,256 to Owen's surprisingly strong showing of 20,864.

But at the moment of Jenkins' triumph, the polls were already turning against the SDP. "Fate dealt us a cruel blow," Steel recalled. "With the sending of the task force in April, British domestic politics were swept aside." By July the patriotism engendered by the Falklands task force took its toll. The centre parties saw their poll showing slump to 24 points, proof of the continuing softness of the centre vote, the age-old problem of the Liberals. The centre was never to recover.

Jenkins went through the election campaign under the awkward title of Prime Minister-designate. Tensions rose during the campaign with Steel, more popular in the polls, being criticised by his Liberal colleagues for relinquishing the leadership to Jenkins. At one point Steel felt sufficiently exasperated to press the Edwardian Jenkins, in effect, to resign the leadership in the middle of the election campaign. Jenkins refused.

Together the Alliance polled nearly 8m votes and came only two points behind Labour. It was an impressive performance by some standards, but given Labour's calamitous campaign and the hopes raised at the time of the SDP's formation, it was a severe disappointment. The SDP complement in the Commons was cut to six and the Liberals only managed 17.

In the wake of the defeat Jenkins immediately resigned, opening the way for Owen to become the party's unopposed leader. His elevation ensured that Steel would face another tough four years of negotiation over policy and distribution of seats. His own party grassroots were in recalcitrant mood. Steel, exhausted by seven years at the helm, disappeared from the political stage to his native Borders for some months amid reports of depression. By contrast, Owen, invigorated by the first taste of party leadership, took Westminster by storm. He developed a reputation for speaking quickly, originally and authoritatively on almost any issue. He immediately decided to give his party a more distinctive flavour by setting it on a strong social market course. Any remnants of Labour statism in economic policy were abandoned. He became the unchallenged figure within his party, making Steel's plan for an eventual merger ever more faint.

For a short period in 1985, as Labour struggled under the weight of the miners' strike, the Alliance took a modest lead in the polls. But like Kinnock, the Alliance was to be undone by defence. A joint Defence and Disarmament Commission, proposed by Owen to take the sensitive issue out of the party's normal policy-making channels, agreed an uneasy compromise designed to carry both Owen's strong instincts on defence and the Liberals' strong CND support. Leaks in July 1986, stemming from Steel, suggested the document would not commit the Alliance to the replacement of Polaris once it ended its useful life in the mid-nineties. Infuriated at the reports, but without contacting Steel, Owen blasted off against the document and, by implication, his own negotiators on the Commission. In matters of defence Owen would have no truck with fudge and mudge. The two party leaders in August travelled to France and emerged with the widely ridiculed idea of the Anglo-French Bombe.

The SDP conference accepted the plan, but it all fell apart when, by a margin of 27 votes out of 1,300, the Liberal Assembly declared any contribution by Britain to a European deterrent must be non-nuclear. The affair underscored the Alliance's problems. Owen regarded the Liberals as woolly, undisciplined and frivolous. Steel, sometimes, did not disagree, but found it increasingly difficult to tolerate Owen's moods. "If we cannot work together in Opposition, how can we be expected to work together in government?"' Steel asked.

Interminable negotiations ended with a new compromise that Owen could wear. In a new document, The Time Has Come, Owen and Steel agreed: "In government we would maintain with whatever necessary modernisation, our minimum nuclear deterrent until it can be negotiated away, as part of a global arms negotiation process, in return for worthwhile concessions by the USSR." Trident would be cancelled, but any modernisation would freeze Britain's nuclear capability at the level of Polaris.

The episode was not terminal to the Alliance, but it foreshadowed the problems the Two Davids experienced in the general election as they offered different answers to questions as fundamental as their approach to a balanced parliament. The campaign was not helped by a dreadful advertising campaign and a failure to stick rigidly to the chosen theme of constitutional reform. The Alliance ended with 23 per cent, 2 per cent down on the previous election.

Steel's immediate response to defeat was to raise the issue of a merger. Reflecting on the campaign, he wrote: "All through the previous parliament David has dragged his feet on joint selection of candidates, joint parliamentary meetings, joint everything and even now when 'jointery' had proved wanting here, he was putting up more obstacles to unity." Steel could not countenance another round of gruelling negotiations over candidate selection. Having failed to act after 1983 – a decision he regretted – he was determined to be decisive on this occasion. The two parties had to merge. No one could sit on the fence any longer.

To Steel's delight, on August 5 1987 the SDP membership voted – with 77 per cent of SDP members taking part – in favour of merger: 57.4 per cent wanted full merger, while 42.6 per cent supported Owen's position of closer constitutional links. Owen resigned the party leadership leaving the SDP to choose the cerebral Bob Maclennan as a caretaker. Maclennan and the pro-unity group demanded full negotiations on policy with the Liberals before merger. A cumbersome negotiating body was established, devoting itself to interminable negotiations on the structure of the new party, leaving policy issues for later. Disastrously, the two parties gave themselves too little time to prepare Maclennan's joint policy prospectus. The Liberal party MPs rebelled and the launch had to be delayed. It was a temporary hitch in the path to merger, but, in the public eye, it only added to the sense of disunity in the centre ground.

The merger went ahead with Owen fighting a doomed rearguard action to keep his Owenite organisation viable. In the winter of 1988 Steel decided, after 12 years, that he did not want to lead the new party. He was replaced by the zestful Paddy Ashdown who defeated Steel's own choice Alan Beith. A former marine, Ashdown had come from the left of the party and had only entered parliament in 1983 as MP for Yeovil. He proved to be a driven man convinced that the new party would die if it became a reheated version of the old Liberal party. A restless thinker, he decided to advance a strategy that the party's long-term aim must be to replace Labour as the party of opposition. He set himself three tasks – to make the party financially viable, provide it with a distinctive radical agenda and to make the party matter in British politics.

Yet, on the ground, the Social and Liberal Democrats, as the new party was named, suffered terribly from the continuing warfare with Owen and ridicule over its incessant name changes. A financial crisis, precipitated by a membership decline, forced Ashdown to make unpopular cuts in headquarters' staff. The party's poll rating slumped to 8 per cent and hit its nadir in the June 1979 Euro-elections when the party came fourth behind the Greens, with lost deposits for 34 of its 78 candidates.

Ashdown ploughed on towards his goal of mounting a policy reconstruction every bit as fundamental as that undertaken by Labour. The process might not have been quite as dramatic as Labour's, but by the beginning of the nineties Ashdown's Liberal Democrat party was unrecognisable from that led by Steel in 1983. It was resolutely federalist on Europe, pro-market, committed to wholesale constitutional change, supportive of the Government's union reforms and pro-tax increases if necessary to fund the decaying public services. As early as 1988 Ashdown predicted: "The role of the state would change from monopoly provider to that of an organisation which ensures distribution, regulation, quality and funds the system in the first place."

Pressed on the party's attitude to hung parliaments, Ashdown insisted only that he could not work with a Thatcher-led Conservative party. On her demise in November 1990 he argued the party could now approach the Tories and Labour even-handedly. In the event of a hung parliament, he warned the leaders of the other two parties, they need not even bother to pick up the phone to offer a coalition unless they were willing to commit themselves to legislation on electoral reform.

By dint of Ashdown's own strong performance as leader and by-election triumphs, the Liberal Democrats had clawed themselves back to respectability. Most polls found them around the 15 per cent mark as parliament ended in July 1991. That put Ashdown pretty well back where the Liberals had been in 1979 when Jenkins first penned his thoughts from Brussels, but, to his credit, he was at the helm of a far more modern and vibrant party. ●

SACKCLOTH AND ERMINE

by David McKie

THIS election more than most will leave the House of Commons transformed. Not because famous heads are likely to roll, though some may; but because so many of the figures who have dominated its affairs over the past decade will have passed on to business and industry, the House of Lords, or their slippers and books. **Margaret Thatcher**, perhaps the most powerful presence the Commons has seen since Churchill, and on her day (the day of her resignation, for example) one of its most scintillating performers, has resolved to go.

But what is perhaps more surprising is that so many of those who surrounded her will be leaving too. Of that first Thatcher Cabinet only John Biffen, David Howell and Michael Heseltine – all either sacked or alienated during her years in power – will be left in the next Parliament. As will Ted Heath, who as Father of the House will outlive her in that sense at least.

The "engine room" of the 1983-87 Parliament, when things went best for her governments, is also much depleted. **Cecil Parkinson**, who joined the Cabinet in April 1982 as chairman of the party and was, according to Nicholas Ridley's memoirs, her chosen successor, is leaving the Commons after a career shipwrecked by his affair with Sara Keays. Forgiven in time, he came back to her Cabinet but in subordinate posts: the great offices of state eluded him. **Norman Tebbit**, once a trusted lieutenant and soulmate until her people second-guessed him during the 1987 election campaign, is quitting, too, partly to spend more time with his wife, grievously injured by the bomb in the Brighton hotel. **Nigel Lawson**, whom she promoted to Chancellor and with whom she fell out spectacularly, has had enough of political life. Also going is **Nicholas Ridley**, in her final days the truest of the Thatcherites, unpicked in the end, as was always likely to happen, by the candour of his tongue.

Others who flickered and faded are going, too: **John Moore**, once a popular choice for a future leadership, with his American training, boyish good looks and impeccably Thatcherite views, came to nothing when he was put to the test at the DHSS. **Sir Geoffrey Howe** claimed to be the architect of Thatcherism long before the lady pursued the strategy on which her success was built. Often her hero as Chancellor, he went to the Foreign Office, transforming himself in her eyes from One of Us to One of Them. Above all, Europe divided them. She demoted and humiliated him, but after the Rome summit he had his lethal revenge. Solid, decent **George Younger** is going, as is **Peter Walker**, who never disguised his dissidence but somehow always survived.

The back benches will also be sapped of character by the loss of **Julian Amery**, once a Suez rebel, who never quite made the Cabinet; **Sir Anthony Meyer**, another FCO spirit, who dared to challenge her when she still looked near-immortal and **Sir Ian Gilmour** who could have been a more formidable challenger but chose not to run; **Sir John Stokes**, that embodiment of Empire, for whom the 20th century is one enormous mistake; and the **Morrison brothers**, one (Charles) ineffably wet, the other (Peter, Mrs Thatcher's Parliamentary Private Secretary and one of the MPs who ran her fatal leadership campaign) as dry as a beggar's crust.

On the Labour side the most famous departure is that of **Michael Foot**, the only MP who was there in 1945. **Merlyn Rees**, a former Home secretary and a man who commands much cross-party affection, is also leaving, as, so he claims, is **Denis Healey**, a man whose wit, erudition and extraordinary talent for reading every word that is printed throughout the western world in good time for lunch, made him a famed assassin of ministers – though few will believe that he has gone until they see him in his ermine. Healey is one of the greatest Labour figures never to have been leader of the party. Even some on the Left used to say that he should have been. Out, too, goes another lost leader - **David Owen:** a Labour Foreign secretary at the age of 38, one of the Gang of Four who founded the SDP, and later, after a spell as the party's leader, the Gang of One who said no to merger with the Liberals, preferring to go it alone under the SDP flag. Brilliant, visionary and famously defiant, he leaves politics early at the age of 53. But his colleagues, John Cartwright and Rosie Barnes, have for once declined to follow him: both are standing again.

The departure of **Jack Ashley** deprives the Commons of one of its most formidable campaigners, champion of the disabled and scourge of Crown Immunity, a living refutation of the view that backbenchers are impotent. Among the younger members who are leaving is **Dafydd Elis Thomas**, who with Dafydd Wigley maintained a lively Plaid Cymru presence in the House since February 1974. Another departure – he has threatened it before, but this time he really is leaving – is that celebrated Lancashire monument, the Liberal Democrat **Sir Cyril Smith**.

But perhaps the most missed of all, not just in the House but by television audiences, including those in America, will be Mr Speaker **Bernard** (commonly known as Jack) **Weatherill**. The Government didn't want him to have the job and its agents sometimes sniped at him, but that mainly reflected his steady unwillingness to make life comfortable for ministers... but then that is not what Speakers are for. ●

RETIRING MPs

CONSERVATIVE

J.Amery (Brighton Pavilion), W.Benyon (Milton Keynes), Sir P.Blaker (Blackpool S), R. Boscawen (Somerton and Frome), Sir B.Braine (Castle Point), Sir A.Buck (Colchester N), Sir W.Clark (Croydon S), Sir P.Dean (Woodspring), Sir J.Farr (Harborough), Sir G.Finsberg (Hampstead and Highgate), Sir I.Gilmour (Chesham and Amersham), Sir A.Glyn (Windsor and Maidenhead), Sir P.Goodhart (Beckenham), Sir E.Griffiths (Bury St Edmunds), C.Hawkins (High Peak), Sir G.Howe (Surrey E), Sir C.Irving (Cheltenham), M.Latham (Rutland and Melton), N.Lawson (Blaby), Sir I.Lloyd (Havant), Sir R.Luce (Shoreham),Sir N. MacFarlane (Sutton and Cheam), Sir M.McNair-Wilson (Newbury), R.Maxwell-Hyslop (Tiverton), Sir A.Meyer (Clwyd NW), Sir H.Miller (Bromsgrove), N.Miscampbell (Blackpool N), J.Moore (Croydon C), Sir C.Morrison (Devizes), Sir P.Morrison (City of Chester), D.Mudd (Falmouth and Camborne), C.Parkinson (Hertsmere), Sir D.Price (Eastleigh), K.Raffan (Delyn), Sir T.Raison (Aylesbury), R.Rhodes James (Cambridge), N.Ridley (Cirencester and Tewkesbury), Sir J.Ridsdale (Harwich), Sir H.Rossi (Hornsey and Wood Green), P. Rost (Erewash), Sir M.Shaw (Scarborough), Sir I.Stewart (Herts N), Sir J.Stokes (Halesowen and Stourbridge), N.Tebbit (Chingford), Mrs M.Thatcher (Finchley), P.Walker (Worcester), Sir D.Walters (Westbury), K.Warren (Hastings and Rye), B.Weatherill (Croydon NE – the Speaker), M.Woodcock (Ellesmere Port and Neston), G.Younger (Ayr). *J.Browne (Winchester), deselected by his local party, may stand as an independent.*

LABOUR

P.Archer (Warley W), J.Ashley (Stoke-on-Trent S), R.Brown (Edinburgh Leith), R.Clay (Sunderland N), S.Crowther (Rotherham), Sir P.Duffy (Sheffield Attercliffe), A.Eadie (Midlothian), H.Ewing (Falkirk E), M.Flannery (Sheffield Hillsborough) M.Foot (Blaenau Gwent), E.Garrett (Wallsend), F.Haynes (Ashfield), D.Healey (Leeds E), D.Howell (Birmingham Small Heath), D.Lambie (Cunninghame S), J.Lamond (Oldham C and Royton), T.Leadbitter (Hartlepool), A.McKay (Barnsley W and Penistone), M.Rees (Leeds S), M.Welsh (Doncaster N). *T.Fields (Broadgreen) and D. Nellist (Coventry SE), expelled by Labour, may stand as independents.*

LIBERAL DEMOCRAT

Sir C.Smith (Rochdale)

IND SOC DEM

Dr D. Owen (Plymouth Devonport)

NATIONALIST

D.E.Thomas (Merionnydd Nant Conwy)

COMING TO THE AID OF THE PARTY

by Martin Linton

THOUGH the two main parties are doing their best to cultivate a modern, classless image, most of their new candidates for the next election continue to be steeped in their parties' traditions – Thatcherites from the Tory party, trade unionists from Labour. If Labour wins the election its crop of new MPs will for the first time have more trade union and party officials than college lecturers; if Major wins he will find himself surrounded by a new generation of young Tory MPs who see themselves as children of the Thatcher "revolution".

Of the 20 Labour candidates picked to succeed retiring MPs in safe seats, nearly half are party or trade union officials, including former party publicity director **Peter Mandelson** (Hartlepool), NUM officials **Eric Clarke** (Midlothian) and **Michael Clapham** (Barnsley W), the EETPU's **John Spellar** (Warley West), Nalgo's **Brian Donohoe** (Cunninghame S), NUPE's **George Mudie** (Leeds E) and **Rachel Squire** (Dunfermline W) and GMB's **Roger Godsiff** (Birmingham Small Heath).

In addition many recent by-election candidates have been party or union officials, including former party organiser **Peter Kilfoyle** (Liverpool Walton), NUM official **Kim Howells** (Pontypridd), the TGWU's **Mike Carr** in the first Bootle by-election and UCW's **Peter Hain** (Neath).

The explanation lies in the party's candidate selection system, which was intended to put a limit on union influence, but has had the opposite effect. At the last election Labour candidates who were college lecturers (102) outnumbered union officials (38) and party workers or MPs' researchers (16) by nearly two to one. At the next election the roles are likely to be reversed, at least among the new MPs Labour will need in order to win a majority. In this group (just one-fifth of the total) it's the people on the Labour movement payroll, trade union officials, party workers and MPs' researchers (24), who outnumber college lecturers (16) by three to two.

The current selection system put an upper limit of 40 per cent on the votes that trade unions could have in the choice of a candidate in order to end a situation where the unions sometimes had a nomination in their gift. But it also allowed union branches to vote without attending a selection conference, which has opened the way for horse-trading between local union branch secretaries on who the candidate should be. The system also extended the vote from party activists to all party members, which has made it even more likely that parties will pick candidates who live locally and are well known to local party members.

Many parties have selected the leader of their council. These include **George Mudie** (Leeds E), **Clive Betts** (Sheffield Attercliffe), **John Harman** (Colne Valley), **Bob Laxton** (Derby N), **Alan Whitehead** (Southampton Test), **Ann Coffey** (Stockport), **Tom Flanagan** (Keighley) and **John Austin-Walker** (Woolwich).

Four constituencies have picked their local MEP: **Llew Smith** (Blaenau Gwent), **George Stevenson** (Stoke-on-Trent South), **Geoffrey Hoon** (Ashfield, Notts), and **Richard Balfe** (Southwark & Bermondsey).

Of all the seats Labour needs to win the next election, 71 per cent have picked candidates who live in the constituency or in an immediately adjacent constituency and most of the remainder live within a few miles. With a stronger tendency now to pick local candidates and trade union officials, Labour has correspondingly fewer candidates who are well known nationally. **Glenda Jackson** (Hampstead & Highgate) is the only example of a candidate well known outside politics.

Only four former MPs are trying to get back into the Commons: **Alf Dubs**, standing again in Battersea, **Bryan Davies**, standing in Oldham Central, **Nick Raynsford**, who won Fulham in a by-election and is now standing in Greenwich, and **John Spellar**, who won Birmingham North-field and is now standing in Warley West.

Of the Tory candidates picked to succeed retiring MPs, some are already closely associated with Thatcher. **John Whittingdale** (Colchester South) and **Oliver Letwin** (Hampstead & Highgate) have worked at Number 10. **Sir Paul Beresford** (Croydon C) and **Eric Pickles** (Brentwood) were leaders of her flagship councils of Wandsworth and Bradford. But many of the younger candidates are "Thatcherites" in a rather different sense. They did not become involved in politics until the mid-seventies, when Thatcher was already the Tory leader, and they did not have a vote until the 1979 election.

Their first taste of politics was the Callaghan Labour government and the "winter of discontent". To them "Thatcherism" was not a radical new creed but the accepted faith of most of their party, so they do not see themselves as "radical Thatcherites" like some of the 1987 intake.

But they would nearly all call themselves "Thatcherite" in the sense that they want a continuation of Thatcherism, or an extension or evolution of it, rather than its abandonment. The younger candidates were infuriated by an article in the Spectator suggesting that the party was "scraping the bottom of the barrel" for candidates and calling for the list of approved candidates to be thinned out to get rid of the "mental porridge".

They can be divided into three groups. The youngest, mainly in their thirties, are the true children of Thatcherism. They caught the political bug early and are the most political group. They include the ablest and most ambitious of the new intake. The youngest is **Dr Liam Fox** (Woodspring), 29, impish, Scottish GP and a strong supporter of the changes in the health service. Also 29 is **David Faber** (Westbury), who first appeared in the limelight as Jeffrey Archer's assistant in the Monica Coughlan affair, but has lived that down to become a Tory candidate. He is Harold Macmillan's grandson but is to the right of centre. **Oliver Letwin** (Hampstead & Highgate), is the nearest thing to a right-wing radical, former adviser to Sir Keith Joseph, then in the Downing Street policy unit, author of a book called Privatising The World, but a loner.

John Whittingdale (Colchester South), 31, is Thatcher's former political secretary and tipped for the top by some, but others find him a bit high-handed and wonder how he'll cope with the parliamentary arena.

Charles Hendry (High Peak), 31, is a former political adviser to Social Security secretary Tony Newton and **David Liddington** (Aylesbury), boyish, state-educated, is a former political adviser to Foreign secretary Douglas Hurd; both are a shade to the right of their ministers.

While Labour has selected mainly local candidates, many Tories have travelled the country in search of a seat. **James Clappison**, 34, is a wealthy Yorkshireman who fought the two Bootle by-elections and has ended up as Cecil Parkinson's successor in Hertsmere, while **Eric Pickles**, 36, Bradford's Thatcherite leader for 18 months, ended up as candidate in Brentwood, Essex.

Alan Duncan (Rutland & Melton), 34, made money as a crude oil broker and lent his Westminster house as Major's leadership campaign headquarters. He runs a dining club for eight of the Young Turks. They include **Edward Garnier** (Harborough), 37, former night lawyer for the Guardian, and **Andrew Robathan** (Blaby), 39, an ex-SAS officer recruited by his boss General de la Billière to run the prisoner-of-war camps in the Gulf war.

Bernard Jenkin, son of former Environment secretary Patrick Jenkin and candidate for Colchester North, is more right-wing, a close ally of Thatcherite ministers. **Nicholas Hawkins** (Blackpool South) is a former president of Oxford University's Monday Club and still solidly right-wing, though mellowed enough to stand for the chairmanship of the Bow Group.

Peter Ainsworth, 34, (Surrey East) is another former Oxford Monday Club chairman who has shifted his position and is now on the soggier wing of his party, at least on social issues, despite being a Tory Wandsworth councillor. **Peter Luff** (Worcester) is a former adviser to Peter Walker and Edward Heath who re-emerged after a period in industry as Lord Young's adviser. By way of compliment his colleagues say he is "no straightforward soggy", and "more robust than his record suggests".

The only genuine Tory wet to have been selected for a seat is **Mark Bishop** (Cambridge), much in the mould of his predecessor Robert Rhodes James and a supporter of the Tory Reform Group.

The next group, mainly in their forties, are not part of the same philosophical thrust. They had other careers and may have drifted into politics late for social reasons. Typical of them are **Geoffrey Clifton-Brown** (Cirencester), an Etonian landowner in Norfolk, and **Iain Duncan-Smith** (Chingford), an old Etonian and ex-Army officer unexpectedly picked to succeed Norman Tebbit, despite being neither a right-winger nor Essex man.

Sebastian Coe (Falmouth) is trying to forget his celebrity status and learn about politics, but no one knows where he stands: least of all himself, say less charitable friends. **Gyles Brandreth** (Chester) is another unknown quantity, but will let no-one forget his celebrity status as a TV presenter, writer, founder of the National Scrabble Championships and the Teddy bear museum.

John Taylor (Cheltenham) has had celebrity status thrust upon him as the first black Tory candidate in a Tory-held seat. Assumed to be liberal, but pro-hanging; some colleagues find him too earnest and humourless.

Among the women selected, Mrs **Jacqui Lait** (Hastings & Rye) has fought her way through the man's world of Tory politics for the last 15 years, contested countless seats, sat on endless committees and has now finally got there. So has the exotic, energetic and apparently fearless **Lady Olga Maitland**, journalist and champion of Nato, now adopted as candidate for Sutton and Cheam.

Others who will be entering the fray are Mrs **Angela Browning**, who will fight Tiverton, Mrs **Angela Knight**, Erewash, and **Judith Chaplin**, 48, Major's political secretary with an office next to the Prime Minister's, who is contesting Newbury. She is popular, powerful and "rightish", but no more so than Major.

The best-known Thatcherite in this group is Wandsworth leader **Sir Paul Beresford** (Croydon C), 45, a New Zealander and a Park Lane dentist with half the Cabinet on his list of patients. Colleagues say he "dispenses ruthlessness and vitriol in equal degrees", and even the Sunday

Telegraph described him in a recent profile as a "Macho-Thatcherite".

The third group are the "retreads", the defeated MPs who are fighting their way back in another seat. **Piers Merchant** (Beckenham) was MP for Newcastle Central from 1983 to 1987, during which time he put his radical right-wing ideas to the test by spending a week on the dole and living on recipes for good, wholesome, cheap meals provided by Edwina Currie.

Warren Hawksley, the former Wrekin MP who was once on the committee of the right-wing and anti-immigration Tory Action group, has succeeded Sir John Stokes as candidate in Halesowen & Stourbridge. Others who have moved south in search of safer seats are **Richard Ottaway**, former Nottingham MP and now candidate for Croydon S, **Derek Spencer**, former Leicester MP and now candidate for Brighton Pavilion, and former Welsh office minister **Mark Robinson**, who has left Newport West to fight Somerton & Frome. **Michael Ancram**, the son of a Scottish earl who was MP for Edinburgh South from 1979 to 1987 and strongly suspected of wetness as a Scottish Office minister, has reappeared as candidate for Devizes.

Both the former Tory MPs for Aberdeen South have moved to England. **Gerald Malone**, MP for Aberdeen South from 1983 to 1987, who has gone to Winchester, and **Iain Sproat**, the MP from 1970 to 1983 who deserted because he expected to lose and was adopted in Roxburghshire which he promptly lost, has been selected in Harwich, Essex. He is the most Thatcherite of the retreads. After a campaign against social security scroungers Thatcher rewarded him with a ministerial post where he became one of the most enthusiastic privatisers; hyperactive, bone dry and belligerently free market. ●

LABOUR CANDIDATES REPLACING LABOUR MPS
GEOFFREY HOON Ashfield *Euro-MP*
MICHAEL CLAPHAM* Barnsley West *TU official*
ROGER GODSIFF Birm Smallheath *TU official*
LLEW SMITH* Blaenau Gwent *Euro-MP*
ROBERT AINSWORTH* Coventry NE *Metal worker*
BRIAN DONOHOE* Cunninghame S *TU official*
KEVIN HUGHES* Doncaster N *Miner*
RACHEL SQUIRE Dunfermline W *TU official*
PIARA KHABRA* Southall *IWF president*
MICHAEL CONNARTY* Falkirk E *Teacher*
PETER MANDELSON Hartlepool *LP official*
GEORGE MUDIE* Leeds E *TU official*
ERIC CLARKE* Midlothian *TU official*
⊕BRYAN DAVIES Oldham Central *PLP official*
JIMMY BOYCE* Rotherham
CLIVE BETTS* Sheff At'cliff *Loc govt*
HELEN JACKSON* Sheff Hillsboro' *Full-time councillor*
GEORGE STEVENSON* Stoke South *Euro-MP*
STEPHEN BYERS* Wallsend *Lecturer*
⊕JOHN SPELLAR Warley West *TU official*

CANDIDATES ON LABOUR'S TARGET LIST
ALASTAIR OSBORNE* Ayr *Community worker*
JOHN HUTTON Barrow *Lecturer*
JOHN POTTER* Basildon *Computer manager*
EUNICE DURKIN* Batley & Spen *Education worker*
⊕ALF DUBS Battersea *Voluntary/charity*
RICHARD BURDEN* Birm Northfield *TU official*
LYNNE JONES* Birm Selly Oak *Housing manager*
ESTELLE MORRIS Birm Yardley *Teacher*
GORDON MARSDEN Blackpool S *Lecturer*
DAVID CRAUSBY* Bolton NE *Engineer*
CLIFFORD MORRIS* Bolton W *Manager*
CHRIS MANN* Brecon *Probation officer*
ANN KEEN* Brentford *Nursing lecturer*
JEAN CORSTON Bristol E *Lawyer*
DOUG NAYSMITH* Bristol NW *Scientist*
JIM DOBBIN* Bury North *Scientist*
HAZEL BLEARS Bury South *Lawyer*
DAVID CHAYTOR* Calder Valley *Lecturer*
ANNE CAMPBELL* Cambridge *Scientist*
TONY WRIGHT Cannock *Lecturer*
JON OWEN JONES* Cardiff C *Teacher*
DAVID ROBINSON* Chester *Teacher*
RAY MCMANUS* Chorley *TU official*
JOHN HARMAN* Colne Valley *Lecturer*

SANDY FEATHER* Corby *TU official*
BOB SLATER Coventry SW *Lecturer*
MALCOLM WICKS* Croydon NW *Voluntary/charity*
ALAN MILBURN* Darlington *Business development officer*
DAVID HANSON Delyn *Voluntary/charity*
BOB LAXTON* Derby N *Engineer*
MARK TODD Derbys S *Publisher*
GWYN PROSSER* Dover *Engineer*
KEVIN LOMAX* Dudley W *Teacher*
TESSA JOWELL Dulwich *Voluntary/charity*
PETER GRANT-HUTCHISON Eastwood *Lawyer*
MARK LAZAROWICZ* Edin Pentlands *Voluntary/chairty*
ANDY LOVE Edmonton *Co-op official*
ANDREW MILLER* Ellesmere Port *TU official*
COLIN BURGON* Elmet *Research officer*
CLIVE EFFORD Eltham
NIGEL BEARD Erith *Industry*
ALAN KEEN* Feltham *Manager*
NICK MOORE* Fulham
GRAHAM GREEN* Gravesham *Lawyer*
⊕NICK RAYNSFORD Greenwich *Housing consultant*
GLENDA JACKSON Hampstead *Actress*
BILL RAMMELL* Harlow *Administrator*
JOHN MCDONNELL* Hayes *Pressure group*
BARBARA ROCHE Hornsey *Lawyer*
GREG POPE* Hyndburn *Loc Govt*
MIKE GAPES* Ilford S *LP official*
JAMIE CANN* Ipswich *Teacher*
TOMMY FLANAGAN* Keighley *Engineer*
ANN HOLMES* Kensington *Housing consultant*
ROGER BERRY* Kingswood *Lecturer*
COLIN PICKTHALL* Lancs West *Lecturer*
RUTH HENIG* Lancaster *Lecturer*
ASHOK KUMAR* Langbaurgh *Scientist*
DAVID TAYLOR* Leics NW *Computer manager*
BRIDGET PRENTICE Lewisham E *Teacher*
JIM DOWD* Lewisham W *Engineer*
NICK BUTLER Lincoln *Economist*
NEVILLE BANN* Lpl Mossley Hill *Lecturer*
BILL MCKENZIE* Luton S *Accountant*
SIOBHAN MCDONAGH* Mitcham *Housing consultant*
IAN GIBSON* Norwich N *Lecturer*
ALAN SIMPSON* Nottingham S *Voluntary/charity*
BILL OLNER* Nuneaton *Engineer*
NICK AINGER* Pembroke *Rigger*
GORDON PRENTICE Pendle *LP official*

JULIE OWENS Peterborough *MP's researcher*
JUDITH CHEGWIDDEN*Putney *Consultant*
GEOFFREY SMITH Ribble South *Retired doctor*
DAVID WILLIAMS* Rochdale *Lecturer*
JANET ANDERSON Rossendale *MP's researcher*
PADDY TIPPING* Sherwood *Full-time councillor*
EDDIE LOPEZ* Slough *LP official*
JOHN DENHAM* Soton Itchen *Voluntary/charity*
ALAN WHITEHEAD* Soton Test *Voluntary/charity*
RICHARD BALFE Southwark *Euro-MP*
KATE PHILLIPS Stirling *TU official*
ANN COFFEY* Stockport *Loc govt*
JOHN SCOTT* Stockton S *Lecturer*
KEITH HILL* Streatham *TU official*
JIM D'AVILA* Swindon *Carworker*
ANDREW MACKINLAY Thurrock *TU official*
PATRICK COSGROVE* Tynemouth *Lawyer*
NEIL GERRARD* Walthamstow *Lecturer*
MIKE HALL* Warrington S *Teacher*
MIKE O'BRIEN Warks N *Lawyer*
JENNY EDWARDS* Westminster N *MP's researcher*
KEN PURCHASE* Wolverhampton NE *Consultant*
HUGH BAYLEY* York *Lecturer*
JOHN AUSTIN-WALKER*Woolwich *Loc govt*
* Local candidate when selected

TORY CANDIDATES SELECTED IN TORY-HELD SEATS
DAVID LIDDINGTON Aylesbury
PHIL GALLIE Ayr
⊕PIERS MERCHANT Beckenham
ANDREW ROBATHAN Blaby
HAROLD ELLETSON Blackpool N
NICHOLAS HAWKINS Blackpool S
ERIC PICKLES Brentwood
⊕DEREK SPENCER Brighton Pavilion
ROY THOMASON Bromsgrove
RICHARD SPRING Bury St Edmunds
MARK BISHOP Cambridge
DR ROBERT SPINK Castle Point
JOHN TAYLOR Cheltenham
GYLES BRANDRETH Chester
IAIN DUNCAN-SMITH Chingford
GEOFFREY CLIFTON-BROWN Cirencester
ROD RICHARDS Clwyd NW
BERNARD JENKIN Colchester N
JOHN WHITTINGDALE Colchester S
SIR PAUL BERESFORD Croydon C
DAVID CONGDON Croydon NE

⊕RICHARD OTTAWAY Croydon S
MICHAEL WHITBY Delyn
MICHAEL ANCRAM Devizes
†NICHOLAS WATERSON Eastbourne
STEPHEN MILLIGAN Eastleigh
MRS ANGELA KNIGHT Erewash
SEBASTIAN COE Falmouth
HARTLEY BOOTH Finchley
⊕WARREN HAWKSLEY Halesowen & Stourbridge
OLIVER LETWIN Hampstead & Highgate
EDWARD GARNIER Harborough
⊕IAIN SPROAT Harwich
MRS JACQUI LAIT Hastings & Rye
DAVID WILLETTS Havant
JAMES CLAPPISON Hertsmere
CHARLES HENDRY High Peak
PETER BUTLER Milton Keynes NE
BARRY LEGG Milton Keynes SW
†ROGER EVANS Monmouth
JUDITH CHAPLIN Newbury
†NIGEL EVANS Ribble Valley
ALAN DUNCAN Rutland & Melton
JOHN SYKES Scarborough
MARK ROBINSON Somerton & Frome
PETER AINSWORTH Surrey East
LADY OLGA MAITLAND Sutton and Cheam
MRS ANGELA BROWNING Tiverton
†WALTER SWEENEY Vale of Glamorgan
DAVID FABER Westbury
⊕GERALD MALONE Winchester
MICHAEL TREND Windsor & Maidenhead
DR LIAM FOX Woodspring
PETER LUFF Worcester

⊕ Retreads
† Seats lost in by-elections

PROMISES, PROMISES...

by Martin Linton

A-LEVELS

CON: The Government remains committed to A-levels. They need to be maintained and improved, not watered down.

LAB: A-level will be reformed in a new unified framework for academic and vocational courses so training credits can count towards A-level.

LIB DEM: A National Council for Tertiary Qualifications will rationalise post-16 qualifications and modularise the post-16 curriculum.

BRITISH TELECOM

CON: The Government is selling part of its remaining stake in BT.

LAB: We will oppose the sale of the rest of the stake.

LIB DEM: We will break up BT.

BUSINESS RATES

CON: The Government does not propose to make any change to Uniform Business Rate.

LAB: Business rates will again become a local rather than a national tax.

LIB DEM: Business rates will be replaced by locally administered rates based on land values.

CARS AND ROADS

CON: British car ownership is the lowest in Europe and certain to rise. That is why we are doubling the trunk road programme over 10 years.

LAB: We want to encourage environmentally responsible car use and review taxation to encourage smaller, fuel-efficient and less -polluting cars.

LIB DEM: We will scale down major road building, abolish tax breaks for company cars, abolish vehicle excise licence and introduce road pricing in urban areas.

CARBON DIOXIDE

CON: We will stabilise carbon dioxide emissions at 1990 levels over the next 15 years. This is a demanding, but realistic target.

LAB: We will freeze carbon dioxide emissions at the 1990 level by the end of the century.

LIB DEM: Our target is to cut carbon dioxide emissions by 30 per cent from their 1990 level by 2005.

CFCs

CON: We will phase out CFC emissions by 2000 and would support a ban by 1997, subject to exceptions.

LAB: We will speed up the timetable for phasing out CFCs and other chemicals which deplete the ozone layer.

LIB DEM: Our target is a total ban on the use of CFCs and halons by 1994.

CHILD BENEFIT

CON: In future it will be increased every year in line with inflation.

LAB: We will restore the real value of child benefit to its April 1987 level.

LIB DEM: We will integrate the tax and social security systems.

COAL

CON: We will privatise British Coal, but plans are still at the preparatory stage.

LAB: We will secure the future of the coal industry by the development of clean-burn technology.

LIB DEM: We would seek to reduce the use of coal – a heavy emitter of carbon dioxide.

COMPULSORY TENDERING

CON: Competitive tendering is compulsory in seven areas and the Government is considering extending it into managerial and technical sectors.

LAB: We will end the system of compulsory competitive tendering except when services consistently fail to come up to standard.

LIB DEM: Competitive tendering can raise the standard of services, but we oppose compulsory tendering, which considers cost and not quality.

DEFENCE CUTS

CON: Defence spending will fall from just under 4 to 3.4 per cent of GDP by 1993-94.

LAB: Arms talks will make substantial defence cuts possible in the future, but it would be irresponsible to give specific commitments while in opposition.

LIB DEM: We will target a 50 per cent reduction in UK defence by 2000.

DEFENCE JOBS

CON: It is inevitable some jobs will be lost, but we will "seek to give the greatest possible warning that we can".

LAB: We will set up a Defence Diversification Agency to help switch the skills and resources of defence work to manufacturing.

LIB DEM: We will set up an Arms Conversion Agency to subsidise arms manufacturers converting out of the business.

ELECTORAL REFORM

CON: Opponents of proportional representation predominate in the Tory party, but strong points can be made on both sides and discussions continue.

LAB: A working party is now considering what systems would be appropriate for the Commons, Scotland, the regions, the Second Chamber and Europe.

LIB DEM: We would introduce proportional representation for all elections, using the single transferable vote wherever possible.

ELECTRICITY

CON: Electricity privatisation greatly benefits customers.

LAB: We will take control of the National Grid.

LIB DEM: We will break up National Power.

EUROPEAN BANK AND CURRENCY

CON: We will not accept the imposition of a single currency and a European Central Bank would remove national control of economic policy.

LAB: A European Central Bank would be needed if there were monetary union, but it should be accountable to finance ministers of the 12 countries.

LIB DEM: Our immediate priorities are economic and monetary union, including, in due course, an independent European Central Bank and a single currency.

EUROPEAN MONETARY UNION

CON: We enthusiastically support stage one of the Delors Report, but part company with Delors over the single currency.

LAB: Closer co-operation on monetary policy is both inevitable and desirable, but we oppose a rigid timetable for monetary union.

LIB DEM: Our immediate priorities are economic and monetary union.

EYE AND DENTAL TESTS

CON: It is not unreasonable to expect people to pay such charges if they can afford to.

LABOUR: We will bring back free eye tests and dental checks.

LIB DEM: We will abolish charges for dental and optical checks.

FREEDOM OF INFORMATION

CON: As much information as possible should be available, but a Freedom of Information Act would undermine ministerial responsibility.

LAB: We will introduce a Freedom of Information Bill in our first parliamentary session.

LIB DEM: We will introduce freedom of information legislation.

GRANT-MAINTAINED SCHOOLS & CTCs

CON: We hope that grant-maintained schools – funded directly by the Government – will become the norm.

LAB: The opted-out schools and CTCs will be returned to the community.

LIB DEM: We will reincorporate grant-maintained schools and CTCs into local education authorities.

GREEN TAXES

CON: Unleaded petrol is an example of how taxation has been used as an instrument of environmental protection.

LAB: Green taxes will mean higher VAT on aerosols with

CFCs and lower VAT on insulation materials.

LIB DEM: Pollution-added tax will be applied to harmful products and subsidies would encourage environment-friendly behaviour.

HOUSE OF LORDS

CON: The House of Lords must be retained because it occupies an absolutely crucial position in the constitution.

LAB: We will establish a new Second Chamber in place of the Lords with power to delay changes dealing with individual or constitutional rights.

LIB DEM: We favour a reformed House of Lords or Senate with about 100 voting members elected by the single transferable vote.

HUMAN RIGHTS

CON: A Bill of Rights could politicise the judiciary and incorporation of the European Convention would be tantamount to a Bill of Rights.

LAB: We will establish a constitutionally entrenched Charter of Rights, going beyond the European Convention on Human Rights

LIB DEM: We will incorporate the European Convention of Human Rights and introduce a UK Bill of Rights.

INCOME TAX

CON: Our objective remains to move towards a basic rate of 20p. This will be achieved as soon as it is prudent and sensible to do so.

LAB: We will move towards a starting rate of 20 per cent with a series of tax bands ending in a top rate ceiling of 50 per cent.

LIB DEM: We will integrate income tax and National Insurance with a top combined rate of 50p in the pound.

INFLATION

CON: Interest rates are the essential instrument of anti-inflation policy. Credit controls would be inefficient, unfair and unworkable.

LAB: We will establish a National Economic Assessment and investigate the possibility of a more co-ordinated approach to collective bargaining.

LIB DEM: Our anti-inflation policy will involve labour market reform, an independent central bank and an active fiscal policy.

LOCAL AUTHORITIES

CON: As a result of the review we are likely to move to a larger number of unitary local authorities replacing the two-tier system.

LAB: We are in favour of unitary authorities below a regional tier, but we will take a flexible approach to get there.

LIB DEM: We support a move to unitary local authorities.

MINIMUM WAGES AND WAGES COUNCILS

CON: Wages Councils should have no permanent place in the labour market, but the Government has not reached a final decision about their future.

LAB: We will introduce a national, legal, minimum hourly wage starting at 50 per cent of men's median earnings and strengthen the Wages Councils.

LIB DEM: We believe in a national minimum income but not a statutory minimum wage. There would be target minimum wages and reformed Wages Councils.

MORTGAGE RELIEF

CON: Mortgage interest relief will continue to be paid at the basic rate of tax and the ceiling on relief remains unchanged at £30,000.

LAB: We will allow first-time-buyers to bring forward their mortgage interest tax relief to the early years when the costs are greatest.

LIB DEM: We would replace mortgage tax relief with housing cost relief, but people with existing mortgages would continue to receive relief.

NATIONAL INSURANCE

CON: We have reformed and simplified the National Insurance system.

LAB: We will abolish the ceiling on National Insurance contributions.

LIB DEM: We will integrate tax and National Insurance which would remove the present N I ceiling.

NATO

CON: Nato will continue to play a major role in the collective defence of the West, but will have to consider what role to play outside Europe.

LAB: Nato will be needed for the foreseeable future, but its role must be fundamentally reassessed.

LIB DEM: There is a key role for Nato in building the CSCE into an effective security structure, which could eventually replace Nato.

NUCLEAR POWER

CON: We will complete the Sizewell B nuclear power station and then review the prospects for British civil nuclear power.

LAB: We will not invest in new nuclear power stations, continue with those in the planning process or extend existing stations beyond their safe span.

LIB DEM: We will phase out the use of nuclear fission by 2020 and cancel construction of Sizewell B.

OVERSEAS AID

CON: We have accepted the UN target of 0.7 per cent of GNP but have no timetable for achieving it. Progress depends on economic circumstances.

LAB: We will meet the UN aid target of 0.7 per cent in five years and set up a new Department of Development.

LIB DEM: We will reach 0.7 per cent in five years and aim at 1.0 per cent in 10 years.

PENSIONS

CON: We will protect the basic state retirement pension against inflation.

LAB: We will increase the pension by at least £5 for a single person and £8 for a couple and thereafter in line with earnings or prices, whichever is higher.

LIB DEM: We will raise the pension by £5 and £8, restore the link with earnings and abolish Serps, the state earnings-related pension.

POLL TAX

CON: We will abolish the community charge and replace it by a new council tax based on the value of the property and the number of people.

LAB: We will abolish the poll tax and replace it with a system of fair rates, a modern property tax linked to the ability to pay.

LIB DEM: We will replace poll tax by local income tax related to ability to pay.

POST OFFICE

CON: We will keep the ownership of the Post Office and the statutory letter monopoly under review.

LAB: We will oppose any plan to sell off the Post Office.

PRIVATISATION

CON: We are selling British Technology Group (BTG). The next two major challenges will be British Coal and British Rail.

LAB: We are strongly opposed to the plans to privatise

BTG. We will set up a new body for investment in high technology and inventions.

LIB DEM: We will consider any further privatisations case by case, but ownership is not the key issue.

PUBLIC EMPLOYEES

CON: The new system for determining civil service pay takes greater account of market forces, staff recruitment and retention.

LAB: We will halt the deterioration in public sector pay and conditions and keep them broadly comparable with equivalent pay movements elsewhere.

LIB DEM: We will give public employees flexible work patterns, including part-time and home working, job sharing and a say in day-to-day decisions.

RANDOM BREATH TESTS

CON: The police have adequate powers to require roadside breath tests.

LAB: We will introduce properly authorised random breath testing and work with the EC to reduce the legal blood alcohol limit to 50 mg per 100 ml.

LIB DEM: We will allow the police to carry out random breath testing and lower the legal blood alcohol limit to 50 mg.

RESEARCH & DEVELOPMENT

CON: We remain committed to maintaining and enhancing the strength and quality of British research.

LAB: We will bring Britain up to competitors' research levels through new research programmes in key technologies.

LIB DEM: We will inject £400m into the science budget to raise it from 0.28 to 0.35 per cent of the gross domestic product.

SCOTLAND, WALES AND THE REGIONS

CON: We support the present constitutional arrangements unequivocally.

LAB: We will establish a Scottish Parliament within a year, a Welsh Assembly, a regional tier of government and an elected strategic body for London.

LIB DEM: We will introduce an elected Scottish Parliament and Welsh Senedd and regional government for England at the speed the regions themselves wish.

SOCIAL CHARTER

CON: Britain will be able to accept, subject to negotiation, the majority of proposals, but has difficulties with a number.

LABOUR: We will sign the European Social Charter.

LIB DEM: We wholeheartedly support the aims of the Social Charter and call for its rapid implementation.

STUDENT LOANS

CON: Student grants will be frozen and top-up loans uprated annually until they reach 50:50 where the Government intends to maintain them.

LAB: We will replace student loans with a fairer system of student grants.

LIB DEM: We will increase student grants to the 1979 level in real terms and restore entitlement to benefit.

TRAINING

CON: We have set up Training and Enterprise Councils so that employers can take over the Government's major training programmes.

LAB: If firms spend less than 0.5 per cent of their payroll on training, they would have to pay the difference as a contribution to Government training.

LIB DEM: We propose that firms should pay a training levy equal to 2 per cent of their payroll minus their approved expenditure on training

TRIDENT

CON: Trident remains vital to our security and the Start arms reduction talks between the US and the Soviet Union will not cover it.

LAB: We will cancel the fourth Trident submarine and the plans to increase the number of warheads compared with Polaris. We will place all of Britain's nuclear capability into international nuclear disarmament negotiations.

LIB DEM: We will continue to build the four-boat Trident, but restrict its warheads to the Polaris level and include them in the Start talks.

1979

MAY: 3 Conservatives win general election with majority of 43. **4** Mrs Thatcher becomes Britain's first woman prime minister. **10** Tony Benn not to stand for Shadow Cabinet: will campaign to shift Labour party to the Left. **JUN: 7** European elections: Conservatives win 60 seats, Labour 17, SNP 1, Ulster Unionist 2, SDLP 1. **12** BUDGET: Income tax rates down from 33 to 30 and 83 to 60 per cent; VAT up from 8 and 12.5 per cent to 15. **JUL: 19** Commons rejects return of capital punishment. **SEPT: 10** Talks on constitution of Zimbabwe open in London. **OCT: 23** All foreign exchange controls scrapped. **NOV: 15** Minimum lending rate rises to 17 per cent, a record. **29-30** Dublin EC summit: Thatcher demands cut in UK contribution. **DEC: 25** Soviet Union invades Afghanistan.

1980

JAN: 2 Steel strike (until Apr 2). **26** BUDGET: Withdrawal of benefit for strikers' wives and families. **APR: 1** Zimbabwe becomes independent. **30** Iranian embassy seized by gunmen. **MAY: 1** British Aerospace Bill, privatising the industry, is enacted. **5** SAS storms and recaptures Iranian embassy. **14** TUC Day of Action against government policies gets muted response. **JUN: 17** Francis Pym, Defence secretary, names Greenham Common and Molesworth as sites for cruise missiles. **JUL: 15** Pym announces choice of Trident as successor to Polaris. **AUG: 8** Housing Bill (includes measures to compel local authorities to sell council houses) enacted. **SEPT: 29** (to Oct 3) Labour conference, Blackpool: votes to establish new broader system for electing party leader and for mandatory reselection of MPs. Also commits party to withdrawal from EC without a referendum. **OCT: 15** Mrs Thatcher, facing some party criticism as recession gathers, tells Conservative conference at Brighton that she is "not for turning". James Callaghan says he is standing down as Labour leader. **NOV: 4** Labour MPs hold first ballot for new party leader: Denis Healey (112 votes) and Michael Foot (83) go on to second ballot. **10** In second ballot, Foot (139) defeats Healey (129). **13** Civil Aviation Bill enacted, privatising British Airways. **24** Chancellor announces £3,000m package of spending cuts and tax increases. **DEC: 8** Thatcher-Haughey summit in Dublin

1981

JAN: 5 Cabinet reshuffle: St John-Stevas dropped. **24** Labour Party special conference at Wembley votes to set up electoral college (unions 40 per cent of the vote, MPs and constituency parties 30 per cent each) to choose future party leaders. **25** Roy Jenkins, former Labour deputy leader, joins Shirley Williams, David Owen and Bill Rodgers (the "Gang of Four") to announce establishment of Council for Social Democracy, seen as staging post to a possible new party. **27** Rodgers leaves Shadow Cabinet: his place goes to Tony Benn. **FEB: 9** Shirley Williams resigns from Labour National Executive. **MAR: 9** Civil service one-day strike: action continues on selected fronts. **10** BUDGET: deflationary measures. **26** Launch of SDP.

All smiles: the "Gang of Four" shot to prominence and fell to earth like a firework party rocket

Victory: the last bastion of a far flung empire was restored by force to expensive sovereign rule

30 364 economists attack Government economic policy. **APR: 11** Brixton riots. **23** Unemployment tops 2.5m for first time since the 1930s. **MAY: 5** Death of Bobby Sands, MP, N. Ireland hunger striker. **7** Labour takes control of Greater London Council. **JUN: 16** Liberals and SDP announce plans to work together in an Alliance. **JUL: 4** Riots in Toxteth area of Liverpool. **8** Riots in London and other cities. **16** Roy Jenkins (SDP) standing for the Alliance comes only 1,759 votes behind Labour in Warrington by-election. **30** End of civil service dispute, longest national pay dispute since 1926. **SEPT: 14** Cabinet reshuffle. Prior sent to N. Ireland; Tebbit takes over Employment. Sir Ian Gilmour dropped; Cecil Parkinson to be party chairman. **14-19** Liberal Assembly meets at Llandudno, votes overwhelmingly for alliance with SDP; told by leader David Steel to "go out and prepare for government". **27** Denis Healey retains post as Labour deputy leader, defeating Tony Benn in vote conducted by party's new electoral college. **OCT: 22** Bill Pitt (Liberal) wins Croydon North West for Alliance from Conservatives. **NOV: 6** Anglo-Irish intergovernmental council announced. **19** Tony Benn voted out of Labour Shadow Cabinet. **25** Scarman report on events in Brixton published. **26** Shirley Williams (SDP) wins Crosby for the Alliance from the Conservatives. **DEC: 8** Arthur Scargill elected to lead NUM. **17** Law Lords declare GLC Fares Fair scheme illegal.

1982

JAN: 26 Unemployment tops 3m. **MAR: 9** BUDGET: Standstill budget; unemployment benefit to be taxed from July. **25** Roy Jenkins (SDP) wins Glasgow Hillhead for the Alliance from the Conservatives. **APR: 2** Argentina invades Falklands and South Georgia. **3** Emergency debate in Commons. **5** Lord Carrington, Foreign secretary, and Foreign Office ministers Humphrey Atkins and Richard Luce resign. Francis Pym becomes Foreign secretary. Fleet sails for Falklands. **25** South Georgia retaken. **MAY: 2** Belgrano sunk. **4** HMS Sheffield sunk. **28** Port Darwin and Goose Green recaptured. **JUN: 3** Angela Rumbold wins Mitcham and Morden for the Conservatives. Previous MP Bruce Douglas-Mann had left Labour for SDP: alone of those who switched, he chose to stand for re-election. **8** Heavy British casualties in Argentinian attack on Bluff Cove. **14** British enter Port Stanley. Argentinian commander surrenders. **JUL: 2** Roy Jenkins elected leader of SDP. **26** Falkland Islands thanksgiving service: controversy over Archbishop of Canterbury's address. **SEPT: 18** Leaked document from Central Policy Review Staff recommends wholesale reconstruction (some say replacement) of welfare state. **OCT: 20** New N. Ireland assembly elected. **28** John Spellar wins Birmingham Northfield for Labour from Conservatives. **NOV: 2** NUM vote rejects Scargill call for strike against pit closures. **DEC: 15** Government defeated by 15 votes on new immigration rules.

1983 **JAN: 6** Cabinet reshuffle: Heseltine to Defence. **11** Start of Sizewell B inquiry. **18** Franks committee clears Government of blame for Falklands invasion. **FEB: 24** Simon Hughes wins Bermondsey for the Alliance from Labour in by-election marred by attacks on Labour candidate's homosexuality. **MAR: 15** BUDGET: tax allowances raised by 14 per cent. **28** Ian MacGregor appointed chairman of Coal Board. **APR: 21** £1 coin introduced. **MAY: 13** Parliament dissolved. **28** In meeting at David Steel's home in Ettrick Bridge, Scotland, Roy Jenkins is asked to stand down as leader of Alliance election campaign, but declines. **JUN: 9** General election: Conservatives returned with majority of 144. Tony Benn and Shirley Williams lose their seats. **11** Cabinet reshuffle: Howe succeeds Pym as Foreign secretary and is replaced as Chancellor by Nigel Lawson. Leon Brittan is Home secretary. **12** News leaks that Michael Foot plans to stand down as Labour leader. **13** Roy Jenkins resigns leadership of SDP and is succeeded by David Owen. **15** Bernard ("Jack") Weatherill becomes Speaker. **JUL: 7** Emergency package of £500m spending cuts. **AUG: 14** John Gummer becomes Conservative party chairman. **OCT: 2** Success of the "dream ticket": Neil Kinnock elected Labour leader, beating Roy Hattersley, Eric Heffer and Peter Shore. Hattersley is deputy leader, beating Michael Meacher, Denzil Davies and Gwyneth Dunwoody. **7** Government announces plans to end GLC and six metropolitan councils. **14** Resignation of Cecil Parkinson because of involvement with Sara Keays. **16** Norman Tebbit replaces Parkinson at Trade and Industry, Tom King takes Employment, Nicholas Ridley enters Cabinet as Transport secretary. **25** US troops invade Grenada. **NOV: 1** Heseltine says demonstrators going too near cruise missile bunker could be shot. **14** Heseltine tells Commons first missiles have arrived. **DEC: 8** Lords vote for experimental televising of proceedings. **9** Lord Carrington appointed general secretary of Nato.

1984 **JAN: 25** Government unilaterally bars union membership at GCHQ. **FEB: 9** On his 90th birthday Harold Macmillan becomes Earl of Stockton. **MAR: 1** Tony Benn returns to Commons as victor of Chesterfield by-election. **12** Start of miners' strike. **13** BUDGET: Radical tax reforms; substantial expansion of Youth Training. **23** Sarah Tisdall sent to prison for leak of Ministry of Defence document to the Guardian. **APR: 2** Norman Fowler announces major review of social security. **17** Woman police constable killed in square outside Libyan embassy. Siege of embassy begins, lasts until Apr 27. **MAY: 29** Police battle with pickets at Orgreave colliery: many hurt. **JUN: 14** European elections: Conservatives 45 seats, Labour 32, SNP 1, Ulster Unionist 2, SDLP 1. Mike Hancock (SDP) wins Portsmouth S. by-election from the Conservatives. **20** Plans announced to abolish GCE O levels

Confrontation: law versus disorder blazed a long and sad trail from the picket line to poll tax riots

Brighton rocked: an IRA active service unit almost brings down the Government

and CSE, to be replaced by new GCSE examination. **26** Agreement reached on Britain's dispute over EC budget (Fontainebleau). **JUL: 18** Report of Warnock committee on human fertility and embryology. **AUG: 6** Appeal Court overturns High Court ruling that Government action at GCHQ was illegal. **SEPT: 4** Norman Willis becomes general secretary of the TUC. **10** Prior leaves N. Ireland office, succeeded by Douglas Hurd. **26** Hong Kong agreement signed. **OCT: 1** Bank of England intervenes after collapse of Johnson Matthey Bankers. **12** Bomb at Grand Hotel, Brighton, kills five. Norman Tebbit badly hurt: Margaret Thatcher among those who escaped. **NOV: 13** In his maiden speech in the Lords, Earl of Stockton (formerly Harold Macmillan) is strongly critical of Government. **26-8** Sale of British Telecom raised over £8,000m. **DEC: 5** Backbench pressure forces Sir Keith Joseph to drop plans to cut student grants, increasing parental contribution. **19** Thatcher in Beijing signs agreement on future of Hong Kong.

1985 **JAN: 1** Jacques Delors becomes President of the European Commission. **23** Televising of Lords begins. **29** Thatcher refused honorary degree at Oxford. **FEB: 11** Clive Ponting acquitted of charge under Official Secrets Act. **26** Start of year-long disruption of schools in dispute over teachers' pay and conditions. **MAR: 3** Miners' strike called off. Vote for immediate return to work (against Scargill's recommendation). **7** End of Sizewell B inquiry **19** BUDGET:

Allowances raised by more than rate of inflation, but indirect taxes go up. **JUN: 3** White paper on future of social security published after Fowler review. **20** Chancellor criticises Bank of England for failure to intervene earlier in Johnson Matthey Bankers crisis. **JUL: 4** Richard Livsey wins Brecon and Radnor for Alliance from Conservatives. **25** Report of committee chaired by Duke of Edinburgh calls for radical shift in housing policy and scrapping of mortgage interest relief. **AUG: 7** Britoil offer heavily oversubscribed. **SEPT: 2** Cabinet reshuffle. Douglas Hurd becomes Home secretary and Norman Tebbit party chairman. **9** Riots in Handsworth area of Birmingham. **13** Britain expels 25 Soviet diplomats: retaliation and counter-retaliation follows. **28** Riots in Brixton. **30** Neil Kinnock attacks Militant at Labour party conference, Bournemouth. **OCT: 1** Riots in Toxteth area of Liverpool. **6** PC Blakelock killed during riot on Broadwater Farm estate in London borough of Haringey. **16-23** Commonwealth conference, Nassau. Thatcher at odds on South African sanctions. **18** Notts miners vote to leave NUM and form Union of Democratic Mineworkers (UDM). **NOV: 15** Signing of Anglo-Irish Agreement. **20** Commons votes against televising proceedings. **DEC: 3** Church of England report calls for greater spending on housing and welfare in inner cities. **13** Westland helicopters announce rescue deal involving US-Italian consortium. Michael Heseltine, Defence secretary, favours sale to European interests. **17** Unionist MPs resign from Commons in protest against Anglo-Irish Agreement.

Debate: the Westland affair highlighted hairline fractures in a divided cabinet

1986

JAN: 6 Letter from Solicitor-General Sir Patrick Mayhew warning Heseltine over Westland is leaked to the press. **9** Heseltine resigns. George Younger becomes Defence secretary. **20** Anglo-French agreement on Channel tunnel. **23** Mini general election in N. Ireland: Unionists retain 14 seats, lose 1. **24** Leon Brittan, Trade and Industry secretary, resigns over Westland. **27** Commons debate on Westland. **28** Green paper on local government finance proposes poll tax for England and Wales. **FEB: 12** Channel tunnel treaty signed at Canterbury. **17** Signing of Single European Act. **MAR: 18** BUDGET: basic rate down from 30 to 29p. **31** GLC and metropolitan councils cease to exist (at midnight Mar 31 - Apr 1). **APR: 10** Nick Raynsford gains Fulham for Labour from Conservatives. **14** Defeat of Shops Bill at second reading. **22** Launching its Freedom and Fairness campaign, Labour adopts a new logo: a red rose. **MAY: 8** Elizabeth Shields takes Ryedale for Alliance from the Conservatives. **21** Kenneth Baker succeeds Sir Keith Joseph at Education. **30** John Stalker is removed from his inquiry into alleged "shoot-to-kill" policies in N. Ireland. **JUN: 12** Dissolution of N. Ireland assembly set up in 1982. **JUL: 3** Report of Peacock committee on future of broadcasting. **11** Inflation falls to 2.5 per cent, best for 19 years. **22** Commons votes to ban corporal punishment in state schools. Liberal Assembly at Eastbourne votes against advice of leadership for motion opposing nuclear deterrent. Steel endorses replacement of Polaris. **SEPT: 28** Kinnock tells party

conference Labour would shut down all US bases in Britain. **OCT: 7-10** Highly successful Conservative conference at Bournemouth, designed by Saatchi and Saatchi around the theme The Next Move Forward, sets out plans for a third term. **11** Plans for nuclear disarmament founder at Reykjavik summit on issue of Reagan's Strategic Defence Initiative (Star Wars). **17** Proceedings open in Australia on UK application to ban publication of Spycatcher. **27** "Big Bang" in City of London. **DEC: 1** Government puts inspectors into Guinness. **8** Sale of British Gas. **22** Liberal MP David Penhaligon, seen as possible future leader, is killed in car crash. **29** Death of Earl of Stockton (formerly Harold Macmillan).

1987

JAN: 8 Government launches AIDS campaign. **26** Layfield inquiry approves Sizewell B power station. **FEB: 11** British Airways share issue: heavily oversubscribed. **26** Rosie Barnes wins Greenwich for Alliance from Labour. **MAR: 6** Zeebrugge disaster: 193 dead. **9** Former leader James Callaghan endorses Trident in Commons debate, against Labour party policy. **12** Government approves Sizewell B. **17** BUDGET: income tax down 2p to 27p. **MAY: 1** Government abandons plans to dump nuclear waste at one of four inland sites. **18** Parliament dissolved. **JUN: 11** Conservatives re-elected with a majority of 101 seats. **13** Cabinet reshuffle: Norman Tebbit leaves the Government, John Moore takes over Social Services. **14** David Steel calls for a "democratic fusion" of the two Alliance parties. SDP responses are divided: Owen hostile, Jenkins favourable. **JUL: 1** Single European Act comes into force. **AUG: 6** Owen resigns as leader of SDP: he opposes merger with Liberals proposed by David Steel. **29** Robert Maclennan succeeds Owen. **31** SDP conference at Portsmouth votes in favour of merger. **SEPT: 17** Liberal Assembly backs merger with SDP. **OCT: 19** "Black Monday" shares crash. **26** Lord Havers resigns as Lord Chancellor because of ill-health; is succeeded by Lord Mackay of Clashfern. **NOV: 10** Deployment of cruise missiles halted. **18** King's Cross disaster, 31 killed. **24** US and USSR reach agreement on intermediate range nuclear weapons (INF agreement). **DEC: 8** INF treaty signed.

1988 **JAN: 10** Lord Whitelaw, deputy Prime Minister, gives up leadership of House of Lords because of ill-health. **12** Revolt on freezing of child benefit: Government majority cut to 47. **13** Steel and Maclennan agree on terms for new merged party, but these are rejected by members. **15** Conservative revolt in favour of private member's bill on Official Secrets introduced by Richard Shepherd. **24** Liberals vote for merger with SDP. **31** SDP votes for merger with Liberals. **FEB: 9** Commons votes to admit TV cameras. **MAR: 3** Formation of Social and Liberal Democrats. Dr Owen and others stay out in a continuing SDP. Nurses and health workers hold one-day strike in support of NHS. **15** BUDGET: 2p off standard rate and top rate cut to 40 per cent. **29** Rover to be sold to British Aerospace. **APR: 18** Rebel Conservative MPs back amendment by Michael Mates to "band" poll tax to make it more equitable, but amendment fails. **JUN: 2** Australian court rules against Government on Spycatcher. **22** TUC votes to suspend EETPU. **28** Bank rate raised for fourth time in month: now 9.5 per cent. **JUL: 6** Publication of Butler-Sloss report on Cleveland child abuse. **19** Government defeated in Lords on eye and dental charges. **25** Cabinet reshuffle: Department of Health and Social Security divided. **28** Paddy Ashdown becomes leader of Social and Liberal Democrats, defeating Alan Beith. **AUG: 22** More liberal licensing laws including all-day opening come into force. **SEPT: 5** TUC Congress expels EETPU. **20** Thatcher expounds her vision of Europe at Bruges. **OCT: 2** Labour party re-elects Kinnock and Hattersley as leader and deputy leader. **13** Law Lords reject Government case on Spycatcher. **19** Home secretary bans radio and TV interviewing of Sinn Fein and other extreme

N. Ireland organisations. **NOV: 1**. Government majority in Commons cut to eight on plan to charge for eye tests. **2** First school votes to opt-out (Skegness Grammer). **9** White Paper proposes student loans. **10** Jim Sillars wins Glasgow Govan for SNP from Labour. **30** Official Secrets Bill published. **DEC: 12** Clapham rail disaster: 35 killed. **16** Edwina Currie, junior Health minister, resigns after ill-judged comments on eggs **21** Terrorist bomb brings down plane over Lockerbie killing 258 on board and 11 on the ground.

1989 **JAN: 8** Plane crash at Kegworth kills 47. **17** Government announces football identity card plan. **26** Report by Lord Windlesham clears Thames TV programme on Gibraltar killings, Death On The Rock; Government rejects the report. **31** White Paper, Working For Patients, foreshadows sweeping changes in NHS. **FEB: 20** Government defeated in Lords on football ID cards. **MAR: 4** Purley rail crash, 5 dead. **14** BUDGET: designed to curb demand in face of renewed inflation. **APR: 1** Poll tax introduced in Scotland. **MAY: 4** John Smith wins Vale of Glamorgan for Labour from Conservatives. **9** Labour NEC votes for policy shift away from unilateral nuclear disarmament. **13** SDP to cease operating as a national party. **16** Labour imposes by-election candidate (Kate Hoey) on local party at Vauxhall. **18** Big expansion announced in road programme; cost doubled to £12 billion. **JUN: 15** In elections for European Parliament, Labour takes 45 seats Conservatives 32, SNP 1, OUP 2, SDLP 1. **JUL: 19** White Paper on reform of legal profession: lawyers horrified. **24** Cabinet reshuffle: Major replaces Howe as Foreign secretary. **OCT: 2** Labour conference abandons commitment to unilateral nuclear disarmament. **19** Court of Appeal frees the Guildford Four. **22** Commonwealth Conference agreement on South African sanctions is immediately repudiated by Thatcher. **25** Announcement that child benefit will be frozen for third year in succession. **26** Chancellor Lawson resigns and is replaced by Major. PM's adviser Alan Walters also goes. **NOV: 21** Televising of Parliament begins. **30** Trade and Industry secretary Ridley admits that BAe was given secret inducements to take over Rover. **31** Lawson makes resignation speech in Commons. **DEC: 5** Thatcher defeats Sir Anthony Meyer in contest for Conservative leadership. **12** Legislation on war crimes approved in principle. **20** Government to grant UK citizenship to 225,000 Hong Kong citizens.

**Loose talk:
cost
livelihoods,
split the
Tories and
ultimately
dislodged the
Iron Lady**

1990
JAN: 3 Norman Fowler, Employment secretary, resigns: replaced by Michael Howard. **9** In speech at Bangor, Brooke foreshadows new round of talks in N. Ireland. **26** Record trade deficit of £20.3 billion reported for 1989. Government drops football ID scheme in light of report by Lord Justice Taylor on Hillsborough disaster. **FEB: 20** Hurd tells Dublin summit that Britain will lift sanctions on South Africa following release of Mandela. **23** Ambulance dispute settled after six months. **MAR: 4** Peter Walker announces impending resignation as Welsh secretary (David Hunt named to replace him on 14). **20** BUDGET: TESSAs launched. **22** Sylvia Heal wins Mid-Staffs for Labour from Conservatives. **31** Many hurt in severe poll tax rioting in central London. **APR: 1** Poll tax starts in England and Wales. Riot in prison chapel at Strangeways, Manchester, spreads through prison causing extensive damage. **6** Separate taxation of married women begins. **23** MPs vote to allow embryo research over 14-day period. **25** MPs vote to cut abortion limit to 24 weeks. Strangeways occupation ended. **MAY: 4** David Hunt becomes Welsh secretary. **JUN: 1** SDP dissolved. David Owen, John Cartwright and Rosie Barnes to sit as Independent Social Democrats. **JUL: 14** Ridley resigns after The Spectator reports his disparaging views on the Germans. **19** £3,000m package to reduce impact of poll tax. **25** Defence review foreshadows 18 per cent cut in armed services. **30** Ian Gow, MP assassinated at his home near

Eastbourne. **AUG: 2** Iraq invades Kuwait. Thatcher calls for a European Magna Carta. **7** US order troops to Gulf. **9** Iraqis annexe Kuwait. UK says it will send forces. **SEPT: 6** Commons recalled to debate Gulf. **25** Publication of Environment White Paper, This Common Inheritance. **OCT: 8** Britain joins ERM. **18** David Bellotti wins Eastbourne for Liberals from Conservatives. **30** Thatcher reports to Commons on Rome summit. **NOV: 1** Sir Geoffrey Howe resigns. **2** John MacGregor becomes Leader of Commons, Kenneth Clarke moves from Health to Education, William Waldegrave takes over Health. **13** Howe's resignation speech berates Thatcher for style of leadership and especially conduct of European policy. **14** Heseltine says he will run for party leadership. **20** First ballot: Thatcher falls 4 votes short of outright victory. **22** Thatcher resigns. **27** Second ballot: Major takes 49.7 per cent of vote. Heseltine and Hurd stand down: third ballot waived. **28** Major becomes Prime Minister. In Cabinet reshuffle, Norman Lamont becomes Chancellor, Baker Home secretary, Patten chairman of the party and Heseltine returns to Environment. **DEC: 5** Electricity privatisation launched: the biggest such operation yet.

1991
JAN: 15 Commons debate on Gulf. On motion for adjournment, 53 Labour MPs oppose Government. **16** First air attack on Iraq. **21** Both Houses debate Gulf. In Commons, 34 Labour members vote against the Government. **FEB: 21** Commons

select committee on trade and industry produces report strongly critical of Lord Young's handling of sale of Rover to BAe. **24** Land war starts in Gulf. **25** Woolf report on prisons published. **28** Iraqis accept all UN resolutions on Gulf and military action ceases. **MAR: 5** Last cruise missiles returned to US. **7** Mike Carr wins Ribble Valley for Liberal Democrats from Conservatives. Baker announces setting up of Royal Commission on criminal justice system under Lord Runciman of Doxford. **19** BUDGET: cuts £140 per head off poll tax, raises VAT to 17.5 per cent. **21** Heseltine announces council tax to replace poll tax. **26** Peter Brooke says basis for talks now exists in N. Ireland. **APR: 18** Full appeal granted in case of Maguire Seven, convicted of terrorist offences in 1976 (one of whom died while in prison). **23** Heseltine reveals details of council tax, based on bands for different property values. **30** Lords rejects War Crimes Bill for second time. **MAY: 3** Major launches Education White Paper foreshadowing end of divisions between universities and polytechnics and between academic and vocational training. **16** Huw Edwards wins Monmouth for Labour from Conservatives. **JUN: 8** Bill Morris (TGWU) becomes Britain's first black union leader. **28** Mrs Thatcher says she won't stand at the next election. **JUL: 3** Peter Brooke calls off N. Ireland talks. **5:** Bank of England closes BCCI. **12** Publication of report by Plant committee, set up by Labour party, on electoral reform. **22** Major unveils his Citizens' Charter. **23** Tom King announces substantial defence cuts and amalgamation of regiments. **AUG: 5** Kenneth Baker says inquiry into escape of two IRA men from Brixton has shown that prison was warned by police five months before. Health minister says 113 more hospitals have applied for self-governing status. **19** Gorbachev ousted in coup. Thatcher says defence cuts should be rescinded. **21** Coup collapses. **22** Gorbachev reinstated. **SEPT: 1** David Owen says he is to leave politics. **3** John Major, in China to sign Hong Kong agreement deal, tells Chinese leaders the world has not forgotten Tiananmen Square. **5** Congress of People's Deputies in Moscow formally winds up Soviet system. **10** Rioting, looting and arson on Meadow Well estate, North Tyneside; follows disturbances at Blackbird Leys estate, Oxford, and Cardiff. **20** Archbishop of Canterbury, George Carey, says Tyneside riots are linked with social deprivation. **24** Major discusses gay rights with actor and leading activist Sir Ian McKellen in Downing Street. **25** Because of alleged links with Militant, Labour MPs Dave Nellist and Terry Fields are barred from holding office in the party and from

attending annual conference. **27** US president Bush announces sweeping cuts in nuclear weapons as part of arms control initiative for post Cold War era. **OCT: 1** Government leaks news that there will be no general election this year. **6** Gorbachev responds to Bush arms package, promising massive cuts. Major says Britain's Trident will stay. **9** Rifkind selects route East of London for Channel Tunnel high speed rail link: service not now expected to open till next century. **16** Health Secretary announces that 99 more hospitals can opt out, but decision on four London hospitals is postponed. Independent Television Commission announces new TV franchises: Thames TV and TV-am among those rejected. **17** Chief executive of TV-am releases letter from Thatcher saysing she is "heartbroken" at their rejection. **28** Major launches Opportunity 2000 scheme for more top jobs for women. Draft text of Maastricht summit treaty offers right to opt out for countries which do not want to commit thenselves to a single currency. **29** Britain says it will not sign EC declaration favouring "swift transition" to monetary union. **31** Queen's speech promises 12 Bills including one to replace poll tax with council tax. **NOV: 6** Chancellor's Autumn Statement announces £11 billion more on public spending, including extra £2.5 billion from privatisation and £3 billion from contingency reserve. Target for Public Sector Borrowing Requirement to rise from £7.9 billion (Budget forecast) for 1991-2 to £10.5 billion (£18.5 billion excluding revenue from privatisation). **7** Conservatives lose Kincardine and Deeside to Liberal Democrats and Langbaurgh to Labour.

LABOUR ISN'T WORKING.
UNEMPLOYMENT OFFICE
BRITAIN'S BETTER OFF WITH THE CONSERVATIVES.

WHAT THEY WANTED, AND WHAT THEY DELIVERED

Conservative economic management in summary

THE Conservatives returned to office in May 1979 determined to break the mould of British politics under Conservative and Labour governments since the end of the second world war. Thatcher believed that government by consensus had wasted too much time and caused too much damage in trying to solve deep-lying problems. Consensus had bred compromise and evaded potentially lethal truths about Britain's decline. Vested interests which stood in the way of modernisation and revival – most conspicuously the trade unions – had to be cut down to size, not placated by deals all too often made on their terms.

The 1979 Conservative manifesto promised to rebuild the economy and reunite a divided and disillusioned people. The first priority in this enterprise would be "to restore the health of our economic and social life by controlling inflation and striking a fair balance between the rights and duties of the trade union movement".

In this new world of rigorous discipline, order would be maintained above all by stricter control of the money supply. Reliance on monetary policy pre-dated Thatcher's arrival at Number 10, but Labour were surreptitious, even shamefaced, about their commitment to monetarism. They regarded it as at most one essential element among many in their economic policy mix. For Thatcher and the Conservatives it was much more than that: an object, in the early days, of an almost evangelistic fervour. The way to kill inflation was not to do deals with the unions, which gave you illusory gains like incomes policies at all too real a cost, but to keep the supply of money so tight that irresponsible settlements could not be funded. The apostles of monetary policy believed they could see an almost clockwork relationship between laxity in control of the money supply and inflation 18 months to two years later. A regime of monetary purity would bring an equally automatic reward.

But the Thatcherite break with the past was intended to go far beyond a mere replacement of weaponry. It was meant to rewrite a whole culture. In the years of consensus politics, the nation had gone soft. That spirit of enterprise for which Britain had once been admired around the world had been sapped in the warm cocoon of state provision. Instead of get up and go, the watchword of the British people now seemed to be: lie back and wait for it. So the second task they set for themselves was "to restore incentives so that hard work pays, success is rewarded and genuine new jobs are created in an expanding economy".

That meant cutting direct taxation, public borrowing and public spending. "The state takes too much of the nation's income," the manifesto said. "Its share must be steadily reduced." It meant putting public assets in private hands, both by selling off state industry and allowing people to buy, on favourable terms, the houses they had been renting from local authorities.

The privatisation of state-controlled industry had a double appeal. Not only would it help to break the culture of state dependency, it would also liberate managers to make the essential changes, drastic and long delayed, which alone would allow adaptation to modern conditions. The strategy was not to shore up jobs which had long since lost their purpose, but to liberate the resources to create new jobs for the world of late 20th-century technology. It meant, too, scrapping controls on money sent abroad, on prices, pay and dividends and on hire purchase arrangements. It meant removing the devices with which providers, from bus operators to High Street opticians and lawyers, tried to shield themselves from the rigours of competition. Competition, argued the Thatcherites, was a far better friend to the public than interference by bureaucrats.

If it isn't hurting, it isn't working

WHEN the Conservatives took office inflation was running at 10 per cent. The pound had halved in value since 1974 and in August 1975 inflation had touched 26.9 per cent. "Inflation on this scale," said the manifesto, "has come near to destroying our political and social stability."

In the first few Conservative months the rate of inflation increased: by December it stood at 17.2 per cent; five months later it was 21.9 per cent. Part of the problem was inherited – the awards by the Clegg Commission on Pay Comparability, set up by Labour, of increases of up to 25 per cent; and the introduction of price increases in nationalised industries, which Labour had postponed before the election. Some of it was home-made, including the decision in Howe's first Budget six weeks after the election to replace the 8 and 12.5 per cent rates of VAT by a uniform rate of 15 per cent. But severe recession in 1980-81 reversed the process: by December 1982 inflation was down to 5.4 per cent, the lowest figure since 1970.

Through Thatcher's second term of office it looked as though the worst was over. Inflation never rose above 7 per cent and in May 1983, on the eve of the election, it fell to 3.7 per cent. The summer of 1986 went even better, with inflation falling to 2.4 per cent. But the Government's response to the great share crash of October 1987 compounded a problem already begun by five years of steady growth. The consequent acceleration of earnings and spending power set off a new bout of inflation, which took the rate back over 10 per cent in August 1990.

As if to prove Thatcher's contention that inflation was a disease which warped all it touched, it began to destabilise the government. The monetarists, whose influence on events had steadily declined, argued, with her apparent approval, that Chancellor Lawson's monetary laxity was building new inflationary pressures which imperilled the Thatcherite enterprise. The eventual Government response was much what it had been in 1980-81: a squeeze on the economy which began to choke inflation, though at the cost of choking more beneficial activity, too. Though the severity of this recession was in part attributable to world conditions, the pain was clearly planned. "If it isn't hurting, it isn't working," said Chancellor Major, who succeeded Lawson.

The unions still won wage increases above the rate of inflation

THE 1979 manifesto's second priority – the assault on what Thatcher saw as the excessive power of the trade unions to determine the course of economic events – was in some respects an extraordinary success. The extent of the Government's inroads would later astonish even some of those who sat in Thatcher's Cabinets and authorised it: the destruction of the closed shop, the imposition of balloting on substantial policy issues and union appointments, and the ruthless defeat of the miners' strike of 1984-85.

But an underlying problem remained. One of the central arguments under successive governments for clipping the wings of the unions was to reduce their power to generate inflation. Yet, weakened as they were, they still succeeded (even during the 1990-91 recession) in winning wage increases well above the rate of inflation. Such success was not restricted to unionised groups – company directors did best of all – but to this extent at least the unions continued to confound those who hoped their power had been broken.

To master inflation, proper monetary discipline is essential

CONTINUING adherents of monetarism – by this time a diminished band – saw the economic disappointments of the early nineties as the direct and predictable consequence of the failure to maintain the true faith with the necessary rigour. The commitment of the 1979 manifesto had been unconditional: "To master inflation, proper monetary discipline is essential, with publicly stated targets for the rate of growth of the money supply."

That philosophy was enshrined in the steersman's manual with which Chancellor Howe equipped himself in March 1980 – the Medium Term Financial Strategy. This set the targets for a steady deceleration of the money supply over a four-year period, coupled with a cut in the size of the underlying budget deficit and a steady reduction in the level of government spending. But targets were regularly missed and as regularly readjusted.

The commitment to monetarism was never formally abandoned, but by the end of the eighties it was clear that Treasury policy was no longer being formulated in such terms. From 1985, when he first became convinced that Britain ought to join the Exchange Rate Mechanism (ERM) of the European Monetary System (EMS), Chancellor Lawson gave increasing attention to the exchange rate of the pound, adopting a policy of shadowing the German Mark (DM), which brought him into bruising conflict with the Prime Minister, while the money supply became, as in Chancellor Healey's day, something you had to watch – but not exclusively or obsessively.

By the end of the eighties the Conservative approach looked much less like a radical break with the past than that which had been signalled. Thatcher's third term, from 1987, was marked by a virtual re-run, on a more dramatic scale, of a story which had been played out over and over again in post-war politics: a burst for growth which ended in overheating, retrenchment and widespread pain. Recession ruled, jobs were lost and companies folded in 1990-91 just as in 1980-81 – or in Labour's recession of 1976-77.

From recession to boom and back again

THE 1980-81 recession was the worst for 50 years. For a time it seemed that no government which presided over such events could survive. In the second quarter of 1981 unemployment topped 2m for the first time in 35 years. By 1982 there were signs of recovery – offset by the backwash of a world recession, which made this one of only two years since 1945 when world output fell. But unemployment did not abate. By January 1983 it was over 3m – and would have been higher had the Government not altered the definition of joblessness.

The process begun in 1980-81 had taken a heavy toll on manufacturing industry, where output collapsed and investment with it. The tide began to subside at the end of 1986: the percentage rate of those out of work fell from 11.7 per cent in the third quarter of that year to 10.7 in the second quarter of the following year, when a general election took place. Lawson's rescue operation after the 1987 market collapse threw the engines into reverse; but with consequences that meant the country moving from recession to boom and back again. Interest rates went up from 7.5 per cent in May 1988 to 13 per cent in November. By the end of 1990 the retraction in the economy had reached the point where by the statistical standard set for these things – six months of negative growth – recession had officially arrived. By the summer of 1991 it looked to be a deeper recession even than that of 1980-81, though by autumn the first signs were appearing that – unemployment apart – the worst might be past. A 0.3 per cent increase in GDP in the third quarter of 1991 meant that the recession was technically over; but even the Chancellor made little of this, since the figures were inflated by a surge in North Sea oil output, and all other indicators showed little if any sign of recovery.

The biggest gainers were the better-off

THE 1979 manifesto promise to cut direct taxation was honoured in Chancellor Howe's first Budget when he cut the 33 per cent rate to 30 (the 25 per cent rate was scrapped the following year) and brought the 83 per cent top rate down to 60. By 1991 the top rate was 40 per cent and the basic rate 25. But indirect taxation increased. VAT, raised to 15 per cent in 1979, was put up to 17.5 per cent in 1991 to fund reductions in the Community Charge (poll tax). National Insurance contributions were also increased. And the incidence of local taxation grew steadily until reversed in the 1991 Budget.

The biggest gainers were the better-off. Yet the tax yield from higher payers actually increased over this period: a clear vindication, ministers argued, for their strategy, and proof of the incentive effects of tax cuts – though it also reflected the very large increases in top people's pay during the Conservative years.

They had spectacular success in cutting the level of public borrowing

IF THE state took too much of the nation's income in 1979, as the Conservative manifesto of that year complained, then it was still taking too much in 1991. Despite several rounds of spending cuts, the Conservative government found the pressure to spend more on public services as irresistible as had their predecessors. Some ministers felt they were getting the worst of both worlds: unable to bring spending down, they denied themselves by their rhetoric the credit for having expanded it.

But they had spectacular success in cutting the level of public borrowing, especially through the growth years of 1982-87. In 1986 the Public Sector Borrowing Requirement (PSBR) was eliminated. Debt was repaid on an impressive scale, thus relieving further interest payments. But as recession grew, the PSBR reappeared. In his Autumn Statement of November 6 1991, Chancellor Lamont estimated an out-turn for 1991-2 of £10.5 billion, or £18.5 billion excluding receipts from privatisation. Thatcher, listening to this announcement from her backbench seat in the Commons, was reported to have looked displeased, and some of her continuing supporters condemned this departure from previous rigour. But the official line on borrowing had changed. What mattered, it was said, was not to eliminate borrowing altogether – that was not realistic in recession when tax revenues fell and spending on benefits swelled – but to do so across the cycle, borrowing in bad times and repaying in good.

The Government's philosophy on public spending had anyway changed. John Major had come to office proclaiming his commitment to raising the standard of public services, partly through devices like the Citizen's Charter but partly by responding more readily to clear evidence of need, as the Autumn Statement did in the case of the NHS. The old right-wing dream of privatising even great services like health and education had faded, both at Westminster and in the grassroots party, as poll after poll demonstrated the dire electoral fate it might invite. When Major declared at the 1991 party conference that there would be no privatisation of the service, "not today, not tomorrow, not after the next election, not ever while I am prime minister" he was rapturously cheered. Even subsidy for public transport was no longer considered indecent.

Deregulation was either an agent of liberty or an engine of licence

THE CONSERVATIVES succeeded in carrying through what looked, at the end of the period, to be a fundamental and probably irreversible transformation in the pattern of ownership. State industries sold off in whole or in part included oil, steel and telecommunications with the promise of the mines and the railways to come. Though Labour talked of restoring telecommunications and water to public ownership, it had no plans to renationalise the rest. Equally sweeping progress was made on deregulation, with controls on pay, prices and dividends immediately abandoned, exchange controls scrapped in 1979 and hire purchase controls removed in 1982.

Ancient restrictive practices were buried. Building societies occupied territory which had hitherto been the preserve of the banks. In 1986 the "Big Bang" radically rewrote the standard practices of the City, with stock exchange jobbers becoming market makers and the computer screen succeeding the Stock Exchange floor. Signalled as a change which alone could enable London to compete with competitors overseas, it produced an explosion in City salaries and led to the age of the loadsamoney, Porsche-driving, mobile phone-toting yuppie: a phase which faded rapidly at the end of the eighties as recession set in. But some other great interests, especially the lawyers, fought off attempts to do much the same to them. And a government attempt to liberalise shop opening hours, especially on Sundays, was wrecked by its own backbenchers.

For its supporters, deregulation was an agent of liberty, to its detractors an engine of licence. They pointed to City scandals: the collapse of Johnson Matthey Bankers in 1984, the collapse of BCCI in the summer of 1991, plus the extraordinary scandal at Guinness, which put its chief executive and two other notable businessmen in jail. They also pointed to the narrowing of economic policy options: shorn of the network of controls they had swept away, the Conservatives, they complained, had only one answer to the explosion of consumer credit, much of it tied to the value of homes, which followed Lawson's post-crash reflation of late 1987 and tax cuts of March 1988. The one response now left to him was to hike interest rates, which in choking the consumer bonanza choked manufacturing industry, too. ●

ANALYSIS

I T HAD often been predicted that the party which won power in 1979 would continue to rule for many years, since these were the years when the windfall of North Sea oil would produce its greatest benefit. This, perhaps, is the context in which judgments need to be made on the issue on which all elections turn – voters' assessments and expectations for the economic well-being of themselves and their families.

Clearly, most people in Britain were far better off by the end of the Thatcher years than at the beginning. Real personal disposable income rose at an annual average rate of 2.8 per cent between 1979 and 1990, not as much as in 1970-74 under Edward Heath when the increase was 3.8 per cent, but better than Labour's average of 2.2 in 1974-79. Spending on essential services also increased by 26 per cent in real terms between 1978-79 and 1989-90.

But some prospered more than others. For the first time in post-war history, Britain found itself in the hands of a government which thought it not only right but actually therapeutic to widen the gap between the prosperous and the poor.

Those in work did much better than the unemployed, an army whose numbers swelled in 1983-86 and again from 1990 onwards. In times of apparent affluence, poverty grew. The theory was that as the successful prospered, the rest of the country also stood to benefit. Prosperity would trickle down from the top of the tree to the bottom. The Government published figures which appeared to show that this had been happening, with the income of the poorest 10 per cent rising twice as fast as the national average. But the statisticians had erred. Work by the Institute of Fiscal Studies for the Commons select committee on the social services showed the reverse had happened. The poorest 10 per cent had done less than half as well as the average.

Supply side constraints were removed, as promised. Most managers agreed that the freedom to manage had been largely restored to them. By the standards of post-war Britain, an uncanny peace prevailed on the nation's shop floors. Borrowing was drastically cut and debt repaid: Britain's overseas assets multiplied. In their times of greatest success, ministers talked with pride of a British economic miracle, admired across a world which had previously come to see us as the sick man of Europe.

"The strategy we have followed since 1979," Chancellor Lawson told the Commons when he presented his public spending plans in 1986, "has brought inflation down to the lowest level for three decades, combined with sustained growth and steadily rising living standards...We have brought it about by the determined pursuit of free markets and sound money, and that is what we shall stick to." But what followed suggested that some of the gains were transient or illusory. Inflation had not been beaten. Growth could not be sustained. And the platform for lasting prosperity was barely detectable. Manufacturing industry, heavily pounded in the 1980-81 recession and thereafter often the victim of high interest rates and an over-valued pound, had shed so much fat that little was left to lose when the 1991 recession began to bite. There were heavy and general casualties, even in the south, which had been spared the worst of the previous recession.

The record of manufacturing investment, research and development and education and training, seen by many as the key to future prosperity, came nowhere near to matching the need in a fiercely competitive world. The record of manufacturing productivity, an equally crucial index, was scarcely more reassuring. There were all the gains that come from a shake-out: as recovery began, more goods were produced by fewer hands just as the text books said. The Conservatives were surely entitled to credit on any accounting basis for the changes that had occurred under their bleak and unforgiving regime in steel, shipbuilding and the coalmines. Yet the record was fitful. Perhaps the most worrying strand was the trade performance. In 1984 the balance of trade on manufactures swung into deficit. And from 1986 onward all previous records were shattered as the deficit on current account built to £19 billion in 1989. Too much of the spending power which had come from the boom had been spent on imported goods: too little had been sold abroad to pay for it. Without the continuing benefit of North Sea oil it would all have looked much worse.

The 1991 recession undid the claim that the Thatcher years had been good for growth. That was true of the middle years: the economy grew by 3.8 per cent in 1985, by 3.6 in 1986, by 4.4 in 1987 and by 4.7 in 1988. But over the full 12 years it was not such a satisfying story.

And yet, as the election approached, the country did not seem convinced that Labour could have done better. Opinion polls indicated a continuing though diminishing preference for the Conservatives as the party best equipped to handle the economy. The party itself pinned most of the blame for what had gone wrong on Chancellor Lawson: for the best of possible reasons – fear of a slump after the October 1987 crash – he had taken too many risks and now we were footing the bill. But Lawson had gone. Now we were under new management. Inflation was falling and interest rates with it and though unemployment was destined to lag behind on the road to recovery, ministers thought in the autumn of 1991 that they could see a further improvement which might carry them through to victory in 1992.

The pages which follow set out some of the essential facts and figures of the Thatcher years. They start, as she did, with economic management and inflation. ●

ECONOMIC MANAGEMENT AND INFLATION

WHAT COMES around goes around: history, fashion, even inflation. Though it has never got back to the Labour peak of 26.9 per cent in August 1975, the inflation roller coaster continues to peak and trough. In May 1980, a year after the Conservatives were elected, inflation climbed to 21.9 per cent. It remained in double figures until April 1982.

The fall which followed, coinciding with the start of the Falklands war, helped put them on course for re-election. Inflation remained in single figures throughout the 1983-87 parliament, touching a low point of 2.4 per cent in July and August 1986. From the summer of 1988 it resumed a steady ascent which took it back into double figures in August 1990 and on to a peak of 10.9 per cent in September and October 1990 before the effects of the 1990-91 squeeze began to reverse the process.

The main instrument for controlling the economy was the manipulation of interest rates, which by making credit costlier calmed down consumer spending. But it also choked off manufacturing investment, thus imperilling the readiness of the domestic market to respond to the upturn when it came.

Opposition parties said the Government had denied itself more flexible weapons, which might have cut discretionary spending without damaging essential spending, by its refusal to consider alternatives like direct controls on credit.

The movement of the exchange rate was in one sense an accidental consequence of the interest rate policy, since high interest rates tended to strengthen the pound. But chancellors also used this weapon in the hope of curbing inflationary expectations.

With high exchange rates, imports became cheaper, but exporters found themselves uncompetitive in world markets. Towards the end of the eighties Chancellor Lawson increasingly relied on the exchange rate as a weapon of economic management, seeing the Exchange Rate Mechanism (ERM) of the European Monetary System as a powerful brake on inflation (countries which had preceded Britain in joining the ERM had dealt more successfully with inflation than we had).

This was one of the reasons for the Chancellor's rift with the Prime Minister in 1987. Mrs Thatcher believed that the pound should be left to find its own level. Lawson thought, as he said in his resignation speech on October 31 1989 that: "The exchange rate should be seen as an essential element of financial discipline...full UK membership of the EMS would signally enhance the credit of our anti-inflationary resolve in general and the role of exchange rate discipline in particular, and thus underpin the Medium Term Financial Strategy." ●

RATES OF CHANGE IN GDP
PERCENTAGE (CONSTANT FACTOR COST AVERAGE ESTIMATE)

1951	1.9	1961	2.7	1971	1.7	1981	-1.2
1952	0.8	1962	1.4	1972	2.8	1982	1.7
1953	3.9	1963	4.0	1973	7.4	1983	3.8
1954	4.2	1964	5.6	1974	-1.5	1984	1.8
1955	3.6	1965	2.9	1975	-0.8	1985	3.4
1956	1.4	1966	1.9	1976	2.6	1986	3.6
1957	1.7	1967	2.2	1977	2.6	1987	4.3
1958	-0.2	1968	4.4	1978	2.9	1988	4.3
1959	4.0	1969	2.5	1979	2.8	1989	1.8
1960	5.6	1970	2.0	1980	-2.0	1990	0.5

averages	1964-70	1974-79	1979-90
	2.6	2.0	2.06

Source: CSO Blue Book

HOW SPENDING POWER GREW 1979-90
1. Rates of change of Personal Disposable Income at constant prices (%)
2. Per capita at constant prices (%)

	1	2
1979	5.8	5.7
1980	1.5	1.4
1981	-0.7	-0.7
1982	-0.2	-0.2
1983	2.8	2.7
1984	2.4	2.2
1985	2.6	2.3
1986	4.5	4.3
1987	3.6	3.3
1988	5.9	5.6
1989	5.3	5.3
1990	3.2	3.2

averages	1	2
1964-70	2.0	2.1
1970-74	3.8	3.5
1974-79	2.2	2.2
1979-90	2.8	2.7

Source: CSO Blue Book

GENERAL GOVERNMENT DEBT
(% OF NOMINAL GNP/GDP)

	1982	1983	1984	1985	1986	1987	1988	1989	1990	Projected 1991	1992
United States	41.3	44.3	45.6	48.8	52.0	52.9	53.8	54.0	54.6	56.2	56.2
Japan	60.9	66.5	67.8	68.5	72.1	74.4	72.4	70.2	66.5	63.2	59.9
Germany	39.6	41.0	41.7	42.5	42.6	44.0	44.5	43.4	43.8	47.6	49.8
France	40.1	41.4	43.8	45.4	45.7	47.3	47.2	46.6	46.9	47.5	47.8
Italy	66.4	72.0	77.2	84.1	88.5	93.0	95.7	98.8	101.1	103.1	104.3
UK	52.9	53.1	54.7	53.1	51.7	49.2	42.8	37.4	35.6	36.0	36.2
Canada	50.1	56.1	58.7	64.6	68.4	68.6	69.0	69.6	72.1	75.6	76.8

Source: OECD

RATINGS IN THE GROWTH LEAGUE 1970-89
GDP PER HEAD, CURRENT PRICES AND PURCHASING POWER PARITIES, (US $)

1970		1974		1979	
1. U.S	4,919	US	6,805	US	10,943
2. Switzerland	4,764	Switzerland	6,637	Canada	9,995
3. Canada	3,881	Canada	5,941	Switzerland	9,474
4. Sweden	3,818	Lux'embourg	5,563	Iceland	8,642
5. Luxembourg	3,676	Sweden	5,332	Norway	8,285
6. Netherlands	3,456	Netherlands	4,987	Sweden	8,232
7. Denmark	3,439	New Zealand	4,916	Luxembourg	8,211
8. Australia	3,406	France	4,817	Germany	8,017
9. Germany	3,381	Australia	4,787	Netherlands	7,897
10. New Zealand	3,320	Denmark	4,769	France	7,889
11. France	3,296	Germany	4,757	Denmark	7,733
12. UK	**3,239**	Iceland	4,743	Australia	7,628
13. Norway	3,063	Norway	4,594	**UK**	**7,384**
14. Belgium	2,953	**UK**	**4,561**	Belgium	7,120
15. Iceland	2,891	Belgium	4,490	Italy	7,024
16. Finland	2,862	Finland	4,342	Austria	7,002
17. Italy	2,848	Austria	4,184	Japan	6,950
18. Japan	2,766	Italy	4,178	Finland	6,927
19. Austria	2,735	Japan	4,012	New Zealand	6,515
20. Spain	2,228	Spain	3,518	Spain	5,258
21. Ireland	1,777	Ireland	2,582	Ireland	4,467
22. Greece	1,540	Portugal	2,402	Greece	4,112
23. Portugal	1,459	Greece	2,330	Portugal	3,788
24. Turkey	945	Turkey	1,438	Turkey	2,344

1983		1987		1989	
1. US	14,265	US	18,254	US	20,629
2. Canada	13,229	Canada	17,145	Canada	19,316
3. Switzerland	12,960	Iceland	15,774	Switzerland	17,696
4. Norway	11,863	Switz'erland	15,734	Luxembourg	17,192
5 Iceland	11,685	Norway	15,493	Norway	16,663
6. Sweden	11,285	Luxembourg	14,553	Iceland	15,767
7. Luxembourg	11,185	Sweden	14,015	Sweden	15,533
8. Germany	10,782	Denmark	13,277	Japan	15,501
9. France	10,749	Germany	13,242	Finland	15,022
10. Denmark	10,603	Japan	13,140	Germany	14,985
11. Japan	10,218	France	12,769	France	14,565
12. Finland	10,200	Finland	12,708	Denmark	14,392
13. Netherlands	10,161	Australia	12,665	**UK**	**14,345**
14. Australia	9,986	**UK**	**12,571**	Australia	14,304
15. UK	**9,861**	Netherlands	12,113	Italy	13,902
16. Belgium	9,834	Italy	12,103	Netherlands	13,709
17. Italy	9,768	Belgium	11,742	Belgium	13,587
18. Austria	9,736	Austria	11,640	Austria	13,407
19. New Zealand	9,061	New Zealand	10,818	New Zealand	11,507
20. Spain	6,992	Spain	8,744	Spain	10,263
21. Ireland	6,134	Ireland	7,557	Ireland	8,984
22. Greece	5,380	Greece	6,349	Portugal	7,360
23. Portugal	5,219	Portugal	6,290	Greece	7,253
24. Turkey	3,154	Turkey	4,170	Turkey	4,484

Source: OECD National Accounts

UK RATINGS IN THE LEAGUE:

1979	1980	1981	1982	1983	1984	1985	1986	1987	1988	1989
13	16	18	18	15	15	15	14	14	14	13

Source: OECD National Accounts

ANNUAL AVERAGE INCREASE IN PRICES

	(average) 1979-82	(average) 1983-6	1987	1988	1989	1990*
US	10.3	3.3	3.7	4.1	4.8	5.4
Japan	4.8	1.6	0.1	0.7	2.3	3.1
France	12.4	10.1	3.1	2.7	3.6	3.4
Germany	5.3	1.9	0.2	2.1	3.8	2.7
Italy	17.6	10.1	4.6	5.0	6.6	6.1
UK	13.0	4.8	4.2	4.9	7.8	9.5
Canada	10.7	4.6	4.4	4.0	5.0	4.8

*12 months to September

STANDARDISED UNEMPLOYMENT RATES
(% BY ILO/OECD GUIDELINES)

	(average) 1979-82	(average) 1983-6	1987	1988	1989	1990
US	7.5	7.7	6.1	5.4	5.2	5.4
Japan	2.2	2.7	2.8	2.5	2.3	2.1
France	6.9	9.7	10.5	10.0	9.4	8.9
Germany	4.1	7.1	6.2	6.2	5.6	5.1
Italy	7.8	9.6	10.9	11.0	10.9	9.9
UK	8.2	11.6	10.3	8.5	7.1	6.9
Canada	8.3	10.7	8.8	7.7	7.5	8.1

TOTAL OUTLAYS OF GOVERNMENT SPENDING AS % OF GDP

	(average) 1979-82	(average) 1983-6	1987	1988	1990
US	34	37	37	36	36
Japan	34	33	33	33	n.a
France	48	52	51	50	50
Germany	49	48	47	47	45
Italy	45	50	51	51	52
UK	46	46	43	41	41
Canada	42	47	46	44	44

GROWTH OF REAL GNP/GDP

	(average) 1979-82	(average) 1983-6	1987	1988	1989	1990
US	0.4	4.1	3.4	4.5	2.5	0.9
Japan	4.1	3.9	4.6	5.7	4.9	5.6
France	2.1	1.6	2.2	3.8	3.6	2.8
Germany	1.1	2.4	1.6	3.7	3.9	4.5
Italy	2.9	2.3	3.0	4.2	3.2	2.0
UK	0.4	3.3	4.7	4.6	2.2	0.6
Canada	1.2	4.4	4.0	4.4	3.0	0.9

Source: OECD Economic Outlook

CONSUMER CREDIT OUTSTANDING AT END OF YEAR (£BN)

1982	1983	1984	1985	1986	1987	1988	1989
16.0	18.9	22.3	26.1	30.2	36.2	42.5	48.2

CENTRAL BANK DISCOUNT RATES, ANNUAL AVERAGE.

	1979	1980	1981	1982	1983	1984	1985	1986	1987	1988	1989
US	12.0	13.0	12.0	8.5	8.5	8.0	7.5	5.5	6.5	6.5	7.0
Japan	6.3	7.3	5.5	5.5	5.0	5.0	5.0	3.0	2.5	2.5	3.8
France	9.5	9.5	9.5	9.5	9.5	9.5	9.5	9.5	9.5	9.5	10.3
Germany	6.0	7.5	7.5	5.0	4.0	4.5	4.0	3.5	2.5	3.5	6.0
Italy	15.0	16.5	19.0	18.0	17.0	16.5	15.0	12.0	12.5	12.5	13.5
UK	17.0	14.0	14.5	10.1	9.0	9.6	11.5	11.0	8.5	13.0	15.0
Canada	14.0	17.3	14.7	10.1	10.0	10.2	9.5	8.5	8.5	8.8	12.5

Source: Annual Register

THE SOARING COST OF LIVING
MONTHLY PERCENTAGE INCREASES ON THE RETAIL PRICE INDEX

	Jan	Feb	Mar	Apr	May	Jun	Jul	Aug	Sep	Oct	Nov	Dec
1975	19.9	19.9	21.2	21.7	25.0	26.1	26.3	26.9	26.6	25.9	25.2	24.9
1976	23.4	22.9	21.2	18.8	15.4	13.8	12.9	13.8	14.3	14.7	15.0	15.1
1977	16.6	16.2	16.7	17.5	17.1	17.7	17.6	16.5	15.6	14.1	13.0	12.1
1978	9.9	9.5	9.1	7.9	7.7	7.4	7.8	8.0	7.8	7.8	8.1	8.4
1979	9.3	9.6	9.8	10.1	10.3	11.4	15.6	15.8	16.5	17.2	17.4	17.2
1980	18.4	19.1	19.8	21.8	21.9	21.0	16.9	16.3	15.9	15.4	15.3	15.1
1981	13.0	12.5	12.6	12.0	11.7	11.3	10.9	11.5	11.4	11.7	12.0	12.0
1982	12.0	11.0	10.4	9.4	9.5	9.2	8.7	8.0	7.3	6.8	6.3	5.4
1983	4.9	5.3	4.6	4.0	3.7	3.7	4.2	4.6	5.1	5.0	4.8	5.3
1984	5.1	5.1	5.2	5.2	5.1	5.1	4.5	5.0	4.7	5.0	4.9	4.6
1985	5.0	5.4	6.1	6.9	7.0	7.0	6.9	6.2	5.9	5.4	5.5	5.7
1986	5.5	5.1	4.2	3.0	2.8	2.5	2.4	2.4	3.0	3.0	3.5	3.7
1987	3.9	3.9	4.0	4.2	4.1	4.2	4.4	4.4	4.2	4.5	4.1	3.7
1988	3.3	3.3	3.5	3.9	4.2	4.6	4.8	5.7	5.9	6.4	6.4	6.8
1989	7.5	7.8	7.9	8.0	8.3	8.3	8.2	7.3	7.6	7.3	7.7	7.7
1990	7.7	7.5	8.1	9.4	9.7	9.8	9.8	10.6	10.9	10.9	9.7	9.3
1991	9.0	8.9	8.2	6.4	5.8	5.8	5.5	4.7	4.1	3.7		

Source: Economic Trends

INCOME AND EXPENDITURE INDEX

	weekly earnings	retail prices: All	retail prices: Food	housing costs	house prices	RPDI
1979	53.9	59.9	67.9	46.2	63.2	93.0
1980	65.0	70.6	76.1	59.6	73.8	93.4
1981	73.3	79.1	82.5	70.3	76.9	92.8
1982	80.2	85.8	88.9	79.2	77.1	92.6
1983	87.0	89.7	91.8	81.2	85.3	95.2
1984	92.2	94.3	96.9	88.7	93.0	97.4
1985			100.0			
1986	107.9	103.4	103.0	105.8	115.7	104.5
1987	116.3	107.7	106.4	114.8	133.5	107.8
1988	126.4	113.0	110.1	125.0	165.1	113.9
1989	137.9	121.8	116.3	150.4	185.0	120.0
1990	133.3	125.7	181.9	n/a	n/a	123.8

INCREASE (%)	weekly earnings	retail prices: All	retail prices: Food	housing costs	house prices	RPDI
1979-83	61.4	49.7	35.2	75.6	35.0	2.3
1983-87-	33.6	20.0	15.9	25.1	56.5	13.3
1987-90*	18.6	23.8	18.1	58.4	116.9	26.2
1979-90*	155.8	122.5	85.1	293.7	192.7	29.2

*or 1989

Source: National Institute Economic Review with additional calculations

HOW EARNINGS OUTSTRIPPED PRICES

	% annual increase in :	
	average earnings	cost of living
1980	12.1	18.0
1981	12.9	11.9
1982	9.4	8.6
1983	8.4	4.6
1984	6.1	5.0
1985	8.5	6.1
1986	7.9	3.4
1987	7.7	4.2
1988	8.8	4.9
1989	9.1	7.8
1990	9.7	9.4

Source: recalculated from Annual Abstract, Monthly Digest of Statistics

THE COST OF BORROWING 1979-91

1979	Base Rate %
April 6	12.0
June 15	14.0
November 16	17.0

1980	
July 4	16.0
November 25	14.0

1981	
March 11	12.0
September 16	14.0
October 1	16.0
October 14	15.5
November 9	15.0
December 3	14.5

1982	
January 22	14.0
February 25	13.5
March 12	13.0
June 8	12.5
July 13	12.0
August 2	11.5
August 18	11.0
August 31	10.5
October 7	10.0
October 14	9.5
November 4	9.0
November 26	10.0 - 10.25

1983	
January 12	11.0
March 15	10.5
April 15	10.0
June 15	9.5
October 4	9.0

1984	Base Rate %
March 7	8.0 - 9.0
March 15	8.5 - 8.75
May 10	9.0 - 9.25
June 27	9.25
July 9	10.0
July 11	10.0 - 12.0
July 12	12.0
August 9	11.5
August 10	11.0
August 20	10.5
November 7	10.0
November 20	9.75 - 10.0
November 23	9.5 - 9.75

1985	
January 11	10.5
January 14	12.0
January 28	14.0
March 20	13.5 - 14 .0
March 21	13.5
March 29	13.0 - 13.5
April 2	13.0 - 13.25
April 12	12.75 - 13.0
April 19	12.5 - 12.75
June 12	12.5
July 15	12.0 - 12.5
July 16	12.0
July 29	11.5 - 12.0
July 30	11.5

1986	
January 9	12.5
March 19	11.5
April 8	11.0 - 11.5
April 9	11.0
April 21	10.5
May 27	10.0
October 14	11.0

1987	Base Rate %
March 10	10.5
March 19	10.0
April 29	9.5
May 11	9.0
August 7	10.0
October 26	9.5
November 5	9.0
December 4	8.5

1988	
February 2	9.0
March 17	8.5
April 11	8.0
May 18	7.5
June 3	8.0
June 6	8.5
June 22	9.0
June 29	9.5
July 5	10.0
July 19	10.5
August 8	10.5 - 11.0
August 9	11.0
August 25	11.0 - 12.0
August 26	12.0
November 25	13.0

1989	
May 24	14.0
October 5	15.0

1990	
October 8	14.0

1991	
February 13	13.5
February 27	13.0
March 22	12.5
April 12	12.0
May 24	11.5
July 12	11.0
September 4	10.5

BANKRUPTCIES
(ENGLAND AND WALES)

	1979	1980	1981	1982	1983	1984	1985	1986	1987	1988	1989	1990	1991*
Personal	3,456	3,986	5,075	5,654	6,981	8,178	6,730	7,093	6,994	7,717	8,138	13,987	11,494
Company	4,537	6,890	8,596	12,067	13,406	13,721	14,898	14,405	11,439	9,427	10,456	15,051	10,833

*1991 first 6 months only
Source: Annual Abstract of Statistics/Association of British Chambers of Commerce

PURCHASING POWER OF THE £

in:	What your 1979 £ would have been worth	What your 1990 £ would have been worth
1979	£1.00	£2.23
1980	85p	£1.89
1981	76p	£1.69
1982	70p	£1.55
1983	67p	£1.48
1984	64p	£1.41
1985	60p	£1.33
1986	58p	£1.29
1987	56p	£1.24
1988	53p	£1.18
1989	49p	£1.10
1990	45p	£1.00

in:	What your 1950 £ would have been worth	What your 1960 £ would have been worth	What your 1970 £ would have been worth	What your 1980 £ would have been worth
1960	72p	£1.00		
1970	49p	68p	£1.00	
1980	14p	19p	28p	£1.00
1990	7p	10p	15p	53p

Source: derived from Economic Trends

FORECASTS OF MONETARY GROWTH, AND WHAT HAPPENED
THE FORECAST OF % GROWTH MADE IN MARCH OF EACH YEAR FOR THE FINANCIAL YEAR JUST BEGINNING (i.e. the 1979 forecast is for the year 1979-80) AND THE OUTTURN AT THE END OF THE YEAR

£M3. Notes and coins in circulation, sterling current accounts of the UK private sector with banks, deposit accounts, public sector accounts

M0. Notes and coins in circulation plus banks' deposits held at the Bank of England.

	£M3		M0	
	forecast	result	forecast	result
1979	7-11	16.2		
1980	7-11	18.4		
1981	6-10	12.8		
1982	8-12	11.1		
1983	7-11	9.5		
1984	6-10	11.9	4-8	5.4
1985	5-9	16.3	3-7	4.1
1986	11-15	18.7	2-6	3.5
1987			2-6	6.4
1988			1-5	6.8
1989			1-5	5.0
1990			1-5	7.2

Source: based on a fuller table in Christopher Johnson, The Economy Under Mrs. Thatcher 1979-1990, Penguin Books.

The forecast figures are the figures given in the Budget by the Chancellor of the Exchequer for the expected percentage increase in the coming year. The results are shown alongside. Thus in 1980 the Chancellor expected an increase in the range of 7 to 11 per cent: in the event the expansion was 7.4 per cent above his top figure.

The Budgets

BUDGETS OF 1979 - 1983 PARLIAMENT

1979

JUNE 12	
CHANCELLOR	Sir G.Howe
HEADLINES	Big tax concessions; big cuts planned in public spending. Interest rates up 2% to 14%. Controls over overseas investment relaxed. VAT increased.

TAX CHANGES	
single person allowance:	up from £985 to £1,165
married person allowance:	up from £1,535 to £1815
additional allowance (single parent premium):	£650
basic rate:	down from 33% to 30%
threshold:	£751-10,000
top rate:	down from 83% to 60%
threshold:	£25,000+
exemptions on capital gains:	£1,000
capital transfer:	£25,000

DUTIES	
alcohol:	no change but VAT effect puts 2p on beer, 28p on spirits
tobacco:	no change but VAT effect puts 6p on pack of 20
petrol:	7p on gallon
diesel:	7p on gallon
road tax:	£50 (no change)

1980

MARCH 26	
CHANCELLOR:	Sir G.Howe
HEADLINES:	Aim to cut PSBR within 2% of GDP by 1984. Social security benefits targeted for cuts: help for jobless to be cut (as incentive to find work). Withdrawal of benefit for strikers' wives and families

TAX CHANGES	
single person allowance:	£1,375
married person allowance:	£2145
additional allowance (single parent premium):	£770
basic rate:	unchanged
threshold:	£11250
top rate:	unchanged
threshold:	£27,000+
exemptions on capital gains:	£3,000
capital transfer:	£50,000

DUTIES	
alcohol:	2p beer, 8p wine, 50p spirits
tobacco:	5p on 20
petrol:	10p on gallon
diesel:	10p on gallon
road tax:	up £10

BUDGETS 1979 - 1990

1981

MARCH 10	
CHANCELLOR	Sir G.Howe
HEADLINES	Public spending excessive and must be drastically cut. Taxes up; allowances frozen instead of being indexed to reflect inflation. Extra revenue to be taken from North Sea oil (following price rises). One-off tax on bank deposits. Big increases on drinking, smoking, motoring.

TAX CHANGES

single person allowance:	£1,375
married person allowance:	£2,145
additional allowance (single parent premium):	£770
basic rate:	unchanged
threshold:	£11,250
top rate:	unchanged
threshold:	£27,000+
exemptions on capital gains:	£3,000
capital transfer:	£50,000

DUTIES

alcohol:	4p beer, 12p wine, 60p spirits
tobacco:	14p on 20
petrol:	20p on gallon
diesel:	20p on gallon
road tax:	up £10

1982

MARCH 9	
CHANCELLOR:	Sir G.Howe
HEADLINES:	Standstill budget. Cut of 1 per cent in National Insurance surcharge. Tax thresholds raised by more than the rate of inflation. Unemployment benefit to be taxed from July 1982.

TAX CHANGES

single person allowance:	£1,565
married person allowance:	£2,445
additional allowance (single parent premium):	£880
basic rate:	unchanged
threshold:	£12,800
top rate:	unchanged
threshold:	£31,500+
exemptions on capital gains:	£5,000
capital transfer:	£55,000

DUTIES

alcohol:	2p beer, 10p wine, 30p spirits
tobacco:	5p on 20
petrol:	9p on gallon
diesel:	7p on gallon
road tax:	up £10

BUDGETS 1979 - 1990

1983

MARCH 15
CHANCELLOR   Sir G.Howe
HEADLINES   A £2,750m reflation. Allowances up by more than the rate of inflation. earlier
                    cut in unemployment benefit is restored. Further cut in National Insurance
                    surcharge. Changes in unemployment registration. Enhanced incentives for new
                    businesses aimed to persuade unemployed to become self-employed. Mortgage
                    interest relief ceiling up from £25,000 to £30,000

TAX CHANGES

single person allowance:	£1,785
married person allowance:	£2,795
additional allowance (single parent premium):	£1,010
basic rate:	unchanged
threshold:	£14,600
top rate:	unchanged
threshold:	£36,000+
exemptions on capital gains:	£5,300
capital transfer:	£60,000

DUTIES

alcohol:	1p beer, 5p wine, 25p spirits
tobacco:	3p on 20
petrol:	4p on gallon
diesel:	3p on gallon
road tax:	up £5

BUDGETS OF 1983 - 1987 PARLIAMENT
1984

MARCH 13
CHANCELLOR: N.Lawson
HEADLINES: "A radical tax-reforming budget".

TAX CHANGES

single person allowance:	£2,005
married person allowance:	£3,155
additional allowance:	£1,150
basic rate:	unchanged
threshold:	£15,400
top rate:	unchanged
threshold:	£38,100+
exemptions on capital gains:	£5,600
capital transfer:	death and lifetime transfers rescheduled. Limit raised to £64,000

DUTIES

alcohol:	2p on beer, 10p on spirits, but wine down 18p (EC ruling)
tobacco:	10p on pack of 20
petrol:	4p on gallon
diesel:	3p on gallon
road tax:	up £5

BUDGETS 1979 - 1990

1985

MARCH 19
CHANCELLOR
HEADLINES

N.Lawson
Aim: to build basis for enterprise to flourish. Substantial expansion of Youth Training to give every 18-year-old a choice of full-time education, job or training (i.e not unemployment)

TAX CHANGES

single person allowance:	£2,205
married person allowance:	£3,455
additional allowance:	£1,259
basic rate:	unchanged
threshold:	£16,200
top rate:	unchanged
threshold:	£40,200+
exemptions on capital gains:	£5,900
capital transfer:	Again rescheduled. Top three bands abolished, highest rate cut from 75% to 60%.

DUTIES

alcohol:	1p beer, 6p wine, 10p spirits
tobacco:	6p on 20
petrol:	4p on gallon
diesel:	3p on gallon
road tax:	up £10

1986

MARCH 18
CHANCELLOR:
HEADLINES:

N.Lawson
Basic rate cut to 29%. No increase on alcohol. Capital transfer tax on lifetime gifts abolished.

TAX CHANGES

single person allowance:	£2,335
married person allowance:	£3,655
additional allowance:	£1,320
basic rate:	down to 29%
threshold:	£17,200
top rate:	unchanged
threshold:	£41,200+
exemptions on capital gains:	£6,300
capital transfer:	Tax on transfer at death becomes inheritance tax. Limit set at £71,000.

DUTIES

alcohol:	no change
tobacco:	11p on 20
petrol:	7p on gallon
diesel:	6p on gallon
road tax:	unchanged

BUDGETS 1979 - 1990

1987

MARCH 17
CHANCELLOR	N.Lawson
HEADLINES	Basic rate cut to 27%. Launch of portable pensions with tax relief. Higher than planned increases in public spending. No increase on alcohol, tobacco, motoring.

TAX CHANGES
single person allowance:	£2,425
married person allowance:	£3,795
additional allowance:	£1,370
basic rate:	down to 27%
threshold:	£17,900
top rate:	unchanged
threshold:	£41,200
exemptions on capital gains:	£6,600
capital transfer:	Previous bands reduced: limit raised to £90,000..

DUTIES
alcohol:	no change
tobacco:	no change
petrol:	no change: unleaded 5p down
diesel:	no change
road tax:	no change

BUDGETS OF 1987 PARLIAMENT
1988

MARCH 15
CHANCELLOR:	N.Lawson
HEADLINES:	Basic rate down 2% to 25%. Top rate cut from 60% to 40%. New standard rate target: 20%. Allowances increased by twice the rate of inflation. Separate taxation for husbands and wives to be introduced in 1990. House purchase tax relief to be limited to one mortgage-payer per home.

TAX CHANGES
single person allowance:	£2,605
married person allowance:	£4,095
additional allowance:	£1,490
basic rate:	down from 27% to 25%
threshold:	£19,300
top rate:	cut to 40%
threshold:	up from £17,900 to £19,300+
exemptions on capital gains:	£5,000
capital transfer:	£110,000

DUTIES
alcohol:	1p on beer,4p on wine, spirits unchanged
tobacco:	up 3p for pack of 20
petrol:	up 5p per gallon, but no increase for unleaded
diesel:	5p per gallon
road tax:	unchanged

BUDGETS 1979 - 1990

1989

MARCH 14	
CHANCELLOR	N.Lawson
HEADLINES	Budget designed to curb demand in face of renewed inflation. Reform of National Insurance system to help diminish poverty trap for low paid. Abolition of earnings rule for pensioners. Tax relief from August 1990 on private health insurance premiums for the over-60s.

TAX CHANGES	
single person allowance:	£2,785
married person allowance:	£4,375
additional allowance:	£1,590
basic rate:	unchanged
threshold:	all intermediate rates between the basic and the top rate were abolished. The basic rate threshold – the point at which taxpayers began to pay more than the basic rate – therefore disappeared.
top rate:	unchanged
threshold:	£20,700+
exemptions on capital gains:	£5,000
inheritance tax:	£118,000
DUTIES	
alcohol:	no change
tobacco:	no change
petrol:	4p on gallon, duty on unleaded cut by 10p
diesel:	no change
road tax:	no change

1990

MARCH 20	
CHANCELLOR:	J.Major
HEADLINES:	"A saver's budget"; launched TESSAs. £500m increase in taxes mostly through duties on alcohol, tobacco and petrol. Cut in pools betting duty

TAX CHANGES	
single person allowance:	(abolition of joint taxation for married couples) £3,005
additional allowance:	£1,720
basic rate:	unchanged
threshold:	unchanged
top rate:	unchanged
threshold:	unchanged
exemptions on capital gains:	£5,000
inheritance tax:	£128,000
DUTIES	
alcohol:	2p on beer, 7p on wine, 54p on spirits
tobacco:	10p on packet of 20
petrol:	11p on gallon, 9p unleaded
diesel:	9p on gallon
road tax:	unchanged

BUDGETS 1979 - 1990

1991

MARCH 19	
CHANCELLOR	N.Lamont
HEADLINES	Poll tax bills to be cut by £140 per head in 1991-92. VAT up to 17.5% to pay for it. End of mortgage tax relief at 40% level.

TAX CHANGES

single person allowance:	£3,295
additional allowance:	£1,720
basic rate:	unchanged
threshold:	unchanged
top rate:	unchanged
threshold:	£23,700+
exemptions on capital gains:	£5,500
inheritance tax:	£140,000

DUTIES

alcohol:	2p on beer, 9p on wine, 56p on spirits
tobacco:	16p on packet of 20
petrol:	4p on a litre (3.5p unleaded)
diesel:	3.5p on litre
road tax:	no change

TAXATION

THE CONSERVATIVES came into office pledged to cut income tax at all levels "to reward hard work, responsibility and success". The top rate, then 83 per cent, must be reduced, they said, to match the average across Europe. They began to redeem these promises within weeks. Chancellor Howe's first Budget, on June 12 1979, cut the standard rate from 33 to 30 per cent and set a target for further cuts to 25 per cent. Top rate was brought down from 83 per cent to 60. Thereafter, cutting became more difficult and in his severely deflationary 1981 Budget, Howe increased taxes by £3.6 billion. Standard rate remained at 30 per cent until 1986, when it was cut to 29 per cent with further reduction a year later to 27 per cent and a third cut in 1988 to bring it to 25. At this point a new target was set: a standard rate of 20 per cent. Top rate was also cut to 40 per cent in the 1988 Budget.

The Conservatives had also promised to bring relief to the poorer taxpayers. From time to time they raised tax thresholds by more than the rate of inflation, so releasing from the tax net more than just those who had been swept into it over the previous year by inflation. But in keeping with their belief that cutting taxes created fresh incentives and liberated the entrepreneur, they gave most help to people at the top. From being the heaviest taxed high wage-earners in Europe, they became among the most favoured. Though the sums forgone by this policy sounded imposing, the Government argued that everyone gained. In 1978-79, they said, when the top rate was 83 per cent, the top 5 per cent of taxpayers contributed 24 per cent of all taxes collected. By the start of the nineties the rate had been more than halved (to 40 per cent), but the yield was actually up, with top taxpayers providing 31.5 per cent of the total contribution.

But other forms of taxation grew heavier. In the first Howe Budget, cuts in direct taxation were offset by increases in VAT. National Insurance contributions also increased. And until the reduction of the poll tax in 1991, – a change paid for by an increase in VAT from 15 to 17.5% – the share of local government costs paid at the local rather than at the national level was steadily increased. Overall taxation, including corporate taxes, accounted for 37.6 per cent of GDP in 1988-89, compared with 33.1 per cent in 1979. ●

THE TAX HAUL
£ MILLION, SHOWING % INCREASE ON PREVIOUS YEAR

	Taxes on income	Taxes on Spending	Social security	Customs & excise	Poll tax
1979	25,239	29,670	11,526	18,347	
1980	31,002	36,474	13,939	22,562	
% increase	*22.8*	*22.9*	*20.9*	*23.0*	
1981	36,134	42,465	15,916	25,809	
% increase	*16.6*	*16.4*	*14.2*	*14.4*	
1982	40,282	46,467	18,095	28,638	
% increase	*11.5*	*9.4*	*13.7*	*11.0*	
1983	43,344	49,500	20,780	31,651	
% increase	*7.6*	*6.5*	*14.8*	*10.5*	
1984	46,655	52,576	22,322	34,997	
% increase	*7.6*	*6.2*	*7.4*	*10.6*	
1985	51,643	56,592	24,210	38,486	
% increase	*10.7*	*7.6*	*9.0*	*10.0*	
1986	52,308	62,909	26,153	42,471	
% increase	*11.2*	*11.2*	*8.0*	*10.4*	
1987	55,812	69,064	28,602	46,320	
% increase	*6.7*	*9.8*	*9.4*	*9.1*	
1988	61,943	76,019	32,176	51,395	
% increase	*11.0*	*10.0*	*12.5*	*11.0*	
1989	69,788	80,136	33,025	54,408	619
% increase	*12.7*	*5.4*	*2.2*	*5.9*	
1990			34,775		8,811
% increase			*5.3*		

Source: Annual Abstract of Statistics

PERCENTAGE OF INCOME GOING IN TAX (T) AND NATIONAL INSURANCE CONTRIBUTIONS (NI)

SINGLE PERSON		1981-2	1985-6	1989-90
½ average earnings	T	17.5	14.9	13.2
	NI	7.7	7.0	6.9
average earnings	T	23.7	22.4	19.1
	NI	7.7	9.0	8.3
2 x average earnings	T	27.3	26.2	22.1
	NI	6.1	7.1	6.1
MARRIED MAN				
½ average earnings	T	10.5	6.3	6.4
	NI	7.7	7.0	6.7
average earnings	T	20.2	18.1	15.7
	NI	7.7	9.0	8.3
2 x average earnings	T	25.1	24.2	20.4
	NI	6.1	7.1	6.1

Source: Social Trends

PUBLIC SPENDING

THE state," said the 1979 manifesto, "takes too much of the nation's income; its share must be steadily reduced. When it spends and borrows too much, taxes, interest rates, prices and unemployment rise so that in the long run there is less wealth with which to improve our standard of living and social services."

In 1978-79, the year during which Labour left office, the Public Sector Borrowing Requirement (PSBR), which is the difference between Government spending and Government receipts, was running at £9.9 billion, or 4.8 per cent of gross domestic product (GDP).

Conservative hopes of bringing that down quickly were not realised, largely because of the cost of the 1980-81 recession, which pushed up the cost of benefits and brought down the yield of taxation. In 1980-81, the PSBR was up to £13.2 billion, or 5.6 per cent of GDP. Thereafter, but for a blip in 1984-85 due mainly to the cost of the miners' strike, the PSBR fell steadily. In 1987-88, there was no need to borrow (the first time this had happened since 1970, when Roy Jenkins was Chancellor) and in the following year receipts exceeded spending by £14 billion.

Part of that was due to the burst of growth which succeeded recession and brought in tax revenues well above expectation. The other helpful ingredient was the programme of privatisation (asset sales), which became a dominant theme of Mrs Thatcher's second term. This brought in some £1.5 billion in 1983-84, rising rapidly to £5.5 billion in 1987-88 and £7.1 billion in 1988-89. What it did not reflect was any overwhelming success in the Government's campaign to hold down public spending. The early years were marked by successive rounds of reductions in planned spending pro-

grammes (usually referred to as "cuts"): in Howe's first Budget only law and order and the armed services were spared. But with spending ministers eager to defend their territories and demand never less than clamorous, expectations were disappointed. The share of GDP taken by public spending rose from 44 per cent in 1978-79 to 47 per cent in 1981-82 and 1982-83 before falling below 40 per cent from 1988 onwards.

Even when recession had cleared, there were areas where costs seemed near-uncontrollable: most of all in the voracious social security budget. In 1982 a Conservative party think tank incited the Prime Minister to think the unthinkable. Only a radical break with whole systems of public provision, it said, would spare her from this burden. But the report was leaked; headlines warned of a threat to the welfare state and the project was buried.

Some services, such as transport and housing, got less, sometimes very much less; but others – law and order, with a 70 per cent increase in real terms between 1978-89 and 1989-90, health (up 35 per cent in real terms), and social security (up 34 per cent) – ground inexorably onwards and upwards. Defence grew in the earlier years, but fell back in the later ones. General government expenditure expanded in real terms between 1978-79 and 1989-90 by 26 per cent. Yet the talk in the outside world was always of cuts: in the NHS; in education, with schools deprived and neglected and the universities starved; in spending on the environment and the infrastructure, which left streets filthy, roads potholed and a sense of public squalor. Public spending had grown fast enough to frustrate Conservative hopes, but not fast enough to meet all the claims made upon it. ●

PUBLIC SPENDING AND BORROWING
GENERAL GOVERNMENT EXPENDITURE AS PROPORTION OF GDP

	% GDP		% GDP
1963-64	36	1978-79	44
1968-69	41	1979-80	44
1973-74	43	1980-81	46
		1981-82	47
		1982-83	47
		1983-84	46
		1984-85	46
		1985-86	45
		1986-87	44
		1987-88	41
		1988-89	39
		1989-90	39
		1990-91	39

Source: Public Expenditure White Paper

PUBLIC SECTOR BORROWING REQUIREMENT

	£bn	as % GDP
1979-80	9.9	4.8
1980-81	13.2	5.6
1981-82	8.8	3.4
1982-83	9.2	3.2
1983-84	9.8	3.2
1984-85	10.2	3.2
1985-86	5.8	1.8
1986-87	2.5	0.6
1987-88	-3.0	-0.7
1988-89	-14.7	-3.0
1989-90	-7.9	-1.7
1990-91	-0.5	-0.2

GENERAL GOVERNMENT SPENDING ON SPECIFIC SERVICES IN REAL TERMS

SHOWING AMOUNTS SPENT ON SPECIFIC SERVICES AS A PERCENTAGE OF GOVERNMENT SPENDING.
£BN (BASE YEAR 1989-90)

	78-79	79-80	80-81	81-82	82-83	83-84	84-85	85-86	86-87	87-88	88-89	89-90	(Est) 90-91	% change on period.
Defence	17.5	18.5	19.0	19.4	20.7	21.3	22.5	22.3	21.9	21.5	20.3	20.8	20.5	+17.1
% Total Govt spend	*11.5*	*11.9*	*12.2*	*12.2*	*12.4*	*12.6*	*13.0*	*12.9*	*12.4*	*12.2*	*11.8*	*11.7*	*11.3*	
Overseas services inc. aid	2.5	2.4	2.3	2.2	2.2	2.3	2.2	2.3	2.3	2.3	2.4	2.5	2.5	nil
% Total Govt spend	*1.6*	*1.5*	*1.5*	*1.4*	*1.3*	*1.4*	*1.3*	*1.3*	*1.3*	*1.3*	*1.4*	*1.4*	*1.4*	
Agriculture Fish Food Forestry	2.4	2.5	2.8	2.6	3.1	3.3	3.2	3.6	2.6	2.7	2.3	2.1	2.7	+12.5
% Total Govt spend	*1.6*	*1.6*	*1.8*	*1.6*	*1.9*	*2.0*	*1.9*	*2.1*	*1.5*	*1.5*	*1.3*	*1.2*	*1.5*	
Trade & industry, energy & employment	9.7	8.4	8.2	9.7	11.7	9.9	10.7	10.3	9.9	7.7	8.8	7.9	7.2	-26.8
% Total Govt spend	*6.4*	*5.4*	*5.3*	*6.1*	*7.0*	*5.9*	*6.2*	*6.0*	*5.6*	*4.4*	*5.1*	*4.4*	*4.0*	
of which:														
Employmnt & training	2.5	2.6	3.3	3.5	3.3	3.8	3.9	3.7	4.1	3.9	3.6	3.2	2.9	+16.0
% Total Govt spend	*1.7*	*1.7*	*2.1*	*2.2*	*2.0*	*2.3*	*2.3*	*2.2*	*2.3*	*2.2*	*2.1*	*1.8*	*1.6*	
Transport	7.0	7.4	7.3	7.4	7.7	7.5	7.5	7.2	6.9	6.6	6.2	6.9	7.4	+5.7
% Total Govt spend	*4.6*	*4.8*	*4.7*	*4.6*	*4.6*	*4.4*	*4.3*	*4.2*	*3.9*	*3.7*	*3.6*	*3.9*	*4.1*	
Housing	10.7	11.3	9.7	6.6	5.7	6.2	6.0	5.2	4.9	4.8	3.5	4.8	5.3	-50.5
% Total Govt spend	*7.0*	*7.3*	*6.2*	*4.1*	*3.4*	*3.7*	*3.5*	*3.0*	*2.8*	*2.7*	*2.1*	*2.7*	*2.9*	
Other environmental services	6.4	6.7	6.6	6.2	6.6	6.4	5.9	5.7	6.5	6.6	6.4	7.4	7.1	+10.9
% Total Govt spend	*4.2*	*4.3*	*4.3*	*3.9*	*4.0*	*3.8*	*3.4*	*3.3*	*3.7*	*3.7*	*3.7*	*4.2*	*3.9*	
Law, order & protection services	5.9	6.4	6.6	7.1	7.3	7.7	8.2	8.0	8.5	9.0	9.3	10.0	10.6	+79.7
% Total Govt spend	*3.9*	*4.1*	*4.2*	*4.4*	*4.4*	*4.5*	*4.7*	*4.6*	*4.8*	*5.1*	*5.4*	*5.6*	*5.8*	
Education & science	22.2	21.9	22.5	22.4	22.5	22.6	22.3	21.9	23.3	24.1	24.2	25.1	25.4	+14.4
% Total Govt spend	*15.5*	*14.1*	*14.4*	*14.0*	*13.4*	*13.4*	*12.9*	*12.7*	*13.2*	*13.7*	*14.1*	*14.1*	*14.0*	
Arts & libraries	0.9	0.9	1.0	1.0	1.0	1.0	1.1	1.1	1.2	1.2	1.2	1.3	1.3	+44.4
% Total Govt spend	*0.6*	*0.6*	*0.6*	*0.6*	*0.6*	*0.6*	*0.6*	*0.6*	*0.7*	*0.7*	*0.7*	*0.7*	*0.7*	
Health & personal social services	21.6	22.2	24.0	24.5	24.8	25.2	25.7	25.8	26.8	27.9	28.8	29.5	30.5	+41.2
% Total Govt spend	*14.1*	*14.3*	*15.4*	*15.3*	*14.8*	*14.9*	*14.9*	*15.0*	*15.2*	*15.8*	*16.7*	*16.5*	*16.8*	
of which:														
Health	18.3	18.7	20.3	20.8	21.2	21.4	21.9	22.0	22.7	23.6	24.3	24.7	25.7	+40.4
% Total Govt spend	*12.0*	*12.1*	*13.0*	*13.0*	*12.7*	*12.7*	*12.7*	*12.8*	*12.9*	*13.4*	*14.1*	*13.9*	*14.2*	
Social security	39.6	40.1	40.9	45.5	48.3	50.6	52.2	53.9	56.1	55.6	53.1	52.9	54.2	+77.1
% Total Govt spend	*22.5*	*25.9*	*26.3*	*28.5*	*28.9*	*29.9*	*30.2*	*31.3*	*31.8*	*31.5*	*30.9*	*29.7*	*29.9*	
Miscellaneous	6.3	6.3	4.9	5.1	5.8	4.9	5.4	5.0	5.6	6.4	5.6	7.1	6.7	+6.4
% Total Govt spend	*4.1*	*4.1*	*3.1*	*3.2*	*3.4*	*2.9*	*3.1*	*2.9*	*3.2*	*3.6*	*3.3*	*4.0*	*3.7*	
Total	**152.7**	**154.9**	**155.6**	**159.7**	**167.4**	**169.2**	**172.7**	**172.4**	**176.4**	**176.4**	**172.1**	**178.2**	**181.4**	**+26.2**

Source: Public Expenditure Analyses 1991

'The early years were marked by successive cuts: in Howe's first budget only law and order and the armed services were spared'

INDUSTRY

"Too much emphasis has been placed on attempts to preserve existing jobs," the 1979 Conservative manifesto declared. "We need to concentrate more on the creation of conditions in which new, more modern, more secure, better-paid jobs come into existence. Government strategies and plans cannot produce revival, nor can subsidies. Where it is in the national interest to help a firm in difficulties, such help must be temporary and tapered." For a start that meant winding down the role of Labour's greatest engine of intervention, the National Enterprise Board. It meant selective denationalisation – for industries directly controlled by the state were most susceptible to political pressure and artificial resuscitation. But the list of candidates marked down for transfer to private hands was short. The high tide of privatisation was not to arrive until Mrs Thatcher's second term.

Initially, though, quite a lot of shoring up of lame-duck industries had to be done. A government which was thought to have foresworn such things found itself *in extremis* putting £880m into a British Steel survival plan and pouring a further £990m into Rolls-Royce (bringing total aid for that enterprise to £2,065m since 1975). But tough managers were installed – John King at British Airways, Ian MacGregor at British Steel and later at the National Coal Board – to cut these industries down to size, gear them to modern conditions and competition with a view to eventual privatisation.

The work was done with a ruthlessness without parallel in recent industrial history and in most of these cases with glowing financial results to show for it. The programme helped to widen share ownership – the proportion of people holding shares in

British companies grew from 5 to 20 per cent between 1979 and 1988 – though in most privatisations, many private subscribers swiftly took their profits and ran, reinforcing Opposition complaints that in most of these cases the sales had been made at heavily discounted prices, to the detriment of the taxpayers. The workforce of the nationalised industries fell by 60 per cent between 1979 and 1989.

By the end of the eighties the Government was running out of industries it could privatise without too much trouble, while opinion polls reported diminishing public enthusiasm. Plans to privatise electricity were drastically revised because no one wanted to buy its nuclear element: first the ageing Magnox reactors had to be removed from the package and in the end, as the truth came to light of the costs of nuclear power, that side of the operation was deleted altogether. The privatisation of water was delayed and partially redesigned because of the heavy cost of meeting anti-pollution requirements laid down by the EC.

Meanwhile, the Department of Trade and Industry, under a succession of ministers (the average length of service of secretaries of state in the Thatcher years was 15 months) had distanced itself from the industries in its charge. Output, employment and investment in manufacturing declined year by year for most of the Thatcher decade. On May 15 1985, a characteristic confrontation occurred in the House of Lords. Chancellor Lawson rebuked members of the Lords' select committee on overseas trade, chaired by the Conservative peer Lord Aldington, for the concern they were

THE PRIVATISATION PROGRAMME

ORGANISATION	STATUS	DATE OF SALE	METHOD OF DISPOSAL
Amersham International	Radiochemicals	Feb 82	sale of shares
Associated British Ports	Runs several big UK ports	Feb 83/ Apr 84	sale of shares
British Aerospace	Aerospace company: 1987 turnover £4,075m	Feb 81/May 85	sale of shares
(£100m of gross proceeds from first sale was put into company as capital injection)			
BAA (British Airports Authority)	Airline company: airports including Heathrow & Gatwick 1988 turnover: £523m.	Jul 7 87	sale of shares
British Airways	Airline company 1988 turnover £3,756m	Jan 87	sale of shares
British Airways Helicopters	BA helicopter fleet Helicopters owned by Scottish Daily Record & Sunday Mail & R.Maxwell	Sep 86	sold to SDR
British Gas	Major UK utility	Dec 86	sale of shares
British Gas Corporation	Onshore Oil Assets (Wytch Farm) Dorset oilfield	May 84	sold to group of bidders
(Initial proceeds of sale retained by British Gas Corporation. Sale allows for further £130m to be paid when production reaches 20,000 barrels per day)			
British Petroleum	Oil company: 1988 turnover £26bn	Oct 79 Jun 81 Sep 83 Oct 87	sale of shares
(First sale of BP shares was in 1977 when Labour reduced the Government holding from 68 to 51%)			
British Rail Hotels	23 hotels	Mar 83- Dec 84	sold to the trade
British Shipbuilders	War & civil shipbuilders warship building side sold:	May 85- Mar 86 -	4 management employee buyouts & 2 trade sales
	3 ship repair yards	Feb 84- Sep 85	2 management buyouts & 1 trade sale
	5 other subsidiaries	Jun 88- Apr 89	2 management buyouts & 3 trade sales
British Steel	Largest UK producer 1988 turnover £4,116m	Dec 88	sale of shares
British Sugar Corporation	Sugar refiner	Jul 81	Government 24 % holding placed with institutions
British Telecom	Telecommunications company: 1988 turn-over of £10,185m.	Nov 84	sale of shares
Britoil	N.Sea production & exploration	Nov 82 Aug 85	sale of shares

expressing over the state of manufacturing industry and their reluctance to accept his view that Britain, like other countries, was simply seeing a perfectly healthy swing from manufacturing to the service sector. He accused peers of "sneering at the service industries" and said he found it distasteful. The resultant committee report was severely critical of the state of manufacturing industry under the Chancellor's stewardship.

An economic policy designed to conquer inflation was throughout the decade taking casualties all down the line. Whole industries had gone to the graveyard, taking with them the ancient slogan: Britain can make it. When the boom years arrived, Japan could make it, but Britain could not. And by 1990-91 recession was again squeezing industry, producing record numbers of business failures.

By the end of the 1980s there was a wide measure of agreement about what had gone wrong in British industry, though much less agreement about what should be done about it.

Investment had been inadequate, as had research and development; in both cases partly because of the lack of confidence induced by recessionary economics. But above all, education and training had been inadequate. Too little heed, it was argued, was still being paid to industry's needs (and too many recruits were coming out of the system unable to meet the required standards). And Britain was still failing to train the men and women whose skills would be needed when the upturn came. All parties signalled this issue as one of the top priorities of the coming election campaign. At the 1990 party conference, Labour paraded its education and training plans as the "big idea", which political commentators had been saying it badly needed to find.

The Conservatives had, since the 1988 White Paper, Employment For The 1990s, pinned much faith chiefly on the creation of a network of 82 Training and Employment Councils (TECs) with a parallel scheme for Scotland. This gave local employers a decisive voice in deploying the Government's £1.7 billion training programme, including control over schemes like Youth Training (for the 16-19 age group) and Employment Training (serving the long-term unemployed) which preceded their creation.

But in July 1991 a leaked Department of Employment document referred to "tensions" and "a deteriorating relationship" between the Department and the TECs, threatening a complete breakdown. ●

ORGANISATION	STATUS	DATE OF SALE	METHOD OF DISPOSAL
Cable & Wireless	Telecommunications company: 1988 turnover £932.4m	Oct 81 Dec 83 Dec 85	sale of shares
Electricity:-			
Regional electricity companies	Utilities in England & Wales	Dec 90	sale of shares
National Power & Powergen	Electricity generating companies	Mar 91	sale of shares
Scottish Power & Hydro-Electric	Scottish electricity companies	Jun 91	sale of shares
Enterprise Oil	N. Sea production & exploration: 1987 turnover £228m	Jun 84	sale of shares
General Practice Finance Corporation	Makes loans to GPs to acquire or improve surgeries	Mar 89	sold to Norwich Union
International Aeradio	Aviation communication subsidiary of BA who resold to British Telecom	Mar 83	sold to STC
(proceeds of £60m sale retained by British Airways)			
Harland & Wolff	Shipbuilders	Sep 89	later passed to holding companies formed by management & employees
Jaguar	Luxury car maker, subsidiary of BL 1987 turnover: £1,002m.	Jul 84	sale of shares
National Bus Company	Local bus operations England & Wales	Jul 86- May 88	trade sales & management buyouts
National Freight Company	Road haulage	Feb 82	buyout by consortium of employees & pensioners
North Sea oil Licences *(special licensing rounds)*	*The government sometimes auctioned licence blocks instead of allocating exploration acreage. Where this occurred the proceeds were classed as privatisation proceeds*		
Rolls-Royce	Civil & military aero engines: 1988 turnover £1,973 m	May 87	sale of shares
Rover Group	Motor manufacturers	Aug 88	sold to British Aerospace

Previous sales of Rover subsidiaries had included Unipart (management-employee buyout by UGC Ltd, Jan 87); Leyland Bus (management-employee buyout, Jan 87); Istel, an information technology company (sold to management consortium, June 87) and Leyland Truck and Freight Rover (sold to DAF, with Rover Group retaining 40 per cent of merged company, April 87).

ORGANISATION	STATUS	DATE OF SALE	METHOD OF DISPOSAL
Royal Ordnance	Artillery, ammunition explosives, ordnance, small arms & rocket motors	Apr 87	sold to British Aerospace
Sealink	Harbour and ferry subsidiary of BR		sold to British Ferries
(Proceeds of £66m retained by BR)			
Short Brothers	Aerospace manufacturers	Oct 89	sold to Bombardier Inc, Canada
Technology Group Holdings *formerly NEB.*	Among other disposals were:		
	ICL (major computer company)	Dec 79	25 % NEB holding sold to institutions
	Fairey (specialised engineering)	June 80	sold to Doulton, a subsidiary of S.Pearson
	Ferranti (electrical & electronic)	July 80	50 % NEB holding sold to institutions
	Inmos (silicon chips) 1983 turnover £38,	Aug 84	75 % BTG holding sold to EMI
	Ferry subsidiary of BR	Jul 84	sold to British Ferries
(Proceeds of £66m retained by BR)			
Water plcs	10 suppliers of water & sewerage	Nov 89	sale of shares

MISCELLANEOUS:
Sale of Professional & Executive Recruitment,
Sales by New Towns Development Corporations,
Oil and commodity stockpiles,
Forestry Commission land,
Crown Agents Holding Board.

Source: Treasury

RECEIPTS FROM PRIVATISATION (£M)

	1979/80 to 1982/3	1983/4 to 1986/7	1987/8 to 1990/91*	ALL YEARS
Amersham International	64	0	0	64
Associated British Ports	46	51	0	97
BAA	0	0	1223	1223
BAe	43	347	0	390
British Airways	0	435	419	854
British Gas -				
sale of shares	0	1820	3467	5287[1]
redemption of debt	0	750	1050	1800
British Petroleum	284	543	5256[2]	6083
British Steel	0	0	2427	2427
British Sugar	44	0	0	44
British Telecommunications				
sale of shares	0	3685	0	3685
loan stock	0	158	200	358
redemption of preference shares	0	250	500	750
Britoil	334[3]	719	0	1053
Cable & Wireless	181	840	0	1021
Enterprise Oil	0	384	0	384
Forestry Commission	14	94	50	158[1]
General Practice Finance	0	0	67	67
Harland & Wolff	0	0	6	6
Land Settlement	0	21	0	21
Motorway service leases	4	3	3	10
NEB Holdings	122	232	0	354
Professional & Executive Recruitment	0	0	5	5
Plant Breeding Institute	0	0	65[4]	65
Rolls-Royce	0	0	1032	1032
Rover Group	0	0	150	150
Royal Ordnance	0	0	186	186
Short Brothers	0	0	30	30
Water	0	0	1903	1903[1]
Wytch Farm	0	18	130	148[1]
Miscellaneous	399	13	3497	3909[1]
Total	1535	10353	21664	33552

[1] Includes sums for 1990-91 which are estimates.
[2] Net of cost of acquiring partly paid shares under support arrangements announced by Chancellor October 29 1987.
[3] Includes repayments of debentures of £88m with interest.
[4] Central government sector received £65m but only £27m was paid to Consolidated Fund

THE ABOVE TABLE EXCLUDES SALES OF SUBSIDIARIES WHERE PROCEEDS WERE RETAINED BY THE PARENT INDUSTRY. THE MAIN SALES IN THIS CATEGORY WERE:

		£m
1982-83	International Aeradio (BA)	60
	British Rail Hotels	30
1983-84	British Rail Hotels	15
1984-85	Jaguar (BL)	297
	Sealink (BR)	40
	Wytch Farm (B Gas)	82
1985-86	Warship yards (B Shipbuilders)	54
	Sealink (BR)	26
1986-87	BA Helicopters	14
	Unipart (Rover)	52
	Leyland Bus (Rover)	4
	British Coal subsidiaries	1
1987-88	British Transport Advertising	40
	Istel (Rover)	48
1988-89	National Bus subsidiaries	24
1989-90	National Bus subsidiaries	1
	Girobank	112
	National Bus subsidiaries	122

Source: Public Expenditure Analyses 1991

DECLINE OF UK MANUFACTURING
1. UK manufacturing production 1979=100
2. UK manufacturing investment 1979=100
3. Employees in employment, manufacturing industry (Thousands)

	1	2	3
1979	100	100	7,107
1980	92	88	6,801
1981	87	69	6,099
1982	87	68	5,751
1983	90	67	5,418
1984	93	79	5,302
1985	96	91	5,254
1986	97	86	5,122
1987	103	91	5,049
1988	110	102	5,089
1989	114	111	5,080
1990	114	n/a	5,046

Source: Annual Abstract of Statistics

CHANGES IN MANUFACTURING PRODUCTION 1979-89

	average 1980-82	average 1983-6	1987	1988	1989	1979-89	1970-89
Japan	+2.1	+4.9	+3.0	+9.7	+6.2	+53.9	+118.2
U.S.	-1.5	+5.3	+5.8	+6.4	+2.6	+35.2	+91.2
Canada	-3.9	+6.4	+5.9	+5.6	+2.7	+26.1	+87.1
Italy	-0.1	+1.5	+1.9	+7.6	+3.5	+20.4	+59.5
France	0	-0.5	+1.0	+5.9	+4.6	+9.7	+46.7
Germany	-1.8	+3.2	0.0	+3.9	+5.6	+17.7	+39.5
UK	-4.3	+2.7	+5.9	+6.5	+4.4	+14.4	+20.9

Source: OECD

CHANGES IN MANUFACTURING INVESTMENT 1979-89

	1982	1983	1984	1985	1986	1987	1988	1989	1981-89
Ireland	+15.7	-6.8	+14.5	+58.7	+9.0	-0.9	+45.4	+31.2	+303.9
Denmark	-2.0	+10.0	+38.2	+31.6	+3.0	+8.7	+6.3	+10.1	+156.9
Belgium	+11.2	-6.1	+4.3	+3.1	+13.0	+7.1	+16.5	+9.9	+74.2
UK	-4.5	0.0	+14.3	+4.2	+5.0	+5.7	+12.6	+7.2	+52.3
France	-2.3	-3.5	+13.3	+6.4	+4.0	+3.8	+13.0	+9.0	+51.1
Italy	-3.0	-9.2	-1.1	+13.6	+7.0	+12.1	+10.0	+12.1	+46.5
Germany	-1.1	-2.3	-1.2	+17.6	+11.0	+2.7	+2.6	+10.3	+44.9
Netherlands	-6.2	+4.9	+26.6	+23.5	+3.0	0.0	-6.8	-2.1	+44.6
Greece	-8.1	-48.8	-53.3	0.0	-27.0	-12.3	+28.1	0.0	-82.0

Source: OECD

MANUFACTURING OUTPUT
1. Index of output in manufacturing industry
2. Output per person employed in manufacturing: 1979=100

	1	2
1979	100	100
1980	91	96
1981	86	99
1982	86	106
1983	89	115
1984	92	122
1985	94	125
1986	95	129
1987	101	138
1988	107	145
1989	112	151
1990	111	152
1991 (2nd qr)	106	149

Source: Economic Trends annual supplement

JOBS IN MANUFACTURING AND SERVICES
1. Employment in manufacturing (Thousands)
2. Employment in services (Thousands)

	1	2	ratio 2 : 1
1979	7,113	13,222	1.86
1980	6,808	13,345	1.96
1981	6,107	13,102	2.15
1982	5,761	13,078	2.28
1983	5,431	13,130	2.41
1984	5,316	13,465	2.53
1985	5,269	13,731	2.61
1986	5,138	13,918	2.71
1987	5,068	14,220	2.81
1988	5,109	14,841	2.90
1989	5,101	15,242	2.99
1990	5,068	15,477	3.05

CHANGING PATTERNS OF EMPLOYMENT
(THOUSANDS)
1. Employment in private sector
2. of which: self-employed
3. Employment in public sector
4. of which: civil service
5. of which: nationalised industry
6. Work-related training
7. Ratio of private to public sector jobs

	1	2	3	4	5	6	7
1979	17,927	1,906	7,449	738	1,849	-	2.4
1980	17,941	2,013	7,387	714	1,816	-	2.4
1981	17,156	2,119	7,185	698	1,657	-	2.4
1982	16,887	2,170	7,021	671	1,554	-	2.4
1983	16,658	2,221	6,952	654	1,465	16	2.4
1984	17,149	2,496	6,911	630	1,416	168	2.5
1985	17,782	2,610	6,579	608	1,137	177	2.7
1986	17,792	2,627	6,546	610	1,065	225	2.7
1987	18,393	2,860	6,370	599	870	311	2.9
1988	19,248	2,986	6,327	593	798	343	3.0
1989	20,219	3,240	6,080	585	727	462	3.3
1990	20,874	3,298	6,040	580	663	424	3.5

% change 1979-90

	+16.4	+73.0	-18.9	-21.4	-64.1	–	–

Source: Economic Trends, Monthly Digest of Statistics

LEGISLATION:

Competition Act 1980
1st reading: July 12 1979
2nd reading: October 23 1979 by 302 (Govt, 5 Lib, 5 OUP) to 235
(Lab , 2 SNP, 1 SNP, 1 SDLP - G Fitt)
Royal Assent: April 3 1980
Provisions: abolished the Price Commission; strengthened powers of the Director-General of Fair Trading and the Monopolies and Mergers Commission to investigate restrictive practices in both public and private sectors; new powers for Secretary of State for Trade to refer nationalised industries to the Monopolies Commission; new procedure for Secretary of State for Trade to ask Director-General to investigate prices causing major public concern.

Shops Bill
1st reading: February 25 1986
2nd reading: April 14 1986. Lost by 296 to 282, a majority against the Government of 14, after a substantial back bench revolt (see voting record section).
Provisions: would have eased restrictions on Sunday opening imposed by the 1950 Shops Act, now regarded by ministers as unenforceable. Its introduction followed the report of the Auld Committee which recommended deregulation. The Home Secretary, Douglas Hurd, was thought to have opened the way for defeat by saying in the debate that the Bill would not be guillotined, which gave it little chance of success even if carried on second reading.

Industry Act 1980
1st reading: October 23 1979
2nd Reading: November 6 1979 by 307 (Government, 3 OUP) to 250 (Lab, Lib, SNP, PC, 1 UU)
Royal Assent: June 30 1980
Provisions: the National Enterprise Board and the Scottish and Welsh Development Agencies were given new functions of "promoting the private ownership of interests in industrial undertakings by the disposal of securities and other property held by [them]". (In November 1979 the membership of the NEB had resigned in a dispute with the Secretary of State for Industry over policy towards Rolls-Royce.) The Act also withdrew regional development grants from intermediate areas.

Competition and Services (Utilities) Bill 1991
Introduced: November 8 1991
2nd reading:
Provisions: The four regulating authorities, Oftel (telecommunications), Ofgas (gas), Offer (electricity) and Ofwat (water) will be empowered to set standards of guaranteed service and ensure that compensation is paid where they are not met. The Bill opens the way for competition in water and gas.

'The new non-interventionist rhetoric never quite squared with what Thatcher's ministers practised in Edinburgh and Cardiff'

REGIONAL POLICY

IN LINE with its conviction that industries could not be saved or sustained for more than a temporary period by government intervention and subsidy, the Conservative government lost little time in winding down the policies it inherited in 1979. (The 1970 Conservative government had done much the same, only to switch back into regional policy as unemployment climbed.) On June 17, the Industry minister, Sir Keith Joseph, one of the chief architects of the new non-intervenionist approach, announced that the "assisted areas" (special development areas, development areas and intermediate areas) which qualified for special government aid to industry would be drastically scaled down over the next three years. Some 40 per cent of the employed population now worked in these areas: his changes would reduce that figure to 25 per cent. A small number of intermediate areas would move up to special development area status. But some special development and development areas would be downgraded.

From August 1 1980, regional development grants would continue to be paid at 22 per cent in special development areas, but the 20 per cent rate in development areas would be cut to 15, and in intermediate areas the grants would disappear altogether. Forms of selective assistance under Labour's 1972 Industry Act would also be reduced or removed.

These changes would reduce government spending by £50m in 1979-80, £138m in 1980-1, £184m in 1981-2 and £233m in 1992-3. From now on, government help would be much more narrowly (and so, it was hoped, much more cost-effectively) targeted. The recession which followed also did much to unpick the effects of earlier regional policies, with large-scale cuts in new plants like Linwood and Bathgate (cars), and Ravenscraig (steel), and the closure of the aluminium smelter at Invergordon. Yet the new non-interventionist rhetoric never quite squared with what Thatcher's ministers practised in Edinburgh and Cardiff.

Under George Younger, Secretary of State for Scotland from 1979 to 1986, what now amounted to heresy continued to flourish, with the Scottish Development Agency, set up in 1974, cheerfully drumming up business as if Labour were still in power. In April 1991 both the SDA and the equally interventionist Highlands and Islands Development Board were replaced by Scottish Enterprise, an organisation more closely influenced by businessmen and run on more Thatcherite lines.

Peter Walker, who became Secretary of State for Wales in 1987, repeatedly boasted of what he had done for Wales by government intervention. Such behaviour was often resented by English Tory MPs, and tensions came to a head when on May 16 1990 British Steel, now privatised, announced its intention to close its hot strip mill at the Ravenscraig works at Motherwell with the loss of 770 jobs.

Malcolm Rifkind, who had succeeded Younger as Scottish secretary in January 1986, joined Labour and Nationalist politicians in condemning the decision and calling on British Steel to reconsider. His anger was all the greater since, as emerged in a Commons debate on May 21, the chairman of British Steel, Sir Robert Scholey, had refused to discuss the closure with him. Rifkind's unThatcherite readiness to intervene upset some backbenchers and got little sympathy from ministerial colleagues.

The Trade and Industry secretary, Nicholas Ridley, was quick to distance himself from Rifkind's protest. At the end of the May 21 debate the Government voted down a motion deploring the closure and saying it threatened the future of steel-making in Scotland, and Rifkind fell into line. ●

UNEMPLOYMENT BY REGION 1979-90
% UNEMPLOYED, SEASONALLY ADJUSTED

	average 1979-82	average 1983-6	1987	1988	1989	1990	Oct 91
East Anglia	5.3	8.1	7.3	5.2	3.6	3.9	6.3
South East	4.7	7.9	7.2	5.4	3.9	4.0	7.6
South West	6.2	9.1	8.1	6.2	4.5	4.4	7.9
East Midlands	6.1	9.8	9.0	7.1	5.4	5.1	7.9
West Midlands	8.1	12.8	11.4	8.9	6.6	6.0	9.2
Yorks. & Humberside	7.4	11.9	11.3	9.3	7.4	6.7	9.1
Wales	10.2	13.3	12.0	9.8	7.3	6.6	9.3
Scotland	10.0	12.8	13.0	11.3	9.3	8.1	9.1
North West	8.8	13.6	12.5	10.4	8.5	7.7	10.0
North	10.2	15.1	14.1	11.9	9.9	8.7	10.7
Northern Ireland	11.4	16.2	17.2	15.6	14.6	13.4	14.1
UK	7.9	10.8	10.0	8.1	6.3	5.8	8.7

Source: derived and updated from from Regional Trends

REGIONAL VARIATIONS

1. Annual rate of growth of regional population 1981-89
2. Average personal disposable income as percentage of UK average,1989
3. Average weekly earnings, men, as percentage of UK average for men, 1990.
4. Average weekly earnings, women, as percentage of UK average for women, 1990.
5. Percentage of over-16s staying on at school, 1989-90.
6. Percentage of working population with degree or equivalent.
7. Perinatal mortality (still births and deaths at under 1 week, per 1,000 live and still births, 1989.
8. Building Society borrowers, average dwelling prices: percentage of UK average, 1990.

	1	2	3	4	5	6	7	8
North	-0.2	88.1	90	89	95	5.5	9.2	73
Yorks. & Humberside	0.1	90.4	90	90	99	5.8	8.7	79
East Midlands	0.5	96.6	91	90	104	7.4	8.2	88
East Anglia	1.0	100.7	95	92	95	8.1	6.7	103
South East	0.3	116.0	117	115	95	11.9†	7.9	136
South West	0.8	102.6	94	93	96	7.6	7.3	109
West Midlands	0.1	92.6	91	90	98	6.4	9.7	91
North West	-0.2	91.8	93	93	102	7.1	8.8	84
Wales	0.3	86.3	87	89	100	5.9	8.3	78
Scotland	-0.2	92.0*	94	93	121	7.0	8.7	70
Northern Ireland	0.4	85.8	86	90	n/a.	n/a.	8.2	53
UK	0.2	100	100	100	63.3xx	8.4xx	8.3	100

Source: Regional Trends bar figures on graduates which come from 1990 Labour Force Survey.

* Scottish figures for 1989 not strictly comparable because of introduction of poll tax.
xx GB figures only
† Greater London 14.5, Rest of South East 10.3.

TRADE

IN 1964 a balance of payments setback, which rapidly became a grave sterling crisis, desta-bilised a new Labour government to a point from which it never quite recovered. The figure which caused the trouble was £800m (and even that was illusory: subsequent recalculations by government statisticians revised most of it away). Yet in the late 1980s Conservative ministers contemplated figures of 25 times that magnitude and declared themselves not to be seriously troubled.

Old and new problems contributed to the opening up of a gap of unprecedented size between what we bought from abroad and what we sold in return (the balance of trade) and in the wider equations which make up the balance of payments, including trade on the so-called invisibles like banking and tourism. One, which had haunted every move in recent years from contraction to expansion, and did so again from 1983 onwards, was the tendency for people to spend more of their additional income in the good years on imported goods than on those produced at home. A tendency now reinforced by the fact that many of the main ingredients of the modern consumer spree – colour televisions, video machines, cameras and computers – are no longer made in Britain. The other, for much of the Thatcher years, was an exchange rate as uncomfortable for exporting manufacturers as the high interest rates which the strength of the pound to some extent reflected.

The full extent of decline was masked by the revenues which came from North Sea oil. But for those who looked beyond the overall figures the portents had soon become troubling. In 1984 the balance between imported and exported manufactured goods swung, for the first time since records began, into deficit, though mercifully for exporters, the strength of the pound, which had helped to price British goods out of foreign markets, was at this point abating.

A surge of imports in 1986 pushed up the non-oil trade deficit by £2,600m to £12,800m. In 1987, with growth accelerating, imports rose a further 11 per cent (by value) producing a worst-ever deficit on manufactured goods of £7,300m. Chancellor Lawson was philosophical. These, for him, were the problems of success. The deficit still amounted to a very modest proportion of GNP, and was offset by the steady growth of overseas assets, now greater than those of any country bar Japan. He saw no cause for remedial action. His 1988 Budget compounded the problem. By May the projected deficit for the year had already been passed. There was no more room for insouciance.

By the time the July results – a record monthly deficit of £2,150m – were logged in late August, Chancellor Lawson was raising interest rates for the eighth time since early June. But the overall result for the year was a current balance deficit of £15,000m.

In his 1989 Budget Chancellor Lawson was still presenting these figures as something far short of disaster. When Lawson left the Treasury in October 1989, Major inherited some even more daunting arithmetic: the trade deficit for that year reached more than £24,000m and the deficit on current account almost £20,000m. That some recovery followed was partly due to a year-long slump in the value of the pound and partly to continued high interest rates damping down the import boom: a remedy which, while diminishing our propensity to enrich foreign manufacturers, was simultaneously eroding that manufacturing base on which any long-term recovery in Britain's competitive trading position would have to be built. ●

TRADE AND THE BALANCE OF PAYMENTS (£M)

	1979	1980	1981	1982	1983	1984
Exports	40,471	47,149	50,668	55,331	60,700	70,265
Imports	43,814	45,792	47,416	53,421	62,237	75,601
Balance	-3,342	1,357	3,251	1,911	-1,537	-5,336
Invisibles balance	2,890	1,487	3,496	2,741	5,325	7,168
Current balance	-453	2,843	6,748	4,649	3,787	1,832

	1985	1986	1987	1988	1989	1990
Exports	77,991	72,656	79,446	80,776	92,831	102,746
Imports	81,336	82,141	90,669	101,854	116,829	120,657
Balance	-3,345	-9,485	-11,223	-21,078	-23,998	-17,911
Invisibles balance	6,095	9,462	7,042	5,927	4,152	4,133
Current balance	3,750	-24	-4,182	-15,151	-19,845	-13,799

Source: Annual Abstract of Statistics, Economic Trends, Monthly Digest of Statistics

CURRENT TRADE BALANCES AS % OF GDP/GNP

	(average) 1979-82	(average) 1983-6	1987	1988	1989	1990
US	0	-2.6	-3.6	-2.6	-2.1	-1.8
Japan	-0.2	+3.2	+3.6	+2.8	+2.0	+1.2
France	-0.7	-0.2	-0.5	-0.4	-0.4	-0.7
Germany	-0.5	+2.4	+4.1	+4.2	+4.6	+3.2
Italy	-1.1	-0.2	-0.2	-0.7	-1.2	-1.3
UK	+1.4	+0.7	-1.0	-3.2	-3.7	-2.4
Canada	-0.5	-0.3	-1.7	-1.7	-2.6	-2.4

Source:OECD

CURRENT BALANCES 1979-89
(GOODS SERVICES AND ALL TRANSFER PAYMENTS) (US $ BILLION)

	average 1979-82	average 1983-6	average 1987-89
United States	0.3	-101.7	-167.6
Japan	-7.8	47.7	74.6
Germany	-4.4	17.8	60.9
France	-4.0	-2.1	-4.6
Italy	-4.6	-0.4	-6.0
UK	6.8	2.9	-21.5
Canada	-2.0	-1.1	-10.1

Source:OECD

GROWTH OF REAL EXPORTS OF GOODS AND SERVICES 1979-90
PERCENTAGE CHANGE ON PREVIOUS YEAR

	average 1979-82	average 1983-6	average 1987-90
United States	4.1	3.1	12.3
Japan	10.7	4.4	10.3
Germany	5.6	3.7	9.4
France	4.4	2.8	6.7
Italy	1.6	4.4	6.4
UK	1.0	4.8	3.8
Canada	2.5	8.7	4.0

Source:OECD

EMPLOYMENT

LONG BEFORE she talked, in the context of the 1984-85 miners' strike, of "the enemy within", Mrs Thatcher had identified excessive union power as a poison in the system second only to inflation, with which it was bracketed in the 1979 manifesto as a top priority for immediate assault. That election took place in the shadow of the strife-ridden 1978-79 "winter of discontent" and opinion polls suggested that many electors echoed the manifesto's sentiments: "we cannot go on, year after year, tearing ourselves apart in increasingly bitter and calamitous industrial disputes." The Conservatives put much of the blame on Labour's favoured treatment of the unions. Labour legislation, they said, had tilted the balance of power in industrial bargaining away from responsible management and towards the unions: the Conservatives would tilt it back.

Part of that would depend on legislation. A succession of Bills progressively tightened the noose on union action, while other legislation hit at the unions' financial base by limiting benefits available to strikers' families. Union protests, even "Days of Action", failed to halt the process. The unions found themselves reduced from their former role as a great estate of the realm to exile on the margins. Rights they had long enjoyed were unilaterally abrogated: the right to union membership at the Government communication headquarters (GCHQ), the teachers' rights to pay bargaining, the dock work labour scheme (a protest strike against its destruction failed). Their influence was further eroded by a steady fall in membership. High and sustained unemployment created a climate of fear which sapped industrial militancy.

The new government's early months had been full of trouble. September 1979 was the worst month for stoppages and 1979 the worst year since 1926. The steel strike of 1980, the civil service dispute the following year and an NHS dispute in 1982 which ran for eight months, making it the longest industrial dispute since 1926, maintained the disruption. Mrs Thatcher's second term produced the biggest conflict of all: the miners' strike of 1984-85.

The miners' strike was fought with a bitterness rare in British industrial history. Things were said and done on the picket lines and in mining communities which would not be forgiven or forgotten. Ostensibly, the Government had no part in it. The dispute, it said, lay between the Coal Board, under Ian MacGregor, and the NUM under Arthur Scargill. But government plans had been laid well before the event (there were exceptionally large stocks at the power stations to see them through the crisis) and throughout the dispute the Government was calling the shots. The stakes were too high to give MacGregor the freedom that ministers claimed was his.

Though gains were claimed, the dispute ended in a drift back to work and a vote to call off the strike against the advice of the NUM executive. The union was left weakened, its membership further reduced by the birth of the UDM, a breakaway union, in Nottinghamshire. In 1974 the power of the miners had helped to bring down a government; in 1985, the power of the state, ruthlessly applied, humbled the NUM.

By the end of the decade much of what the Conservatives promised in 1979 had come about.

STRIKES AND WORKING DAYS LOST
1. Stoppages beginning in year.
2. No. of workers involved (Thousands)
3. Working days lost (Thousands); of which:
4. Working days lost (Thousands), in mining & quarrying

	1	2	3	4
1979	2,080	4,583	29,474	128
1980	1,330	830	11,964	166
1981	1,338	1,499	4,266	237
1982	1,528	2,101	5,313	374
1983	1,352	573	3,754	591
1984	1,206	1,436	27,135	22,484
1985	887	643	6,402	4,143
1986	1,053	538	1,920	143
1987	1,004	884	3,546	217
1988	770	759	3,702	222
1989	693	727	4,128	52
1990	620	285	1,903	94

Source: Employment Gazette

UK EMPLOYMENT AND UNEMPLOYMENT, QUARTERLY, SINCE 1979*
THOUSANDS, SEASONALLY ADJUSTED

		employed	unemployed			employed	unemployed
1979	I	23,072	1,100.7	1985	I	21,397	2,994.1
	II	23,145	1,087.6		II	21,414	3,031.5
	III	23,190	1,064.6		III	21,427	3,025.0
	IV	23,206	1,052.5		IV	21,418	3,040.9
1980	I	23,115	1,072.5	1986	I	21,395	3,076.2
	II	22,965	1,184.5		II	21,379	3,111.5
	III	22,689	1,341.2		III	21,380	3,124.0
	IV	22,386	1,595.1		IV	21,389	3,080.4
1981	I	22,115	1,859.8	1987	I	21,416	3,042.6
	II	21,870	2,066.7		II	21,575	2,944.3
	III	21,731	2,225.4		III	21,740	2,793.5
	IV	21,580	2,340.8		IV	21,955	2,641.0
1982	I	21,514	2,424.2	1988	I	22,126	2,519.4
	II	21,395	2,475.9		II	22,269	2,390.4
	III	21,225	2,551.6		III	22,437	2,241.1
	IV	21,101	2,639.6		IV	22,518	2,133.0
1983	I	21,026	2,715.9	1989	I	22,680	1,981.6
	II	21,054	2,764.6		II	22,757	1,846.8
	III	21,107	2,807.8		III	22,868	1,766.2
	IV	21,169	2,819.2		IV	23,023	1,670.4
1984	I	21,204	2,850.4	1990	I	22,802	1,615.8
	II	21,229	2,876.5		II	22,864	1,607.0
	III	21,281	2,913.1		III	22,796	1,632.1
	IV	21,363	2,965.3		IV	22,622	1,704.8
				1991	I	22,372	1,891.6
					II		2,173.6

Source: Economic Trends Annual Supplement, Monthly Digest of Statistics

* On the basis now used to calculate the figures, i.e. those claiming benefits only. The totals which appeared at the time may have been higher. For international comparisons see page 71.

The balance of power had been tilted back towards the employers and away from the unions. The whole of that change was coloured by unemployment.

A famous poster in the 1979 election showed a dole queue winding into the distance under the slogan: Labour isn't working. When that was pasted on to the hoardings the number of those out of work stood at 1.3m. That was greatly multiplied under the Tories. Unemployment went on climbing long after the 1980-81 recession had ended, not reaching its peak until 1986. And those figures understated the problem. Certainly 600,000 people,

probably many more, had disappeared from the register through job creation schemes and changes in definitions. The toll of lost jobs alarmed a good many Conservatives and not just for electoral reasons.

Yet in 1983 Thatcher defied predictions, winning a 144-seat majority with unemployment standing at over 3m on the basis of calculation then in use. The end of the decade saw some recovery; in the first quarter of 1989 the number out of work fell below 2m. But before long the 1990-91 recession was doing its work, biting this time even in the south, which in all past recessions had come through relatively unscathed. ●

STANDARDISED UNEMPLOYMENT RATES

	average 1979-82	average 1983-6	1987	1988	1989
US	7.6	7.8	6.2	5.5	5.3
Japan	2.2	2.7	2.9	2.5	2.3
France	7.0	9.7	10.5	10.0	9.4
Germany	3.5	6.8	6.2	6.2	5.6
Italy	8.3	10.4	12.1	12.1	12.1
UK	7.5	11.5	10.4	8.2	6.2
Canada	8.4	10.8	8.8	7.8	7.5

Source: OECD

UNEMPLOYMENT BENEFIT AND AVERAGE EARNINGS

	SINGLE PERSON			MARRIED MAN WITH TWO CHILDREN		
	Standard Rate UB Income	Average Weekly Earnings	Benefit as a % of net income	Standard Rate UB Income	Average Weekly Earnings	Benefit as a % of net income
Oct 1972	£13.75	£39.70	47.7%	£22.10	£42.60	68.0%
Nov 1979	£31.79	£114.10	39.8%	£54.64	£122.10	59.7%
Nov 1982	£31.45	£224.00	20.2%	£65.35	£138.50	36.8%
Apr 1989	£34.70	£269.50	18.1%	£70.60	£284.00	33.1%

* Earnings related is included in UB rate up to November 1892. Income for married man includes Family Allowance/Child Benefit. Net income is after tax and NI deductions

Source: Hansard: WA col 521, June 19 1990

PERCENTAGE IN EMPLOYMENT GETTING JOB-RELATED TRAINING

age	1984	1987	1989
16-19	20	21	23
20-24	14	17	19
25-29	11	14	17
ALL	9	12	14

Source: Social Trends

EMPLOYMENT BY SEX, FULL AND PART-TIME
GB (MILLIONS)

	MEN		WOMEN	
	full	part	full	part
1986	12.7	1.1	5.7	4.5
1987	12.7	1.3	5.8	4.7
1988	13.1	1.3	6.2	4.7
1989	13.3	1.4	6.6	4.9

Source: Social Trends

DECLINE OF TRADE UNION MEMBERSHIP
TOTAL MEMBERSHIP OF UNIONS AFFILIATED TO TUC ON DECEMBER 31 EACH YEAR

	No. of unions	members (millions)	as % of work force in employment	% change in membership year on year
1979	454	13.3	52.7	+1.3
1980	438	12.9	52.9	-2.6
1981	414	12.1	50.9	-6.5
1982	408	11.6	49.7	-4.2
1983	394	11.2	47.3	-3.1
1984	375	11.0	45.4	-2.2
1985	370	10.8	44.4	-1.6
1986	335	10.5	43.0	-2.6
1987	330	10.5	41.4	-0.6
1988	315	10.4	38.8	-0.9
1989	309	10.2	38.0	-2.1

Source; Employment Gazette

LEGISLATION

Since the Conservatives came to power in 1979 there have been eight Acts of parliament including the Wages Act 1986 and the Public Order Act 1986 which have effected radical changes to employment law. Subsidiary legislation includes codes of practice on picketing and industrial action ballots.

Employment Act 1980
1st reading: December 6 1979
2nd reading: December 17 1979, by 315 (Government, 8 Libs) to 245 (Lab, PC, SNP)
Royal Assent: August 1 1980
Provisions: introduced a limited definition of lawful picketing; required an 80 per cent ballot for a closed shop; offered unions funds to pay for ballots

Employment Act 1982:
1st reading: January 28 1982
2nd reading: February 8 1982, by 348 votes to 241 (with the Government: 17 SDP, 9 Liberals, J.Kilfedder UPU; against: Lab, 5 SDP, G. Cunningham (Ind), Plaid Cymru, 1 SNP, G. Fitt (Socialist)).
Royal Assent: October 28 1982
Provisions: introduced further restrictions on secondary action and compensation for dismissal because of a closed shop, and gave employers the right to take legal action for damages against trade unions.

Trade Union Act 1984
1st reading: October 26 1983
2nd reading: November 8 1983, by 362 (Govt, Lib, SDP, 1 OUP) to 189 (Lab, PC, SNP, SDLP)
Royal Assent: July 26 1984
Provisions: made executive committee elections by postal ballot compulsory every five years; introduced ballots on political funds and before industrial action and sequestration of union assets.
Rebellion: On April 2 1984, 40 Conservative MPs supported an amendment from John Townend (Con Bridlington) requiring union members to "contract in" to pay to a political fund. The amendment was defeated by 472 (Government, Lab, PC) to 57 (40 Con, 12 Lib, 4 SDP, 1 OUP).

Employment Act 1988
1st reading: October 22 1987
2nd reading: November 3 1987, by 335 (Government) to 233 (Lab, Lib Dem, SDP, SNP, Plaid Cymru J. Kilfedder (UPUP))
Royal Assent:May 26 1988
Provisions: gave members the right to ignore a union ballot decision on industrial action, not be disciplined by their union, and to inspect their union's accounts. It specified that members would not have indemnity against unlawful conduct and had the right to stop employers deducting union dues (check off). It outlawed industrial action to establish or preserve closed shops and introduced new restrictions on industrial action and election ballots.

Employment Act 1989
1st reading: November 30 1988
2nd reading: January 11 1989, by 290 (Government plus UPUP) to 216 (Lab, Lib Dem, SDP, SNP, Plaid Cymru, 1 DUP, 1 SDLP)
Royal Assent: November 16 1989
Provisions: introduced a pre-hearing review of cases going to Industrial Tribunals and a £150 deposit to prevent groundless applications; removed restrictions on the work of women and children; exempted employers with fewer than 20 staff from including disciplinary procedures in employment contracts; restricted time-off for union representatives; required employees to have two years' service before being given written reasons for dismissal; abolished redundancy rebates; and abolished the Training Commission.

Employment Act 1990
1st reading: November 21 1989
2nd reading: January 29 1990, by 255 (Government plus SDP) to 198 (Lab, Lib Dem, SNP, Plaid Cymru)
Royal Assent: November 1 1990
Provisions: constrained the closed shop by making it unlawful not to employ non-union members; made all secondary action other than picketing unlawful; ballots on industrial action must include regular, casual workers; more stringent measures requiring unions to repudiate unofficial action and allowing for the selective dismissal of staff taking unofficial action.

'The jewel in the crown for the Government was nuclear power... over the years they celebrated its advantages'

ENERGY

THE ENERGY policy outlined in the Conservative manifesto in 1979 had three components: oil, where they promised to end the government interference which under Labour had held the industry back; coal, which had to be made efficient and competitive; and nuclear power, which had to make "a proper contribution". Alternative sources, much favoured by environmentalists, did not merit a mention.

Not surprisingly oil came first. It was frequently said in the 1970s that big political dividends awaited whichever party was in government through the eighties, when the unplanned bonus of North Sea oil would be at its peak. The Conservatives had that honour; though whether they put it to maximum use as a long-term regenerator of the British economy remains in dispute. To prolong North Sea productivity the Conservatives introduced measures to try to increase the incentive to continue exploration. Concessions in the 1983 Budget, including a phased reduction of Petroleum Revenue Tax and the promise of its abolition in 1986, together with exemptions from royalties in most new fields, led to exploration in places where it had previously been judged not worth the risk. The other main objective was to get as much of the industry out of public and into private hands, again in the hope of greater efficiency, productivity and financial yield .

The objective in the coal industry was to push up productivity and produce a greater yield from far fewer pits – an aim in which the industry largely succeeded, though at the cost of heavy redundancies which blighted mining communities. Productivity doubled in the seven years after the 1984-85 coal strike, but over 100 pits closed and some

120,000 jobs were lost. It was the threat of closures which had led to the year-long dispute with the NUM, led by Arthur Scargill, during which the National Coal Board, with a surreptitious orchestration of tactics by ministers, maintained a bleak and uncompromising refusal to yield. The strike was a failure and was followed by closures on much the pattern that Scargill had predicted: though the weakening of the NUM by the strike, and the appearance of the UDM, a rival union in the Nottingham coalfield, made the programme of closures easier to implement. But while jobs dwindled, productivity soared.

The jewel in the crown for the Government was nuclear power. At first ministers hoped to build at least one new nuclear station a year. Over the years, they celebrated its advantages:

● It was cheap. The stations were costly to build, but cheaper than coal to run and its output was not subject, like oil, to seismic price disturbances.

● It was safe. That was firmly maintained, even after the Chernobyl disaster of April 26 1986. With our higher safety standards, such an event could never happen here. And even the death rate at Chernobyl, it was said, paled beside the toll taken each year by pollution from coal-fired stations.

● It was clean, unlike fossil fuels. It didn't defile the atmosphere, or cause global warming (the "greenhouse effect"). As Environment secretary Ridley argued this case with crusading zeal. Conservationists, he said, could not have it both ways. If arguments in favour of cutting the amounts of carbon dioxide and sulphur dioxide from coal-burning power stations were accepted, the only viable alternative was a huge expansion of nuclear power.

MAIN SOURCES OF POWER

1.% SHARE OF INLAND CONSUMPTION OF MAIN SOURCES OF FUEL AND EQUIVALENT FOR ENERGY USE.

	coal	petroleum	natural gas	nuclear electricity
1979	36.4	39.1	20.0	3.9
1982	35.5	35.6	23.0	5.1
1985	32.2	35.2	25.2	6.8
1988	32.9	34.1	24.0	6.7
1989	31.8	34.7	23.7	7.6

2. % SHARE OF MAIN SOURCES FUEL INPUT FOR ELECTRICITY GENERATION.

	coal	petroleum	nuclear
1979	71.6	14.7	11.1
1982	73.2	9.7	14.6
1985	63.1	15.5	18.9
1988	70.3	7.8	19.5
1989	68.0	7.9	21.9

Source: Digest of UK Energy Statistics

COAL: PRODUCTION, EMPLOYMENT AND PRODUCTIVITY

1. Coal production (million tonnes)
2. Average number of wage earners (thousands) on colliery books
3. Output per man-shift (tonnes) (GB)

	79-80	80-81	81-82	82-83	83-84	84-85*	85-86	86-87	87-88	88-89	89-90
Production	108.6	109.6	108.2	104.3	89.5	27.6	87.8	87.1	81.8	84.4	73.6
Wage earners	232.5	229.8	218.5	207.7	191.5	175.4	154.6	125.4	104.4	86.9	69.8
Output per M/S	2.31	2.32	2.40	2.44	2.43	2.08	2.72	3.29	3.62	4.14	4.32

* year of miners strike. *Source: Digest of UK Energy Statistics*

GOVERNMENT REVENUES FROM NORTH SEA OIL (£BN)

	PRT and supplementary petroleum duty	royalties	corporation tax	TOTAL	as % of Govt revenue
1982-83	5.7	1.6	0.5	7.8	6.0
1983-84	6.0	1.9	0.9	8.8	6.5
1984-85	7.2	2.4	2.4	12.0	8.5
1985-86	6.4	2.1	2.9	11.3	7.5
1986-87	1.2	0.9	2.7	4.8	3.0
1987-88	2.3	1.0	1.4	4.7	2.7
1988-89	1.4	0.6	1.2	3.2	1.6
1989-90	1.2	0.4	0.8	2.4	1.2
1990-91	1.4	0.6	0.9	2.9	1.3

Source: Goldman Sachs UK Economics Analyst January 1991

Also, though this argument wasn't put in quite such crude terms, it was less vulnerable to union action than coal. Nuclear power had no known equivalent of Arthur Scargill. There had been two oil price explosions and a miners' strike, Cecil Parkinson, then Energy minister, told the Commons in April 1989: but for nuclear power Scargill might have won.

The option of moving to the American system of pressurised water reactors (PWR) had been examined by Labour before they left office. The Conservatives lost little time in picking it up. Plans by the Central Electricity Generating Board (CEGB) for its first PWR, Sizewell B on the Suffolk coast, were the subject of Britain's longest-running public inquiry, from January 11 1983 to March 7 1985. (The French, who proceed more directly without such public examination, were planning their 70th PWR by the time the Sizewell verdict emerged.)

The judgment was on balance favourable. Yes, said the Layfield inquiry, in the national interest, the project should go ahead. The potential benefit outweighed any possible safety hazard. Three more PWRs were proposed: one, at Hinkley Point in Somerset, was approved in September 1990. But the Government's hopes for nuclear power were not to last.

They survived the fears about safety, which arose not just from distant experience like the Chernobyl disaster but also from problems much nearer home, chiefly at Sellafield (formerly Windscale) on the Cumbrian coast, where a leak led in 1985 to the prosecution of British Nuclear Fuels (BNFL) for negligence and mismanagement. The high incidence of childhood leukaemia in the area close to Sellafield led to two inquiries. One, by Sir Douglas Black, confirmed the unusual incidence but found no concrete evidence to link it with nuclear power. A subsequent inquiry by the Medical Research Council suggested that the problem might have something to do with the sperm of the children's fathers.

None of that seemed to shake the Government's faith in nuclear power. What did, however, was a series of revelations about the true costs of the enterprise, brought to light, ironically, by

another of the Government's enthusiasms, electricity privatisation. The first warnings that the cost of the PWRs might be higher than predicted seeped out in January 1989. Next the aged Magnox stations had to be withdrawn from the privatisation programme because of the deterrent effect of their decommissioning costs.

Then the whole nuclear element was deleted from the sale. The accountants' explorations connected with privatisation had uncovered a frightening story: it was estimated, for instance, that the base cost per kilowatt hour of the Hinkley operation would be two and three quarter times as much as the figure put before the inquiry. "It feels in retrospect," said a leader in the Guardian, "like one of the most expensive con tricks (or self-delusions) of the century."

Sizewell B, it was decided, should go ahead: but nothing else for the moment. This was not a new experience. The story of nuclear power in Britain had been littered with disappointments. Britain's five Advanced Gas-cooled Reactors (AGRs) had, the CEGB admitted, fallen well short of expectations. Because of technical faults they were often out of commission and had produced less than half their predicted output. There were similar stories of woe from the USA, where every reactor ordered in 15 years had been cancelled, and from countries like Sweden and Italy which by the end of the decade had already abandoned their programmes – though apparently not in France, whose nuclear power exports we might shortly be buying, some now predicted, on a substantial scale.

No party could take pleasure in this outcome. Labour and the Social and Liberal Democrats were pledged to phase out nuclear power. But any incoming government now faced this problem. All estimates suggested a rocketing demand for energy, both at home and even more urgently across the developing world. If nuclear power was not to provide it, what would? Fossil fuels? But that could only be done at a vast environmental cost. Could some way be found to expand supply? Or as the Green movement argued, would it soon become inevitable to put limits on demand? ●

'The one place where rail prevailed over road was in the building of the Channel Tunnel'

AGRICULTURE

THE years of Conservative government produced an inevitable but disconcerting reversal of agricultural policy which left much of the industry feeling more than normally battered and apprehensive. The industry the Conservatives inherited in 1979 was still operating under the imperatives which, first under domestic policies and later under the Common Agricultural Policy (CAP) of the European Community, had held sway since the second world war: the modernisation and maximisation of production, the search for higher productivity, with machines increasingly replacing men, all cushioned by subsidy and protection, tax reliefs and even relief from rates. The results were spectacular. Between 1945 and 1991, the work force fell by two thirds yet the volume of agricultural production almost doubled. Dependence on imports was steadily reduced: by 1986, Britain was producing 80 per cent of its temperate food needs, a rise of 20 percentage points since 1973. "Our agriculture and food industries" said the 1979 Conservative manifesto "are as important and efficient as any we have". And apart from promises to seek radical change in the CAP, including devaluation of the "green pound" to put British producers on level terms with those across the Community, there seemed at this stage little sign of what was to come.

Yet change was inescapable. Protection and subsidy, whether home or EC-grown, were dirty words for this government. EC over-production was an open scandal. A Euro-landscape dotted with grain mountains and wine lakes was a natural target for Thatcher's reforming zeal. On other grounds too there was a revolt against over-production: the damage it did to the environment,

through nitrate pollution and the vandalising of the countryside as hedges gave way to cost-efficient prairies; revulsion against the cruelty done to animals by factory farming methods. Even the fabled gains in productivity began to be questioned. Output per man had soared: but so had energy costs.

"The basic change that has taken place" said the Agriculture secretary, John Gummer, reflecting on these years in a Commons debate in April 1991, "has not been our joining the Community or any particular system or change in system; it has been the move from a world in which the West was afraid of shortages of food to a world in which those who can afford it can buy as much food as they need".

In 1984 the imposition of quota limits on milk producers signalled what was coming. By late 1985 a fundamental debate was under way in Europe over the future of the CAP, now costing £12bn a year, with a general shift in philosophy, in line with Thatcherite teachings, from continuing subsidy to the therapeutic disciplines, as they saw them, of market forces. In December 1986, with the grain mountain standing at 16.8m tonnes and the wine lake one third of a billion gallons deep, EC agricultural ministers reached agreement on further cuts in production of milk and beef, though still not of grain. In June 1988, following guidelines agreed by the EC in February, the British government announced its "set-aside" scheme, under which farmers would be paid to take arable land out of production, though the NFU found the Government's scale of payments niggardly. Farmers were encouraged to explore the possibilities of the bed

THE CONTRACTION OF FARMING
1 Total agricultural area UK(excludes some minor holdings in Scotland and N.Ireland)- thousands of hectares
2 Work force employed: farmers, partners, directors, full time- thousands
3 Work force employed: farmers, partners, directors, part time- thousands
4 Work force employed: hired full time- thousands
5 Work force employed: hired part-time- thousands
6 Index for income from farming to farmers, non-principal partners and directors and their spouses and family workers, 1979=100
(work force statistics as at June each year)

	Area	Farmers Full Time	Farmers Part Time	Hired Full Time	Hired Part Time	Income
	1	2	3	4	5	6
1979	18,936	215	89	152	45	100
1980	18,953	208	90	145	44	84
1981	18,808	205	89	140	43	95
1982	18,783	204	89	135	42	108
1983	18,735	203	87	133	41	87
1984	18,720	202	91	126	41	117
1985	18,702	199	93	121	41	72
1986	18,676	197	94	112	41	85
1987	18,622	194	95	106	40	85
1988	18,595	192	93	101	40	66
1989	18,553	189	94	99	39	74
1990	18,525*	184	98	97	40	63
1991		178	99	92	39	

*77 per cent of total area of UK

Source: MAFF and NFU

GOVERNMENT SPENDING ON AGRICULTURE FISHERIES FOOD AND FORESTRY
1 Total spending on agriculture etc at current prices.
2 % of government expenditure
3 % of GDP

	1978-1979	1979-1980	1980-1981	1981-1982	1982-1983	1983-1984	1984-1985	1985-1986	1986-1987	1987-1988	1988-1989	1989-1990	1990-1 estimate
1	1.0	1.3	1.6	1.7	2.2	2.4	2.4	2.9	2.2	2.4	2.2	2.1	2.9
2	1.6	1.6	1.8	1.6	1.9	2.0	1.8	2.1	1.5	1.5	1.3	1.2	1.5
3		0.6	0.6	0.6	0.7	0.7	0.7	0.7	0.5	0.5	0.4	0.4	0.5

and breakfast business or the transfer of land to leisure pursuits. New golf courses proliferated.

Though across much of the world, as famine followed famine, the problem remained too little food, not too much, few challenged this strategy. All political parties, even the National Farmers Union (NFU) accepted it: the debate was about how the change should be organised. Labour advocated less reliance on market forces and more on "managed change"; both they and the Liberal Democrats wanted greater emphasis and greater reward for good environmental practices. Like many of the farmers themselves, they feared that falling prices would drive the industry towards worse practice rather than better.

The EC, which was where these matters were settled (80 per cent of our agricultural spending was now determined in Brussels) increasingly favoured guaranteeing farmers' incomes rather than price support. The pressures increased as the Americans and their allies demanded drastic cuts in subsidy and protection at meetings of GATT (the General Agreement on Tariffs and Trade). It was on this issue that four years of trade talks aimed at reducing protection in world trade foundered in Brussels in December 1990 as the EC argued that really radical cuts could bankrupt millions of farmers.

But Britain was unhappy too with the EC's own plans. In July 1991, with the grain mountain now swollen to 20m tonnes, the beef surplus to 750,000 tonnes, and the surplus in dairy products to 900,000 tonnes, the agriculture comissioner, Ray McSharry, from the Republic of Ireland, produced a formula which won strong support across member nations for direct income subsidies and incentive payments to offset cuts in production subsidy and reductions in quotas. He proposed a 35 per cent cut in the price paid for cereals, 15 per cent cuts for butter and beef, and 10 per cent for milk.

There would be incentive payments to take land out of production, accept early retirement, and switch to environmentally friendly uses like the planting of forests. The programme would be costly: it would mean the EC farm budget topping £26bn in 1992. But in the following four years, the growth of the budget would be less than if present practices continued. Gummer opposed it vehemently, saying that it discriminated in favour of countries with large numbers of small farmers and against Britain, where farming units were much larger than average (175 acres against an overall EC average of 41 acres).

The approach of the election found agriculture in a state of gloom and uncertainty. Incomes had fallen by 22 per cent in real terms in 1990 to their lowest level in the whole post-war period (though some of this loss has been offset by the development of alternative sources of income). Between June 1990 and June 1991, over 7,000 full time farmers – about 4 per cent – left the industry. It was commonplace to say that the farmers were always complaining: but with such a shake-up in the industry, together with the consequences of a period of high interest rates and the effects of recession, all political parties accepted that they had more cause than usual for doing so now. ●

'It was commonplace to say farmers were always complaining, but they had more cause than usual for doing so now'

TRANSPORT

TRADITIONALLY something of a governmental byway, transport took on a distinctly higher profile during the Conservative years. This was an area of life where the Thatcherite agenda – the assault on monopoly, the liberation of competition, the lifting of the shackles of the state – could, they hoped, be widely applied. Most of the transport proposals in the 1979 manifesto appeared in its section on denationalisation. The 1980 Transport Act set the pattern, engineering the reconstruction of the National Freight Corporation to prepare it for sale, and deregulating long-distance bus operation by lifting restrictions on new entrants, intercity services, tours and excursions.

There was an immediate and positive consumer response as coach fares dropped and new services opened. In succeeding years this dual approach was continued in road, rail and air. On the roads, National Bus and its Scottish equivalent were privatised. The 1985 Transport Act adopted a market approach and municipal authorities ceased to operate their own transport fleets, which became arm's-length operations competing with the private sector. Only services where a social need existed, but no independent operator came forward, could be subsidised, and they had to be put out to tender. Rival companies could despatch their buses on identical routes: all you needed to do was to register your route and observe the regulations. These measures did not apply to London, though deregulation there was promised later on. But the 1984 London Regional Transport Act took London Transport away from the GLC and entrusted it to a Government-appointed executive.

By the end of the eighties private capital was being persuaded to take on projects like the Dartford-Thurrock bridge across the Thames east of London, a second Severn crossing, and a toll motorway in the Midlands. In the air British Airways (BA) and the British Airports Authority (BAA) were privatised, though here the attempt to break down protection and open up competition made slower progress, since it had to be negotiated internationally. On the railways British Rail (BR) was made to sell subsidiaries like its engineering arm BREL, its hotels and its catering operation Travellers Fare. The ultimate aim was to privatise BR itself, but no date was ever put on it.

Meanwhile, the Government sought to cut it free from extensive subsidy. "Lower subsidy," said the 1991 Conservative Campaign Guide hopefully "reflects greater efficiency"; though that was not how travellers invariably saw it. By 1991 the taxpayer subsidy to BR was half what it was in 1983, and in real terms, its lowest ever. The subsidy to the great commuter region Network SouthEast was due to disappear altogether by 1993.

BR did its best to cope on the reduced level of public investment, which fell far below its assessment of what a modern rail network needed. But the 1990-91 recession pushed it back into the red as revenues fell and the property market slumped.

In the eyes of the Opposition that reflected a less advertised theme of the Conservative attitude to transport: a bias towards roads. Mrs Thatcher very rarely travelled by train.

In her mind the private motor car was a form of liberation; it gave you both responsibility and freedom. In the war between individualism and collec-

GOVERNMENT SPENDING ON TRANSPORT
1. Total spending on transport at current prices (£bn).
2. % increase on previous year in real terms.
3. % of government expenditure.
4. % of GDP.

	1978-1979	1979-1980	1980-1981	1981-1982	1982-1983	1983-1984	1984-1985	1985-1986	1986-1987	1987-1988	1988-1989	1989-1990	1990-1 estimate
1	3.0	3.7	4.3	4.8	5.3	5.5	5.7	5.8	5.7	5.8	5.8	6.9	8.0
2		+6.0	-1.0	-11.0	+4.0	-3.0	0.0	-4.0	-4.0	-4.0	-6.0	+11.0	+7.0
3	4.6	4.8	4.7	4.6	4.6	4.5	4.3	4.2	3.9	3.7	3.6	3.9	4.1
4		1.8	1.8	1.8	1.9	1.8	1.7	1.6	1.5	1.3	1.2	1.3	1.5

GRANTS TO BRITISH RAIL
(£ MILLION)

	1979	1980	1981	1982	1983	1984	1985	1986	1987	1988	1989
Grants to British Rail	691	718	933	1002	1033	1013	1014	897	946	654	703
index of real value: *(1979 = 100)*	100	87	101	101	99	93	88	75	76	49	49
of which:											
Public Service Obligation:	505	597	800	831	855	827	832	737	775	473	501
index of real value: *(1979 = 100)*	100	99	119	115	112	104	99	85	85	49	48

ANNUAL INVESTMENT IN BRITISH RAIL
(£ MILLION)

	1979	1980	1981	1982	1983	84-85	85-86	86-87	87-88	88-89	89-90
Investment	248	304	277	243	252	280	399	399	526	570	700
index of real value: *(1979 = 100)*	100	102	84	68	67	71	95	92	115	117	135

Source: derived from Digest of Transport Statistics

GOVERNMENT SUPPORT FOR RAILWAYS IN BIGGEST EC COUNTRIES 1988

	Support (£m equivalent)	Support per head of population (£ equiv)
W Germany	3,509.4	57.34
France	3,005.0	53.79
Italy	4,006.6	69.75
GB	634.4	11.43

FINANCIAL SUPPORT RECEIVED EXPRESSED AS % OF GDP

	average 1979-82	average 1983-86	1987	1988
W.Germany	0.89	0.77	0.68	0.67
France	0.73	0.76	0.68	0.66
Italy	0.62	0.87	0.89	0.89
GB	0.31	0.28	0.21	0.14

Source: British Railways Board

INDEX OF TRANSPORT OF FREIGHT:
(1979=100)
1. Rail (BR freight traffic : commodity measure)
2. Road (carriage by heavy goods vehicles)

	1979	1980	1981	1982	1983	1984	1985	1986	1987	1988	1989
Rail	100	91	91	84	86	46*	72	82	83	88	85
Road	100	90	91	92	93	97	100	102	109	126	133

* depressed by coal strike

Source: derived from Digest of Transport Statistics

tive values, the car represented self-help and self-determination. The car, unlike the train, couldn't be used by the unions to prosecute their wage claims. Even the commitment to save the environment, which road travel did so much to pollute, was abated in this cause. "We are not going to do away with the great car economy," the Prime Minister pledged. At the height of the Government's move towards green values, spending on the road programme was doubled to £12 billion over 10 years.

The one place where rail prevailed over road was in the building of the Channel Tunnel. At Lille in Northern France on January 20 1986, Mrs Thatcher and President Mitterrand announced that the contract would go to a rail-only scheme put forward by the Channel Tunnel Group and France-Manche. The cost would be £5,300m (by 1990 it had already risen to £7,200m) and the first train would run in 1993. Thatcher was thought to have favoured a road scheme and the winning contractors were required to come forward with plans to provide one by the year 2000.

It was a matter of pride to the Government that this historic enterprise would be paid for by private money. But that created problems. Where the French went ahead with ambitious plans for appropriate high-speed rail links, their British equivalents foundered. A consortium formed by BR and private companies found the cost of a rail link beyond them, especially because of the cost of environmental safeguards. Their appeal for an injection of public money was rejected in June 1990.

The political salience of transport was heightened over the period by several disasters: a horrific fire in the Underground station at King's Cross (November 18 1987: 31 dead), a crash outside Clapham Junction (December 12 1988: 35 dead) followed by further deaths in rail accidents at Purley, south of London (March 4 1989: five dead), and Bellgrove in Strathclyde (March 6 1989: two dead); at sea, the loss of the ferry Herald of Free Enterprise at Zeebrugge (March 6 1987, 193 dead); and in the air the Kegworth crash of January 8 1989 (47 dead). Labour blamed some of these on Government neglect. "The tragedies of the 1980s – Zeebrugge, Lockerbie, Clapham, King's Cross – are

symbols of a government which has put cost cutting before people's lives," said a policy document of May 1990. The Conservatives were outraged: a blatant attempt, they said, to exploit human suffering for party gain – especially since the air crash at Lockerbie was the work of terrorists.

And then, at the end of the period, the argument suddenly changed. Malcolm Rifkind became Transport secretary under a new Prime Minister and used a speech to a London conference on May 28 1991 to signal new directions, even to preach what in Mrs Thatcher's day might have sounded like heresy. "I must declare myself, enthusiastically and unequivocally," he said, "as desiring to see far more traffic, both pasenger and freight, travelling by the railways."

As Opposition spokesmen noted, there was no pledge of powerful new public investment in the railways to underline this conversion. The £1.4 billion extra for transport in the 1991 Autumn Statement was to compensate for revenues lost because of the recession and depressed property values, rather than to fund new projects. It averted cuts on loss-making lines, but did not unfreeze BR's investment plans. And the speech marked no wholesale retreat from private provision. Rifkind committed the Government to ending the BR monopoly on the provision of freight and passenger services, though his approach to the eventual wholesale privatisation was pragmatic, not ideological. "If it won't help the travelling public," he told the Financial Times, "then it would be a bloody silly thing to do." Yet before long Rifkind was even prepared to consider the use of road pricing to deter people from entering city centres.

Labour had already moved towards the understanding that you couldn't go on building more and more roads to cope with more and more traffic, not least because new roads may attract new traffic. A left-of-centre think tank, the Institute for Public Policy Research, had specifically endorsed road pricing. The most radical proposals came from the Liberal Democrats, who in line with their strong environmental commitments, favoured road pricing, costlier petrol and the total abolition of tax privileges on company cars. ●

LEGISLATION

Transport Act 1980
1st reading: November 15 1979
2nd reading: November 27 1979, by 314 (Government, 6 Lib, 1 OUP) to 250 (Lab, SNP, 1 PC)
Royal Assent: June 6 1980
Provisions: major reform of the bus licensing system (established under 1930 Road Traffic Act) to allow new private operators; and reconstruction of the National Freight Corporation as a company under the Companies Act. (On February 22 1982 NFC was bought out by management, staff and pensioners for £53.5m and renamed National Freight Consortium.)

Transport Act 1981
1st reading: December 12 1980
2nd reading: January 13 1981, by 312 (Government, Lib, OUP, James Kilfedder) to 235 (Lab, PC, SNP)
Royal Assent: July 31 1981
Provisions: private capital was to be introduced into the Sealink ferry and hotel businesses and other BR subsidiaries; the British Transport Docks Board to be replaced by a two-tier organisation and a new holding company would be established in which the government would retain a 51% shareholding; the National Ports Council to be abolished; a points system would be created for road traffic offences; taxation of heavy lorries would be related to the damage they did to roads.

Transport Act 1985
1st reading: January 31 1985
2nd reading: February 12 1985, by 288 (Government, OUP) to 205 (Lab, Lib, SDP, SNP, PC).
Royal Assent: October 30 1985
Provisions: the National Bus Company was to be privatised; the Act also set a "deregulation day" (October 1 1986) on which local authority-owned bus services would have to become Companies Act companies and compete on fair terms with other operators. Road service licensing was to be abolished outside London; operators wishing to run a local service had to register a route with the local traffic commissioner. Local authorities were no longer required to co-ordinate public transport and their powers to limit taxi licences was restricted. The British Railways Board was empowered to put forward proposals for bus substitution where rail routes were considered uneconomic.

EDUCATION

THE 1979 Conservative manifesto declared its dissatisfaction with a system of state education run at high cost but apparently unable to deliver even the most basic of standards. This was not a new theme: in 1976 James Callaghan had set his Education secretary Shirley Williams to launch a "great debate" into educational standards in response to public concern.

The manifesto proclaimed that the Conservatives would halt the destruction of good schools (by which they meant the replacement of grammar schools with comprehensives), promote higher standards of achievement in basic skills and increase parental influence over what happened in schools. The aim was to create a serene and well-ordered system less open to what they saw as malign political influence. But in practice these were years of conflict, with the Government at odds with teachers and teaching unions, who claimed that the service was underfunded and that Conservative reforms put intolerable burdens on schools and staff, and also with local authorities, whose control over education was progressively transferred, in part to the schools themselves but also to central government.

A Bill to prevent local councils compelling schools to go comprehensive was rushed through before the 1979 summer recess. By the end of the first term the Government had brought in legislation to introduce an Assisted Places scheme, designed to help families who could not afford to send bright children to independent schools; to give parents the right of representation on school governing bodies; and to augment parents' right to choose their children's schools.

Conflict with the teachers developed fast after the 1983 election. In 1984 the Education secretary Sir Keith Joseph announced plans to amend teachers' conditions of service and to replace the Burnham Committee, an unwieldy forum in which pay and teachers' conditions were negotiated. Already discontented over the erosion of their earning power since the new deal for teachers which was supposed to have followed the report of the Houghton Committee in 1974, teaching unions began a wave of selective stoppages and work-to-rules which were to disrupt teaching and examination processes through 1984 and 1985.

The pace of change, and with it the teachers' resistance, increased when Kenneth Baker succeeded Joseph in May 1986. His Teachers' Pay and Conditions Bill unilaterally abolished the Burnham Committee, replacing it with an advisory committee to which the teaching unions were allowed to make representations, and built on a new framework of incentives for teaching responsibilities. In 1988 he introduced an Education Reform Bill, advertised as the most fundamental reconstruction of the system since the Butler Act of 1944. This established a core curriculum setting out a basic course of study to be followed by all pupils between 5 and 16, monitored by testing at 7, 11, 14 and 16.

Schools would be entitled to opt out of local authority control and assume grant-maintained status, becoming virtually self-governing within DES rules. In schools which remained within the system, control of budgets would be delegated to governing bodies – on which, because of their

GOVERNMENT SPENDING ON EDUCATION
1. Total spending at current prices, £bn.
2. Percentage increase on previous year in real terms.
3. Percentage of government expenditure.
4. Percentage of GDP.

	1978-1979	1979-1980	1980-1981	1981-1982	1982-1983	1983-1984	1984-1985	1985-1986	1986-1987	1987-1988	1988-1989	1989-1990	1990-1 estimated
1	9.5	10.9	13.3	14.5	15.6	16.4	17.0	17.6	19.3	21.1	22.8	25.1	27.5
2		-2.0	+2.0	*	*	*	-1.0	-2.0	+6.0	+3.0	+4.0	+4.0	+1.0
3	14.5	14.1	14.5	14.0	13.4	13.4	12.9	12.7	13.2	13.7	14.1	14.1	14.0
4		5.2	5.6	5.6	5.5	5.3	5.1	4.9	4.9	4.9	4.7	4.8	5.0

* less than 1% per cent

STUDENT AWARDS - REAL VALUE AND PARENTAL COSTS
(ENGLAND AND WALES) SHOWING VALUE OF GRANT DEFLATED BY:
1. Retail Price Index and
2. Average earnings

	standard maintenance grant (£)	index of real value compared with RPI (Feb 1980=100)	index of real value compared with Average Earnings (Feb 1980=100)	average assisted contribution by parents (%)
1979-80	1,245	100	100	13
1984-85	1,660	92	89	25
1988-89	2,050	90	74	31
1989-90	2,155	88	n/a	n/a

Source: Social Trends

PUPIL-TEACHER RATIOS

	1971	1981	1989
public sector:primary	27.1	22.3	21.9
public sector:secondary	17.8	16.4	15.0
all public (inc. nursery)	23.2	19.0	18.3

Source: Social Trends

EXPENDITURE PER PUPIL.
(ENGLAND) £s PER PUPIL 88-89 PRICES, SHOWING MAIN DESTINATIONS OF SPENDING

	PRIMARY		SECONDARY	
	1980-81	1988-89	1980-81	1988-89
Teaching	613	775	863	1,206
Educational support	32	48	30	40
Premises-related	56	56	67	74
Admin, clerical etc	20	56	28	67
Premises	118	123	166	196
Books, equipmt	26	32	47	70
Net spending per pupil*	870	1,102	1,217	1,692
% increase, real terms		26		39

* less certain charges

Source: Social Trends

greater representation, parents would be taking an increasingly dominant role. A network of City Technology Colleges would be introduced, also outside local authority control and relying heavily on business expertise and money, though still having access to public funding on a level which Opposition parties were soon to describe as excessive and a drain on the funding of conventional schools. The Inner London Education Authority would be phased out (a backbench revolt led by Norman Tebbit and Michael Heseltine got that changed to instant eradication) and local authorities were required to relinquish controls over polytechnics and higher education colleges.

Some of the changes proved to be too ambitious and had to be watered down by Baker's successor, John MacGregor, in his brief tenure of the department in 1989-90. Teacher appraisal was postponed and the programme of CTCs, which had not taken off on the scale which Baker had hoped for, was scaled down. Despite all this sometimes frenetic activity, public disquiet over standards and spending on schools failed to abate. Though spending per pupil increased sharply in real terms – by 27 per cent in primary schools and 39 per cent in secondary – not enough of this seemed to be feeding through to the classrooms, where, despite the increase in budgets, redecorations and repairs were postponed from year to year and there always seemed to be a shortage of textbooks. In July 1988, Her Majesty's Inspectors found that a quarter of schools were unsatisfactory. That statistic, according to Baker, proved the need for his reforms. But opinion polls continued to show high levels of public disapproval, with Labour leading the Conservatives as the party regarded as best-equipped to run education.

Higher education was one of the areas identified by Mrs Thatcher's governments as pitted with institutional inefficiencies and restrictive practices and assiduous empire-building. The distrust was reciprocated. From 1981 onwards, higher education was required to make sweeping cuts, starting with a demand for 15 per cent economies over three years, to be settled within a month.

Student numbers were to be cut by 5 per cent by 1984-85. In November 1984 Joseph attempted to raise charges for higher education, abolishing the minimum student grant and the automatic payment of tuition fees and effectively stiffening the scale for parental contributions.

Conservative MPs rose in revolt on behalf of their constituents who had university-bound children and Joseph retreated. In January 1985 an attempt at Oxford to confer an honorary degree on Mrs Thatcher was thwarted by a dons' revolt fuelled by the fury of the scientists, who felt especially under-funded and beleaguered.

Baker's reform programme of 1988 extended to higher education, too. Though he shrank from the wholesale replacement of student grants by student loans, which some of his backbenchers favoured, he announced the freezing of grants, with the shortfall to be made up by a system of "top-up" loans. There would be new funding arrangements for universities and polytechnics, and polytechnics and higher education colleges would pass from local authority control to become independent institutions run by their own boards of governors. The system known as academic tenure, which made it difficult to remove university teachers from their posts even in cases of known incompetence, would no longer apply to appointments made after November 20 1987: a necessary contribution, the Government maintained, to making higher education more efficient, though some in the universities saw it as a dangerous attack on academic freedom.

But the biggest problem was that so few went into higher education compared with the practice in comparable countries. This was one of the considerations which led Major, himself an early dropout whose higher education was conducted by correspondence, to intervene directly in education policy, taking over the presentation of the Government's Education White Paper of May 1991. This proposed the ending of two famous divisions in education: that between the universities and the polytechnics and that between academic and vocational education. ●

PERCENTAGE OF 16 TO 18-YEAR-OLDS IN EDUCATION AND TRAINING*
BY AGE AND TYPE OF STUDY; INTERNATIONAL COMPARISON 1986

	Full-time	Part-time	All
Germany	47	43	90
USA	79	1	80
Japan	77	3	79
France	66	8	74
Italy	47	18	65
UK	33	31	64
UK 1988	35	34	69

Source: Social Trends

LEGISLATION

Education Act 1979
1st reading: May 17 1979
2nd reading: June 19 1979, by 307 (Government, 5 OUP, 1 UU, 3 Lib) to 237 (Lab, 6 Lib, 1 PC).
Royal Assent: July 26 1979
Provisions: removal of the compulsion dating from the 1976 Education Act on local authorities and governors of grammar schools to reorganise along comprehensive lines.

Education (No2) Act 1980
1st reading: October 25 1979
2nd reading: November 5 1979, by 305 to 253 (Lab, 8 Lib, PC, SNP)
Royal Assent: April 3 1980
Provisions: schools normally required to have own governing body containing two elected parents and two elected teachers; parents given statutory right to express a preference about where their child should be educated; established an assisted places scheme under which government would meet fees of pupils selected to study at top independent schools where parents could not afford to pay; local education authorities given greater discretion in setting school meal prices.

Education Reform Act 1988
1st reading: November 20 1987
2nd reading: December 1 1987, by 348 (Government) to 241 (Lab, Lib, SDP, SNP, Plaid Cymru, SDLP, UPUP)
Royal Assent: July 29 1988
Provisions: introduced national curriculum, attainment targets, testing at 7, 11, 14 and 16. Control of school budgets passes to governing bodies. Schools may opt out and apply for grant-maintained status. Polytechnics and the larger colleges of higher education pass out of local authority control, becoming free-standing bodies whose governors are to include representatives of commerce and industry. Universities Funding Council to replace University Grants Committee. City Technology Colleges to be set up outside local authority control, run by independent bodies linked with industry and commerce.

Education (Student Loans) Act 1990
1st reading: November 22 1989
2nd reading: December 5 1989, by 301 (Government) to 220 (Lab, Lib Dem, SDP, OUP, DUP, SDLP, UPUP and three Conservatives: D.Dover (Chorley), D.Knox (Staffs Moorlands) and R.Rhodes James (Cambridge)).
Royal Assent: April 26 1990
Provisions: introduced loans to supplement higher education grants.

Schools Bill 1991
Introduced: November 6 1991
2nd reading:
Provisions: All parents to get a written report at least once a year on child's progress including exam and test results and comparisons with national benchmarks. Governors must supply annual report on school performance including levels of attendance and destinations of school leavers. Local authorities required to produce league tables of school performance. New national schools inspectorate to be established: present inspectorate to be reduced; teams of inspectors will compete for contracts awarded by schools.

Further and Higher Education Bill 1991
Introduced: November 4 1991
2nd reading:
Provisions: 450 further education colleges and 113 sixth form colleges to be moved out of local authority control. Further Education Funding Councils and Higher Education Funding Councils to be established for England and Wales. Colleges must publish reports on their results, including destinations of leavers.
Polytechnics and the larger HE colleges may call themselves universities and award their own degrees. The Council for National Academic Awards (CNAA) will be wound up.

HEALTH

"I N OUR National Health Service," said the 1979 Conservative manifesto, "standards are falling; there is a crisis of morale; too often patients' needs do not come first." Throughout the last 12 years precisely these complaints have been made about the NHS. The predominant judgment, among other parties, among people working in the service and among those who use it, was that there has been a crisis of underfunding. The Conservative diagnosis was different. The core of the problem, they said, was that a service designed in the 1940s was inadequate to cope with the needs of the 1990s. Resources were inaccurately targeted and often wasted. Spending more money was no guarantee that you would deliver more satisfaction.

Throughout these years there were high levels of public discontent with the Government's running of the service and much suspicion about its deeper intentions. At one point in the 1983 election campaign the Conservatives called an emergency press conference to answer charges that they were plotting the dismemberment of the service. "I have no more intention of dismantling the health service," Mrs Thatcher retorted, "than I have of dismantling Britain's defences."

As always, spending totals were at the heart of the dispute. Though the NHS was not spared in the cuts in spending programmes ordered during this period, health spending increased by well over the rate of inflation – by 35 per cent in real terms between 1978-79 and 1989-90. As Mrs Thatcher repeatedly said at question time in the Commons, there were more doctors, more nurses, more patients being treated, more treatments becoming available, and much higher spending all round

than when Labour was in power. But as anyone who visited hospitals knew, it was not enough. The demands of the service were famously insatiable and three factors – the change in the balance of the population as people survived in greater numbers into old age; the advance of expensive but much sought-after technologies; and the need to comply with specific Government policy objectives – meant costs were escalating far faster than the general cost of living.

A further developing problem was the growing incidence of the Human Immuno-Deficiency Virus (HIV) with its fatal consequence, the Acquired Immune Deficiency Syndrome, Aids. Unrecognised before 1981, it began to multiply first mainly among homosexual men but then among heterosexuals also. As alarm over the implications grew, the Social Services secretary Norman Fowler in November 1986 launched a £20 million publicity campaign to draw attentions to its dangers and to the need for safe sex: the candour of its language shocked some of his colleagues.

One group won particular sympathy. About 1,200 haemophiliacs had been given contaminated blood while in NHS care. At first the Government resisted pressure to pay them more than a £34m ex gratia payment announced in March 1990. But after the judge hearing the case had issued a statement drawing the Government's attention to the "moral dimension" of the claim, John Major, newly arrived in Downing Street, sanctioned a further payment of £42m. By September 1991, the number of cases of Aids in Britain had risen to 5,065 and the number of resulting deaths had reached 3,156. Total government spending on Aids had topped £600m.

GOVERNMENT SPENDING ON HEALTH AND PERSONAL SOCIAL SERVICES
1. Total spending at current prices, £ bn.
2. % increase on previous year in real terms.
3. % of government expenditure.
4. % of GDP.

	1978-1979	1979-1980	1980-1981	1981-1982	1982-1983	1983-1984	1984-1985	1985-1986	1986-1987	1987-1988	1988-1989	1989-1990	1990-1 estimated
1	7.8	9.3	12.0	13.5	14.7	15.5	16.7	17.7	18.9	20.7	22.8	24.7	27.8
2		+2.0	+9.0	+2.0	+2.0	+1.0	+2.0	*	+3.0	+4.0	+3.0	+2.0	+4.0
3	12.0	12.1	13.0	13.1	12.7	12.7	12.7	12.7	12.9	13.4	14.1	13.9	14.2
4		4.5	5.1	5.2	5.2	5.0	5.0	4.9	4.8	4.8	4.7	4.8	5.1

* less than 1 per cent

STAFFING AND SERVICES IN THE NHS
(UK, THOUSANDS)
1. average number of beds available daily
2. average number of beds occupied daily
3. NHS hospital waiting lists UK
4. number of doctors in practice UK
5. average patients per doctor

	beds available	beds in use	on waiting lists	no. of doctors	patients per doctor
1979	461	374	828	26.4	2.23
1983	440	354	855	28.7	2.06
1987	392	317	806	30.7	1.97
1988	373*	n/a	828	31.2	1.94
1989	n/a	n/a	827	31.5	1.91
1990	n/a	n/a	842	n/a	n/a

* 1988-9 figure

Source: Social Trends

GOVERNMENT SPENDING ON AIDS
MONEY MADE AVAILABLE TO REGIONAL HEALTH AUTHORITIES FOR HIV PREVENTION AND TREATMENT, COUNSELLING AND SUPPORT FOR VICTIMS OF HIV AND AIDS

	(£m)
1987-88	25.1
1988-89	61.7
1989-90	122.5
1990-91	129.5
1991-92	137.3

Source: written answer from Mrs Virginia Bottomley, Health minister, to Mrs Teresa Gorman (Con Billericay) May 17 1991.

LEGISLATION

Health Services Act 1980
1st reading: December 7 1979
2nd reading: December 19 1979, by 320 (Government, 5 Lib, 4 unionists) to 250 (Lab, SNP, PC)
Royal Assent: August 8 1980
Provisions: restoration of pay beds in NHS hospitals; eased controls on private hospitals (allowing them up to 120 beds instead of 100 in London and 75 elsewhere); imposed cash limits on health authorities and permitted them to engage in voluntary fund-raising activities.

National Health Service and Community Care Act 1990
1st reading: November 22 1989
2nd reading: December 7 & 11 1989, by 323 (Government) to 247 (Lab, Lib Dem, SDP, SNP, Plaid Cymru, OUP, DUP and two Conservatives: M.Morris (Northampton S) and N.Winter-ton (Macclesfield).)
Royal Assent: June 29 1990
Provisions: extensive reform of NHS including right for hospitals to opt out and become self-governing trusts, transferred controls of budgets to larger general practices which want to take it, and reorganised the system of local community care on the lines recommended by the Griffiths Report giving local authorities responsibility for care of the elderly and handicapped in the community. Abolished most remaining instances of Crown Immunity (immunity against prosecution) in the service allowing normal health and safety regulations to apply.
Rebellion: On March 13 1990, 33 Conservative MPs voted against the Government to carry a Labour amendment on income support for the elderly to ensure that the costs of their care were fully covered. But immediately afterwards the Commons declined, by a majority of 27, to add this new clause to the Bill.

The pressures came to a head in the winter of 1987-88 as reports flooded in from hospitals of shortage of staff, shortage of beds, patients prematurely discharged and patients turned away. The heads of three of the royal colleges of medicine made an unprecedented public complaint that the NHS was "in crisis" and close to breaking point. An all-party Commons select committee on the social services estimated that the NHS had been underfunded since 1981 to the tune of £2,000m.

But the Government remained unconvinced that the remedy lay in spending more money. As the clamour continued, so signs developed that the Government actually welcomed it as the preface for a kind of sweeping reform, which until then had been rejected as politically unacceptable. Radical solutions involving a general switch towards private provision, favoured by right-wing think tanks and by some Conservative MPs, were still judged impossible. (A report in 1982 from the Government's Central Policy Review Staff had suggested a switch to a system of private health insurance, which could save, it suggested, £3billion on a budget of £10billion; there could also be charges for doctors' visits and higher charges for drugs.) But greater commercial discipline, a greater responsiveness to market forces, a fuller accountancy of what was being spent where and to what effect – all these were very much on the agenda.

The result was the 1989 White Paper, Working For Patients, setting out what the Health secretary, Kenneth Clarke, described as "the most fundamental reform programme in the history of the NHS". It was built upon a favourite theme of the Thatcher governments: drawing a dividing line between providers and clients choosing between competitive services. GPs and health authorities would be clients, hospitals the providers. Hospital services would be costed and priced as never before, while health authorities mapped out their likely needs and negotiated with hospitals to meet them. Up to 320 of the country's 2,000 hospitals would be given the chance of self-governing status as NHS hospital trusts, able to borrow money and fix their own wages, still within the NHS but outside the jurisdiction of its system of health authorities. (In fact, 57 opted to do so from the opening of the scheme on April 1 1991.) All NHS hospitals, whether opting

out or not, would be empowered to sell services to any health authority or to the private sector. The biggest GP practices could now apply for their own NHS budgets and obtain a defined range of services for hospitals of their choice, whether or not their local district health authority had a contract with it. The BMA, an old assailant of change in the service, opposed this one with particular virulence. The Liberal Democrats said it undermined the founding principles of the NHS; Labour, that it opened the door for eventual privatisation.

Particular fear was expressed that groups like the mentally ill and the aged, with no great market appeal, would be neglected. One general theme of the protest was that pilot schemes should be run before such extensive changes. That was rejected, not least on the grounds that it might prolong uncertainty. By April 1991, when the new pattern came into being, apprehension over the NHS had become the biggest political issue of the day, blamed for losing the Government a by-election in Monmouth and feared by some MPs as the biggest potential vote-loser since the poll tax.

Opinion polls showed that many voters, and even up to a quarter of Conservative supporters, believed Labour claims that if re-elected the Conservatives would privatise the health service. John Major disclaimed this intention: "There will be no charges for hospital treatment, no charges for visits to the doctor, no privatisation of health care, neither piecemeal nor in part, nor in the whole" he told the Conservative Party conference on October 11. "Not today, not tomorrow, not after the next election, nor ever while I am prime minister". On October 20 the health secretary William Waldegrave hinted that tax concessions for private health insurance for the elderly, introduced at Thatcher's insistence, might be withdrawn: he later retracted.

Despite all the pressures, the Government pressed ahead with its reforms. On October 16, Waldegrave anounced that a further 99 hospitals would be allowed to opt out – though four teaching hospitals in the capital, where some of the early opt-out hospitals had run into financial trouble, were told they would have to wait until the completion of an inquiry into London's hospitals. Conservative unease on this issue helped to produce an unusually generous deal for the NHS in the Chancellor's Autumn Statement of November 6. An estimated £2.7 billion was added to the planned expenditure total for 1992-3, bringing it to £34 billion, or £36 billion including receipts. That brought the projected increase on spending on the NHS in real terms since 1978-9 to 55 per cent. Though some in the NHS still found these sums inadequate, the Institute of Health Services Management called them "a welcome recognition of the financial strain under which the NHS has been operating", and even the Labour spokesman, Robin Cook, accepted that they ought to preclude any further cuts. "A death-bed repentance of a government that knows it is about to meet the electorate" he called it. ●

WELFARE

THE DEMANDS of welfare, like the demands of health, are infinite and insatiable. And they are destined to get worse: the numbers of old people, who are net recipients, are destined to increase, while the proportion of those in work, who need to sustain them, diminishes. That problem was not foreseen in the 1979 Conservative manifesto, whose prescriptions were designed to balance the need to help those genuinely in want with the need to end the climate of dependency.

As Conservative party conferences so often reminded them, the work shy, as well as the poor, were always with us. Their aims were to simplify a system grown so complex that even those who ran it could not always fathom it; to reduce the poverty trap, to bring effective help to the needy, but also to restore the incentive to work – which meant cutting taxes, bringing unemployment and short-term sickness benefit into the tax net, putting greater pressure on the unemployed to find work, and clamping down on fraud. The best hope of reconciling demand with supply, in other words, lay through much more rigorous targeting.

The 1980-81 recession and the high rate of unemployment it left behind inevitably meant a sizeable rise in social security spending. Together with the increase in the number of people of pensionable age, that helped to swell social security spending as a proportion of general government expenditure. In the peak year of 1986-87 it accounted for 31.8 per cent of general government spending. This happened despite the Government's attempts to tailor some benefits. In 1980 several benefits, including sickness and unemployment payments, were raised by less than the rate of infla-tion; the abatement was restored in 1983 but at this point the benefits were made subject to tax. From 1980 the system inherited from Labour in which pensions and unemployment benefit were increased annually in line with both the cost of living and the increase in wages was abandoned: from now on, pensions would increase in line with the cost of living (normally the more modest increase) alone. As promised, unemployment pay and short-term sickness benefit were brought into the tax net. Earnings-related supplements for the unemployed, the sick, and widows were dropped.

The Government had rejected the recommendations of the CPRS in 1982 for a radical recasting of the system, but it could not allow things to go on as they were. In April 1984 the Social Services secretary Norman Fowler announced a fundamental review – to be conducted, as was always Mrs Thatcher's preference, in-house, rather than by some outside commission. The results fell far short of the extensive excursion into Thatcherite territory that some had predicted. The most striking conclusion was that the Government should abandon the State Earnings Related Pension Scheme (Serps) brought in by Labour in 1975.

But this aroused so much protest, not just from the Opposition but from the pensions industry and some Conservative MPs, that Fowler abandoned it, deciding instead to keep Serps alive but dilute it. It was also proposed to give every worker due to retire after the year 2000 the right to a private pension – a move condemned by Labour as a bribe and in practice a much more expensive enterprise than its authors expected.

GOVERNMENT SPENDING ON SOCIAL SECURITY
1. Total spending on social security at current prices.
2. % increase on previous year in real terms.
3. % of government expenditure.
4. % of GDP.

	1978-1979	1979-1980	1980-1981	1981-1982	1982-1983	1983-1984	1984-1985	1985-1986	1986-1987	1987-1988	1988-1989	1989-1990	1990-1 estimate
1	16.9	20.0	24.2	29.4	33.5	36.7	39.8	43.3	46.6	48.7	49.9	52.9	58.6
2		+ 1.0	+ 2.0	+ 11.0	+ 6.0	+ 5.0	+ 3.0	+ 3.0	+ 4.0	- 1.0	- 4.0	*	+ 2.0
3	25.9	25.9	26.3	28.5	28.8	29.9	30.2	31.3	31.8	31.5	30.8	29.7	29.9
4	9.6	10.2	11.3	11.7	11.9	12.0	11.9	11.9	11.3	10.4	10.2	10.7	

* less than 1 per cent

WEEKLY RATES OF BENEFITS (£)

	Unemployment benefit	Sickness benefit	Retirement pension single*	Retirement pension married	invalidity pension	child benefit
November 1979	18.50	18.50	23.30	37.30	23.30	4.00
November 1980	20.65	20.65	27.15	43.45	26.00	4.75
November 1981	22.50	22.50	29.60	47.35	28.35	5.25
November 1982	25.00	25.00	32.85	52.55	31.45	5.85
November 1983	27.05	25.95	34.05	54.50	32.60	6.50
November 1984	28.45	27.25	35.80	57.30	34.25	6.85
November 1985	30.45	29.15	38.30	61.30	38.30	7.00
July 1986	30.80	29.45	38.70	61.95	38.70	7.10
April 1987	31.45	30.05	39.50	63.25	39.50	7.25
April 1988	32.75	31.30	41.15	65.90	41.15	7.25
April 1989	34.70	33.20	43.60	69.80	43.60	7.25
April 1990	37.35	35.70	46.90	75.10	46.90	7.25
April 1991	41.40	39.60	52.00	83.25	52.00	8.25**
April 1992	43.10	41.20	54.15	88.95	54.15	9.65**

* rates of widow's pension are identical
** for first-born child only: There was an interim rise to £9.25 in 1991

Source: Annual Abstract of Statistics; press reports

Until 1980 pensions were raised annually to keep pace with prices and earnings. The Conservative government altered the rule and linked pensions with prices only. The following table, taken from a Commons written answer from Treasury minister Mrs Gillian Shephard to Andrew Bowden (Con, Brighton Kemp Town) shows how pensions would have risen had the link with earnings been maintained.

	SINGLE PERSON		MARRIED COUPLE	
Uprating date	Actual (linked with RPI)	If linked with earnings	Actual (linked with RPI)	If linked with earnings
November 1980	27.15	27.45	43.45	44.00
November 1981	29.60	30.75	47.35	49.30
November 1982	32.85	33.30	52.55	53.40
November 1983	34.05	36.20	54.50	58.05
November 1984	35.80	38.05	57.30	61.00
November 1985	38.30	41.40	61.30	66.35
July 1986	38.70	43.70	61.95	70.05
April 1987	39.50	45.60	63.25	73.15
April 1988	41.15	49.20	65.90	78.95
April 1989	43.60	53.45	69.80	85.75
April 1990	46.90	58.65	75.10	94.05

Mrs Shephard said that to pay pensions at the level required to keep pace with earnings would have meant an increase of £3.18 a week in the National Insurance contribution paid by each employee and of £4.35 per employee in the contribution paid by the employer.

The full effects of the Fowler review did not begin to bite until after the 1987 election. Then they bit hard. In April 1988, claimants who had been entitled as of right to one-off payments to provide necessities like clothing and furniture had now to apply for payments from a Social Fund, which came in the form of loans: whether or not you qualified was left to the discretion of whoever you met on the other side of the counter.

There were sharp reductions in housing benefit and rent rebates and free school meals were abolished. The measures were condemned by a gallery which ranged from the Government's own independent Social Security Advisory Committee to the Bishop of Durham, who called them "verging on the wicked". "At the furthest perimeter of society," wrote Hugo Young in One Of Us, his classic account of Mrs Thatcher's years in government, "the squeeze was now discernibly applied against a disease long identified in Thatcherite rhetoric as the 'dependency culture', but hitherto thought too dangerous to try to cure by deprivation."

The protest was heightened by the fact that these changes came within weeks of a Budget which had brought large relief to the rich. That Budget had also failed fully to uprate child benefit. Its effect, ministers said, was too indiscriminate, available to rich as well as to poor, a misuse of resources they intended for the needy. Despite Conservative back-bench protests, there was again no full uprating in 1989 or 1990. In 1991, after Mrs Thatcher's departure, child benefit was raised by £1 – but for the first child only.

The return of recession put new pressures on the social security budget. The Chancellor's last autumn Statement, on November 6 1991, saw a £4.2 billion increase on planned spending for 1992-3 to a new total of £70.6 billion. This reflected new and gloomier calculations of the expected level of unemployment for the year, now put at 2.5 billion. ●

LEGISLATION

Social Security Act 1980
1st reading: November 29 1979
2nd reading: December 20 1979, by 312 (Government, 2 OUP) to 255 (Lab, Lib, SNP, PC, DUP, G Fitt (Ind), J Kilfedder (UPUP).)
Royal Assent: May 23 1980
Provisions: changes in method of calculating pensions and other long-term benefits; Supplementary Benefit Commission abolished and new Social Security Advisory Committee created; new framework for supplementary benefit claims and entitlements; school leavers' entitlement to supplementary benefit deferred until beginning of new school term; equal treatment introduced for men and women in social security.

Social Security (No2) Act 1980
1st reading: March 28 1980
2nd reading: April 15 1980, by 299 to 244 (Lab, Lib, SNP, PC, OUP, G.Fitt, UPU).
Royal Assent: July 17 1980
Provisions: changes in entitlement to social security incorporated in new Act, designed to make net saving of £270m in 1981-82 and £480m in 1982-83. Controversy over regulation cutting supplementary benefit entitlement of family of person on strike by £12pw.

Social Security Act 1985
1st reading: November 15 1984
2nd reading: November 26 1984, after rejection of Labour reasoned amendment: Lib, SDP, OUP voted with Government and Plaid Cymru with Labour
Royal Assent: July 22 1985
Provisions: protection of personal occupational pension rights of workers who changed jobs before retirement age; extension of statutory sick pay to cover the first 28 weeks of an illness and employers relieved of National Insurance contributions on their share of sick pay. At report stage changes were made in the structure of National Insurance contributions outlined in the 1984 budget.

Social Security Act 1986
1st reading: January 17 1986
2nd reading: January 28 1986 by 278 (Government) to 201 (Lab, Lib, SDP, SNP, Plaid Cymru, SDLP)
Royal Assent: July 25 1986
Provisions: additional state pensions to be based on lifetime average earnings rather than the best 20 years; made it possible to contract-out personal pension schemes in the same way as as occupational pension schemes; abolished maternity pay and wound up the Maternity Pay Fund.

Social Security Act 1988
1st reading: October 22 1987
2nd reading: November 2 1987, by 328 (Government) to 238 (Lab, Lib, SDP, SNP, Plaid Cymru, OUP, SDLP, UPUP).
Royal Assent: March 15 1988
Provisions: altered eligibility for income support and pattern of benefit contributions. Withdrew benefit from unemployed school-leavers who do not join YTS. Put cold-weather payments on a statutory basis. Tightened the law on payment of attendance allowance after a court ruling which the Government said interpreted it as being more generous than the legislation had intended.

POVERTY

THE EXTENT of real poverty in Britain in the early 1990s was a matter of contention: what the evidence plainly suggested was that the poor in these years had fallen further behind the rich. This did not imply the kind of abject poverty which existed across much of the third world (which also grew worse in these years), but relative poverty in which the have-nots saw the haves pulling further and further away. According to EC figures, the rise in poverty in Britain between 1975 and 1985 was greater than in any other member state. The number of households defined as "poor" by the EC grew by one third in these 10 years.

A report prepared for the European Poverty programme published in 1991 suggested that 10.3m people (3.8m households) were living in relative poverty (the measure adopted being a disposable income less than half the national average) in mid-decade. Though ministers disputed the methodology, Social Security minister Nicholas Scott told BBC radio: "The Government deliberately set out in 1979 to increase the ability of people to earn more, to retain more of what they earn and to contribute to the general prosperity. That has happened. There have been some people who in a sense have been left behind in that movement. Their standard of living has still gone up, but not nearly as fast, and the gap has widened..."

For a time the Government invoked the "trickle down" theory, which held that the greater prosperity of the rich was seeping through to lift the poor. Official statistics suggested that the poorest one-tenth had been doing twice as well as the national average. But this claim was abandoned after work by the Institute of Fiscal Studies for the Commons

social services committee showed that in fact the poorest one-tenth had done less than half as well as the average.

There was a particular concern at the end of the decade about the fate of children in poor households. In July 1991 a report from the National Children's Home said 10 per cent of under-fives in low income families were going without food at least once a month. The withdrawal of their automatic right to benefit meant that 16- and 17-year-olds who were unwilling or unable to live at home had to subsist on pitiful levels of income. Unprecedented numbers slept on the streets or resorted to begging.

The greatest single curse of poverty, Professor David Piachaud reported in a paper for the Campaign for Work, was not being old, sick or part of a one-parent family, but living in a household smitten by unemployment. That had a particularly strong influence in the creation of relative poverty because of the changes the Conservatives made in the system of unemployment benefit.

Benefits were now tied to the rate of inflation, but not any longer to the level of earnings. Benefits therefore held their own in real terms – the standard unemployment benefit in 1990 was £37.35, against £38.41 at 1990 prices in 1979 – but failed to keep pace with the incomes of those in work: in 1979 a married claimant qualified for 35 per cent of average earnings, in 1990 for only 27 per cent. Around three-quarters of unemployed men were now means-tested, against approximately half in 1979.

But times were not much better for some of

**NUMBER OF FULL-TIMERS WITH GROSS WEEKLY EARNINGS BELOW THE
COUNCIL OF EUROPE'S "DECENCY THRESHOLD" 1979-90***
(MILLIONS/PERCENTAGE OF WORKFORCE)

	1979		1982		1988		1990	
	m	%	m	%	m	%	m	%
Full-time women	3.00	57.6	2.75	55.6	2.91	55.0	3.29	53.8
Full-time men	1.64	14.6	1.83	17.7	2.77	26.7	2.93	28.1
All full-time workers	4.64	28.3	4.58	30.0	5.68	36.2	6.12	37.0

Source: Low Pay Unit estimates based on New Earnings Surveys

NOTE: The figures for 1979 and 1983 are for men aged over 21 and for women aged over 18: the figures for 1988 and 1989 include all workers "on adult rates". Overtime earnings are excluded
* The rate for 1990/91 is £178.91 a week.

INCOMES OF THE POOR 1979-88
% GROWTH OF REAL INCOME 1979-88 BEFORE HOUSING COSTS FOR:

average of total population	poorest 10 per cent
31.8	9.5

% GROWTH OF REAL INCOME 1979-88 AFTER HOUSING COSTS

average of total population	poorest 10 per cent
33.5	2.0

NUMBER OF INDIVIDUALS WITH REAL INCOMES BELOW THE CONSTANT 1979 LEVEL OF HALF AVERAGE INCOME

before housing costs (million)		after housing costs (million)	
1979	1988	1979	1988
3.7	2.5	9.4	8.7

NUMBERS LIVING ON BELOW HALF AVERAGE INCOME

before housing costs (million)		after housing costs (million)	
1979	1988	1979	1988
3.8	9.1	4.9	11.8

*Source: 1st report of House of Commons Select Committee on Social Security April 1990;
based on research by Institute for Fiscal Studies commissioned by the committee.*

(These figures show that the poorest households are in real terms better off than they were in 1979, but because their incomes have grown much less fast than those of the better-off, more people were living on less than half average income in 1988 than was the case in1979. In other words, while actual poverty lessened, relative poverty increased.)

those in work. In its drive to enhance incentives, the Government helped bring about a worsening in the distribution of disposable income (after tax and benefits): the top 20 per cent saw their share of income rise from 39 to 42 per cent while the bottom 20 per cent slipped further down, from 6.5 per cent in 1979 to 6.1 in 1987. Only Spain and Italy, according to EC figures, had fewer workers attaining two-thirds of national average earnings than the UK.

Calculations of this kind helped to persuade the Labour party to commit itself to establishing a national minimum wage, while the Liberal Democrats promised a basic minimum income. Some unions, led by the AUEW and EETPU, strongly opposed the national minimum wage and Conservatives condemned it as a dangerous delusion. The Employment secretary, Michael Howard, predicted it would destroy up to 2m jobs.

Similar policies were already in force across the EC. France, Luxembourg, the Netherlands, Portugal and Spain have a national minimum wage. In Belgium and Greece general minimum wages are fixed by national agreement. Denmark, Italy and West Germany set legally binding minimum wages by collective agreements covering most of the workforce. But ministers argued that British conditions and practices were not comparable. They feared that inflationary pressures would be increased and our competitive position weakened. ●

DISTRIBUTION OF WEALTH IN THE UK

In 1988 the wealthiest 10 per cent of the adult population owned more than half the marketable wealth of the United Kingdom.

MARKETABLE WEALTH: (% OF WEALTH OWNED BY THE MOST WEALTHY:-)

	1976	1981	1986	1988
1%	21	18	18	17
5%	38	36	36	38
10%	50	50	50	53
25%	71	73	73	75
50%	92	92	90	94

TOTAL MARKETABLE WEALTH £bn

	1976	1981	1986	1988
	280	565	955	1,317

MARKETABLE WEALTH LESS VALUE OF DWELLINGS (% OF WEALTH OWNED BY THE MOST WEALTHY)

	1976	1981	1986	1988
1%	29	26	25	27
5%	47	45	46	50
10%	57	56	58	63
25%	73	74	75	80
50%	88	87	89	93

Source: Social Trends

COMMUNITY CARE

THAT MORE and more people were living longer in late 20th-century Britain was both a cause for celebration and stress: stress because the demographic trends were projecting increasing numbers of people who would need to be cared for and a decreasing proportion of people in work and able to pay for them. Already the number of citizens aged 80 or more had risen by 50 per cent between 1961 and 1989 and official predictions suggested a further 30 per cent increase by 2025. That growing population was reflected in the demand for places in nursing or residential care and an extraordinary growth in demand for public funds to pay for such people: from 12,000 claims in 1979 to 189,000 in 1990. Social security subsidies to these places rose from £10m in 1979 to £1,000m in 1989. A system where responsibility was uneasily divided between government agencies and local authorities was increasingly showing the strain.

Concern about the open-ended cost of this care was compounded by an Audit Commission report which suggested that much of the £6,000m a year being spent on community care was going to waste. There was also increasing evidence from the private and public sectors that the standard of care in some of these institutions was lamentable, even wicked. It was more and more obvious, too, that the gap was widening between what even the most solicitous homes were having to charge and the level of financial support available from government agencies.

The result was an inquiry carried out by Roy Griffiths, the Prime Minister's adviser on health, which reported in March 1988. He recommended the unification of the present divided service and said that local authorities ought to take charge of it. That swam against a tide in Government opinion which distrusted local government and sought to reduce its powers, not to enhance them. For over a year, the Government failed to respond. But in

June 1989, Health secretary Clarke announced that the lead role in provision would after all be given to local authorities, with a new care pattern established, repeating yet again that division between purchaser and provider which so often coloured Government thinking.

From April 1991 local authorities would have to decide who needed to go into private and voluntary sector homes. These homes would be the providers: the council would be the purchaser, buying their service – and normally only providing its own if there was no alternative. Where such a course seemed feasible, councils might decide instead to let people remain in their homes, but give them the comprehensive back-up needed to make that possible.

The original deadline had to be deferred. Full implementation was deferred by two years, from April 1991 to April 1993: the cost would have added 30p a week to the poll tax. And apprehensions persisted about the level of support which people would get if they chose to stay at home. There was worrying evidence from other sectors that the funding available to make care in the community work might not be enough.

For many years under successive governments it had been official policy to remove the mentally handicapped and all but the most severely affected of the mentally ill out of their institutions and into society. Between 1977 and 1987 the number of mentally ill patients in hospital declined from 84,000 to 60,000; but the number of places available to them in residential accommodation rose by only 5,000, to 9,000. An estimated 30 per cent of those sleeping rough in Britain in 1991 were thought to be schizophrenic. Though in 1991 the Government gave local authorities £21m to tackle this problem, the voluntary organisations said it was still nowhere near enough. ●

AGE STRUCTURE OF THE POPULATION (MID-YEAR ESTIMATES)
(MILLIONS)

	under 16	16-39	40-64	65-79	80plus	ALL
1981	12.5	19.7	15.7	6.9	1.6	56.4
1986	11.7	20.6	15.8	6.8	1.8	56.8
1989	11.5	20.4	16.3	6.9	2.1	57.2

projected

	under 16	16-39	40-64	65-79	80plus	ALL
1991	11.7	20.2	16.5	6.9	2.2	57.5
2001	12.8	19.2	18.0	6.7	2.5	59.2
2011	12.1	18.1	20.2	7.0	2.7	60.0

Source: OPCS/Social Trends

The number of people aged 80-plus was just over 50% greater in 1989 than in 1961. Population in this group is expected to grow steadily to 2.9m in 2025.

GROWTH OF CLAIMS FOR RESIDENTIAL AND NURSING HOME CARE
(THOUSANDS)

	residential care homes	nursing homes	TOTAL
1979 Dec	*	*	12
1983 Dec	*	*	26
1987 May	84	32	117
1990 May	125	64	189

Source: written answer Gillian Shephard to J. Cousins, November 16 1990

* Figures before 1985 are not considered reliable enough to be sub-divided between nursing and residential care homes. Figures may not add up because of rounding

CHILDREN

THE YEARS of Mrs Thatcher's government were punctuated by outbursts of public concern about the welfare of children, usually triggered by the disclosure of a specific malpractice or tragedy. Like the case of Maria Colwell before it, which helped to prompt the Children Act of 1975, the cases of Jasmine Beckford, Kimberley Carlile and Tyra Henry – only three of more than 20 inquiries into child deaths between 1974 and 1988 – produced anguished public inquests and declarations that things of this kind must never happen again.

Where social workers were often condemned in such cases for their failure to intervene, in another crop of cases there was outrage at allegedly precipitate and authoritarian intervention. That was what happened in Cleveland after reports from two doctors, Marietta Higgs and Geoffrey Wyatt, led to more than 120 children being identified as victims of sexual abuse and summarily removed from their homes.

A series of other cases of abuse, some said to have involved Satanic practices, in Rochdale, Nottingham, Orkney and elsewhere, led to irreconcilable disputes between those who believed intervention had been right and necessary and those who could not accept that these children had been genuinely at risk. Cleveland, the Guardian said in a leader on July 7 1988, following the report of an inquiry headed by Lord Justice Butler-Sloss, had proved to be a double tragedy: for parents whose children were summarily removed and wrongly diagnosed as suffering from sexual abuse, and for those children across the country who were genuinely suffering from abuse, because of the swing in public attitudes against intervention which Cleveland had produced.

The Cleveland case, along with a series of reports from the Law Commission, helped engender the 1989 Children Bill, which Lord Mackay, the Lord Chancellor, described as the most far-reaching reform of child law in living memory. It brought together the private and public elements of the law and sought to balance the sometimes conflicting interests of children, parents, local authorities and the courts in a framework which, to a greater extent than any previous legislation, made the child's interests paramount. The period for which children could be held under emergency powers would be cut from 28 days to eight (with a possible seven-day extension). New rights of appeal and access would be given to parents whose children were taken from them. Councils would have to go to the courts to gain custody rather than simply acting on a council resolution and the grounds on which care orders could be made would be widened to give more weight to the threat of abuse as against its actuality. A general duty would be placed on every local authority to provide services for children in need and their families.

What worried the Opposition parties most was what the Bill omitted, especially the failure to commit substantial new resources to match new obligations, and the continued rejection of the proposal for non-adversarial family courts, backed-up by a family welfare service, made by the Finer committee on one-parent families in 1972.

But children remained at risk in less spectacular ways than those revealed by cases like Beckford

LEGISLATION

Children Act 1989
1st reading: March 20 1989
2nd reading: April 27 1989, unopposed
Royal Assent: November 16 1989
Provisions: an eight-day emergency protection order
replaced the 28-day place of safety order. Parents could challenge the orders after 72 hours and be represented at proceedings. They would have new rights of access
to children in care. Children would have stronger rights of representation in care proceedings. Councils would have to
obtain court approval before removing a child. Courts would
have to observe more rigorous criteria before agreeing. Councils could no longer take children into care on a "parental resolution". There would be restrictions on the use of wardship to
give councils compulsory powers over a child. Unmarried
cohabitees would have right to assume joint responsibility for
a child – a gain for unmarried fathers. The law on private fos-
tering of children and on children's homes was reformed.

Rebellion: on April 24 1989 19 Conservatives opposed the
Government on a Conservative backbench amendment to the
Social Security Bill to index-link child benefit, which had been
frozen in two consecutive budgets. The rebels were: W. Beny-
on (Milton Keynes), J. Critchley (Aldershot), H. Dykes (Harrow
E), Sir I. Gilmour (Chesham), R. Hicks (Cornwall SE), Dame
E. Kellett-Bowman (Lancaster), D. Knox (Staffs Moorlands),
J. Lester (Broxtowe), Sir R. McCrindle (Brentwood), D. Madel
(Beds SW), T. Marlow (Northampton N), Sir A. Meyer (Clwyd
NW), T. Raison (Aylesbury), T. Rathbone (Lewes), Sir G.
Shaw (Pudsey), R. Squire (Hornchurch), C. Townsend (Bex-
leyheath), Sir D. Walters (Westbury), Sir G. Young (Acton).

Child Support Act 1991
1st reading: February 14 1991 (Lords)
2nd reading: February 18 1991, unopposed
Royal Assent: July 25 1991
Provisions: to enforce maintenance payments for children
and trace errant fathers. Linked with establishment of Child
Support Agency starting work in 1993 to track down fathers
defaulting on payments. Mothers refusing "unreasonably" to
identify fathers may face reductions in benefit.

and Carlile, Nottingham and Cleveland. The number of children living in poverty increased in these years; by 1990, one in 10 children lived in households whose head was out of work. According to the Family Policy Studies Centre, one-parent families fared worse than any other group in the first six years of Conservative government, their non-benefit income falling 38 per cent in real terms and their income, even with benefits and tax allowances, declining by 11 per cent. The number living in bed and breakfast accommodation rose to 11,000. More children were thrown into insecurity by marriage break-up. The numbers registered as "at risk" reached frightening levels: research in 1989 estimated that three out of every 1,000 children were now registered by a local authority as in need of protection (many of whom still had no social worker assigned to them). The numbers of children leaving home rose, too. A Children's Society report in 1990 estimated that 98,000 children were running away every year. Joan Lestor, Labour's spokesperson on children, called in vain for the establishment

of a register. Many such children ended up living in squats, shop doorways and cardboard cities.

In a speech on January 17 1990 Mrs Thatcher said the weakening of family life now represented a greater threat to children's well-being than the deterioration of the environment. Some blamed these ills on poverty or on affluence: but "don't blame freedom and prosperity for faults ingrained in human nature," she said.

There were suggestions from some Conservative MPs, which John Moore, as Social Services secretary, appeared to endorse, that levels of benefit were helping to swell unemployment and even encouraging unmarried girls to become pregnant. But other Conservative backbenchers were disturbed by family poverty and especially the refusal in 1988, 1989 and 1990, to uprate child benefit – a policy defended by ministers on the grounds that this benefit was indiscriminate and the money could be more effectively targeted to those in need through income support and family credit. ●

'One visible sign of the Thatcherite revolution was the porches and coach lamps grafted on to what had once been a council house indistinguishable from its neighbour'

HOUSING

NOWHERE outside the privatisation programme did Mrs Thatcher's governments break more sharply with the past than in housing. Spending on housing was cut far more drastically than spending in any other category, though the figures were distorted by changes in the subsidy system: cuts in housing subsidy led to increases in the social security budget as other benefits were increased to cover the shortfall. The number of housing starts in the public sector fell by 80 per cent in the 10 years from 1979. In 1979 the private sector built twice as many houses as the public sector; in 1989 it built 12 times as many.

The 1979 manifesto committed the party to creating a property-owning democracy. "Unlike Labour," it said, "we want people to have the security and satisfaction of owning property." Some might be deterred by the thought of expensive mortgages – but that arose from Labour mismanagement. Conservative plans for cutting government spending and borrowing would bring mortgage rates down. For council tenants the restrictions which Labour councils had put on buying their homes would be swept away. There would be a Bill in the first session of the new Parliament to establish the right to buy – and at handsome discounts.

That promise was carried out in the 1980 Housing Act which also improved tenants' rights to speedy repairs and maintenance. With the help of generous subsidies to first-time buyers specifically and to all home buyers through tax relief on mortgage interest (MIRAS), which expanded mightily while other forms of housing subsidy dwindled, home ownership boomed. That owning your own home brought a feeling of liberation was widely attested not least by Labour's readiness to abandon its old opposition to the sale of council houses.

But not all that exuberance lasted. The pledge to keep mortgage rates down was not similarly honoured: as interest rates climbed, so the cost of a mortgage soared to a point where the "satisfaction and security" of the manifesto promise were diminished, not enhanced. By 1990-91 the rate of repossessions was climbing fast. The Conservative defeat in the Mid-Staffs by-election of March 1990, though mostly blamed on the poll tax, looked to those on the ground to owe a lot to the cost of mortgages, too.

But times were not good, either, for those who remained in the public sector. Council rents were pushed up, not least, it was sometimes suspected, to enhance the incentive to buy. Subsidies were cut: in the 1988 social security changes, 1m people who had previously been eligible for benefit had it taken away because their savings exceeded £8,000. The council house building programme was largely abandoned, in line with the provider/client distinction which permeated so much government thinking: the local authority's role was to measure the need and make strategic arrangements not to build houses. Even councils which wished to spend were hampered by new restraints on the use they made of their money. In a bid to reduce still further council control of housing, provision was made in the 1988 Housing Act for the setting up of Housing Action Trusts: people on council estates could be asked to choose whether to continue in municipal tenancy or trans-

GOVERNMENT SPENDING ON HOUSING
1. Total spending on housing at current prices £bn.
2. % increase on previous year in real terms.
3. % of government expenditure.
4. % of GDP.

	1978-1979	1979-1980	1980-1981	1981-1982	1982-1983	1983-1984	1984-1985	1985-1986	1986-1987	1987-1988	1988-1989	1989-1990	1990-1 estimated
1	4.6	5.6	5.7	4.3	3.9	4.5	4.5	4.2	4.1	4.2	3.3	4.8	5.7
2		+1.0	-14.0	-32.0	-14.0	+9.0	-3.0	-13.0	-6.0	-2.0	-27.0	+37.0	+10.0
3	7.0	7.3	6.2	4.1	3.4	3.7	3.5	3.0	2.8	2.7	2.1	2.7	2.9
4		2.7	2.4	1.7	1.4	1.5	1.4	1.2	1.1	1.0	0.7	0.9	1.0

INVESTMENT IN PUBLIC AND PRIVATE HOUSING:
1. Gross domestic fixed capital formation £m 1985 prices: private and public dwellings
2. Housing starts, thousands, by (a) private enterprise (b) housing associations (c) local authorities, new towns, government departments

	1. INVESTMENT		2. HOUSING STARTS GB			
	investment in housing: private	investment in housing: public	private sector (a)	housing assocs. (b)	local authorities (c)	ratio (a) : (c)
1979	9,665	3,615	144.0	15.9	65.3	2.2
1980	9,134	3,198	98.8	14.7	41.5	2.4
1981	8,149	2,155	117.2	12.9	26.0	4.5
1982	8,680	2,282	140.7	17.8	34.8	4.0
1983	9,323	2,924	172.2	14.3	36.9	4.7
1984	9,737	2,825	158.1	12.6	27.3	5.8
1985	9,323	2,536	165.5	12.5	21.9	7.6
1986	10,347	2,536	180.0	12.9	20.2	8.9
1987	10,964	2,741	196.6	12.8	20.0	9.7
1988	12,310	2,556	221.2	14.1	16.3	13.1
1989	11,565	2,836	170.3	14.0	15.0	12.2
1990	n.a	n.a	134.1	17.3	8.6	11.0

Derived from Economic Trends Annual Supplement

HOUSING STRESS

	no. of mortgages at end of period	properties repossessed	%	no. mortgages 6-12 months in arrears	%
1980	6,210,000	3,480	0.06	15,530	0.25
1981	6,336,000	4,870	0.08	21,540	0.34
1982	6,518,000	6,860	0.11	27,380	0.42
1983	6,846,000	8,420	0.12	29,440	0.43
1984	7,313,000	12,400	0.17	48,270	0.66
1985	7,717,000	19,300	0.25	57,110	0.74
1986	8,138,000	24,090	0.30	52,080	0.64
1987	8,283,000	26,390	0.32	55,490	0.67
1988	8,564,000	18,510	0.22	42,810	0.50
1989	9,125,000	15,810	0.17	66,800	0.73
1990	9,415,000	43,890*	0.47	123,110	1.31

* In the first half of 1991, repossessions totalled 36,610

Source: Council of Mortgage Lenders

fer to the independent HATs.

Though the rules for making this choice were tilted in favour of change, most of the local ballots ended in a decision to stick to the status quo. And in further deference to another strand of prevailing philosophy – private provision good, public provision bad – plans were laid to revive the private rented sector, which now accounted for only 6 per cent of the housing market. The "fair rents" provisions of Labour legislation were abolished for new lettings, though preserved for existing ones. Picking up a scheme of the maverick Conservative backbencher Sir Brandon Rhys Williams, the Government introduced in its 1980 Housing Act a new form of letting called shorthold – a form of assured tenancy over a limited time-span (more than six months to a maximum of three or four years). Yet these measures were basically modest. The wholesale reinvigoration of private renting, which some of the think tanks demanded, was never engineered.

One visible sign of the Thatcherite revolution in housing was the new suburban estate with the gleaming car in the drive: another, the fancy windows and porches and coach lamps grafted on to what had once been a council house indistinguisable from its neighbours. But a third was the cardboard city, the vagrant in the doorway, the proliferation of homelessness not just in London but in other cities and the countryside. Some Conservatives blamed this on people's reluctance to take the jobs available; others rated it the consequence of cuts in social security benefits and especially the removal of automatic rights to benefit for 16- and 17-year-olds.

The attacks on the policies held to have caused these developments went far wider than the political parties. In July 1985 a committee chaired by the Duke of Edinburgh called for radical change in the subsidy system for rented property, to be balanced by phasing out MIRAS. In December that year Faith In The City, a report published by a group set up by the Archbishop of Canterbury, Dr Robert Runcie, explored the social conditions of city dwellers as well as the spiritual. That, too, recommended higher welfare payments to alleviate need and fearlessly made the case for the sort of collective action which Mrs Thatcher distrusted. ●

MORTGAGE INTEREST TAX RELIEF BY INCOME RANGE 1989-90 UK (£)

	average value of relief per mortgage	total cost of relief
under £5,000	420	190m
£40,000 plus	1,360	570m
all mortgages	470	6,900m

(Between 1981-82 and 1989-90 the real cost of mortgage relief rose from £3.5bn to £6.9bn) *Source: Social Trends*

FORMS OF HOUSING TENURE (%)

	1979	1983	1987	1988
owner-occupied owned outright	22	24	24	24
owner-occupied with mortgage	30	33	39	40
rented with job or business	3	2	3	2
rented from local authority or new town	34	32	26	26
rented from housing assoc or co-op	1	2	2	2
private rent unfurnished	8	5	4	4
private rent furnished	2	2	2	2

Source: General Household Survey

PEOPLE IN BED AND BREAKFAST, HOSTELS, AND OTHER TEMPORARY ACCOMMODATION
31 DECEMBER EACH YEAR

	B & B	hostels	other
1980	1,330	3,380	
1981	1,520	3,320	
1982	1,640	3,500	4,200
1983	2,700	3,400	3,740
1984	3,670	3,990	4,640
1985	5,360	4,730	5,830
1986	8,990	4,610	7,190
1987	10,370	5,150	9,240
1988	10,970	6,240	12,890
1989	11,480	8,020	18,400
1990	11,130	9,010	25,030

Source: written answer, Timothy Yeo, junior environment minister, to Jeremy Corbyn (Lab, Islington N) April 17,1991

LEGISLATION

Housing Act 1980
1st reading: December 20 1979
2nd reading: January 15 1980, by 319 (Government, 5 UU) to 267 (Lab, 8 Lib, PC, G. Fitt, 1 Con - W. Benyon (Buckingham)
Royal Assent: August 8 1980
Provisions: gave local authority and new town tenants the right to buy their homes (Secretary of State for the Environment had the power to take over the sale if the local authority was not facilitating it); public sector tenants' rights were outlined in a new tenants charter (including right to have lodgers and do own improvements); the 1977 Rent Act was amended to encourage letting and expand the private rented sector. Shorthold tenancies were introduced.

Housing Act 1988
1st reading: November 19 1987
2nd reading: November 30 1987 by 324 (Government) to 214 (Labour, Lib Dem, SDP, Plaid Cymru)
Royal Assent: November 15 1988
Provisions: introduced system of Housing Action Trusts which could take over estate management where tenants voted for this to happen. After refurbishment the stock would be transferred to the private or voluntary sector. Minimum period for shorthold tenancy cut to six months.

Housing (Scotland) Act 1988
1st reading: December 3 1987
2nd reading: January 11 1988
Royal Assent: November 2 1988
Provisions: established body called Scottish Homes with housing powers including ability to acquire public sector homes occupied by secure tenants; local authority grants to enable tenants to secure housing other than public sector housing.

SOCIAL REFORM

THOUGH by now 20 years old, the three great social reforms of the sixties – the liberalisation of the laws on divorce, abortion and homosexuality – were not the end of the story. Through the years of the Thatcher government there was pressure for change in all three areas.

The rising rate of divorce – by the end of the period, one in five children could expect their parents' marriages to end before they were 16 – was much deplored, but no practical course was suggested to reverse it. Instead what activity there was concentrated on trying to civilise the rougher effects of the 1969 reform. The 1984 Matrimonial and Family Proceedings Act cut the minimum period for divorce from three years to one, and ended the system of lifelong maintenance payments known as "the meal ticket for life". In 1988 a Law Commission report suggested one of two courses: to allow divorce on demand after a nine- or 12-month waiting period; or to make a fixed period of separation – say a year – the sole grounds for divorce. Initially the Government response was broadly favourable but in a report published by the Family Policy Studies Centre in December 1991, the Lord Chancellor, Lord Mackay, unexpectedly raised objections to it. He argued that the courts ought to retain the power to refuse an application where one partner in the marriage was innocent, and objected to the divorce. This objection cut across the philosophy of the Law Commission recomendations which sought to remove the concept of guilt and innocence from divorce altogether. "There is quite a strong feeling in some people's minds" said Lord Mackay "that the Law Commission did not recognise sufficiently clearly the need

to strengthen the institution of marriage."

Predictions that the changes of the sixties would open the floodgates to equal treatment for homosexuals with heterosexuals, or to exhibitions of flagrant behaviour in public places, were scarcely sustained by what followed: gay people continued to feel beleaguered and persecuted. Two pieces of legislation were seen as especially threatening. One was an amendment written into the Local Government Bill which said that local authorities must neither promote homosexuality nor promote the teaching in any maintained school of the acceptability of homosexuality as a pretended family relationship.

There were fears that good books would be banned and that a wave of prosecutions would follow, though in practice this did not occur. Similar fears arose in 1991 over clause 25 of the Criminal Justice Bill, which enabled courts to deal with quite minor kinds of sexual behaviour by gays: even holding hands in public could be treated on the same level as such serious offences as illegal intercourse with a girl under 16 or indecency with young children. After widespread protests the provisions were eased, but here, too, fears continued of a new wave of persecution and prosecution. John Major's approach, however, differed from Thatcher's. To the dismay of some of the Conservative Right, he invited the actor and gay rights campaigner Sir Ian McKellen to Downing Street to discuss the fears and preoccupations of gay people.

The campaigners who had fought so fiercely against the abortion reforms of the sixties never accepted that they were irreversible. A private

DIVORCE

	total divorces (thousands) GB	persons divorcing per thousand married people Eng and Wales
1961	27.0	2.1
1971	80.0	6.0
1976	135.4	10.1
1981	155.6	11.9
1986	166.7	12.9
1989	162.5	12.7

Source: Social Trends

LEGAL ABORTIONS
(THOUSANDS)

1971	101.0
1976	109.0
1981	139.0
1986	158.0
1989	181.0

Source: Social Trends

LEGISLATION

Homosexual Offences (Northern Ireland) Order 1982
laid before Parliament: July 14 1982
approved: October 25 1982, by 168 votes to 21 (against: OUP, DUP, 15 Conservatives)
Provisions: a homosexual act between two consenting men aged 21 or over would cease to be an offence. Brought the law on homosexual acts into line with the rest of the UK, incorporating parts of the 1967 Sexual Offences Act and 1980 Criminal Justice (Scotland) Act.

Unborn Children (Protection) Bill (Private, sponsor Enoch Powell)
1st reading: December 5 1984
2nd reading: February 15 1985 by 238 to 66 (free vote)
May 3 1985, debate adjourned at report stage. Failed for lack of time.
Provisions: would have outlawed use of embryos for research.

Surrogacy Arrangements Act 1985
1st reading: March 28 1985
2nd reading: April 15 1985 unopposed
Royal Assent:July 16 1985
Provisions: outlawed financial gain through payment or advertising where arrangements were made for one woman to bear another's child.

Abortion (Amendment) Bill (private, sponsor David Alton)
1st reading: October 28 1987
2nd reading: January 22 1988 by 296 to 251, 36 Labour MPs supporting it against party policy. Progress prevented by a filibuster.
Provisions: would have cut the period for legal termination of a pregnancy from 28 to 18 weeks, except where two doctors certified that the mother's life was imperilled, or the child

would be born dead or incapable of independent life.

Licensing Act 1987
1st reading: October 29 1987
2nd reading: November 9 1987 by 293 to 87. Labour not whipped; Sir Bernard Braine (Con, Castle Point) voted against the Government.
Provisions: allowed pubs in England and Wales to remain open for 12 hours a day and for an extra hour on Sundays.

Human Organ Transplants Act 1989
1st reading: April 20 1989
2nd reading: May 22 1989 (formal)
Royal Assent:July 27 1989
Provisions: prohibition of commercial deals in human organs and restriction of transplanting of organs between people not genetically related. Followed press reports of trade in organs for transplant particularly from Turkey.

Human Fertilisation and Embryology Act 1990
1st reading: November 22 1989 (Lords)
2nd reading: April 2 1990, unopposed
Royal Assent:November 1 1990
Provisions: implements many findings of Warnock Report, including regulations for research using human embryos and creation of new offence of unlicensed use or storing of an embryo. In a free vote on April 23 the Commons voted by 362 to 189 in favour of clause 11 of the Bill allowing regulated research using embryos. On the night of April 24-25 a series of votes was taken on abortion. The outcome was: for an 18-week limit (as in the Alton Bill) 165, against 375. To retain the status quo (28 weeks): for, 141, against 382. To cut the limit to 20 weeks: for, 189, against 358. To set it at 26 weeks: for, 156, against 372. To reduce it to 22 weeks - the anti-abortionists' main hope of success: for, 255, against 302. A period of 24 weeks was then approved by 335 to 129. (See section on MPs' voting records).

member's bill introduced by the Liberal Democrat David Alton, which would have cut the limit for legal abortions to 18 weeks, won a majority of 45 (296 to 251) on its second reading on January 22 1988, but failed for lack of time. This issue now became intertwined with another, which arose from the report of the Warnock committee on Human Fertilisation, published on July 18 1984. This recommended a ban on agencies offering surrogate motherhood services and called for the legitimisation of children born after artificial insemination by a donor. A majority concluded that it would be right to allow researchers to use surplus human embryos for up to 14 days. The Government implemented the finding on surrogate motherhood agencies in the 1985 Surrogacy Arrangements Act, but for some time made no move on the issue of embryo research.

In the absence of government legislation, backbench MPs hostile to the Warnock finding decided to act. The former Conservative minister, now an Ulster Unionist, Enoch Powell, introduced the Unborn Children (Protection) Bill, which would effectively have banned all such research except in a few very specific cases. It was given a second reading on February 15 1985 by 238 votes to 66, but was foiled by a filibuster – the Government refusing, as was its invariable practice with private members' bills, to provide extra time to save it. The Government's own Bill to implement Warnock, the Human Fertilisation and Embryology Bill, finally appeared in the 1989-90 session and was given an unopposed second reading on April 2 1990. On April 23, in a free vote during the committee stage of the Bill (which because of its exceptional nature was taken on the floor of the House) the Commons approved the research use of embryos up to 14 days by 364 to 193. In the early hours of April 25, after seven hours of debate and two and a half hours of continuous voting, the Commons defeated attempts to achieve a significant tightening of the abortion law, settling instead by 335 votes to 129 for a reduction of the latest permissible time from 28 weeks to 24. But in so doing they also approved two exemptions, which in the view of both sides further liberalised the law, allowing abortion at any time to prevent grave permanent damage to the physical health of the pregnant woman or in cases of foetal abnormality.

The anti-abortionists claimed this outcome was the result of widespread confusion in the Commons during voting on April 25 and sought to reopen the issue. On June 21 they failed on the casting vote of the Deputy Speaker, Sir Paul Dean, to make it more difficult to get a late abortion in cases of severe foetal abnormality. The vote was tied 197-197. An attempt earlier in the evening to reintroduce upper time limits in such cases was defeated by 229 to 215. ●

R.C. Cathedral

NO RETURN TO BACKSTREET ABORTIONS

OUR BODIES
OUR LIVES
OUR RIGHT
TO DECIDE

' A private member's bill would have cut the limit for legal abortions to 18 weeks'

WOMEN

MRS THATCHER was no feminist. It never seemed likely that Britain's first woman prime minister would go about promising dazzling new deals for women in a country where, on almost every available test, women had come nowhere near to equal opportunity. Few institutions proved that as blatantly as parliament. Politics was by no means alone in rigorously excluding women from jobs at the very top: there were precious few women industrialists, permanent secretaries, judges, consultants, or chief constables – let alone women bishops. But a study by the Hansard Society in January 1990 put politics alongside the academic life and the law as the territory which was toughest for women to penetrate. Women made up 52 per cent of the British electorate but even in 1987, their best election is history, they took only 6 per cent of seats in the Commons. Apart from the brief flowering of Lady Young – made Leader of the House of Lords in September 1981 but dropped in June 1983 – Mrs Thatcher's administrations found room for only one women cabinet minister: herself. Major's first cabinet failed to include a woman.

There have certainly been signs of advance. There are now women in the Appeal Court; and several women editors on national newspapers. By 1991, almost half the students entering universities, medical schools and law schools were women, suggesting a much greater presence at the top of each profession in the near future. But the catalogue of measures specifically taken to benefit women during the Thatcher years was fairly meagre. At the top came the decision announced by Lawson in the 1988 Budget to tax husbands and wives separately. Until then a wife was taxed at her husband's marginal rate. If she didn't work, but saved, the interest on her savings was taxed with his income, too; a discouragement of thrift by a government which claimed to prize it. Lawson's reform, which came into force in April 1990, was estimated to have benefited 3m wives, roughly half of all wives who paid tax.

More women found jobs in this period, sometimes from choice and sometimes from necessity. The number of women classed as "economically active" rose by 12 per cent in the five years to 1989 before recession arrived, giving Britain a higher proportion of women in work than any EC country but Denmark. Equal pay for equal work, however, remained a distant ambition, despite 16 years of Barbara Castle's equal pay legislation – policed by an Equal Opportunities Commission which repeatedly complained of its impotence. According to an EC survey in July 1990 the gap between men's and women's wages in Britain was wider than most in the community: in the UK, women were earning 68 per cent of what men got, against 85 per cent in Denmark and Italy and 80 per cent in France and Greece. On October 28 1991 Major launched a campaign called Opportunity 2000, designed to ensure that more top jobs would go to women.

Some of the strongest pressure for change came from Europe. In the 1985-86 session the Government brought in a Sex Discrimination Bill to take account of European Court judgments and to bring the Sex Discrimination Act of 1975 into line with EC directives; and then had to amend it to take account of the case of Helen Marshall, who successfully took her employers, the South West

NUMBER OF WOMEN MPS ELECTED IN UK ELECTIONS SINCE 1918

1918	1	1955	24
1922	2	1959	25
1923	8	1964	29
1924	4	1966	26
1929	14	1970	26
1931	15	1974	23
1935	9	1974	27
1945	24	1979	19
1950	21	1983	23
1951	17	1987	41

WOMEN MPS IN EUROPE (%)

Sweden	38	Luxembourg	13
Norway	34	Portugal	10
Denmark	31	Belgium	9
Netherlands	25	Ireland	8
Germany	16	UK	7
Italy	13	France	6
Spain	13	Greece	5

EMPLOYMENT IN GREAT BRITAIN BY SEX, FULL AND PART-TIME
GB (MILLIONS)

	MEN		WOMEN	
	full	part	full	part
1986	12.7	1.1	5.7	4.5
1987	12.7	1.3	5.8	4.7
1988	13.1	1.3	6.2	4.7
1989	13.3	1.4	6.6	4.9

Source: Social Trends

AVERAGE GROSS HOURLY EARNINGS
(EXCLUDING THE EFFECTS OF OVERTIME) FULL-TIME EMPLOYEES AGED 18 AND OVER, 1979-1989

Year	Men (pence)	Women (pence)	Women's earnings as % of men's
1979	226.9	165.7	73.0
1981	322.5	241.2	74.8
1983	387.6	287.5	74.2
1985	445.3	329.9	74.1
1986	481.8	358.2	74.3
1987	521.3	383.8	73.6
1988	568.3	426.8	75.1
1989	622.8	475.6	76.4
1990	676.4	520.0	76.9

(Men earn on average £90 a week more than women)   *Source: New Earnings Survey*

THE SEX DIVIDE ON THE GULF WAR
WHICH OF THE FOLLOWING COMES CLOSEST TO YOUR OWN VIEW?

	MEN	WOMEN
Base (number of respondents)	684	740
Britain should do everything it can, including the use of force, to get Iraq to withdraw from Kuwait	67	42
Britain should do everything it can, short of using its armed forces, to get Iraq to withdraw from Kuwait	22	41
Britain should not get involved in trying to get Iraq to withdraw	10	16

(all figures except base figures are percentages. They may not add up to 100 per cent because of rounding.)

Source: ICM Poll for the Guardian. Sample 1,424, Fieldwork January 11-12 1991.

Hampshire Health Authority, to the European Court for ordering her to retire at the age of 62.

Though the rate of women returning to work after pregnancy sharply accelerated, many who wanted to do so were hampered by the lack of suitable arrangements for placing their children. As Education secretary in the early seventies, Mrs Thatcher had talked of creating nursery or child-care places for 50 per cent of three-year-olds and 90 per cent of four-year-olds; but at the end of the nineties that still remained a dream. Her view appeared to have shifted: "the idea that we might have a whole generation of creche children is not one I think would be right for the next generation, or for each individual," she told a BBC interviewer in June 1990. "I don't think you can have a child in nursery all day". (Quoted by Susan McRae in Contemporary Britain, An Annual Review, 1991, Blackwell). In his 1990 Budget Major removed nurseries, creches and playgroups provided by employers from the list of taxable perks. In July 1991 the Government hinted at further changes to extend tax concessions to working mothers who made arrangements outside the workplace for placing their children.

L egislation was introduced to enforce the payment of maintenance by errant fathers, though the requirement that mothers could have their benefits docked for failing to name their children's fathers was attacked as a serious infringement of liberty. A computerised call and recall breast cancer screening service was introduced for women between 50 and 64, the most vulnerable group, and a general system of cervical smear tests for all women between 20 and 24 was due to be in place by 1993. But the Government declined to follow Labour in promising a specific minister for women with Cabinet rank.

All this may seem to assume that women's political fates hang simply on "women's issues". That is clearly not the case: other issues were at least as influential in improving or worsening women's lives. High rates of inflation worried women more than they worried men. The lack of financial help for carers hit women rather than men, since the job of caring fell more often on women. Changes on welfare benefits cut both ways: when family credit was raised by more than the rate of inflation, they gained; when child benefit was frozen, they lost. Mothers of young children suffered disproportionately more from poverty and homelessness. And women were more fearful than men of the prospect of nuclear war, as the long women-only occupation at Greenham Common symbolised.

A ll that made the under-representation of women in parliament even more of a blot on democracy. In other ways, too, male domination may have skewed the balance of political debate. The House of Commons which in January 1991 twice debated the war in the Gulf was especially unrepresentative of the people who sent it there, in that this was an issue where, more than most, the opinions of men and women were sharply divided. An ICM poll carried out for the Guardian on January 11-12 1991, shortly before the bombing began, told the story graphically.

All three main political parties were much concerned about the under-representation of women in parliament. In the selection of candidates for by-elections, where the party headquarters exert more influence than they do in run-of-the-mill selections, women did much better: 12 of the 55 by-elections between June 1979 and July 1991 were won by women. Labour and the Liberal Democrats now require the inclusion of at least one woman on every constituency short-list. The Conservative party has yet to follow – though in July 1991 Major was reported to favour changing the Commons' hours, the greatest single deterrent for women who contemplate standing for parliament. ●

LEGISLATION

Sex Discrimination Act 1986

1st reading: February 6 986 (Lords)
Second reading: May 22 1986 after rejection of Labour
amendment by 166 (Government, Lib, SDP) to 55 (Lab)
Royal assent: November 7 1986
Provisions: implemented European court judgments on
equal treatment of men and women. Updated 1975 Sex Discrimination Act in line with EC directives. Removed restrictions on women's work, especially shift work, Sunday working, working at night, maximum hours, hours of finishing. Second reading passed unopposed after rejection of Labour
amendment regretting failure to cover collective agreements
and removal of some restrictions on working hours and conditions. During the second reading the Minister undertook to
introduce amendments to end discrimination between obliga-
tory retiring ages for men and women in the light of a European court judgment.

RACE RELATIONS AND IMMIGRATION

ALL BRITISH citizens, said the 1979 Conservative manifesto, were equal before the law and should have equal opportunities. But, not least in the interests of good community relations, immigration must be firmly controlled and new measures would need to be introduced, including the redefinition of British nationality, tougher action to prevent illegal entry and a register of those entitled to come.

The Conservatives were more successful in the second aim than the first: the inflow of Commonwealth migrants to the UK was sharply reduced in the Thatcher years. William Whitelaw, Mrs Thatcher's first Home secretary, a more emollient figure than she, succeeded in losing the commitment to the register, but new immigration rules approved in December 1979 removed the automatic right of husbands or fiancés of women settled here to join them. He also put new restrictions on the admission of other would-be entrants.

In 1981 the British Nationality Bill, attacked by Labour as pure race discrimination, opposed in the Lords by five bishops led by the Archbishop of Canterbury Dr Robert Runcie, and strongly condemned by Commonwealth governments, especially India, diluted the value of British citizenship for many not born here. A further attempt to change the immigration rules ran into trouble in 1982 as the Left condemned it for being too harsh and the Right for being too soft, producing a rare Government defeat in the Commons.

By the 1983 election the Government was able to claim that it had cut immigration to the lowest level since controls began 20 years before. No further measures were promised, but the 1987 manifesto promised still more stringency and a 1988 Immigration Act removed specific concessions which until then had been extended to those who had arrived in Britain before 1973. The impositions of mandatory visas on a number of Commonwealth countries between 1985 and 1989 also made entry more hazardous, and the 1987 Immigration (Carriers Liability) Act imposed fines on air and shipping companies who brought in passengers who lacked proper documents. In 1990 the immigration issue came back to the boil at Westminster with the Government's decision that 50,000 Hong Kong citizens with their families should be allowed full British citizenship if they had the right qualifications. The purpose of this discrimination was to ensure that in the interests of a well-ordered transfer to China, such people would feel able to stay in the colony through the period of transition rather than leaving early to make new lives elsewhere. This solution was bitterly attacked by the Liberal Democrat leader Paddy Ashdown, for making the limit on entry to Britain too tight, and by a phalanx of Conservative MPs including Norman Tebbit for letting too many immigrants in. Forty four MPs (Hansard lists 43) were reported to have opposed the Government on the Bill's second reading. Some Labour MPs would have liked to see their leaders taking the Ashdown line rather than voting against the Bill along with people like Tebbit: more than 50 abstained.

Like most Governments in the West, the British government became increasingly disturbed in the late eighties by the numbers seeking asylum. Applications for admission rose from 1,563 in 1979

MIGRATION IN AND OUT OF UK
(THOUSANDS) MINUS FIGURE MEANS OUTFLOW EXCEEDS INFLOW

COMMONWEALTH	75-79	80-84	85-89
Australia	-7.3	-22.1	-17.0
Canada	-15.6	-8.6	- 3.3
New Zealand	-1.1	- 2.4	3.7
African countries	5.0	3.2	5.2
Bangladesh, India, Sri Lanka	11.8	11.6	10.0
Pakistan	10.8	9.2	7.1
Caribbean	1.3	0.3	0.2
other	6.8	0.8	1.8
EC	- 8.0	1.1	6.6
USA	- 8.2	- 8.3	- 4.1

Source: Social Trends

LEGISLATION

Immigration Rules
Outlined in White Paper November 14 1979
Debated: December 4 1979, approved by 294 (Government, 5 OUP) to 252 (Lab, Lib, SNP).
Provisions: inter alia ended the automatic right of entry of husbands or fiancés of women settled in the UK; further restrictions on entry of parents, grandparents and children over 18; ended practice of allowing permanent settlement for those who originally came to UK for temporary stay.
An Opposition amendment that the rules violated the "principle that the rights of all British citizens legally settled here are equal before the law whatever their race colour or creed" was defeated 296 to 251.
Rebellion: it was estimated that 17 Conservative MPs deliberately abstained, including Cyril Townsend (Bexleyheath), who resigned his post as PPS.

British Nationality Act 1981
1st reading: January 13 1981
2nd reading: January 28 1981, by 292 votes to 242 (against: Lab, 10 Lib, SNP, 1 Plaid Cymru, G.Fitt (Socialist), James Kilfedder, (UPUP), UU, DUP).
Royal Assent: October 30 1981
Provisions: superseding 1948 Nationality Act, replaced the status of citizen of the UK & Colonies with three categories of citizenship: British, citizen of British dependent territories and British overseas citizenship. It revoked the automatic right to British citizenship of any child, including those born in the UK, unless at least one of his or her parents was a British citizen by birth. Children born overseas to parents of patrial or naturalised British citizenship could be refused entry to the UK. The Bill was attacked as racially discriminatory. A Lords amendment by Lord Elwyn-Jones (Lab) declared "the Bill would result in injustice, would greatly increase the number of stateless men, women and children, would create uncertainties and feelings of insecurity and would exacerbate racial tension". It was rejected by 149 votes to 92 despite the support of five bishops, including Dr Robert Runcie, Archbishop of Canterbury.

Rebellion: on December 15 1982 the Government was defeated in the Commons on its Statement of Changes in the Immigration Rules (designed to take account of the proposals of the 1981 British Nationality Act and principally regulating the admission to the UK of husbands or fiancés of women already living here). A motion opposing the statement, proposed by Roy Jenkins (SDP), was carried by 290 to 272 with 23 Conservative backbenchers (some of whom thought the proposals were still not strict enough) voting with Labour, SDP, Lib, SNP, PC, OUP, and G Fitt (Ind), against the Government.

Immigration Act 1988
1st reading: November 5 1987
2nd reading: November 16 1987 approved by 258 (Government) to 221 (Lab, Lib Dem, SDP, SNP, Plaid Cymru)
Royal Assent: May 10 1988
Provisions: designed to meet the 1987 Conservative manifesto pledge to make controls on settlement still tighter. Removed concession previously given to men who settled here before 1973 whose wives and children had been able to enter without marriage tests or financial and accommodation tests. All claims to British citizenship must now be established before travelling. Grounds for appeal against deportation narowed to the facts, not the merits, of the decision.

to 15,530 in 1989: in the first six months of 1991 they were running at 1,000 a week. Though many were genuinely fleeing political persecution, the Government said such claims were often a cover for economic betterment.

In July 1991 Home secretary Baker increased concern on this score by proposing that legal aid should no longer be available to people fighting such cases. In November 1991 the Government published an Asylum bill designed to bring about a substantial reduction in the number of asylum-seekers allowed to stay in Britain. Baker argued that the Bill drew a necessary distinction between political refugees, leaving their home countries because of a threat to their lives, and economic refugees, whose real motive was a better standard of living. The Bill was publicly criticised by the Archbishop of Canterbury, George Carey, and the Roman Catholic Archbishop of Westminster, Cardinal Hume. Baker said his bill was "colour blind": some Labour MPs called it racist.

Opposition parties complained that the Government's commitment to better race relations fell far short of its sense of urgency on restricting immigration – reflecting, perhaps, the priorities of a Prime Minister who in her days as Opposition leader had talked in a television interview of Britain being "swamped". A report from the Policy Studies Institute in 1991 confirmed that members of ethnic communities were still far more likely to be jobless, dependent on social security and living in poverty. The Commission for Racial Equality in a consultation document said Major's hopes of a country "at ease with itself" could not be met without dealing with the stress and injustice suffered by people denied equal opportunity because of race or ethnic origin. It called for the law to be extended to cover all areas of government and regulatory activity, including immigration control and the work of the police and prison services.

An NOP poll for the Independent on Sunday in July 1991 showed that Britain was seen as a racist society by 79 per cent of blacks, 56 per cent of Asians and 67 per cent of whites. Sometimes the tensions exploded on to the streets. Rioting in Brix-

ton in the spring of 1981 led to an inquiry by a Lord of Appeal, Lord Scarman, who in his report put a lot of the blame on deprivation in the black community. In language very different from that adopted by ministers, most of whose emphasis had been on reimposing law and order, Lord Scarman wrote: "Unemployment and poor housing bear on them very heavily; and the educational system has not adjusted itself satisfactorily to their needs. Their difficulties are intensified by the sense they have of a concealed discrimination against them, particularly in relation to job opportunities and housing..." Such conditions could create a precondition towards violent protest, especially since it caught media attention. To attack racial disadvantage, he warned, might mean, for a time at least, policies of positive discrimination.

Much of this was ignored. Further riots occurred, in Moss Side, Manchester, Toxteth, Liverpool, Handsworth, Birmingham, St Paul's, Bristol, and again in Brixton, but the trouble remained sporadic. The grievances, though, were not.

There were repeated complaints of police harassment and discrimination, especially in London, despite the best attempts of police chiefs like Sir Peter Imbert in London to police these areas more sensitively and to recruit more officers from the ethnic communities. There were incidents which heightened the tension: the Rushdie affair, for instance, when a handful of leaders of ethnic minorities endorsed the Ayatollah Khomeini's call for the writer to be killed; or the bizarre case of Norman Tebbit's "cricket test", when on the eve of the vote on the Hong Kong Bill he suggested that many in immigrant communities owed no real allegiance to Britain, as shown by the way they supported visiting sides from India, Pakistan and the West Indies against England in Test matches. In December 1990 members of the local Conservative party in Cheltenham opposed the selection of John Taylor, a black lawyer, as their prospective candidate, some on the grounds that he wasn't local, others overtly because he was black. But his nomination was confirmed. ●

British Nationality (Hong Kong) Act 1990

1st reading: April 4 1990
2nd reading: April 19 1990, by 313 (Government plus Lib Dem, SDP, 1 OUP, 1 Plaid Cymru, 1 SNP, UPUP) to 216 (Lab, 2 DUP, 43 Conservatives)
Royal Assent: July 26 1990
Provisions: extended British citizenship to 225,000 Hong Kong residents in four categories: general (including business, management, accountancy, medicine, the law, engineering) 36,200; key entrepreneurs 500; disciplined services 7,000; sensitive services 6,300. Assessments to be made on a points system with scores for age, education and training, experience, links with Britain, fluency in English, etc.

Conservative MPs opposing the Government were: R. Adley (Christchurch), J. Arnold (Gravesham), J. Aspinwall (Wansdyke), V. Bendall (Ilford N), D.G. Bevan (Birmingham Yardley), J. Biffen (Shropshire N), Sir N. Bonsor (Upminster), R. Boyson(Brent N), J. Browne (Winchester), N. Budgen (Wolverhampton SW), J. Carlisle (Luton N), Dr M. Clark (Rochford), S. Coombs (Swindon), J. Cran (Bridlington), D. Dover (Chorley), D. Evennett (Erith), Sir J. Farr (Harborough), G. Gardiner(Reigate), C. Gill (Ludlow), Mrs T. Gorman (Billericay), C. Gregory (York), P. Griffiths (Portsmouth N), Mrs M. Hicks (Wolverhapton NE), M. Irvine (Ipswich), T. Janman (Thurrock), Mrs E. Kellett-Bowman (Lancaster), R. Knapman (Stroud), Sir N. Macfarlane (Sutton), P. Marland (Gloucs W), T. Marlow (Northampton N), D. Mudd (Falmouth), J. Pawsey (Rugby), M. Shersby (Uxbridge), I. Stanbrook (Orpington), Sir J. Stokes(Halesowen), N. Tebbit (Chingford), N. Thorne (Ilford S), J. Townend (Bridlington), J. Ward (Poole), J. Watts (Slough), B. Wells (Hertford), Mrs A. Winterton (Congleton), N. Winterton (Macclesfield).

Asylum Bill 1991

Introduced: November 1 1991
2nd reading: November 13 1991 by 311 (Government, OUP, 1 DUP, J.Kilfedder (UPUP) to 233 (Lab, Lib Dem, Ind SDP, SNP, PC)
Provisions: Would reduce number of asylum seekers admitted to Britain. Under previous system, about 25 per cent of asylum seekers had been admitted as genuine refugees, but a further 65 per cent had been admitted under ELR (Exceptional Leave to Remain) status. Kenneth Baker, Home secretary, said that under the Bill's provisions, only "a substantial minority" in this group would qualify in future. New grounds for refusal were also added in the Bill, including failure to apply immediately on arrival and failure to seek refuge either in a safer part of home territory or in a neighbouring country.But processing of cases would be greatly speeded up and a new right to seek leave to appeal would be provided.

LAW AND LIBERTY

THE CONSERVATIVES came into office in 1979 determined to turn back the rising tide of crime, which Labour, they said, by neglect and laxity, had helped to create. Their first priority was to build up the police, increasing numbers, raising pay, giving them better back-up and so, they hoped, restoring crushed morale. The manifesto echoed the familiar Conservative conference call for tougher sentences – but only where appropriate: in many cases, it said, long terms in prison were not the answer. For some young offenders the party favoured a short, sharp, shock regime: for others, community service. But punishing crime was only half the equation: prevention deserved a high priority, too. In line with all previous practice, the return of capital punishment – of which Mrs Thatcher was strongly in favour – would be left to a free Commons vote.

The Conservatives were true to their word: law and order was one of the very few fields exempted from public expenditure cuts when they first took office, and spending in real terms was increased between 1978-89 and 1989-90 by 70 per cent.

They built up police numbers and pay: their first pay award to the police came within a week of their election victory. They equipped the police with new powers, some of them contentious. And they produced new measures to encourage crime prevention, like Neighbourhood Watch.

But the tide was not rolled back. The number of notifiable offences recorded by the police in England and Wales rose from 2,536,700 to 3,870,700 in the decade from 1979 – an increase of over 50 per cent. The clear-up rate fell – from 41 per cent of notifiable offences in 1979 to 32 per cent in 1986,

though the next three years saw some improvement. The biggest rises were in rape, robbery and trafficking in controlled drugs, where notified offences rose at a rate of more than 10 per cent a year. The proportion of notified offences which involved the use of firearms rose by 45 per cent in these years.

Conservative conference-goers, who had expected a drastic turn for the better, made their displeasure plain at the seaside each year, venting their wrath on successive Home secretaries. "Too soft" was the general verdict. But one measure introduced in deference to that feeling, the short, sharp, shock regime for young offenders, collapsed ignominiously; and Home Office ministers stuck doggedly to the view that too many people were going to prison, not too few. Since they could not be seen as interfering with judicial independence, their campaign to reduce custodial sentencing was largely based on pumping out advice, though new legislation was tailored to minimise the use of imprisonment. The prison population continued to climb for most of these years and with it the number of those detained on remand, though both trends showed signs of being reversed at the end of the eighties.

Despite overwhelming popular support, MPs, allowed free votes, continued to reject the return of hanging whenever they voted on it.

Though the 1983 manifesto was able to point to the biggest programme of prison building and modernisation this century, an exceptionally forceful HM Chief Inspector of Prisons in England and Wales, Judge Stephen Tumim, submitted repeated

GOVERNMENT SPENDING ON LAW AND ORDER

1. Total spending on law and order and protection services at current prices £bn.
2. % increase on previous year in real terms.
3. % of government expenditure.
4. % of GDP.

	1978-1979	1979-1980	1980-1981	1981-1982	1982-1983	1983-1984	1984-1985	1985-1986	1986-1987	1987-1988	1988-1989	1989-1990	1990-1 estimated
1	2.5	3.2	3.9	4.6	5.1	5.6	6.2	6.5	7.1	7.9	8.8	10.0	11.4
2		+8.0	+3.0	+8.0	+3.0	+5.0	+6.0	-2.0	+6.0	+6.0	+3.0	+8.0	+6.0
3	3.9	4.1	4.3	4.4	4.4	4.5	4.7	4.7	4.8	5.1	5.4	5.6	5.8
4		1.5	1.6	1.8	1.8	1.8	1.9	1.8	1.8	1.8	1.8	1.9	2.1

ATTEMPTS TO REINTRODUCE THE DEATH SENTENCE

	FOR	AGAINST	MAJORITY AGAINST
July 19 1979. Debate on motion "that this House believes that the sentence of capital punishment should again be made available to courts"	243	362	119
May 11 1982. New clauses on Criminal Justice Bill death for persons convicted of murder	195	357	162
involving: terrorism	208	332	124
firearms/explosives	176	343	167
police/prison officers	208	332	124
armed robbery/burglary	151	331	180
July 13 1983. Motions to restore death penalty for persons convicted of murder	223	368	145
involving: terrorism	245	361	116
police officer	263	344	81
prison officer	252	348	96
shooting/explosion	204	374	170
course of theft	194	369	175
April 1 1987. Motion calling for death penalty in cases of "evil" and premeditated murder where jury verdict is unanimous	230	342	112
June 7 1988. Amendment to Criminal Justice Bill to reintroduce the death penalty for murder, and to allow juries to recommend it to the judge	218	341	123
December 17 1990. New clauses on Criminal Justice Bill – death sentence to be mandatory for murder, but Court of Appeal may substitute a life sentence	182	367	185
death for persons convicted of murder involving: police officer	215	330	115
firearm/explosive/police/prison officer	186	349	163

(The Commons also debated abolition of the death penalty for offences of treason or piracy. Voting was: for abolition, 257; against, 289; majority against abolition 32.)

reports condemning conditions and calling for reform. In 1990 there were riots in eight prisons, the most serious of which was at Strangeways in Manchester. It began with a disturbance in the chapel on April 1, lasted for 25 days, caused extensive damage and led to the death of a prisoner. In a report published on February 25 1991, Lord Justice Woolf blamed "intolerable" conditions, including gross overcrowding and a degrading regime (not the fault, he said, of the then governor). Woolf made 12 recommendations covering the prison service generally, including stricter limits on numbers accommodated, the appointment of a prison ombudsman and an improved system for dealing with prisoners' grievances, and a commitment to end slopping out within five years. Home secretary Baker promised to better that date with a target of 1994 and announced more generous arrangements for prison visiting, but the implementation of the whole Woolf programme of prison reform was judged to be unrealistically expensive.

Confidence in the criminal justice system was badly impaired by a number of miscarriages of justice. In October 1989 the Lord Chief Justice found that convictions of four men said to have carried out the Guildford and Woolwich pub bombings of 1975 were "unsafe and unsatisfactory". That led to renewed demands for the reopening of the case of six men convicted for the bombings in Birmingham in 1975. Home secretary Hurd declined to do so since the case had already been back to the Appeal Court in 1987-88, when Lord Chief Justice Lane had rejected it with visible distaste. But the campaign persisted and the Birmingham verdicts were discovered to be unsafe too.

Throughout the Conservative years activists complained that the war on crime and on Irish terrorism had eroded civil liberties. Mrs Thatcher preached freedom and believed her years in office had done much to widen it. Freedom to choose which hospital you used, which school your children went to; freedom to own your own home; freedom to work as you wished without union constraint or interference; freedom from meddling government; freedom from Soviet tyranny. Opponents accused her of trampling on freedom: the removal of the right to union membership at GCHQ; the prosecution of Sarah Tisdall, who leaked Ministry of Defence plans to handle the arrival of cruise missiles at Greenham, and the failed prosecution of civil servant Clive Ponting, who, angry that questions by the Labour MP Tam Dalyell about the Belgrano incident were not being fairly answered, sent him some of the documents.

Perhaps the most spectacular case of all was the Government's obsessive attempt to ban publication of Spycatcher, Peter Wright's memoirs of his years in the security services. The case went to the highest court in the land, but the book was by now so well known and so widely available, the Law Lords ruled, that such damage as it could do had been done already. At one point Lord Bridge, senior Law Lord and former chairman of the Security Commission, said he could not help thinking the absolute protection of the service for which the Cabinet secretary, Sir Robert Armstrong, was asking "could not be achieved this side of the Iron Curtain".

Later the Government took the fight to Australia and lost there as well. The response was a Bill to reform the law on Official Secrets, hailed by its authors as libertarian, but seen by critics as designed to claw back the Government's losses on Spycatcher, imposing the blanket ban on publication of such disclosures which they had failed, at great expense, to win in the courts. Though legislation was introduced to put the security services on a statutory basis, the Government resisted all demands that they be supervised either by a parliamentary select committee or by Privy Councillors.

In 1990 the Government brought forward a Bill to extend the jurisdiction of British courts so that prosecutions might be brought against suspected Nazi war criminals living in Britain. The War Crimes Bill was bitterly contested across party lines, with some arguing that there should be no prosecution for crimes, however heinous, which occurred so long ago. On December 12 1989 the Commons voted in favour of legislation by 348 to 123 and on March 19 1990 the Bill was given a second reading by 273 votes to 60. The Lords rejected the Bill on June 4 1990 by 207 votes to 44 and it had to be brought back in the following session. On April 30 1990 the Lords again rejected it by 131 to 109, but the Commons insisted and under the terms of the Parliament Act of 1911 the bill then passed to the statute book. ●

NOTIFIABLE OFFENCES RECORDED BY POLICE
ENGLAND AND WALES (THOUSANDS)

	1979	1984	1989	1990-91*	% increase 1979/1991
Theft and handling stolen goods	1,416.1	1,808.0	2,012.8	2,583.3	+82.4
Burglary	544.0	892.9	825.9	1,113.8	+104.7
Criminal damage	320.5	497.8	630.1	779.0	+143.1
Violence against the person	95.0	114.2	177.0	186.4	+96.2
of which: more serious offences	5.9	7.2	13.9	n/a	–
Sexual offences	21.8	20.2	29.7	29.3	+34.4
of which: rape	1.2	1.4	3.3	n/a	–
TOTAL	2,536.7	3,499.1	3,870.7	4,928.7	+94.3

* June 1990 to June 1991

PROPORTION OF OFFENCES CLEARED UP BY THE POLICE (%)

	1979	1984	1989
Theft and handling stolen goods	40	35	31
Burglary	31	27	27
Criminal damage	30	23	23
Violence against the person	77	74	77
Sexual offences	75	72	75
TOTAL	41	35	34

Source: Home Office

PEOPLE IN PRISON 1979-89
ENGLAND AND WALES

	1979	1984	1989
All in prison	42,220	43,295	48,500
men	40,762	41,822	46,736
women	1,458	1,473	1,764
All on remand	6,438*	8,741	10,499
of whom: untried	3,921*	7,173	8,576

* 1979 figure unavailable: this is 1980 figure

Source: Home Office

OFFENCES IN ENGLAND AND WALES CURRENTLY RECORDED AS HOMICIDE

	TOTAL	per million population
1969	332	6.8
1979	546	11.1
1980	549	11.2
1981	499	10.1
1982	557	11.2
1983	482	9.7
1984	537	10.8
1985	537	10.8
1986	568	11.4
1987	602	12.0
1988	560	11.8
1989	576	11.4

Source: Social Trends

LEGISLATION

Protection of Information Bill
November 20 1979: in the wake of the Blunt affair the Bill, which was designed to replace Section 2 of the 1911 Official Secrets Act and instead to prevent disclosure of a limited range of specified information, was withdrawn.

Criminal Attempts Act 1981
1st reading: December 19 1980
2nd reading: January 19 1981, unopposed but altered under new experimental system of special committees being tried on unopposed legislation.
Royal Assent: July 27 1981
Provisions: repeal of Section 4 of the Vagrancy Act 1824, the "sus" law. The Opposition protested that a new offence of "interference with a motor vehicle in a public place" would perpetuate many of the features of the "sus" law.

Criminal Justice Act 1982
1st reading: December 2 1981
2nd reading: January 20 1982, no division
Royal Assent:October 28 1982
Provisions: increased flexibility in sentencing and treatment of offenders. New clauses were introduced at report stage proposing to make capital punishment available as a penalty for murder and certain categories of murder. All were defeated on a free vote .

Police and Criminal Evidence Act 1984
1st reading: October 26 1983
2nd reading: November 7 1983, by 339 (Government) to 188 (Lab, SNP, PC, D. Alton - Lib, J. Hume - SDLP)
Royal Assent:October 31 1984
Provisions: detailed police powers to stop and search, carry out road checks and of entry, search and seizure; procedures for questioning and treatment of persons in police detention, including conduct of intimate searches and taking of intimate and non-intimate samples; defined "serious arrestable" and "arrestable" offences; laid down criteria relating to admissibility of evidence in criminal proceedings; established Police Complaints Authority and, following Lord Scarman amendment, made racially discriminatory behaviour a police disciplinary offence; ordered arrangements to be made for community policing.

Data Protection Act 1984
1st reading: November 3 1983
2nd reading: January 30 1984, by 226 (Government, Lib, SDP) to 104 (Lab, PC, SNP, D. Alton - Lib)
Royal Assent: July 12 1984
Provisions: legislation designed to "regulate the use of automatically processed information relating to individuals and the provision of services in respect of such information". Established post of Data Protection Registrar to maintain a register of personal data users and computer bureaux and ensure that data is used in accordance with the principles of the legislation; the decision of the Registrar could be appealed to a Data Protection Tribunal; "data subjects" were given legal rights, including right of access; there were specific exemptions from the provision of the legislation to safeguard national security or the detection or prevention of crime or assessment of tax or duty, etc. The Act enabled ratification of the Council of Europe's Convention for the Protection of Individuals.

Interception of Communications Act 1985
1st reading: February 14 1985
2nd reading: March 12 1985, approved after rejection of Labour amendment declining 2nd reading by 278 (Government) to 175 (Lab, Lib, SDP, SNP, PC).
Royal Assent: July 25 1985
Provisions: created new offence of unlawful interception. But interception was allowed under certain conditions, most importantly if carried out under a ministerial warrant. Warrants could be issued in the interests of (i) national security, (ii) the prevention or detection of serious crime or (iii) safeguarding the economic well-being of the UK. Labour's amendment opposing the 2nd reading claimed the Bill "gives statutory authority to interception of communications on criteria at once so vague and so sweeping as to permit interception on an unacceptably wide basis and which provides insufficient safeguards for those adversely affected by unlawful interception".

Public Order Act 1986
1st reading: December 5 1985
2nd reading: January 13 1986, by 292 (Government) to 201 (Lab, Lib, SDP, SNP, PC)
Royal Assent: November 7 1986
Provisions: abolished the common law offences of riot, rout, unlawful assembly and affray and created new public order offences of riot, violent disorder, affray and disorderly conduct; new regulations on processions and assemblies required organisers to give police seven days' notice; an extension of the ban on material likely to stir up racial hatred and of police powers to seize such material; persons convicted of football-related offences could be banned from attending matches for up to three months. The legislation was passed in the wake of urban riots.

Criminal Justice Act 1987
1st reading: November 14 1986
2nd reading: November 27 1986 after defeat by 219 to 160 of Labour amendment calling for its rejection
Royal Assent: May 15 1987
Provisions: relating to investigation and trial of fraud.

Criminal Justice (Scotland) Act 1987
1st reading: February 26 1987
Scottish Grand Committee: March 23 1987
Royal Assent: May 15 1987
Provisions: included measures on recovery of proceeds of drug trafficking in Scotland.

Criminal Justice Act 1988
1st reading: December 9 1987
2nd reading: January 18 1988 by 285 (Government) to 225 (Lab, Lib Dem, SNP, Plaid Cymru, OUP)
Royal Assent: July 29 1988

Provisions: made fresh provisions for extradition; gave Attorney-General right to challenge lenient sentences; abolished defence's right to peremptory challenge of jurors. Amended rules of evidence for criminal proceedings. Extended power to seize assets of convicted offenders, which already applied to drug traffickers under the Drug Trafficking Act, to cover serious crimes such as robbery, fraud and counterfeiting. Changes in the law on jurisdiction and power of criminal courts, the collection, enforcement and remission of fines imposed by coroners, juries, supervision orders, the detention of children and young persons, probation and the probation service, criminal appeals, anonymity in rape and similar cases; amendments and fresh provisions relating to witnesses, compensation under the Criminal Injuries Compensation Board, compensation for wrongful conviction, creation of summary offence of possessing indecent photograph of a child.

Protection of Information Bill (private sponsor: Richard Shepherd Con, Aldridge-Brownhills)

1st reading: October 28 1987

2nd reading: January 15 1988: lost 234 to 271.

Provisions: would have repealed Official Secrets Act of 1911. Built on distinction between severe breaches of security and lesser offences deserving lesser penalties, reserving heavy penalties for the protection of information on defence, international relations, security and intelligence where unauthorised disclosure would be likely to cause serious injury to the nation or to the safety of a citizen. It would be a defence to show that the information was widely available already. The Home secretary, Douglas Hurd, argued that this was not a suitable matter for private member's legislation. The Government imposed a three-line whip to vote it down, but 20 Conservative MPs (including a teller) voted in favour and 50 more abstained. The rebels were: J. Aitken (Thanet S), R. Allason (Torbay), J. Biffen (Shropshire N), Sir R. Body (Holland), Sir N. Bonsor (Upminster), Sir A. Buck (Colchester N), N. Budgen (Wolverhampton SW), T. Devlin (Stockton S), D. Dover (Chorley), H. Dykes (Harrow E), Sir I. Gilmour (Chesham), J. Gorst (Hendon N), E. Heath (Old Bexley), J. Lester (Broxtowe), R. Rhodes James (Cambridge), P. Rost (Erewash), R. Shepherd (Aldridge), R. Squire (Hornchurch), T. Taylor (Southend E) with T. Marlow (Northampton N) a teller.

Official Secrets Act 1989

1st reading: November 30 1988

2nd reading: December 21 1988, by 298 (Government plus UPUP) to 221 (Lab, SDP, Lib Dem, Plaid Cymru, SNP, R. Shepherd (Con) and T. Taylor (Con))

Royal Assent: May 11 1989

Provisions: following Ponting and Spycatcher cases in which prosecutions failed, and the defeat of the Shepherd Bill, replaced the 1911 Official Secrets Act with two classes of offence of disclosing information on security and intelligence: the first a blanket ban on disclosure by all present or former members of the service, the second prohibiting any government servant or contractor from disclosing information which might damage the work of the intelligence and security services, or information on international relations which might

jeopardise UK interests. An amendment to include a "public interest" defence was lost 267-169, 13 Conservatives voting against the Government.

Security Service Act 1989

1st reading: November 23 1988

2nd reading: December 15 1988, 204 (Government plus SDP and OUP) to 105 (Lab, SLD, 1 SNP, 1 Plaid Cymru)

Royal Assent: April 27 1989

Provisions: placed the security services on a statutory basis and provided for investigation of complaints about the service to be undertaken by a new tribunal or commissioner. On January 16, amendments to put the service under the control of a Commons select committee or a committee of privy councillors were defeated by 232 (Government and UPUP) to 163 (Lab, Lib Dem, SDP, SNP, Plaid Cymru plus 3 Conservatives – J. Aitken, R. Allason and R. Shepherd).

Criminal Justice Act 1991

1st reading: November 8 1990

2nd reading: November 20 1990, by 350 (Government plus Liberal Democrats, SDP, OUP, DUP, UPUP) to 190 (Lab plus 1 Plaid Cymru).

Royal Assent: July 25, 1991

Provisions: to ensure greater consistency in sentencing, reduce the use of jail for minor offences, replace the parole and remission system by new arrangements for early release. Range of "community" penalties extended (with possible use of electronic tagging). Parents might now be required to pay fines of offenders aged 16 and 17. Changes to make it easier to bring cases of child abuse, including use of videos. Clause 25 was strongly opposed by homosexuals as making minor sexual practices equivalent to serious heterosexual offences.

War Crimes Act 1991

2nd reading: March 19 1990, 273-60 on free vote (see section on MPs' voting records). The principle of legislating on the issue had been approved by the Commons on December 12 1989 by 348 to 123 on a free vote. Lost on second reading in the Lords on the night of June 4-5 by 207 votes to 74. Under the Parliament Act, the Commons insisted on the Bill, overriding a further Lords vote against it on April 30 1991, and it automatically passed to the statute book.

Provisions: following a report by Sir Thomas Hetherington (former Director of Public Prosecutions) and William Chalmers (former Crown Agent in Scotland) it allowed the prosecution within the UK of people resident here who were suspected of war crimes on German or German-occupied territory in the second world war.

THE ARTS

AS with health, education, housing, social security, transport, science and much else, so with the arts: the constant theme of the Conservative years was a barrage of complaint against alleged Government stinginess, together with many wistful comparisons with the way these things were ordered across the Channel. There were ceaseless disputes not just about the level of public provision but about the way in which it was disbursed. While great national institutions like the Royal Opera House and the National Theatre protested against being expected to live in near penury, organisations in the regions condemned an excessive concentration of resources on a few fat cats in the capital.

The return of the Conservatives in 1979 seemed to begin propitiously with the appointment as arts minister of Norman St John-Stevas, a notable aesthete and the first arts minister to hold a Cabinet seat, who was given an independent department, the Office of Arts and Libraries. But within six weeks, the first Conservative Budget brought reductions of some £5m in arts provision, including cuts in grants for all galleries and museums and a £1m reduction in the Arts Council budget. The raising of VAT added a further burden. Six days later, St John-Stevas announced the dawn of a new regime for the arts. The cuts in personal and corporate taxation in the Budget, he said in a newspaper interview, had opened the way for much greater private giving. There would now be a major shift from public to private patronage.

St John-Stevas's tenure was in any case brief. In January 1981 he was dropped from the Government and replaced by a minister outside the Cabi-

net; the Office of Arts and Libraries was brought within the Department of Education. Though sceptical, the arts world began to respond to the new philosophies. In 1982, the Arts Council chose as its new director-general the director of the Association of Business Sponsorship of the Arts, Luke Rittner. The level of business interest increased. Lord Gowrie, arts minister in 1984-5 (which meant that the arts once more had Cabinet representation) developed a Business Investment Sponsorship Scheme which by the 1987 election had raised the level of sponsorship to £25m, against half a million a decade before.

The theme of self-help was reinforced after that election by Richard Luce, who had succeeded Gowrie in 1985 (a change which again took responsibility for the arts outside the Cabinet). On June 8, he told a conference of the Regional Arts Association that it was time to abandon the "welfare state mentality" which infected the arts. Traditional patterns of public support had created a dependency culture which must now be replaced by an enterprise culture. Peter (later Lord) Palumbo, a notable private patron who became chairman of the Arts Council in 1989, warned that public subsidy tended to breed bureaucracy.

These shifts were denounced as philistine by great figures in the arts world like the former National Theatre director, Sir Peter Hall (who was known to have voted Conservative in 1979). In June 1989, the chairmen of five national museums and galleries wrote to the Prime Minister saying that if their grants continued to fall behind the rate of inflation they would not be able to pay their staff or

GOVERNMENT SPENDING ON ARTS AND LIBRARIES
1 Total spending on arts and libraries at current prices.
2 % of government expenditure
3 % of GDP

	1978-1979	1979-1980	1980-1981	1981-1982	1982-1983	1983-1984	1984-1985	1985-1986	1986-1987	1987-1988	1988-1989	1989-1990	1990-1 estimated
1	0.4	0.5	0.6	0.7	0.7	0.8	0.8	0.9	1.0	1.0	1.1	1.3	1.4
2	0.6	0.6	0.6	0.6	0.6	0.6	0.6	0.6	0.7	0.7	0.7	0.7	0.7
3	0.2	0.2	0.3	0.2	0.2	0.2	0.2	0.2	0.2	0.2	0.2	0.2	0.2

ARTS COUNCIL SPENDING IN ENGLAND:
INDEX OF ARTS COUNCIL SPENDING IN REAL TERMS, (1983-84=100)

	1984-85	1985-86	1986-87	1987-88	1988-89	1989-90
National companies*	101	99	96	93	88	86
Regional arts assocns	105	129	192	204	201	196
Other	99	91	132	125	124^	127
TOTAL	100	99	127	124	122^	122
Welsh Arts Council	104	100	104	100#	101	98
Scottish Arts Council	96	100	99	99	99	96
TOTAL ARTS COUNCIL GB	101	99	122	120	118^	117

Source: Cultural Trends 1991:9 Policy Studies Institute, based on annual reports of Arts Council of GB. By permission.
* main revenue grant only; excludes grant from Arts Council Touring Department (included in Other)
^ excludes £2.411m towards Royal Opera House Development Trust
# excludes funds towards purchase of Sherman Theatre by Welsh Arts Council
NB ARTS COUNCIL RECEIVED FROM OAL £25m 1986-7 £24m in 87-88 and £23m 1988-89 to cover loss of funding by GLC and Mets.

CENTRAL GOVERNMENT MAIN FUNDING DEPARTMENTS
EXPENDITURE ON ARTS, MUSEUMS AND GALLERIES
IN REAL TERMS (1984-85 PRICES), £THOUSANDS

	1984-5	1985-6	1986-7	1987-8	1988-9	1989-90
ARTS SUPPORT						
Office of Arts & Libraries	110,328	111,837	136,356	132,682	135,229	131,944
Scottish Office Education Dept	388	584	494	494	479	484
Welsh Office	490	564	578	579	571	587
NI Dept of Education	2,849	3,052	2,982	3,281	3,211	3,603
TOTAL ARTS SUPPORT	114,055	116,037	140,410	137,036	139,489	136,617
MUSEUMS AND GALLERIES						
Office of Arts & Libraries	60,458	58,548	69,535	69,578	75,472	71,119
Scottish Office Education Dept	7,178	7,460	7,796	7,708	8,472	8,742
Welsh Office	6,233	6,369	6,431	6,201	6,540	6,701
NI Dept of Education	3,636	3,695	3,843	4,090	3,787	4,019
TOTAL MUSEUMS & GALLERIES	77,505	76,071	87,605	87,578	94,271	90,581

Source: adapted from fuller tables, also showing spending at current prices and indices of annual change in real terms, and government spending other than though main funding departments,Cultural Trends 1991:9, Policy Studies Institute. By permission. Figures exclude spending on administration, heritage, libraries and professional training in the arts (including National Film and TV School). The Natural History Museum has been excluded from OAL figures 1988-9 - 1989-90. Museum expenditure figures include purchase grants.

keep up their buildings, while Luke Rittner warned that with Arts Council grants to clients running 6 per cent behind the rate of inflation, the arts were facing "disaster". In November 1990, the Royal Shakespeare Company said its financial shortfall had reached such a pitch that its theatre in the Barbican would have to go dark for the winter, and unless its Arts Council grant was increased it might have to quit altogether. The Council itself was thrown into turmoil when in line with reports from the retiring head of the Office of Arts and Libraries, Richard Wilding, and the National Audit Office, Luce announced that the Council would have to cede much of its present authority to regional arts boards. Palumbo backed this change but Rittner, who believed such fragmentation must diminish the arts world's political clout, resigned.

By now, the case for greater public funding was argued in different and rather more practical terms. In 1988 a report from the Policy Studies Institute pointed out that the arts was big business, employing some 500,000 people, accounting for 1.2 per cent of GDP, and even more to the point, making a solid contribution to Britain's overseas earnings: rather more, in fact, than the motor industry and exceeded only by banking, shipping and travel.

The talk of gathering crisis across the arts coincided with a sorry decline in the British film industry. For a time the Thatcher years had been good for the industry, with productions like Gandhi and Chariots of Fire breaking records across the world. But it did not last. The Films Act 1985 was a text book Thatcherite enterprise. It abolished the Eady Levy, then worth some £4.5m a year, which required exhibitors to pay a share of their takings from seats to the industry, abolished the quota requirement which guaranteed a share of showings in British cinemas for British-made films, and wound up the National Film Finance Corporation in favour of a private film funding company with some state support.

The decline, even near-collapse, of production and investment at the end of the decade led to a meeting at Downing Street in June 1990 between Margaret Thatcher and leaders of the industry, headed by Sir Richard Attenborough. The response was much warmer than they had expected. The Government promised £5m over three years to support UK producers in European co-productions, while a series of working parties was arranged to enable the Government and the industry to explore new sources of investment and possible tax concessions. But in his March 1991 budget, Chancellor Lamont, who as a junior minister had put the Films Bill through parliament, rejected all the proposals for tax incentives which had come from the working parties. Some of the cries of anguish, though, were stifled in November 1991 when the Government announced the largest ever increase in the Arts Council's funding: a rise of £27m, or 13.9 per cent, almost 10 per cent more than the rate of inflation. The arts minister, Tim Renton, said he wanted the money to go on artists and performing companies, not administration. The regions were expected to fare rather better than the capital. Museums and galleries, however, were given a more modest increase. Labour put this unexpected generosity down to electioneering. ●

LEGISLATION

Films Act 1985

Introduced: November 8 1984

2nd reading: November 19 1984 by 216 (Government) to 106 (Lab, Lib)

Provisions: abolished Eady Levy on cinema admissions. National Film Finance Corporation to be abolished and its assets vested in the Trade and Industry secretary who would then make available £1.5m a year to encourage British film production.

Ended quota system requiring cinemas to show minimum proportion of British-made films.

During the committee stage an amendment was carried to introduce a levy to be paid by BBC and independent channels to producers of films shown on TV. This was reversed on report stage by 224 votes to 164.

BROADCASTING

GOVERNMENT policy on broadcasting reflected a familiar dichotomy of the Conservative years: deregulation in some areas, more extensive regulation in others. The Government was committed to open up the airwaves to enable entrepreneurs to broaden public provision. It began the process with the Broadcasting Act 1980, which established a fourth channel, to be operated not by the Open Broadcasting Authority earlier proposed by Labour on the lines recommended by the Annan Committee in 1977, but by the Independent Broadcasting Authority (IBA). Even so, it was given a mandate which safeguarded minority interests not widely catered for on its existing channel, as well as providing for a Welsh language channel. The solution seemed to reflect the less than Thatcherite preferences of the Home Secretary, William Whitelaw.

Channel Four, which opened on November 2, 1982, was followed by the arrival of TV-am, which was awarded the breakfast-time slot in the reshuffle of television franchises in December 1980. These years were also expected to see a big expansion in cable television, but it failed to catch on. Of 137 franchises awarded between 1983 and 1991, only 49 reached the construction stage: roughly one in a thousand homes took the service in Britain, compared with six in ten in the United States.

In December 1986, a contract for direct broadcasting by satellite (DBS) was awarded to BSB (British Satellite Broadcasting) but their arrival was pre-empted by the launch in November 1988 of the Astra satellite, owned by a company based in Luxembourg, which enabled Rupert Murdoch's Sky TV to start satellite transmissions in February 1989.

BSB did not open up until April 29, 1990, but with both stations losing money, a merger was concluded on November 2, producing an organisation (BSkyB) heavily dominated by Sky. This upset the IBA, which had not been consulted and objected that a DBS contract awarded to one organisation had effectively been transferred without its consent to another. And it outraged the Opposition, which complained that Rupert Murdoch, whose newspapers were strongly committed to the Conservative Party, was being permitted to reverse the franchise award.

The Sky/BSB deal was also seen by Labour, and others, as a breach of the spirit of Britain's cross-media ownership regulations, under which the owner of a national newspaper (and Rupert Murdoch owns five) cannot own more than 20 per cent of a television company. The ruling will come into force in 1993, under the Broadcasting Act of 1990, the most radical shake-up of independent television since its inception.

In March 1985, a committee under Sir Alan Peacock was set up to examine alternatives to the licence fee to finance the BBC. Some of its findings disappointed market-minded Conservatives. It did not believe the BBC should be forced to take advertising and recommended that the licence fee should continue for 10 years linked to the rate of inflation. More radically, however, a majority of members suggested that ITV franchises, instead of being awarded at the IBA's discretion, should be put out to competitive tender.

The Broadcasting Bill built on this proposal. It created a new authority, the Independent Televi-

TELEVISION FRANCHISES
THE FIRST FRANCHISES TO BE DECIDED ON THE NEW BASIS WERE AWARDED ON OCTOBER 16 1991.
FOUR INCUMBENT CONTRACTORS WERE REJECTED. THE RESULTS WERE:

	winners	bid	losers
North of Scotland	*Grampian	£702,000	†North of Scotland TV (£2.71m), †C3 Caledonia (£1.13m)
Central Scotland	*STV	£2,000	unopposed
Borders	*Border TV	£52,000	unopposed
Northern Ireland	*Ulster TV	£1,03m	TVNI (£3.1m), †Lagan TV (£2.71m)
North West	*Granada	£9m	†North West TV (£35.3m)
North East	*Tyne Tees	£15.06	North East TV (£5.01m)
Yorkshire	*Yorkshire TV	£37.7m	†Viking TV (£30.12m), White Rose TV (£17.40m)
Wales & West	*HTV	£20.53m	Merlin (£19.37m), †Channel 3 Wales & West (£18.29m), C3W (£17.76m)
Midlands	*Central TV	£2,000	unopposed
East of England	*Anglia TV	£17.80m	Three East (£14.078m), †East of England TV (£10.13m)
South & South East	Meridian	£36.52m	*TVS (£59.76m), Carlton TV (£18.08m), †Sth of England TV (£22.105m)
London (Weekend)	*LWT	£7.59m	†London Independent Broadcasting (£35,41m)
London (Weekday)	Carlton TV	£43.17m	Greater London TV (£45.319m), *Thames TV (£32.70m), †CPV-TV (£45.32m)
Breakfast	Sunrise	£34.61m	*TV-am (£14.13m), Daybreak (£33.26m)
South West	West Country TV	£7.82m	*TSW (£16,117m), †TeleWest (£7,266m)
Channel Islands	*Channel TV	£1,000	†CI 3 TV (£102,000)

* denotes incumbent contractor
† failed to meet quality standard

LEGISLATION

Broadcasting Act 1980
Introduced: February 5 1980
2nd reading: February 18 1980, unopposed, after rejection by 179 (Government) to 139 (Lab, Lib, PC) of a Labour amendment opposing second reading because the Bill failed to set up an Open Broadcasting Authority
Provisions: established fourth channel, to be operated by IBA, and single Broadcasting Complaints Commission for both BBC and independent channels. Imposed a levy on independent sound radio contractors.

Broadcasting Act 1990
Introduced: December 7 1989
2nd reading: June 6 1990 by 310 (Government, 1 SDP, UPUP) to 238 (Lab, Lib Dem, OUP, DUP, SDLP, SNP, PC)
Provisions: Created Independent Television Commission to replace IBA and Cable Authority, to be licensing body for Channel 3 (formerly ITV), Channel 4, a new Channel 5 and possible later Channel 6, cable and satellite television. At least 25 per cent of relevant output to be bought in from independent producers.

Licences to be awarded to the highest bidder passing a quality threshold, but a lower bid could also be taken in "exceptional circumstances".
A new Radio Authority would allocate up to three national commercial stations, awarding the licences by competitive tender, and supervise all independent radio. Broadcasting Standards Council to be put on statutory basis.
During committee stage in the Lords, the Government endorsed an amendment by Lord Wyatt of Weeford (Ind) to set up an impartiality code for broadcasters. The Government introduced its own clause based on the amendment, which was carried in the Commons on October 25 by 268 (Government, OUP, UPUP) to 181 (Lab, Lib Dem, SNP and 3 Con- J.Critchley (Aldershot), R.Shepherd (Aldridge-Brownhills and G.Walden (Buckingham)).

sion Commission (ITC) to succeed the IBA and Cable Authority, which except in "exceptional circumstances" would award television franchises to the highest bidder who was able to satisfy quality standards.

The Bill was modified in committee to include new safeguards for quality, especially to defend children's and religious programmes. The first award of franchises under this system, in October 1991, produced widespread dismay. Some companies failed the quality test, some lost their contracts by bidding too low, while others were held to have imperilled programme standards by bidding too high. Among those who were most dismayed was Margaret Thatcher, who wrote to TV-am, a company she greatly admired for its robust resistance to union power, deploring the loss of their franchise – though in this case the ITC had been true to her own free market principles, rejecting TV-am simply because someone else had put in a higher bid.

While the Conservatives hoped to see entrepreneurship flourish, they also feared an impairment of moral standards, and believed that some broadcasters exploited freedom of speech in ways detrimental to the national interest. This led to a series of bruising clashes. In August 1985, after protests by Thatcher, the Home Secretary, Leon Brittan, asked the BBC not to transmit a programme in its series Real Lives, which contained an interview with a leading IRA figure. The programme was withdrawn, but later shown in amended form.

In October 1986 the party chairman Norman Tebbit sent a dossier to the BBC containing what he said were instances of bias in its coverage of the US action in Libya.The BBC denied bias. In January 1987 after Government protests, the BBC halted a programme in a series called "Secret Society" compiled by the New Statesman journalist Duncan Campbell, about a satellite surveillance project. The offices of the New Statesman and those of BBC Glasgow were raided by police.

There were furious government protests in 1988 about a Thames Television documentary, Death on the Rock, about the killing of three IRA activists in Gibraltar. An inquiry by the former Conservative minister Lord Windlesham, set up by the company, found in its favour, but the Government rejected its findings.

On October 19 1988 the Government banned face to face television interviews with spokesmen of the IRA and equivalent organisations. During the Lords proceedings on the 1989 Broadcasting Bill, the Government accepted in principle the case made by a right-wing Independent peer, Lord Wyatt of Weeford, to establish a code for broadcasting impartiality and introduced an amendment to the Bill incorporating a modified form of his proposals.

Conservatives also complained of excessive sex and violence on television, and failure to maintain standards of taste and decency. In line with a 1987 manifesto commitment they created, alongside the existing Broadcasting Complaints Commission, a Broadcasting Standards Council which the 1980 Broadcasting Act put on a statutory basis, charged with laying down suitable codes of practice, monitoring programmes and examining complaints. ●

'Margaret Thatcher wrote to TV-am, a company she greatly admired, deploring the loss of their franchise'

CONSTITUTIONAL REFORM

FOR MOST of this century constitutional reform in general and electoral reform in particular have been the exclusive and unchallenged cause of the Liberal party and its various heirs and successors. Not only on the grounds of equity, including equity for the Liberals whose national support has been under-represented in every general election since 1910, but as the key to better government. A fair electoral system, a reformed House of Commons with powerful select committees, democratically elected Second Chamber, decentralisation to Scotland and Wales and the English regions, a written constitution, a Bill of Rights based on the European Convention, a Freedom of Information Bill in place of the Official Secrets Act: these, it was argued, were not peripheral issues but part of the central agenda of any attempt to reverse Britain's long decline.

Towards the end of the eighties that cause was taken up by a broad coalition of interests, with the pressure group Charter 88 at its heart. By the end of the decade it looked to have won the battle for public support on most of these issues; though whether the majority of voters yet thought these things urgent as well as desirable was another matter. On May 24 1991 an opinion poll commissioned by the Rowntree Trust and carried out by MORI demonstrated wide public backing for almost all the ingredients which made up the reformers' case. Support was especially strong among Labour voters, who had swung towards constitutional change far faster than their parliamentary leadership. On October 4 1990 the Labour party conference voted to examine the merits of a new electoral system not just for the European parliament, its planned Second Chamber and its parliaments for Scotland and

Wales, but for Westminster, too. A committee set up under the chairmanship of Professor Raymond Plant of Southampton University produced interim findings on July 1991 which were broadly favourable to reform, though they held open the possibility of retaining "first past the post" for Westminster elections while using other systems for regional, Second Chamber and European elections. The party also began to advocate a Bill of Rights, though in a modified form, fearing the power of judges override progressive legislation. Its ambitious constitutional package also included reform of the Commons, an elected Second Chamber to replace the Lords, devolution first to Scotland and later to Wales and the regions, a statutory "right to know", and curbs on prime ministerial patronage.

Some in the Labour party thought this agenda too limited: it ought also, said Tony Benn, who introduced a private member's bill on these lines in May 1991, to look at such issues as the future of the monarchy and the disestablishment of the Church of England. Others viewed these events with scepticism. They were all got up, they said, by the chattering classes. The folks in the pub and the shopping precinct were not that interested. When they saw beyond the slogans, when they began to look at the practicalities of change, the enthusiasm they expressed to pollsters would swiftly wane.

The Conservatives were the most resistant of all. One of their first acts of Government was to repeal the two Labour Bills on devolution for Scotland and Wales, which had failed to survive the test of popular referendums. No less revered a figure than Sir Alec Douglas-Home had assured Tory devolutionists during the Scottish referendum of

PUBLIC OPINION ON CONSTITUTIONAL CHANGE
(RESULTS OF MORI POLL FOR ROWNTREE TRUST, TOTALLY AND BY PARTY).

Should there be :	Yes	No	Don't know
elections on a fixed date?	56	23	21
proportional representation?	50	23	27
compulsory voting?	49	42	9
elected second chamber in place of Lords?	40	29	31
voting on Saturdays or Sundays?	37	24	39

	Yes	No	Don't know
Freedom of Information Act?	77	9	14
referendums on important issues?	75	20	5
a Bill of Rights?	72	11	17
magistrates elected?	60	31	9
greater powers of government for Wales?	42	40	18
same for Northern Ireland?	42	43	16
same for regions of England?	27	61	12

Should Scotland be :	Scots	Rest
part of UK with devolved assembly?	51	41
independent but part of EC?	23	11
independent and outside EC?	9	4
no change	16	32

If the Tories win, should Scots MPs:		
accept Tory rule?	26	39
present a bill for a Scottish Assembly?	62	39
refuse to take their seats?	6	5
no opinion?	6	17

In election campaigns should there be	Yes	No	Don't know
a limit on national spending by parties?	81	14	5
public money to finance party campaigns?	39	53	8
a ban on publication of opinion polls?	21	74	5
a ban on party political broadcasts?	8	79	3
a ban on TV and radio coverage?	14	84	2
a ban on newspaper coverage?	10	88	2

Do you support proportional representation?	Support	Oppose	No Preference
All	50	23	27
Conservative	39	36	25
Labour	53	18	29
Liberal Democrat	70	12	18
Middle class	55	23	22
Working class	47	23	30
Trade unionists	59	22	19

Do you support a Bill of Rights?	Support	Oppose	No Preference
All	72	11	17
Conservative	62	18	20
Labour	83	5	12
Liberal Democrat	74	9	17
Middle class	63	19	19
Working class	76	8	17
Trade unionists	79	9	12

Source: MORI for Rowntree Trust. Sample 1,547 Fieldwork, March 3-25 1991.

1979 that the Tories, if elected, would produce a better package. But none materialised. Though the fall in the Conservative vote since 1955, when they out-polled Labour, continued through the period, reducing them at the 1987 election to 10 seats out of 72, they stood by the status quo, refusing to join the Scottish parties in the constitutional convention which met to debate Scotland's future, from March 30, 1989, producing a "Claim of Right" asserting the right of the Scottish people to determine the form of government best suited to their needs. (The Nationalists, who were founder-members, later withdrew.) By the autumn of 1991 the Convention had agreed on plans for a Scottish Parliament with powers to legislate and to raise revenue, elected by a system not yet specified but certainly more broadly representative than first-past-the-post. The loss of Kincardine and Deeside at the by-election of November 7 reduced the Conservatives to only nine seats in Scotland against Labour's 48 and the Liberal Democrats' 10. An ICM/Scotsman poll showed that three quarters of Scottish electors regarded the Conservatives as an English party.

The opposition parties in Scotland saw the Kincardine result as another landmark along the road to a Scottish Parliament which they now regarded as inevitable: the Conservatives were left more than ever divided. Some, fearing still further losses at the coming election, urged the Government to reconsider its long rejection of devolution. Others continued to argue that any move in that direction would undermine the union. The only option was to stand firm. On November 14, John Major told the Commons: "The self-styled Scottish Constitutional Convention is self-appointed and unrepresentative, and the introduction of tax-raising powers would make Scotland the highest taxed part of the United Kingdom and destroy inward investment that has done so much for their standard of life."

A party which had come into office condemning the over-powerful, over-centralised state in some ways compounded it. Local government, one alternative focus of power, was reduced and humbled: powers it had once enjoyed were in some cases delegated but in others seized by Whitehall. "Whatever else this might be," Hugo Young said of this process in his book One Of Us, "it was not an exercise in reducing the power of the central state.

Rather, bodies that might rival the central state were emasculated or dismantled. The idea of genuine independence, even of competing sources of wisdom and advice, became increasingly uncongenial to a government which was so little obliged to attend to them in Parliament itself." Large Conservative majorities, won in three successive elections, made for a complacent Commons. Backbenchers dutifully voted through measures they did not believe in, such as the poll tax. The Official Secrets Act, long discredited and virtually written off after the failure to convict Clive Ponting, was replaced, not with a Freedom of Information Act, but with new legislation which in some ways tightened the noose. A private member's bill by the Conservative back bench MP Richard Shepherd had offered a compromise formula for safeguarding state security which commanded cross-party support, but the whips moved in to crush it.

Rejecting a Bill of Rights, the Government offered an alternative route for enhancing the rights and powers of the people: a Citizen's Charter, very much John Major's own initiative and published by him in July 1991. Some of its provisions were embodied in the Bills anounced in the Queen's Speech in November. But rival parties were working on these lines too. The Liberal Democrats, especially, complained that Major had cribbed the idea from them.

Thatcher's first government had laid some claim to be parliamentary reformers with the setting up in 1979 by the Leader of the House, Norman St John-Stevas, of a network of new select committees. But in times of crisis, like that over Westland, attempts were made to fob these committees off and slight them, depriving them of witnesses they wanted to hear – though the Defence committee's inquiry into Westland produced some of the toughest invigilation yet mounted by any Westminster committee. The Conservatives, like Labour before them, denied these committees the level of staff and research back-up they needed. One reform which did arrive after two decades of debate was the admission of television cameras to the Commons, decided by a free vote of the House on February 9 1988 (voting was 318 to 264). The cameras began to operate on November 21 1989, at last allowing the public to see for themselves what the people they had elected were up to. ●

THE CITIZEN'S CHARTER AND THE LABOUR AND LIBERAL DEMOCRAT ALTERNATIVES

CONSUMER RIGHTS

CONSERVATIVES:	End Post Office monopoly; stronger powers for gas, water and telephone watchdogs. No new powers over rest of private sector.
LABOUR:	Consumer Protection Commission to monitor prices; tough new laws over labelling and private businesses, particularly second-hand car dealers; Ombudsmen to handle disputes in utilities. New Department of Consumer Affairs to empower consumer groups to take up grievances and organise campaigns.
LIB-DEMS:	Strengthen labelling of goods and consumer information. Increased competition, reform of Mergers and Monopolies Commission and Office of Fair Trading.

FREEDOM OF INFORMATION

CONSERVATIVES:	Publication of exam results in newspapers and national league tables of schools and hospitals. Obligation on local authorities to publish adverse criticisms of their services by the Audit Commission and the remedies they have taken.
LABOUR:	New Freedom of Information Act to cover everything except matters of national security.
LIB-DEMS:	New Freedom of Information Act similar to Labour's.

EDUCATION

CONSERVATIVES:	More schools to opt out of local authority control; examination results, truancy rates to be published; inspectorate to be more independent; lay members to be involved in appeals over admission, exclusion and identification of children with special needs.
LABOUR:	Plans to end the opting out of schools; introduce free nursery education for all; extend higher education; set up Education Standards Commission; introduce new rights for parents, governors and teachers to object to school reorganisations or closures.
LIB-DEMS:	Introduction of free nursery education for all; expansion of higher education; consumer panels to monitor local education service.

HEALTH

CONSERVATIVES:	Guaranteed time limits for operations and day-care treatment after maximum 21-month waiting period; patients' Charter; individual care plan for the elderly and handicapped; guaranteed standards at doctors and dentists.
LABOUR:	Patients' Charter, No-fault compensation when operations go wrong; new powers for community health councils; more rights for the disabled.
LIB-DEMS:	Patients' Charter; comprehensive complaints procedure; operations guaranteed within specific period; choice of place for operation or care.

TRANSPORT

CONSERVATIVES:	Privatise British Rail; introduce performance pay for rail staff taking into account absenteeism and punctuality; compensate season ticket holders and Inter-City rail users for poor service. More convenient driving tests; fewer cones on motorways.
LABOUR:	Enhanced rail and ferry safety; improved road safety; more cycle routes; tougher laws for heavy lorries. Compensation scheme for poor rail services.
LIB-DEMS:	Open British Rail to competition from new operators; money back guarantee for poor public transport services; help for rural transport.

VOTES AND SEATS AT ALL ELECTIONS SINCE 1945
SHARE OF VOTE AND SHARE OF SEATS AT GENERAL ELECTIONS SINCE 1945
1. Share of seats in the new Parliament
2. What the share of seats would have been if the parties had taken the same share of seats as their share of the vote.

| | 1 | | | | 2 | | |
	Con	Lab	Lib/All		Con	Lab	Lib/All
1945*	210	393	12		253	307	58
1950**	298	315	9		271	288	57
1951**	321	295	6		300	305	16
1955**	345	277	6		313	292	17
1959**	365	258	6		311	276	37
1964**	304	317	9		273	278	71
1966**	253	364	12		264	302	54
1970	330	288	6		292	272	47
1974[1]	297	301	14		241	236	123
1974[2]	277	319	13		227	249	116
1979	339	269	11		279	234	88
1983	397	209	23		276	179	165
1987	376	229	22		275	200	146

Source: based on figures in FWS Craig, British Electoral Facts & Britain Votes 4
* Conservative plus Lib Nat and Nat ** Conservative plus Lib Nat

LEGISLATION

SCOTLAND AND WALES ACTS 1978
Following the March 1 1979 referendums on devolution both these Acts were repealed by Commons votes. June 20 1979: order repealing Scotland Act approved by 301 to 206 (Lab, SNP, Lib opposing). The Opposition was against repeal before all party talks had been held on the future of government in Scotland.
June 26 1979: order repealing Wales Act approved by 191 to 8 (Lib, PC opposing). A select committee was set up to examine Welsh affairs.

'The opposition parties in
Scotland saw the
Kincardine result as
another landmark along
the road to a Scottish
Parliament'

LOCAL GOVERNMENT

FOR MUCH of its time in office the Conservative government was at odds, even it sometimes seemed at war, with local government. In one sense there was nothing new about that: it was a Labour Environment secretary, Anthony Crosland, who in 1976 warned high-spending town halls: "the party is over". Local government is big business: the budget of the GLC, before the Conservatives closed it, was bigger than that of some nation states. No central government trying to run an economy could afford to ignore the money which councils raised and spent. But what was new this time was the sheer amount of clanking machinery invented and wheeled into action to try to impose more rigorous central control.

Michael Heseltine, Mrs Thatcher's first Environment secretary, set himself the objective of reducing local spending by manipulating the levels of the rate support grant which every council received from central government. To do this, he introduced an elaborate mechanism for assessing how much each council ought to be spending. Any authority exceeding its figure would lose grant.

The attempt failed. In the short term it was always more likely to push up the budgets of low-spending authorities faster than it squeezed the overspenders. But it also coincided with an upsurge of left-wing influence in Labour local government. For these councillors, to go back on election pledges because of Government pressure to cut spending was exactly the kind of sell-out for which they condemned Labour's national leadership.

So the Government moved to a tightening of the grant mechanism and the introduction in its 1984 Rates Act of rate-capping: the introduction of a ceiling on the rate which a council might legally raise.

Many Conservatives in the boroughs and shires, and some at Westminster, were apprehensive over this incursion into local democracy, and the Bill had a troubled passage. Its enactment led to a series of battles with Labour councils, including the biggest of all, the GLC, under a charismatic young left-wing leader, Ken Livingstone, which refused to make the cuts they needed to fix a legal rate.

Some of these councils had earned a reputation for profligacy. Yet central government, too, had contributed to the pressure to raise more money locally: the Conservatives, continuing a practice begun by Labour, were steadily reducing the central government contribution to local government finances while passing legislation which imposed new obligations and new financial burdens on local government. And the councils' record of overspending was, outside of a handful of recalcitrant local authorities, no worse than the Government's.

The offensive now moved from the councils' powers to their very existence. A late amendment to the 1983 Conservative manifesto committed the party to abolish the GLC and the six metropolitan councils (Greater Manchester, Merseyside, West Midlands, West Yorkshire, South Yorkshire, Tyne and Wear). Events had shown them, the party said, to be an unnecessary and wasteful tier of government. The Inner London Education Authority was spared – but that, too, was to go before long.

Meanwhile, the powers of local government

MAIN SOURCES OF LOCAL AUTHORITY RECEIPTS
(£ MILLION)

	central funding	rates	poll tax	TOTAL	central funding as % of total
1979	11,272	6,567		22,043	51
1980	13,233	8,261		26,545	50
1981	15,201	10,194		30,849	49
1982	16,190	11,732		33,473	48
1983	18,703	12,219		36,115	52
1984	19,908	12,767		37,871	53
1985	20,438	13,638		39,699	52
1986	21,813	15,251		42,912	51
1987	23,277	16,777		46,123	51
1988	23,452	18,726		48,614	48
1989	24,043	19,913	619	51,802	47
1990	38,088	5,126	8,811	59,529	64

Source: Blue book

GENERAL GOVERNMENT FINAL CONSUMPTION AT MARKET PRICES
CENTRAL AND LOCAL ELEMENTS (£M CURRENT PRICES)

	Central	% of total	Local	% of total
1979	23,401	60.2	15,482	39.8
1980	29,989	61.2	19,029	38.8
1981	33,879	61.1	21,573	38.9
1982	37,000	61.2	23,440	38.8
1983	40,654	61.7	25,212	38.3
1984	43,142	61.8	26,715	38.2
1985	45,879	62.1	28,000	37.9
1986	48,806	61.3	30,839	38.7
1987	52,059	60.9	33,481	39.1
1988	55,721	60.7	36,126	39.3
% change				
1979-1988		+ 138.0		+ 133.0

Source: Economic Trends Annual Supplement

COUNCIL TAX: VALUATION BANDS PROPOSED IN LOCAL GOVERNMENT
FINANCE BILL 1991

	VALUATION	% OF TAX PAYABLE
A	UP TO £40,000	100
B	£40,001-52,000	117
C	£52,001-68,000	133
D	£68,001-88,000	150
E	£88,001-120,000	183
F	£120,001-160,000	217
G	£160,001-320,000	250
H	ABOVE £320,000	300

LEGISLATION

Local Government, Planning and Land Act 1980
1st reading: January 24 1980
2nd reading: February 5 1980, by 315 to 260 (Lab, 7 Lib, 4 UUs, SNP, 1 PC)
Royal Assent: November 13 1980
Provisions: repealed 300 ministerial controls over local authorities in England and Wales covering education, libraries and museums, licensing, transport, etc, and 170 similar controls in Scotland; increased accountability of local authorities by requiring them to publish information about their activities and by requiring direct labour organisations to compete with private sector; new powers to order rate revaluations when deemed appropriate; extended domestic rate relief; replaced rate support grant with single block grant system and prescribed ceilings with authorities spending above "standard" level carrying more of burden themselves; speeded up planning system, including relaxing controls on historic buildings and conservation sites; established urban development corporations for rundown docklands areas in London and Merseyside.

had been progressively diminished or transferred to other unelected authorities. Urban development schemes in areas like the docklands and the inner cities were entrusted not to councils but to development corporations, who, it was assumed, were likely to be far more vibrant and innovative. Schools were allowed to opt out of town hall control and new institutions like CTCs were created outside their purlieu. Polytechnics and colleges of higher education were lost to them; in May 1991, the Prime Minister announced that further education would also be taken from them. They lost their representation on health authorities. They were ordered to sell council houses and would have had to surrender control of many large estates had tenants voted in greater numbers for Housing Action Trusts (HATs). Services formerly run by direct labour had now to go out to tender.

But the greatest battles of all came over what ministers called the Community Charge and the rest of the world called the poll tax. This was the latest device to squeeze local authority spending and increase council accountability. The theory was simple enough. Councils, the Conservatives argued, had been able to pitch the rates as high as they liked, knowing that much of their revenue came from business, which could not vote them out; while those too poor to pay the rates could vote for high-spending parties (ie Labour), safe from the fear of facing the financial consequences.

Change to a tax on people, rather than property, and all would have to pay: so all would have the incentive to elect parties (like the Conservatives) who sought to keep spending down. So legislation was introduced first for Scotland and then in England and Wales. Hardly anyone outside the Conservative party liked it; some Conservatives were hostile and tried in vain to amend the Bill to relate it more closely to people's ability to pay. There were several Commons rebellions: on April 18 1988 the Government's majority was cut to 25 on an amendment from the senior Tory backbencher Michael Mates to establish a system of banding in the interests of greater equity.

The poll tax came into force in Scotland on April 1 1989 and in England and Wales a year later. The results were explosive. They included riots in London and other cities (even Tunbridge Wells took to the streets in rather more decorous protest), a 24-point Labour lead in the polls, and the loss to Labour of one of the safest Conservative seats in the country, Mid-Staffs. Refusal to pay was widespread, which helped to push the levels of tax even higher. Additional money was found to cushion its worst effects, even at the cost of delaying much needed changes in the system of community care. Once Mrs Thatcher, who described the community charge as her "flagship", had gone, the poll tax was doomed.

On April 23 1991 Michael Heseltine, now at Environment with a brief to defuse or get rid of it, announced a change to a new Council Tax, which was mainly a form of property tax but with some mitigation for the smallest households. A bill to bring in the Council Tax was introduced in November 1991. Even before that, however, Chancellor Lamont's 1991 Budget announced a £140-a-head cut in the levels of poll tax for 1991-92. At a stroke the flagship was scuppered, as was the 12-year dictum that local government had to stand on its own two feet and cease to be so dependent on the largesse of the taxpayers. ●

Rates Act 1984
1st reading: December 19 1983
2nd reading: January 17 1984, by 346 to 247 (Lab, Lib, SDP, PC, OUP, J. Kilfedder – UPUP, 13 Conservatives)
Royal Assent: June 26 1984
Provisions: introduced "rate-capping of overspenders" by allowing central Government to limit the rates made and precepts issued by local authorities in England and Wales. The Environment secretary was empowered to prescribe a maximum rate and local authorities were required to consult industrial and commercial ratepayers before reaching expenditure decisions.
Financial powers of local government had already been curtailed by the 1981 Local Government and Finance Act.

Rating and Valuation (Amendment) (Scotland) Act 1984
1st reading: November 24 1983
2nd reading: December 5 1983, by 277 to 198 (Lab, Lib, SDP, OUP, SNP, PC)
Royal Assent: June 26 1984
Provisions: extended essential powers of Rates Act to Scotland by empowering the Secretary of State for Scotland to control the rate levels of all local authorities.

Local Government (Interim Provisions) 1984
1st reading: March 30 1984
2nd reading: April 11 1984, by 301 (Government, OUP) to 208 (Lab, Lib, SDP, PC, 18 Conservatives)
Royal Assent: July 31 1984
Provisions: provided for the cancellation of May 1985 elections for the Greater London Council and the six metropolitan county councils in advance of legislation proposing their abolition to be introduced early in the next session of Parliament. Amendments in the Lords allowed current membership of the bodies to continue rather than have transitional bodies appointed.
Rebellion: the 18 Conservative MPs who voted against the Government included Edward Heath, Sir Ian Gilmour, Francis Pym and Geoffrey Rippon.

Local Government Act 1985
1st reading: November 22 1984
2nd reading: December 3/4 1984, by 354 (Government, OUP, 1 Lib - Cyril Smith) to 219 (Lab, Lib, SDP, PC)
Royal Assent: July 16 1985
Provisions: the abolition of the GLC and six metropolitan county councils on April 1 1986 and the transfer of their functions to other bodies (most would go to the London boroughs and the metropolitan district councils). The Inner London Education Authority was to become a directly elected body. The Bill's passage was stormy, especially in the Lords where the Government met with defeats and much reduced majorities.
Rebellion: at committee stage the first clause (abolition) was taken on the floor of the House. The Government's majority was cut to 23 (233 to 210) on an amendment proposed by Patrick Cormack (Con) seeking to replace the GLC with a new, elected authority with powers to be decided by Parliament. 17 Conservatives joined Lab, Lib, SDP and PC to vote with Cormack; two other Conservatives acted as tellers.

Local Government Act 1986
1st reading: November 7 1985
2nd reading: November 18 1985, by 285 (Government, Lib, SDP) to 176 (Lab, SNP, PC)
Royal Assent: March 26 1986
Provisions: local authorities to be prohibited from publishing material which appeared to be designed to affect support for a political party. The Secretary of State for the Environment could issue codes of recommended practice relating to the content, style, distribution and cost of local authority publicity and local authorities would be required to keep separate accounts of expenditure on publicity; rating authorities in England and Wales would be required to set a rate on or before the first day of the financial year.

Abolition of Domestic Rates etc (Scotland) Act 1987
1st reading: November 27 1986
2nd reading: December 9 1986 by 258 (Government) to 204 (Lab, Lib, SDP, 1 SNP, PC, JE Powell (OUP))
Royal Assent: May 15 1987
Provisions: abolished the domestic rating system in Scotland and provided for the finance of local government there by the imposition of the Community Charge or poll tax.

Local Government Act 1988
1st reading: June 26 1987
2nd reading: July 6 1987 by 286 (Government) to 212 (Lab, Lib, SNP, PC, J.Fookes (Con))
Royal Assent: March 24 1988
Provisions: regulated local and public authorities' functions in connection with public supply or works contracts; financial assistance for housing purposes; provisions on publicity, administration and auditing. Clause 28 of the Act outlawed the "promotion" of homosexuality by local authorities.

Local Government Finance Act 1988
1st reading: December 3 1987
2nd reading: December 16/17 1987 by 341 (Government) to 269 (Lab, Lib Dem, SDP, SNP, Plaid Cymru, OUP, DUP, UPUP and 17 Conservatives)
Royal Assent: July 29 1988
Provisions: replacement of the rating system with the poll tax or Community Charge. Nicholas Ridley, Environment secretary, said the Bill aimed to "abolish the inequities of the present domestic rating system".
Rebellion: Conservative MPs led by Michael Heseltine criticised the new charge in the debate. Edward Heath said it would be "unfair and unworkable". 17 Tories voted against the second reading, reducing the Government majority to 72. Conservative rebels were: A. Beaumont-Dark (Birmingham Selly Oak), W. Benyon (Milton Keynes), P. Cormack (Staffs SW), J. Critchley (Aldershot), Sir I. Gilmour (Chesham), P. Goodhart (Beckenham), A. Hargreaves(Birmingham Hall Green), B. Hayhoe (Brentford), E. Heath (Old Bexley), M. Irvine (Ipswich), D. Knox (Staffs Moorlands), J. Lester (Broxtowe), Sir A. Meyer (Clwyd NW), C. Morrison (Devizes), P. Temple-Morris (Leominster), R. Squire (Hornchurch), Sir G. Young (Acton).
On April 18 at beginning of report stage, Michael Mates (Con)

proposed an amendment creating a banded system related to ability to pay: 38 Tories voted against the Government in favour of the amendment and at least 10 abstained, cutting the Government majority to 25. (See section on voting records).

Local Government and Housing Act 1989
1st reading: February 1 1989
2nd reading: February 14 1989, by 279 (Government plus OUP, UPUP) to 203 (Lab, Lib Dem, SDP, SNP, Plaid Cymru)
Royal assent: November 16 1989
Provisions: restrained political activity of local government employees in line with the Widdicombe Report of 1986. Extensive changes to housing finance including a "ring fence" system to stop councils subsidising rents out of rates/ community charge. Local authorities no longer required to maintain a housing stock.

Local Government Bill 1991
Introduced: November 5 1991
2nd reading:
Provisions: Local Government Commission for England (Scotland and Wales to be reviewed separately) will recommend changes in structure, including creation of more single-tier unitary authorities. League tables of councils' performance to be compiled by Audit Commission.Additional council services must be put out to tender, including architectural engineering and property management, police support, school transport, theatre and arts management.

Local Government Finance Bill 1991
Introduced: November 1 1991
2nd reading: November 11-12 1991 by 339 (Government, J.Kilfedder(UPUP)) to 245 (Lab, Lib Dem, Ind SDP, SNP, PC)
Provisions: Abolishes community charge (poll tax) to be replaced by new council tax, based on value of a home within eight bands. Home will be assumed to contain two people: one person households will qualify for 25 per cent rebate. Councillors who fail to pay poll tax or council tax will not be allowed to take part in votes on financial issues.

'Once Mrs Thatcher, who described it as her "flagship" had gone, the poll tax was doomed'

INNER CITIES

THERE ARE two kinds of political issue: those the parties choose to promulgate and those that are forced upon them. The state of the inner cities was forced on to the agenda by the wave of rioting which began in Brixton, south London, on the night of April 11 1981 and spread through the hot nights of summer to Toxteth, Liverpool, and Moss Side, Manchester, in July. Brixton got Lord Scarman, whose report blamed the violence on grievances over housing, unemployment and lack of political clout, particularly in the black community. Liverpool got Michael Heseltine, who descended on the city with a sense of reforming passion which even opponents admired. The resurrection of Liverpool, the Environment secretary said, was not a matter for the Government alone: it could only be done in partnership.

But the Government's vision of partnership had more place for business and industry than it had for local government. In Glasgow a harmonious collaboration between central and local government was transforming the city: but elsewhere, first in the London docklands and Liverpool, and later in other centres, the strategy of renaissance left local government in the cold. By 1989 urban development corporations were directing the fortunes of eight more blighted areas: Trafford Park, in Manchester, Teesside, Tyne and Wear, the Black Country, Sheffield, Bristol, Leeds and Central Manchester with Government financial backing which amounted to £543m in 1990-91.

Some, like Lord Scarman in Brixton, favoured different solutions; solutions which implied a radical shift in Government thinking. In December 1985 a Church of England report, Faith In The City, called for increased Government spending to erad-icate need: spending on job creation and on higher welfare payments, including a sharp increase in child benefit. One way to raise this money, it dared to suggest, was to cut back on tax relief on mortgage interest. A Government spokesman (or according to some reports, a senior Government minister) condemned the report as "Marxist".

By now the inner city was the stuff of promises, assigned a separate section in the Conservative manifesto of 1987. "We must do something about the inner cities," Mrs Thatcher declared as she stood on the staircase at Conservative Central Office on June 12 after her re-election. And though closer scrutiny seemed to suggest that the problem she had in mind was the state of the Tory vote in those cities, she embarked a fortnight later on a personal fact-finding mission. On September 16 the cameras caught her standing in a wasteland which had once been the site of one of the largest engineering works on Teesside, and pledging that the great days would return – through a partnership of Government, local councils and industry. She returned determined to strengthen the inner city strategy, which she put in the hands of a thrustful younger minister, Kenneth Clarke.

The result, launched by Mrs Thatcher amid great fanfares on March 7 1988, was the Action on Cities programme, worth £3 billion in 1988-89 and £4 billion in 1990-91.

But that was not by any means all new money, since it incorporated a variety of programmes already under way. The success of the programme was clearly going to depend on the involvement of the private sector, marshalled by a new organisation called British Urban Development, to be run

DECLINE OF CONSERVATIVE SUPPORT IN THE BIG CITIES
% OF VOTE IN GENERAL ELECTIONS:

	Birmingham			Manchester			Liverpool			Leeds			Glasgow			
	Con	Lab	L/A	Con	Lab	L/A	Con	Lab	L/A	Con	Lab	L/A	Con	Lab	L/A	Nat
1970	48	49	2	44	53	3	44	51	4	43	50	7	32	50	0	17
1983	39	42	18	30	50	19	29	47	20	35	36	29	19	52	21	8
1987	39	45	16	28	54	18	17	57	26	34	40	26	13	62	15	10

SEATS HELD ON COUNCIL
(END OF MAY)

	Birmingham			Manchester			Liverpool			Leeds			Glasgow			
	Con	Lab	L/A	Con	Lab	L/A	Con	Lab	L/A	Con	Lab	L/A	Con	Lab	L/A	Nat
1971*	81	67	8	68	81	0	82	67	7	71	45	4	16†	66	-	1
1976	66	52	8	45	54	0	17	42	40	50	38	8	17	55	-	-
1981	52	68	6	23	72	4	21	40	38	29	62	8	11	58	3	-
1986	43	70	4	7	86	6	7	54	37	28	58	11	5	59	2	-
1991	32	71	12	5	85	9	2	62**	27‡	21	67	10	4	59	2	-

* before reorganisation of local government. † There were also 28 Progressives: this party later merged with the Conservatives.
** Also 5 Broad Left (Militant suported). ‡ Also 1 Liberal and 1 SDP.
L/A denotes councillors of Liberal Party, then of Alliance, then of Social and Liberal Democrats.

by Hartley Booth (who in July 1991 would be named as her successor as Conservative candidate for Finchley). It sought to persuade 11 large companies to invest £5m apiece. But the whole ambitious enterprise was the prisoner of the climate when it was launched. It was not designed for recession. Just as recession transformed the image of London docklands from a 21st-century venture in modern entrepreneurship to a tract of empty offices and unlettable upmarket housing, so BUD found itself loaded with land it could not sell. Its operations were scaled down and in two cases taken over by local Labour councils.

Yet Heseltine, back at Environment, found much to celebrate when he toured the inner cities in May 1991. He called them "deserts of dereliction transformed into modern human society".

In an attempt to rekindle local business enthusiasm, he staged a competition: 16 councils, of which 11 were chosen, would be invited to bid for a share of £75m to be spent on neighbourhood programmes over five years. Those selected, he announced on July 31, were Bradford, Dearne Valley (including Rotherham, Doncaster and Barnsley), Lewisham, Liverpool, Manchester, Middlesbrough, Newcastle, Nottingham, Tower Hamlets,

Wirral and Wolverhampton: those disappointed were Birmingham, Bristol, Salford, Sheffield, Stockton and Sunderland.

Heseltine also insisted that the Government wanted to work with local councils, but some of them were wary. They cited cuts in public expenditure which had cramped their ambitions and offset the Government's publicised aid for the cities. The development corporations, they claimed, had grabbed too great a share of the action. Jeremy Beecham, the Labour leader in Newcastle, complained that councils had been painted out of the picture in much the same way that people who fell out of favour used to disappear from the photographs in the Kremlin.

In the late summer of 1991, urban riots unexpectedly flared again; first in Cardiff, then on the Blackbird Leys estate in Oxford where the trouble was caused by joy-riders, and finally in a week of trouble on and around the Meadow Well estate on North Tyneside. To the fury of some Conservatives, the new Archbishop of Canterbury, Dr George Carey, linked the Tyneside disturbances with high levels of unemployment, poverty and social deprivation in the area. ●

'She was determined to strengthen the inner city strategy with a £3 billion Action on Cities programme'

THE ENVIRONMENT

TO JUDGE by the party manifestos, the condition of the environment did not matter very much in the politics of 1979. The Conservatives allotted it just 91 words; Labour thought "this important issue" worth about 150. The Liberals were rather more generous. The Ecology party's entire manifesto was devoted to the environment, but few had heard of them.

All that changed dramatically by the end of the Thatcher years. A variety of factors, including disasters like Chernobyl in April 1986, pressures from the EC, and the increasingly effective operations of pressure groups at home, helped propel the issue close to the top of the political agenda, particularly for young voters. An ICM poll for the Guardian in September 1990 put it second to the poll tax as the most serious issue facing the country. And of all the great issues, it was the one where the electorate had least faith in the conventional political parties to get things right. In May 1991, when the Green party was in decline, a MORI poll graphically demonstrated this point. Asked which party had the best policies on unemployment, education, health care and managing the economy, respondents overwhelmingly chose either the Conservatives or Labour, whose joint ratings varied from 56 to 71 per cent. But on the environment, only 23 per cent chose the main parties: 44 per cent preferred the Greens.

Great numbers of people who had never even considered them now became deeply concerned about three issues in particular.

● Global warming, or the greenhouse effect, where gases, of which the chief was carbon dioxide, trapped heat reflected back from the earth, causing substantial change in the nature of the climate, threatening a rise in sea levels which could cause extensive flooding in coastal areas across the world.

● Degradation of the ozone layer, eating away at our natural shield against ultra-violet radiation, so increasing our vulnerability to conditions like skin cancer. The main agent was CFCs, a man-made gas, widely employed to make refrigerators and air conditioners efficient.

● Acid rain, the main agent being sulphur dioxide, especially from coal-fired power stations, motor vehicles and some kinds of industrial plant; a particular offender being power stations using fossil fuel.

In the early years of the decade the Government was repeatedly asked to react to such threats with rather more urgency. Thus in 1984 the Commons select committee on the environment declared itself "gravely disturbed" by Government policy on atmospheric pollution and especially by its lack of serious research. Though sulphur dioxide emissions had been reduced by 37 per cent since 1970, mainly because of the collapse of our heavy industry, we were still the worst offenders in Europe apart from Italy. The Royal Commission on Environmental Pollution – a permanent body – complained in the same year that policy on pollution control suffered from lack of resources, lack of planning, lack of continuity and secretiveness. And Britain declined to join the Thirty Per Cent Club, a group of countries pledging themselves to reductions of at least 30 per cent in sulphur dioxide.

Government moves to reduce the permitted

SULPHUR DIOXIDE (SO²) EMISSIONS.
ESTIMATED EMISSIONS BY SOURCE AND TYPE OF FUEL, (THOUSAND TONNES)

	1979	1984	1989	% of all, 1989
Domestic	264	158	135	4
Commercial:				
public service	221	148	88	2
power stations	3,242	2,589	2,644	71
refineries	228	115	109	3
agriculture	30	10	7	-
other industry	1,409	593	595	16
railways	14	6	3	-
road	55	43	60	2
civil air	2	2	1	-
shipping	67	55	57	2
TOTAL	5.531	3,719	3,699	

CARBON DIOXIDE (CO²) EMISSIONS.
(MILLION TONNES)

	1979	1984	1989	% of all, 1989
Domestic	25	22	23	14
Commercial:				
public service	10	9	8	5
power stations	62	49	52	33
refineries	5	5	5	3
agriculture	1	1	1	*
other	53	36	36	23
rail	1	1	1	*
road	21	23	29	19
civil aircraft	*	1	1	*
shipping	2	2	2	1
TOTAL	181	148	157	100

Source: Digest of Environmental Protection and Water statistics

LEGISLATION

Environmental Protection Act 1990
1st reading: December 20 1989
2nd reading: January 15 1990 by 288 (Government, Lib Dem) to 202 (Lab, SDP)
Royal Assent: November 1 1990
Provisions: stricter controls over pollution through inspection of air, water and land pollution by the same agency (Her Majesty's Inspectorate of Pollution) rather than three separate organisations as before. Stricter measures on litter. New controls over who can operate waste sites and the rules they must observe. Separate agencies for England, Wales and Scotland to replace the Nature Conservancy Council (attacked by opponents as a weakening of protection).
Rebellion: on April 30 1990 a move by Dame Janet Fookes (Con Plymouth Drake) to force the Government to draw up a scheme for compulsory registration of dogs was defeated by 275 to 263. Fifty Conservatives voted against the Government. On July 5 a Lords amendment to the same effect was carried against the Government by 155 to 83, but on October 29 this was reversed in the Commons by 274 to 271, a majority of three, with 43 Conservatives voting against the Government.

levels of lead in petrol reflected a response to three different sorts of pressure: the requirements of the EC – "now arguably the single most important and effective influence in British environmental policy and politics", according to John McCormick in his book British Politics And The Environment (Earthscan Publications); the activities of a pressure group called Clear, directed by the veteran campaigner Des Wilson; and the advice of the RCEP. And though at the end of the decade the Government could fairly claim to have gone further than most of its EC counterparts in providing tax incentives for motorists to switch to unleaded fuel, it had done so later than some others. A Government pledge to clean-up Britain's polluted beaches followed EC pressure and a threat to prosecute after a quarter of beaches had been found to be below the standards set by an EC directive in 1975. It was pressure from Europe, too, which did most to ensure the cleaning-up of water.

Recycling in Britain remained well behind the best practices in Europe. The safe and efficient treatment of waste generally, including the dangers of methane from landfill sites, are being tackled seriously, although local authorities complain they are badly short of resources. There is still no solution to the problems of dealing with nuclear waste, becoming more acute as decommissioning of nuclear power stations begins and Britain imports more spent fuel for reprocessing. The import of toxic waste for incineration continues to be a profitable and contentious business.

By the late eighties there was clearly a growing awareness of environmental dangers, and a greater sense of urgency was developing at Westminster and in Whitehall. At Montreal in 1987 a British government which until then had seemed reluctant to set hard targets for phasing out CFCs, reversed its position and offered to stage the follow-up conference in London. The former factories, mines and nuclear inspectorates were reorganised into a new monitoring organisation, Her Majesty's Inspectorate of Pollution.

In June 1988, in approving an EC directive on levels of emission from large combustion plants, the Government promised a 60 per cent reduction in sulphur dioxide emissions by 2003 – a tougher target than some it had previously rejected. In speeches to the Royal Society and the Conservative party conference Mrs Thatcher seemed to put herself at the head of a great international crusade to save the threatened environment. On April 26 1990 a seminar on the greenhouse effect was held at 10 Downing Street; in May Mrs Thatcher committed Britain to pegging carbon dioxide emissions by 2005; and in June the world was summoned to London to discuss the ozone layer. Agreement was reached on June 30 1990 to phase out CFCs completely by the end of the century.

The conversion was under way even before the totally unexpected success of the Green party (formerly the Ecology party) in the European elections of June 15 1989 when it captured 15 per cent of the vote and finished ahead of the Social and Liberal Democrats. The Prime Minister's interest may even have helped the Greens by making their case look more mainstream and politically legitimate. Environment secretary Ridley continued to disparage the Greens as the marginal inhabitants of a fantasy land, but a month after the European elections he was replaced by a greener, younger Chris Patten, who believed that green values must not just decorate but permeate the whole of Government policy.

The high point of the new environmentalism came with the publication in 1989 of a consultative paper called Blueprint For A Green Economy prepared by Patten's adviser David Pearce – commissioned by Ridley, but seized on and thrust into prominence by Patten. This called for greater weight is to be attached to environmental values throughout government, and advocated the creation of incentives which, as with the preferential taxation of unleaded petrol, would harness the purchasing power of the consumer to propel manufacturers into better ecological practices. This was followed by committed green-values speeches, quite unlike anything heard from Environment secretaries before, delivered by Patten at the Conservative party conferences of 1989 and 1990 in which he promised to rid Britain of its tag "The dirty man of Europe".

In some senses the rhetoric was running ahead of reality, especially where green philosophy collided with the free market economy. One example was water, where demands from Europe for higher British standards, again with a threat to prosecute, gravely embarrassed the Government and even forced a delay in the privatisation programme. It was originally intended that the new privatised water authorities should regulate their own standards, but that was successfully challenged as a breach of EC law, and a National Rivers Authority was created to control discharges into rivers.

Yet even at its peak the new governmental commitment to environmental concern fell far short of the full green agenda. It would not, for a start, take on the motor car. ("We are not going to do away with the great car economy!" Mrs Thatcher promised in March 1990: a £12.4 billion road-building programme over the next 10 years was part of the proof of that.)

Patten's White Paper, This Common Inheritance, published in September 1990, disappointed the pressure groups, not so much for what it said, since it represented the strongest programme of environmental philosophy yet published by any British government, but because of the solid new commitments that had been hoped for but failed to appear.

It endorsed the philosophy of sustainable development advanced by the UN World Commission on Environment and Development headed by the Norwegian prime minister Gro Harlem Brundtland in April 1987 called Our Common Future, and in a bid to ensure that green values permeated the whole of Government thinking promised that every department would have one minister with environmental responsibilities.

But the Cabinet committee, chaired by Mrs Thatcher, which supervised it had struck out provisions said to have been in Patten's own strategy, particularly those, like a projected Carbon Tax, which could have been construed as anti-motorist.

As the nineties began the environmental tide was clearly receding. Green party support had fallen back to 1 or 2 per cent in the polls and the onset of recession had switched public concern back towards economic issues. Growth, which in the boom years of the later eighties had come to be widely seen as a bit of a problem, was once more sought after with urgency and desire. ●

EUROPE

IT BEGAN with a row over money. Mrs Thatcher went to the European Community summit in Dublin in November 1979 determined to get her rights. Britain, she told her fellow heads of government, had been paying far too much to the Community and wanted a £1,000m reduction. In language whose brutality caused diplomats to wince, she told them: "We want our money." They offered her, at the end of the meeting, a meagre £350m. She rejected it. At the Luxembourg summit of April 1980 they upped the offer to £760m. Again, nothing doing.

A bargain was eventually struck at a meeting of EC foreign ministers in Brussels in May 1980. Britain's net contribution would be cut from £1,000m to £371m in 1980 and £445m in 1981. Mrs Thatcher was still not satisfied. The terms of the deal, she told her Foreign secretary Lord Carrington, were not even as good as the ones she had rejected in Luxembourg. The Cabinet overruled her. But she still wasn't finished. At the Stuttgart summit of July 1983 Mrs Thatcher said there could not be progress until Britain's just claims were met. In December the Athens summit failed on this account even to produce a communique. Brussels, in March, was another failure, amid reports that Britain might withhold all contributions unless it got its way. The dispute continued to rage until the Fontainebleau summit (June 1984). There they finally hit on a formula. Britain would get a rebate based on a fixed percentage of the difference between what it paid into the Community and what the Community spent in Britain. The figure arrived at was 66 per cent, the one Mrs Thatcher had gone there to get.

Even then she wasn't happy. Your wasteful ways, she continued to tell her EC colleagues, are costing Britain dear. She kept Britain out of ventures like the European Space Agency, since she could not be sure that they represented value for money.

But by now the core of the argument had explicitly shifted from mere financial wrangling to something more profound – a debate about the nature and the future of the Community: whether it should press on towards closer and closer integration, even finally federation; or whether it should remain, as Mrs Thatcher believed, a looser form of alliance, independent nations working together, what de Gaulle had called a "*Europe des patries*". That debate was to colour the whole of British politics for the rest of her government's life, to disturb and disrupt Thatcher's party and to bring about her downfall.

In 1986 it added a whole new dimension to an otherwise minor dispute about a helicopter manufacturer who had run into trouble. The company, Westland, planned a deal with an American rescuer. Defence secretary Heseltine, who believed that Britain's industrial future lay predominantly in collaboration with Europe, thought Westland should find a European partner. When none came forward he set out to create one.

That led to a grinding clash between two philosophies: Heseltine's Europeanism and the view of Mrs Thatcher and Industry secretary Leon Brittan that markets should rule, and that if Westland wanted a deal with Sikorski, that was what it should have. On January 9 1986. Heseltine left the

TRANSACTIONS WITH EC (£M)

	payments	receipts	net outflow
1979	1,626	550	1,076
1980	1,783	958	825
1981	2,188	1,675	513
1982	2,878	2,154	724
1983	2,994	2,235	759
1984	3,213	2,392	821
1985	3,789	1,760	2,029
1986	2,812	2,138	674
1987	4,066	2,282	1,784
1988	3,555	2,115	1,440
1989	4,443	2,143	2,300

LEGISLATION

European Communities (Amendment) Act 1986
1st reading: March 27 1986
2nd reading: April 23 1986 by 319 (Government 13 Lib) to 160 (Lab, 10 Con, 2 PC, 1 SNP, JE Powell (OUP))
Royal Assent: November 7 1986
Provisions: changed UK legislation to comply with the Single European Act, agreed at Luxembourg summit in December 1985 and signed in February 1986. The Act rewrote the definition of "the Treaties" and "the Common Treaties" in line with plans for the next stage in European harmonisation.
Ten Conservative MPs opposed the Bill on second reading. They were: J. Aitken (Thanet S), M. Brown (Brigg), N. Budgen (Wolverhampton SW), D. Conway (Shrewsbury), E. du Cann (Taunton), N. Hamilton (Tatton),R. Moate (Faversham), H. Proctor (Billericay), T. Taylor (Southend E), B. Walker (Tayside N).

Rebellion: Conservative MPs voting against the Government on motion approving ERM entry, October 23 1991:. J.Biffen (Shropshire N), Sir R.Body (Holland with Boston), J.Browne (Winchester), N.Budgen (Wolverhampton SW), T.Dicks (Hayes and Harlington), Mrs T.Gorman (Billericay), T.Janman (Thurrock), D.Mudd (Falmouth and Camborne), R.Shepherd (Aldridge Brownhills);T.Taylor (Southend East);N. Winterton (Macclesfield).

On November 21 1991,the Commons approved by 351 to 250 a Government motion endorsing the line to be taken at the Maastricht summit the following month. The motion said that Britain should be at the heart of Europe, while avoiding a federal Europe. Six Conservative MPs voted against the motion. They were:J.Biffen (Shropshire N), Sir R.Body (Holland with Boston), J.Browne (Winchester), Sir N.Fairbairn (Perth and Kinross), R.Shepherd (Aldridge-Brownhills) and N.Winterton (Macclesfield).
Since abstentions are not registered in the Commons it was not clear how many Conservatives deliberately abstained. But some who had voted immediately before on a Labour amendment failed to support the Government in this division. They included:W. Cash (Stafford), J.Cran (Beverley), A.Favell (Stockport), C.Gill (Ludlow), T.Jessel (Twickenham),

R.Moate (Faversham), Sir T.Taylor, (Southend East), N.Tebbit (Chingford) and Mrs A.Winterton (Congleton).
A Labour amendment said the Government's divisions were preventing the UK from exercising a decisive influence on the EC's future. It called for an extension of majority voting on social and environmental issues. Labour MPs reported to have abstained on this amendment were: T.Benn (Chesterfield), D.Canavan (Falkirk), R.Clay (Sunderland North), J.Corbyn (Islington North), R.Cryer (Bradford South), Mrs G.Dunwoody (Crewe and Nantwich), T.Fields (Liverpool, Broadgreen), J.Hughes (Coventry North East), D.Lambie (Cunninghame South), R.Leighton (Newham NE), M.Madden (Bradford West), B.Michie (Sheffield Heeley), A.Mitchell (Great Grimsby), D.Nellist (Coventry South East), P.Shore (Bethnal Green and Stepney), D.Skinner (Bolsover), N.Spearing (Newham South) and D.Winnick (Walsall North).

CRITERIA FOR 'CONVERGENCE'
The tests of convergence agreed at Maastricht on December 9 and 10, 1991, were:
- no annual budget deficit over 3 per cent of GDP
- national debt reduced to 60 per cent of GDP
- no devaluation within the ERM
- the national rate of inflation in the year preceding the decision most be not more than 1.5 per cent above the average of the three states with the lowest rates, and the rate must be sustainably low
- Government bond interest rates most be not more than 2 per cent above the average of the three best performances in the Community.

QUALIFIED MAJORITY VOTING. (QMV)
It was agreed at Maastricht to give wider application to this system, first introduced in 1986 for legislation on the single market, in place of the national veto. Voting power reflected the size of each member country, as follows:

Germany, France, Italy, the United Kingdom	10
Spain	8
Belgium, Greece, Netherlands, Portugal	5
Denmark, Ireland	3
Luxembourg	2

Cabinet, claiming debate had been stifled. In the subsequent inquest, Brittan had to go, too; at the height of the crisis, it even seemed briefly possible that Mrs Thatcher herself might not survive.

The signing in February 1986 of the Single European Act, implemented in Britain after ill-attended debates in the Commons by the European Communities (Amendment) Bill of 1986, created far less excitement: yet it helped to account for much of the trouble which later engulfed the party. Its primary purpose was to establish a free internal market in the Community by the end of 1992. But it had other clear implications of a much less Thatcherite kind: the three-stage plan for progress towards economic and monetary union produced by the President of the Commission, the French socialist Jacques Delors, in April 1989 flowed directly, he insisted, from the Single European Act. Stage one was no great problem: it was mostly about breaking down barriers and opening up markets and there was no more avid supporter of that than Mrs Thatcher. Even this part of the package had its unacceptable propositions: it said, for example, that all member countries should be members of the Exchange Rate Mechanism (ERM) of the European Monetary System, a view she had specifically rejected at the Hanover summit of June 1988 which had set Delors in motion.

But the more substantial problems came later. Stage two demanded the operation of a common monetary policy and a European planning machinery: stage three transferred even greater control over national budgets to Brussels, demanded a single currency, and went right to the threshold of economic and monetary union.

To Mrs Thatcher such things were anathema. She had run up her standard in a speech at Bruges on September 20 1988. "Willing and active cooperation between independent sovereign states," she said, "is the best way to build a successful European community. To try to suppress nationhood and concentrate power at the centre of a European conglomerate would be highly damaging and would jeopardise the objectives we seek to achieve...We have not successfully rolled back the frontiers of the state in Britain to see them reimposed at a European level with a European super-

state exercising a new dominance from Brussels ...Enterprise is the key...the lesson of the economic history of Europe in the 1970s and 1980s is that central planning and detailed control don't work."

The Bruges speech irrevocably established Mrs Thatcher's position as leader of the Euro-sceptics rather than the unifying and healing leader most of her predecessors would have preferred to be. The ERM, which required subscribing members to keep their currencies within prescribed bands, became an increasingly bruising issue. Chancellor Lawson and Foreign secretary Howe were eager to join: Lawson, indeed, had adopted a policy of shadowing the German Mark, which was a kind of surrogate for ERM membership. Mrs Thatcher would not have it; her personal economic adviser, Sir Alan Walters, seemed all too clearly to speak for her when he called it "half-baked".

But at the Madrid summit of June 25-27 1989 the Prime Minister, under pressure from Lawson and Howe, conceded. For the first time she set out the terms on which Britain might be ready to join: tough terms, certainly, whose fulfilment looked distant – but at last some commitment was there. The Government also undertook to produce alternative recommendations for the EC's future development to those of Delors.

The removal of Howe from the Foreign Office on July 24 was seen as the price for the ground he had taken from her in Madrid. And frustrations over this issue, brought to a head by the way he was openly second-guessed by Alan Walters, helped to account for the resignation of Chancellor Lawson on October 26 1989.

But the change in these two top offices did little to resolve the tensions in the party. Hurd at the Foreign Office and Major at the Treasury were by no means Euro-fanatics and certainly not federalists, and they moved with more caution than the men they succeeded. But both were plainly more ready than Mrs Thatcher to let the process of integration evolve and to take a more constructive line in Europe than her instincts allowed. The new triumvirate of Thatcher, Hurd and Major settled into an uneasy accommodation.

British membership of ERM was announced on October 8 1990. Delors was still resisted, but resisted more constructively. Britain remained opposed to instituting a single currency, but Major came up with a plan for a hard Ecu as a 13th community currency which might supersede the pound and its fellows one day, if the people of Europe wished it.

The compromise stuck, more or less, until the Rome summit of October 27-28 1990 and the statement Mrs Thatcher made to the Commons on her return. The statement itself was unexceptional and stuck close to the Cabinet's unwritten concordat. But Mrs Thatcher's impromptu answers to the questions which followed were not. Here she simply let rip, delighting her ultras and leaving others aghast, even managing to disparage Major's pet scheme for the Ecu.

Howe resigned on November 1 and in a venomous personal statement to the Commons on November 13 accused her, in effect, of sabotaging her colleagues. Heseltine, out of office since Westland, said he would run for the leadership: and the contest began which sank her.

All of this was in striking contrast to the way the Opposition parties had handled the issue. In 1988 Jacques Delors had enthused the TUC with his vision of a European social charter: socialism by the back door, as Mrs Thatcher's acolytes called it – which was one reason why Labour liked it. By the time the issue began to break the Conservative party, Labour, which as late as the 1983 election had still been committed to pulling Britain out, had become a largely Europhile party, committed to ERM well before the Government and constantly chiding the Cabinet for being bad Europeans. But they stopped far short of federalism. That cause was left to the Liberal Democrats, who alone had been a party of Europe all along.

John Major thus went to the Maastricht summit of December 9 and 10 1991 far less committed to the project of economic, monetary and political union than either Kinnock or Ashdown would have been. The outcome was agreement on a treaty, but with two substantial exemptions to meet British reservations. The first was on the **single European currency**. By December 31, 1996, EC finance ministers would be empowered to decide that at least seven states had met the terms of economic "convergence" (see page 195) necessary for the project to go ahead. If these tests were satisfied in 1996, then a date would be set for these states to adopt the Ecu as their common currency. If that proved impossible, then an automatic process would begin which would produce the single currency in 1999, even if only five states qualified. The United Kingdom, however, was exempted from these arrangements. It would not be required to adopt the single currency unless the British Parliament voted to do so.

The second was the **social chapter** of the treaty, which included provisions on workers' rights to consultation, guaranteed working conditions, maximum hours and a minimum wage, and equal opportunities for women. Britain opposed the chapter because of feared effects on industrial competitiveness and a wish to safeguard the rolling back of union power achieved in the Thatcher years. The Liberal Democrats also opposed the social chapter. To meet these objections the other 11 member states agreed to delete the chapter from the Treaty and to develop their own regulations outside it.

Britain also succeeded in deleting from the draft treaty all reference to a **federal** destiny for the Community. Instead it expressed the intention to move to "ever closer union", which many who signed believed was much the same thing.

John Major described the deal as the best possible outcome for Britain and for the Community. Labour and the Liberal Democrats objected that it effectively created a two-tier community with Britain as the sole occupant of the lower tier. Opting out of the social chapter approach, Labour added, would relegate British working people to the status of second class citizens within the Community. Conservative anti-federalists, though welcoming the exemptions, feared that Britain was still aboard what they called a conveyor belt to eventual federalism. ●

FOREIGN AFFAIRS

MRS THATCHER'S instinctive approach to foreign affairs grew out of her concept of freedom. It coloured her judgment of the three great powers with whom she had to deal: America, Russia and the developing power of Europe. The United States, especially under Reagan, was the sort of society she admired: a land with a culture of self-help and free enterprise, suspicious of government and every form of collectivism, proud of the kind of success that comes from tough individual endeavour. The Soviet Union, at least in her early years, was much as Reagan had depicted it: an evil empire, for the destruction of whose system all true lovers of freedom must urgently pray. The invasion of Afghanistan in December 1979 looked like proof of all she had ever feared and warned against. After the empire had crumbled, prominent anti-Communists from the former Iron Curtain countries gathered at the Conservative party conference in Brighton in 1990 as if to pay fealty to her for the part her example had played in ensuring their liberation; which was no doubt how she saw it too.

Europe, with its weakness for building bureaucracies and dabbling in socialist solutions, came somewhere between the two poles of the Soviet Union and America. Those who thought the greatest issue in British foreign policy was the choice that would have to be made between the special relationship and our role in Europe were asking a question she could scarcely comprehend. Both intuitively and intellectually she found the sacrifice of the relationship with Reagan's, or even Bush's, America too high a price to pay for any cause. Moments of trial confirmed what she had always

known: Britain and America stood solidly shoulder to shoulder; the Europeans could not be relied on.

On most of the foreign tests she faced – the Falklands, the American bombing of Libya, South Africa, the Gulf – she simply followed her instincts. To the outside world, British foreign policy must often have looked like little more than what Mrs Thatcher happened to be saying at the time. Yet sometimes she took advice and tempered her original preferences, as she did on Zimbabwe; as she also did on the Soviet Union once she had decided that Gorbachev was a man she could do business with.

Over Zimbabwe her preference must have been to recognise the Government of the black prime minister Bishop Muzorewa installed by the Smith regime. The Conservatives in opposition had come very close to endorsing him. Instead she deferred to the guidance of her Foreign secretary, Lord Carrington, and of Commonwealth leaders. When a constitutional conference called at Lancaster House in London in the autumn of 1979 arrived at a formula for free elections in Zimbabwe, she stood firm in its defence against old political friends who sought to reverse it. A senior Cabinet minister, Lord Soames, was despatched to Salisbury to manage the transition and supervise the elections of March 1980. Zimbabwe became independent on April 22 at the end of a process which even Opposition leaders in Britain found hard to criticise.

More often, though, the Commonwealth riled her, and never more than on South Africa, where the British Government did its utmost to scuttle the sanctions policy supported by everyone else.

OFFICIAL DEVELOPMENT ASSISTANCE FROM OECD MEMBERS AS % OF DONOR GNP

	1980	1985	1989
Canada	0.43	0.49	0.50*
Denmark	0.74	0.80	0.93
France	0.63	0.78	0.72*
Germany	0.44	0.47	0.41
Italy	0.15	0.26	0.39*
Japan	0.32	0.29	0.32*
Sweden	0.78	0.86	0.98
UK	0.35	0.33	0.31
United States	0.27	0.24	0.21*

* 1988 figure

Source: World Development Report 1990

UK AID AS % GNP 1979-1989

1979	1980	1981	1982	1983	1984	1985	1986	1987	1988	1989
0.52	0.35	0.43	0.37	0.35	0.33	0.33	0.31	0.28	0.32	0.31

Source: OECD

TOP 10 RECIPIENTS UK OVERSEAS AID FROM 1979
(INDIVIDUAL YEARS MAY BE UNREPRESENTATIVE BECAUSE OF RESPONSE TO PARTICULAR CRISES).

	Average 1979-83		Average 1984-88		1989 (£m)
1. India	118.0	India	115.2	India	99.5
2. Bangladesh	36.3	Bangladesh	38.3	Nigeria	63.0
3. Kenya	34.8	Kenya	37.0	Bangladesh	54.8
4. Tanzania	28.8	Sudan	28.4	Kenya	53.9
5. Sudan	28.2	Zambia	27.2	Ghana	50.2
6. Sri Lanka	27.2	Tanzania	25.4	Malawi	43.1
7. Zimbabwe	26.5	Malawi	24.4	Tanzania	38.1
8. Pakistan	22.0	Pakistan	20.4	Sudan	31.4
9. Zambia	20.7	Indonesia	20.1	Pakistan	31.1
10. Malawi	17.8	Sri Lanka	20.0	St Helena & dependencies	28.7

Source: derived from Annual Abstract of Statistics

LEGISLATION

Hong Kong Act 1985
1st reading: January 10 1985
2nd reading: January 21 1985, unopposed
Royal Assent: April 4 1985
Provisions: gave effect in UK law for the provisions of the UK-China agreement on the handover of Hong Kong in 1997 (signed December 19 1984 in Beijing). Though the Bill was unopposed, reservations were expressed in Parliament over plans to create a new nationality status for Hong Kong by Order in Council rather than by an Act of Parliament.
The order was published on October 17 1985 entitled The Nationality Provisions Of The Hong Kong Act 1985. It created a new category of citizenship, that of British National (Overseas), for the 3,250,000 people who held British Dependent Territories Citizenship. But BN(O) did not carry the right of abode in the UK nor was it transmissible by descent.

British Nationality (Hong Kong) Act 1990
1st reading: April 4 1990
2nd reading: April 19 1990, by 313 (Government, Lib Dem, SDP, 1 OUP, 1 Plaid Cymru, SNP, UPUP) to 216 (Lab, 2 DUP, 44 Con)

Royal Assent: July 26 1990
Provisions: provided for the acquisition of British citizenship by up to 50,000 selected Hong Kong residents, their spouses and children.
MPs – (all Labour) – voting against Government motion expressing full support for British forces in Gulf, modified by Labour amendment calling for minimum casualties, January 21 1991
Ms D. Abbott (Hackney N), T. Banks (Newham NW), H. Barnes (Derbyshire NE), T. Benn (Chesterfield), R. Brown (Edinburgh Leith), B. Clay (Sunderland N), H. Cohen (Leyton), J. Corbyn (Islington N), T. Dalyell (Linlithgow), T. Fields (Liverpool Broadgreen), Mrs M. Fyfe (Glasgow Maryhill), G. Galloway (Glasgow Hillhead), Mrs M. Gordon (Bow), B. Grant (Tottenham), D. Hinchcliffe (Wakefield), J. Hood (Clydesdale), J. Hughes (Coventry NE), D. Lambie (Cunninghame S), J. Lamond (Oldham C), K. Livingstone (Brent E), E. Loyden (Liverpool Garston), J. McAllion (Dundee E), J. McFall Dumbarton), W. McKelvey (Kilmarnock), M. Madden (Bradford W), Mrs A. Mahon (Halifax), C. Mullin (Sunderland S), D. Nellist (Coventry SW), R. Parry (Liverpool Riverside), Ms D. Primarolo (Bristol S), D. Skinner (Bolsover), G. Strang (Edinburgh E), Mrs A. Wise (Preston), J. Wray (Glasgow Provan). Tellers were D. Canavan (Falkirk W) and R. Cryer (Bradford S).

At Nassau in 1985 she stood alone against tough economic sanctions, eventually did a deal which mildly watered down her colleagues' intentions, then publicly rubbished what they had agreed. "If it is one against 48," she said at her press conference after the Kuala Lumpur summit on October 24 1989, "then I am very sorry for the 48." Across the third world she was sometimes reviled as a friend of apartheid. That she fiercely rejected. The difference between Britain and those who disagreed with it was not in their views of apartheid, she said, but in their commitment to practicality.

Early in 1982 Nicholas Ridley returned from the Falklands proposing that sovereignty be transferred to Argentina, which would then lease the islands back to Britain. This in part reflected a Whitehall assumption that continued British rule of these distant outposts was no longer realistic and a deal would have to be done some time.

The Argentinian invasion of the islands on April 2 1982 put paid to all that. When the House of Commons met in emergency session on Saturday April 3 the mood was overwhelmingly for resolute action. While the task force steamed southwards, the search began for diplomatic solutions, but all failed: because of Argentinian intransigence, said the British and Americans, though some Opposition MPs suspected the British government did not wish to be denied its military triumph. South Georgia was reclaimed on April 25 (it was then, and not as is sometimes supposed after the sinking of the Belgrano on May 2, that Mrs Thatcher commanded: "Rejoice"). The Argentinians surrendered on June 14. Two hundred and fifty five British servicemen lost their lives and 600 Argentinian servicemen. The war was conducted on a high tide of public approval, though hard questions were still being asked. A committee under Lord Franks was told to inquire into events leading up to the Argentinian invasion, but the issues pursued by MPs like Tam Dalyell – especially the charge that the Belgrano was sunk not just outside the exclusion zone but while steaming away – was never investigated or even, some complained, fully answered in Parliament. And Britain was left with the task of rehabilitating and garrisoning the islands at enormous cost

for an indefinite period, since the islanders had been promised that their wishes would be paramount; and their wish was to stay with Britain.

Another invasion on October 25 1983 – that of Grenada by America where the Government had been ousted and the Prime Minister murdered – was a different matter. Britain was not consulted, though this was a Commonwealth country and the Queen was the Head of State. The British government had rejected intervention and signalled its displeasure in language entirely foreign to the usual dulcet exchanges between Mrs Thatcher and President Reagan.

But there were no such exchanges or doubts when in April 1986 Reagan asked for the use of British bases for America's bombing raid on Libya. Though Britain was never a friend of Colonel Gadafy – especially since the siege at his London embassy in April 1984 after a British policewoman was shot in the square outside – but London had reservations about rumoured American plans for an air strike. Yet when the call came, Mrs Thatcher's response was swift and unconditional: though once the dust had cleared it was made clear to Washington that further cooperation in enterprises of this kind was not to be taken for granted.

The question of Hong Kong and the New Territories was the subject of a high profile visit by Thatcher to Beijing in September 1982. Britain tried to secure either the status quo or a lease-back arrangement, but China insisted on the return of its "sovereign territory". Britain settled for the orderly transfer of the whole area in 1997, with guarantees for the future, and the Sino-British Joint Declaration was initialled in Beijing on September 26 1984. The Chinese government agreed that Hong Kong's capitalist character would be preserved for at least 50 years, with its free port and role as a financial centre, together with guarantees of freedom of speech and other basic rights.

But China soon sought to influence British policies *before* it took control in 1997. Beijing disliked plans for Hong Kong to move towards democracy (an enterprise, to be honest, for which neither Whitehall nor the Hong Kong establishment had shown much enthusiasm before). Direct elections for part of the Legislative Council were postponed from 1988 to 1991. Apprehensions about Chinese rule led to a brain drain of many professional people from Hong Kong. Their migration to Britain had been precluded by the British Nationality Act of 1981 which changed the status of the majority of residents from citizens of the UK and its colonies to citizens of British Dependencies and Territories, without the right of entry.

Britain was forced to respond to the popular outcry in Hong Kong following the Tienanmen Square massacre of June 1989. A compromise plan offered full rights of entry for a maximum of 50,000 heads of household and 175,000 dependants. These were people whose continuing presence in Hong Kong would be needed during the transition. There were disputes with Beijing over political protest in Hong Kong, and disagreement over the Basic Law which China was drafting to govern Hong Kong after 1997. It would only allow for an element of direct election to the Legislative Council by 2003, and an eventual fully-elected system, which after Tienanmen Square seemed unlikely.

The final showdown came in June 1991 with the dispute over Hong Kong's plan for a new airport. Intended to boost Hong Kong confidence, the project had been denounced by Beijing. Britain now climbed down, allowing China a substantial say in the airport plans and, more significantly, the right to be "consulted" on all Hong Kong issues of importance before 1997. Hong Kong accepted, more wearily than bitterly, that London had once again fatally failed to stand up to Beijing.

The mightiest conflict of a troubled 12 years under the Conservatives was presaged on August 2 1990 when the Iraqis invaded Kuwait and declared it part of their state. A UN demand for immediate withdrawal was ignored. Sanctions were imposed and the US, UK and other countries began military preparations. The UN set a deadline of January 15 1991 for withdrawal.

Intense activity, both official and unofficial (including visits to Baghdad by senior British politicians like Edward Heath and Tony Benn), failed to move the Iraqi president, Saddam Hussein.

An air bombardment began on the night of January 16-17 and lasted for five weeks. It was followed on February 24 by a land assault which swiftly destroyed Iraqi resistance. This was called off on February 28 when Iraq agreed to comply with UN resolutions. It was judged at this point that the war aims had been met. Prime Minister Major had told the Commons that these were to remove Iraq from Kuwait, restore its legitimate government, re-establish peace and security in the area and uphold the authority of the UN: they did not include the removal of Saddam, who remained in power in Baghdad. Because of the threat this created for some of his population, especially the Kurds in the North, the Allies remained in the area to give them protection, creating "safe havens" along lines proposed by Major; but their safety looked far from secure as the Allied withdrawal proceeded through the summer of 1991.

At the peak of the war 43,000 British troops were deployed. On January 15 the Commons debated events in Iraq on a motion for the adjournment which was carried by 534 votes to 57, effectively endorsing Government policy. On January 21 the Commons approved a Government motion expressing full support for Britain's troops in the Gulf, and incorporating a Labour amendment saying casualties should be kept to a minimum. This was carried 563-34. Fewer than 150 Allied lives were lost, including 17 Britons, nine killed by US "friendly fire". Iraqi casualties were estimated at 150,000, perhaps even more. Extensive environmental damage was done thoughout the region: when the Iraqis left Kuwait they fired some of its oil wells, with consequences it would take decades to eradicate.

France is the only country of the world's most powerful industrial nations to achieve the UN target for overseas aid of 0.7 per cent of gross national product. Britain, which in 1979 was second to France among the Group of Seven nations, had sunk by the end of the eighties to sixth place. The decline was sharpest in the early years, when Sir Geoffrey Howe cut aid along with everything else: more easily, some believed, because overseas aid had ceased to be a separate ministry as it had been under Labour.

The slide continued until 1987 when the figure was 0.28 per cent. Spending on aid went up in real terms that year, but because it did not keep pace with the boom, the share of GNP for which it accounted was less.

The Western aid performance is even worse than it looks in that its outflow is offset by inflows of debt repayment – though it became more and more clear as the eighties progressed that some of these debts could never be repaid. Britain took several initiatives to try to redress this process. At the Venice summit of 1987 Chancellor Lawson proposed that interest on loans to the poorest countries of Africa should be paid at well below market levels. Major as prime minister suggested a two-thirds cut in bilateral debt of the poorest countries. In July 1991 the Government promised to write off £327m owed by Egypt, one of the biggest such concessions ever made to a third world country.

Few years produced such a crisis of need as 1991, with disasters in Bangladesh, the Sudan and across much of Africa. Though new tranches of aid were announced, most of it came out of existing budgets: only £30m was new money wrung out of the Treasury, and £10m, controversially, went to a fund-raising project run by the former deputy chairman of the party, Jeffrey Archer.

Three quarters of the contingency budget of the ODA (Overseas Development Administration) had gone in the first four weeks of the new financial year. Labour, who had never delivered the UN's 0.7 per cent, and the Liberal Democrats blamed Treasury stinginess rather than the minister, the liberal Lynda Chalker. Both were specifically pledged to hit the UN target if they came to office. Major promised more cautiously that it would be done when economic circumstances permitted. The judgment that the electorate might not favour higher spending on aid was somewhat contradicted by the huge sums raised by the likes of Bob Geldof with ventures like Band Aid.

Apart from the level of spending, there was contention between the parties over the basis on which claimants for aid were judged. The test was said to be "good government", economic and social, which Chalker said was simple good sense: there was no point in pouring in money which would be misused. The Opposition parties feared the test of good government tended to put too much weight on a British-style commitment to market economics. The Opposition also complained that nationally and internationally the response to disasters was too slow; Labour wanted an organisation geared to rapid reaction on the lines of France's Médecins Sans Frontières. British proposals to strengthen the UN's capacity to respond were endorsed at the G7 summit in July 1991. ●

'Heseltine warned
that anyone who
got too close to the
cruise bunkers
could be shot'

DEFENCE

DEFENCE was one of the five great issues listed in the statement of intent at the start of the
1979 Conservative manifesto. During the
past five years, the manifesto said, the military
threat to the world had steadily grown as the Communist bloc established virtual parity in strategic
nuclear weapons and substantial superiority in
conventional ones. Labour had cut down our
forces, weakened our defences, cut our contribution to Nato: the Conservatives would strengthen
our protection in an increasingly threatening
world.

Who better to execute such a commitment than
a leader already known around the world as the
Iron Lady? And almost immediately an issue
appeared that would let her demonstrate that resolution, contrasting it with the faint hearts of the parties opposite. In December 1979 Nato adopted
what was known as its twin-track policy. It called
for US-Soviet negotiations on arms control, but said
that if these failed Nato would modernise and augment its nuclear capability. The outgoing Labour
government under James Callaghan carried some
responsibility for the process. "Although Callaghan
had been spared the need to agree to accept US
cruise missiles into Britain," wrote Lawrence Freed-
man in The Thatcher Effect - A Decade Of Change
(edited by Denis Kavanagh and Anthony Seldon,
Oxford University Press), "his role at the four-
nation Guadeloupe summit at the start of 1979 was
central to the development of Nato policy." But
now, in opposition, Labour was moving to a
strongly unilateralist position on nuclear weapons,
which would bring it by 1983 to pledge a Labour
government to remove all nuclear bases from

British soil. Initially the Liberals opposed deployment, but their partners in the Alliance, the SDP,
were in favour, though on condition that a dual-key
system was provided, ensuring that the UK government had an effective veto over their use. Its 1983
manifesto did not commit the parties either way.

It was always expected that the arrival of cruise
missiles, first at Greenham Common in Berkshire
and later at Molesworth near Huntingdon, would
be a difficult and contentious moment which might
feed the demand for unilateral nuclear disarmament. In January 1983 Heseltine was chosen to
replace John Nott at Defence very much on that
consideration. The first cruise missiles reached
Greenham in November. Picketing, mainly by
women who, in a prolonged and largely peaceful
demonstration quite unlike any staged in Britain
before, took up permanent residence round the
perimeter, continued all the time they remained
there. (Heseltine had warned on November 1 that
anyone who got too close to the cruise bunkers
could be shot.)

A second issue, again very much to Mrs Thatcher's taste, was the replacement of the ageing
Polaris nuclear force, Britain's independent deterrent.

Again, the preparatory work had been done
under Callaghan, but now Labour was wholly
opposed to the Government's solution, announced
by Mrs Thatcher's first Defence secretary, Francis
Pym, to buy the Trident missile system from America, at a cost which before long had risen to £7.5 billion. The Liberal Social Democrat Alliance initially
opposed the purchase of Trident, though later,

GOVERNMENT SPENDING ON DEFENCE
1. Total spending on defence at current prices, £bn.
2. % increase on previous year in real terms.
3. % of government expenditure.
4. % of GDP.

	1978-1979	1979-1980	1980-1981	1981-1982	1982-1983	1983-1984	1984-1985	1985-1986	1986-1987	1987-1988	1988-1989	1989-1990	1990-1 (est)
1	7.5	9.2	11.2	12.6	14.4	15.5	17.1	17.9	18.2	18.9	19.1	20.8	22.1
2		+6.0	+3.0	+2.0	+7.0	+3.0	+6.0	-1.0	-2.0	-2.0	-6.0	-2.0	-1.0
3	11.5	11.9	12.2	12.2	12.4	12.6	13.0	12.9	12.4	12..2	11.8	11.7	11.3
4		4.4	4.7	4.8	5.0	5.0	5.2	4.9	4.7	4.4	4.0	4.0	4.0

INTERNATIONAL COMPARISONS OF DEFENCE SPENDING
1. Defence spending as percentage of GDP (market prices) 1990
2. Defence spending per head (US dollars) 1990

	1		2
Greece	5.6	US	1,208
US	5.5	Norway	844
Turkey	4.5	France	759
UK	4.0	UK	670
France	3.6	Germany	550
Norway	3.3	Denmark	508
Portugal	3.0	N'lands	497
Germany	2.9	Belgium	474
N'Lands	2.7	Italy	430
Belgium	2.5	Canada	425
Italy	2.3	Greece	375
Spain	2.0	L'bourg	262
Denmark	2.0	Spain	243
Canada	2.0	Portugal	165
L'bourg	1.2	Turkey	87

Source: Nato/MoD

These figures do not necessarily reflect the relative purchasing power of individual currencies and are therefore not a complete guide to comparative resource allocation.

under the influence of the former Labour Foreign secretary Dr David Owen, its position shifted.

In the early years of her Government Mrs Thatcher was closely in accord on defence issues with US President Ronald Reagan. But as the thaw in the Cold War began, tensions appeared. Mrs Thatcher might be able to do business with Mikhail Gorbachev, but that in her book was no grounds for relaxing one's guard. Reagan appeared to think otherwise. In her terms, he began to go soft on the nuclear issue. "A world without nuclear weapons," she said "would be less stable and more dangerous for all." But at his Reykjavik summit with Gorbachev in October 1986, Reagan confirmed Mrs Thatcher's worst fears by appearing to commit himself to the elimination of all nuclear weaponry, beginning with intermediate range missiles but going on to abolish the lot. What obstructed that intention was his determination to hang on to his Strategic Defence Initiative (SDI), popularly known as Star Wars, providing the Americans with a shield in space which would blunt any nuclear attack. To Gorbachev that meant the Americans handing themselves an advantage which the Soviet Union could not possibly match. Without the abandonment of SDI, he said, there could be no deal. The threat to Nato's nuclear strategy, and to Britain's Trident, was thus averted.

But there was no attempt to obstruct the process of the talks on intermediate range weapons (the INF talks), which in 1987 succeeded in sweeping away a whole class of weapons and meant the end of the presence of nuclear cruise missiles on British soil. Indeed, these were claimed as a vindication of the firm stand which Britain, along with its allies, had taken in the face of Soviet threats a decade before. Britain also supported the negotiations to bring about deep cuts in strategic armouries. But the Government continued to emphasise the need for vigilance, especially in the light of uncertainty about Gorbachev's future and events like war in the Gulf. Certainly there was no intention of parting with Trident, except in the distant context of extremely deep cuts in the US and USSR nuclear arsenals.

The domestic political argument, meanwhile, had been transformed. Digesting the lessons of

previous elections, when the commitment to unilateral nuclear disarmament had plainly cost it votes, Labour under Neil Kinnock formally abandoned the policy (though in terms which the Conservatives claimed were still dangerously ambiguous). The shift was confirmed by a vote at the Labour party conference in October 1989.

The Alliance also suffered all kinds of trouble over defence policy. The most serious occurred at their annual assembly at Eastbourne in 1986. On September 23 the conference insisted, against the advice of the platform, that a European defence force, on which the Liberals and SDP had agreed, would have to be non-nuclear. This vote destroyed the compromise worked out by a joint commission of the parties to reconcile differences which had arisen between Steel and the Liberals and Owen and the SDP on the replacement of Polaris. In his speech three days later Steel reasserted the commitment to update nuclear defences if disarmament talks failed. The party's MPs then devised a compromise formula emphasising the commitment to disarmament, but saying that a minimum deterrent, at most equivalent to the Polaris system, would be retained until the disarmament process succeeded.

The crumbling of what Reagan once called the "evil Empire" and the formal dissolution of the Warsaw Pact raised profound questions about the future pattern of Western defence. What was Nato now for? Who were we defending ourselves against? And did we really still need to do so at such a crushing cost? The heavy cost of Britain's defence, for which we continued to pay well above the European average, was an inescapable issue throughout these years. The Conservatives had come in on the Nato commitment to an annual increase of 3 per cent, but once the set term was over they soon began to look hard for cuts.

In 1980 it took the chiefs of staff and a threat of resignation by Defence secretary Pym to avert substantial cuts in their budget, and the threat returned the following year as Nott, Pym's successor, prepared a programme of cuts which reduced the size of the Navy and the role of the surface fleet. There was strong constituency opposition to cuts in the dockyards affecting Tory marginals in places like Portsmouth and Chatham.

The Falklands war impeded that process and much of the programme of cuts ordered by Nott was quietly reversed. But by 1990 the whole scale of British defence was again under review. A week before the Iraqis went into Kuwait the Defence secretary Tom King had set out "Options for Change" in the structure and deployment of British forces as a result of a five-month defence review. In July, a Defence White Paper foreshadowed substantial cuts. The total strength of the armed services would be cut from 308,000 to 246,000 by the mid-nineties; the RAF would lose seven frontline squadrons including Tornado bomber squadrons which had fought in the Gulf and two of its four German bases; the Navy would lose eight surface escorts cutting the number of frigates and destroyers to 40, and the submarine force could be cut from 27 to 16.

These cuts were nowhere near as drastic as a programme which, according to leaks, had earlier been devised by the minister for defence procurement, Alan Clark, but the services were seriously alarmed. King came back to the Commons in July with a White Paper which confirmed the main elements of his "Options for Change" document of a year earlier - though there was still no sign of the financial "peace dividend" that both the public and the other big spending departments in Whitehall had been hoping for. He followed this with the announcement that the Rosyth naval base in Scotland would not be closed, as expected, but merely reduced in size. A week later he announced plans for the restructuring of the army's regiments to cut

manpower by 40,000 in four years. The unpleasant job of deciding which historic regiments should go was left to the Army Board, which succeeded in avoiding the extinction of any of the infantry or armoured regiments – though some were to amalgamate. Opposition parties, though accepting the need for cuts in defence, said the Government's choices had been precipitate and ill-considered. The cuts were sharply criticised by the all-party Commons Select Committee on Defence. The planned merger of the Gordon Highlanders with another regiment became an issue in the Kincardine and Deeside by-election of November 1991 which the Conservatives lost. Some ministers, including the Scottish secretary, Ian Lang, were reported to believe that the merger might yet be averted, but this was denied by Downing Street and the Defence secretary, Tom King.

At the end of July 1991, US and Soviet negotiations were at least ready to initial the Start treaty, after nine years of negotiation on the reduction of strategic arms capacities. The cuts averaged 30 per cent, though this did little more than cancel out the growth of the strategic arsenals in the years while these talks had been taking place. But the coup which removed Gorbachev and his subsequent reinstatement very much on others' terms threw the future of disarmament negotiations back into deep uncertainty. Thatcher's immediate response to news of the coup was to call for all defence cuts to be rescinded; Major and King thought it better to wait and see how events developed.●

NORTHERN IRELAND

THERE WERE two governmental approaches to Northern Ireland in the seventies and eighties. One of them said: you will never solve this problem by military means alone. While political grievances remain, there will always be violence. The job of politicians is to maintain the most effective possible security and look for a new political settlement. The other, exemplified by the Labour Northern Ireland secretary Roy Mason, in charge of the province from 1976 to 1979 and in the view of some Conservative MPs the best secretary of state the province ever had, concentrated almost exclusively on security and regarded the search for political solutions as a dangerous distraction. Every such exercise, it was argued, carried with it the suggestion that the union of Great Britain and Northern Ireland was less than permanent and indissoluble, and thereby gave aid and comfort to the Provisional IRA.

That, had he survived the bomb which killed him as he drove out of the Commons car park on March 30 1979, might have been the preference of Airey Neave, Mrs Thatcher's close friend and counsellor who was expected to become her Northern Ireland secretary. It was what many had expected of Thatcher herself. Nonetheless, a succession of Northern Ireland secretaries during her premiership launched political initiatives, none of which succeeded.

In July 1980, the first, Humphrey Atkins, produced (after a constitutional conference boycotted by the Unionists) plans for an 80-member assembly elected by Single Transferable Vote and with some form of guarantee for minority community influence in the work of its executive. The initiative collapsed. His successor, James Prior, against the background of his prime minister's barely disguised scepticism, began all over again with a scheme of what he called "rolling devolution" built round a 78-seat assembly, again elected by PR. The theory was that the parties would examine areas of the province's life, like education or housing, to see if they might be suitable for devolution. If 70 per cent of assembly members agreed on its suitability, the Secretary of State might devolve it into their hands. Elections to this assembly took place on October 20 1982, but it failed to make much progress. The SDLP and Provisional Sinn Fein refused to attend from the start, as for a time in 1983 after the death of three Protestants in an attack on a gospel hall at Darkley, did the Official Unionists. The OUP resumed their seats in May 1984.

But in December 1985 the Alliance party withdrew after the OUP and Dr Paisley's Democratic Unionist Party voted to suspend normal business and debate the rights and wrongs of the Anglo-Irish Agreement. That was the end of that: on June 19 1986 the Commons approved an order winding up the Prior assembly.

These events were overshadowed by the developing process which in November 1985 produced the Anglo-Irish Agreement. In 1980 talks between Mrs Thatcher and Charles J. Haughey, the Taoiseach (prime minister) of the Republic, produced an agreement that at further talks the leaders would discuss "the totality of relationships between these islands", a phrase which Dublin saw as a distinct advance on the role which London usually sought to assign it in the context of Northern Ire-

DEATHS IN NORTHERN IRELAND

	CIVILIAN	POLICE	ARMY	UDR
1969	12	1	0	0
1970	23	2	0	0
1971	115	11	43	5
1972	321	17	103	26
1973	171	13	58	8
1974	166	15	28	7
1975	216	11	14	6
1976	245	23	14	15
1977	69	14	15	14
1978	50	10	14	7
1979	51	14	38	10
1980	50	9	8	9
1981	57	21	10	13
1982	57	12	21	7
1983	44	18	5	10
1984	36	9	9	10
1985	25	23	2	4
1986	37	12	4	8
1987	66	16	3	8
1988	54	6	21	12
1989	39	9	12	2
1990	48	13	7	8

Source: Northern Ireland Office

ELECTIONS IN NORTHERN IRELAND
SHARE OF THE VOTE 1985-90

	District** 1985	General* 1987	District** 1989	European** 1989
Ulster Unionist	29.8	37.8	31.0	22.2
Dem Unionist	23.4	11.7	17.8	29.9
SDLP	17.6	21.1	20.9	25.5
Sinn Fein	11.8	11.4	11.1	9.2
Alliance	7.1	10.0	6.9	5.2
Others	10.3	8.0	6.4	7.9

* first past the post basis ** PR   *Source: Conservative Campaign Guide for 1991.*

IDENTIFIABLE PUBLIC GOVERNMENT EXPENDITURE PER HEAD OF POPULATION 1989-90
(ON AN INDEX WHERE UK AVERAGE = 100)

	England	Scotland	Wales	N. Ireland
Agriculture, fisheries, food forestry	76.4	176.9	150.7	471.9
Trade, industry, energy employment	81.1	134.2	132.6	499.3
Roads and transport	95.7	135.1	119.0	81.6
Housing	90.8	163.1	76.0	217.2
Other environment	94.4	119.0	132.6	149.7
Law, order, protective	93.5	109.2	78.8	303.3
Education and science	95.4	131.9	96.7	141.1
Arts and libraries	103.1	107.2	91.1	n/a.
Health, personal social services	96.5	125.1	103.2	118.4
Social Security	97.9	108.1	110.8	117.7
ALL EXPENDITURE	95.4	121.8	106.8	155.1

Source: Public Expenditure Analyses

land. That led to the establishment of an Anglo-Irish intergovernmental council to meet regularly at both ministerial and official levels. This deepened Unionist fears: Mrs Thatcher's assent, Dr Paisley stormed, had made her a "traitor". But the process was gathering momentum, especially after the election of Dr Garret Fitzgerald as Taoiseach in November 1982. On November 15 1985, at Hillsborough Castle, Mrs Thatcher and Dr Fitzgerald put their names to an agreement whose chief effects were these: that there would be no change in the status of Northern Ireland without the consent of its people (thus strengthening the existing border guarantee, now underwritten by Dublin); there would be regular consultations on Northern Ireland between the London and Dublin governments, serviced by a permanent joint secretariat (giving Dublin a stake in the province's government, which Dr Fitzgerald defined as "going beyond a consultative role but necessarily...falling short of an executive role"); and cross-border collaboration on security would be enhanced.

The deal commanded overwhelming support at Westminster, approved in the House of Commons on November 27 1985 by 473 votes to 47. In Dublin it was more contentious: Haughey began by attacking it, calling it a severe blow to the concept of Irish unity and a sad day for Irish nationalism – but his party did not oppose it in the Dail, and after returning as Taoiseach in February 1987 he firmly upheld the agreement. But in Protestant Belfast it was greeted with fury, not least because of its origins, hatched up by London and Dublin behind the backs of the Unionists.

Even under so explicitly Unionist a premier as Mrs Thatcher, the landscape had changed irrevocably. "The Thatcher effect on Northern Ireland," wrote D. George Boyce (The Thatcher Effect – A Decade Of Change, edited by Dennis Kavanagh and Anthony Seldon, Oxford University Press), "was to make it clear that the British government did not see constitutional nationalists, Northern or Southern, as the central difficulty any more. They were part of the solution, while Ulster Unionists were now identified as part of the problem." Enoch Powell called Mrs Thatcher a "Jezebel" and the 15 Ulster Unionist MPs resigned their seats and fought

them in a mini-general election on January 23 1986 on the issue of the agreement. One lost to the SDLP; the rest, though re-elected, for some time rarely appeared at Westminster. Several went to jail for offences committed in defiance of the agreement. But a bid to break the agreement by a Protestant strike, a tactic effectively used to wreck the power-sharing system agreed in 1973 at Sunningdale, was this time a failure.

This hostility never abated. As late as 1991 Dr Paisley described the agreement as "the great wrong perpetrated upon us by a wilful and headstrong woman intoxicated with the poisoned chalice of the Foreign Office".

Yet, gradually, the existence of the agreement began to alter the terms of political debate. Younger Unionist politicians, like Dr Paisley's turbulent deputy Peter Robinson, found the continuing suspension of the province's political life increasingly irksome. They began to talk in terms of accommodation with the minority community. In a speech at Bangor on January 9 1990 Peter Brooke, who succeeded Tom King at the Northern Ireland Office in July 1989, suggested the time might have come for a new round of talks on new ways of restoring political power to the province. The talks, he proposed, should concern themselves with three sets of relationships: those within the province; those between the North and the South; and the London-Dublin relationship. The first "strand" of the talks would involve the province's parties (but excluding those linked with violence, which ruled out Provisional Sinn Fein), and he would chair it. But the timing of Dublin's involvement in the sequence produced irreconcilable differences, which in July 1990 forced Brooke to abandon a promised Commons statement on the launch of the process.

It was not until March 26 1991 that he finally announced to the Commons that the basis for formal talks now existed; and even then there were further delays, especially over the choice of an independent chairman for the later stages when Dublin became involved. Then the Unionists announced that they could not continue unless an imminent meeting of the Anglo-Irish conference was called off; at which point Brooke pre-empted

SECURITY EVENTS IN NORTHERN IRELAND AND ON THE MAINLAND

1979
March 30: Airey Neave MP (Con) killed at Westminster by bomb attached to his car.
August 27: 18 soldiers killed at Warrenpoint. Earl Mountbatten and two others killed by bomb explosion aboard his fishing boat off County Sligo (fourth victim died later)

1981
January 16: Mrs Bernadette McAliskey, who as Bernadette Devlin was MP for Mid Ulster from 1969 to 1974, and her husband Michael seriously wounded by gunmen.
January 21: Former Stormont Speaker Sir Norman Stronge and his son shot dead in Co. Armagh.
May 5: Death of Bobby Sands, elected the previous month as MP for Fermanagh and S. Tyrone, on hunger strike in Maze prison. Nine other hunger strikers had died by the end of August. The prisoners were demanding political status, a demand refused by the Government, whose stand was supported by the Labour leader Michael Foot.
August 8-9: Over 1,000 petrol bombs thrown at security forces in protests marking the death of hunger striker Thomas McElwee and the anniversary of internment.
October 10: Two killed by bomb at Chelsea Barracks.
November 14: Robert Bradford MP (Official Unionist) shot dead with another man at a community centre.

1982
April 19: Steven McConomy (11) dies after being hit by plastic bullet fired by security forces. On May 13 a resolution of the European Parliament called for the banning of plastic bullets.
July 20: Bomb explodes in Hyde Park as detachment of Household Cavalry passes by. Two people killed and 23 wounded; two more died later. Bomb in Regent's Park bandstand kills six and injures 28 (a seventh died later).
November – April 83: Security force killings of 10 people suspected of terrorist activity leads to allegations by SDLP, Provisional Sinn Fein and others of a "shoot-to-kill" policy.
December 6: 17 people, 11 of them servicemen, killed by bomb in bar at Ballykelly – claimed by INLA.

1983
May 25: Mass escape from Maze prison. Prison governor resigned after critical report by Chief Inspector of Prisons for England and Wales.
December 17: Bomb outside Harrods department store in Knightsbridge kills six.

1984
October 12: Bomb at Grand Hotel, Brighton, kills five people, including Conservative MP Anthony Berry and Mrs Roberta Wakeham, wife of a Cabinet minister; Mrs Margaret Tebbit, wife of Cabinet minister, is grievously injured. Mrs Thatcher, who was in the hotel, escapes unharmed.
1985
February 20: Four members of RUC killed in vehicle explosion on border near Killeen.

February 28: Nine members of RUC killed in mortar attack on Newry police station.

1986
December – March 1987: Eleven killed in INLA internal feud.

1987
April 25: Lord Justice Gibson and wife killed by IRA bomb on Belfast-Dublin road.
October 31: French seize arms apparently en route from Libya to IRA.
November 8: Eleven killed more than 60 injured by bomb explosions during Remembrance Day celebration at Enniskillen.

1988
March 6: Daniel McCann, Mairead Farrell and Sean Savage, believed to be on IRA bomb mission, are killed by security forces, apparently SAS, in Gibraltar.
March 16: Three killed by Loyalist gunman who attacks mourners at IRA funeral.
March 19: Two British soldiers, whose car for unexplained reasons comes upon IRA funeral procession, are pulled out and killed.
May 1: Three British soldiers killed in Netherlands.
May 16: Three killed by loyalist gunman in a Catholic pub in Belfast.
June 16: Six British soldiers killed at charity event at Lisburn.
July 23: Three members of Hanna family killed during attempt to assassinate judge.
August 20: Eight British soldiers killed when military bus is blown up on Ballygawley-Omagh road.
October 30: Three IRA members killed in ambush between Omagh and Carrickmore.

1989
September 22: Ten bandsmen killed by bomb at Deal barracks, Kent; another died later.

1990
April 9: Four members of UDR killed by landmine at Downpatrick.
May 27: Two Australian tourists killed in Netherlands – mistaken for British soldiers.
July 24: Landmine on road near Armagh kills three RUC officers and a nun.
July 30: Ian Gow, Conservative MP, killed by terrorist bomb at his home near Eastbourne.

1991
February 7: Mortar bomb attack on Downing Street. One bomb explodes in garden of Number 10 during meeting of war cabinet.
February 18: Bombs at Paddington (no casualties) and Victoria (1 dead, more than 40 injured) stations.
November 13: Following spate of sectarian killings, IRA kill 4 in Belfast.
November 14: Loyalist gunmen kill 3 (one proves to be a Protestant) bringing total deaths in year to 84.

them and wound up the process – though expressing hopes in the Commons that it might one day be resumed.

Throughout this time, the carnage continued, as did the towering cost of maintaining security and sustaining an economy which the troubles inevitably sapped. There were episodes of tension which at other times might have shaken the London-Dublin relationship. One of the worst was the fate of the Stalker inquiry. The deputy chief constable of Manchester, John Stalker, was asked to investigate allegations that the security forces had operated a policy of "shoot to kill" in 1982. But in May 1986 Stalker was abruptly withdrawn from the inquiry after allegations about contacts with criminals during his service in Manchester. The SDLP MP Seamus Mallon spoke of "sinister forces" trying to impede the inquiry.

Stalker said in February 1988 that he believed he had been removed because had his inquiries continued the consequences for the Royal Ulster Constabulary could have been "disastrous". The inquiry was continued by another officer – the same man, bizarrely, who was also investigating charges against Stalker in Manchester. Though it was later claimed that the Stalker-Sampson inquiry had produced recommendations that prosecutions should be instituted, Attorney General Sir Patrick Mayhew announced in January 1988 that none would be brought, on grounds of national security.

After many rejected protests, three cases which had led to long sentences for alleged terrorist activities – those of the Birmingham Six, the Guildford Four and the Maguire Seven – had to be reopened, with the evidence on which the convictions were based officially declared to be unsafe and unsatisfactory.

The Court of Appeal had also to order the release of the "Winchester Three", convicted of conspiring to murder the then Northern Ireland secretary, Tom King: comments made by King during the trial were found to have been prejudicial.

The continuing security problems in Northern Ireland also restricted civil liberties – unnecesarily so, in the eyes of the Labour party, which in 1982 ceased to support the continuation of emergency legislation introduced by a Labour government in 1978. Even so, Northern Ireland policy remained broadly bipartisan, except for a group on the Labour Left who supported British withdrawal. Official party policy favoured eventual reunification – but only with the consent of the people of the province.●

LEGISLATION

Northern Ireland Act 1982

1st reading: April 20 1982

2nd reading: May 10 1982, by 291 votes to 29 (against: 20 Conservatives and most Unionist MPs).

Royal Assent: July 23 1982

Provisions: based on the White Paper Northern Ireland: A Framework For Devolution for progressive transfer of powers to the 78-member Northern Ireland Assembly and the end of direct rule.

After the passage of the Bill elections were set for October 20. Twenty Conservatives rebelled against the legislation on the grounds that the Bill lacked the broad support of the Northern Irish people.

Nicholas Budgen (assistant government whip), Peter Lloyd (PPS to Adam Butler, Minister of State at the Northern Ireland Office) and Viscount Cranborne (PPS to Cranley Onslow, Minister of State at the Foreign and Commonwealth Office) resigned.

The Labour opposition criticised the Bill for failing to secure cross-community support and abstained in most divisions.

MPs voting against the Anglo-Irish Agreement, November 27 1985:

Conservative: J. Amery (Brighton Pavilion), J. Biggs-Davison (Epping Forest), M. Brown (Brigg), J. Browne (Winchester), P. Bruinvels (Leicester E), N. Budgen (Wolverhampton SW), T. Dicks (Hayes), D. Dover (Chorley), Sir J. Farr (Harborough), I. Gow (Eastbourne), M. McNair-Wilson (Newbury), M. Morris (Northampton S), C. Murphy (Welwyn), B. Porter (Wirral S), R. Shepherd (Aldridge), T. Skeet (Beds N), I. Stanbrook (Orpington), B. Walker (Tayside N), Mrs A. Winterton (Congleton), N. Winterton (Macclesfield). Viscount Cranborne (Dorset S) was a teller.

Labour: T. Benn (Chesterfield), B. Clay (Sunderland N), H. Cohen (Leyton), J. Corbyn (Islington N), T. Dalyell (Linlithgow), T. Fields (Liverpool Broadgreen), J. Lamond (Oldham C), Miss J. Maynard (Sheffield Brightside), D. Nellist (Coventry SE), R. Parry (Liverpool Riverside),M. Redmond (Don Valley), E. Roberts (Hackney N), D. Skinner (Bolsover).

Unionist: R. Beggs (UUP, Antrim E), C. Forsythe (UUP, Antrim S), J. Kilfedder (UPUP, North Down), K. Maginnis (UUP, Fermanagh), Rev. R. McCrea (DUP, Mid Ulster), H. McCusker (UUP, Upper Bann), J. Molyneaux (UUP, Lagan Valley), J. Nicholson (UUP, Newry), Rev. I. Paisley (DUP, Antrim N), E. Powell (UUP, South Down), P. Robinson (DUP, Belfast E), Rev. M.Smyth (UUP, Belfast S), J.D. Taylor (UUP Strangford), C. Walker (OUP, Belfast N). W. Ross (UUP Londonderry E) was a teller.

Fair Employment (Northern Ireland) Act 1989

1st reading: December 15 1988

2nd reading: January 31 1989 by 272 (Con, Lib Dem, SDP) to 192 (Lab, OUP, DUP, 1 SNP, 1 Plaid Cymru)

Royal Assent: July 27 1989

Provisions: created a Fair Employment Tribunal for Northern Ireland and promoted the equality of opportunity in employment in Northern Ireland between persons of different religious beliefs.

NORTHERN IRELAND POLITICAL INITIATIVES

1. The Atkins initiative.

October 25 1979. Humphrey Atkins tells House of Commons that after talks in the province he plans to convene a constitutional conference. He says: "It is right to transfer back to locally elected representatives some at least of the powers of government at present exercised from Westminster."

November 20. The Government publishes a White Paper as basis for the work of the conference. Debated in Commons on **November 29.** OUP leader James Molyneaux is very hostile.

November 22. Gerry Fitt resigns as leader of SDLP, after rejection of working paper prepared for the conference on the grounds that no account is taken of Irish dimension. The party also condemns the Government's reduction of power- sharing from a necessary condition of devolution to just one option.

November 23. OUP decides not to attend. Molyneaux tells Atkins: "far from bringing the parties together, a conference and the attendant publicity would drive them further apart".

December 15. SDLP, now led by John Hume, agrees to attend the conference.

January 7 1980. Conference opens. Boycotted by Official Unionists, but DUP, SDLP and Alliance (APNI) attend.

March 24. Adjourned because of deadlock on role of minority community in devolved administration.

July 2. Further consultative document published. Recommends transfer of powers to single assembly elected by single transferable vote. Powers would be broadly those transferred in 1973: agriculture, commerce, education, employment, environment/housing, health and social services. Interests of minority community could be safeguarded by (a) guaranteed places on executive or (b) ensuring that chairmanships and deputy chairmanships of committees were allocated equally to members supporting and opposed to the party running the executive. These people would form a Council of the Assembly with blocking powers, thus requiring Executive to get at least some support from opposition ranks in order to proceed. Debated in Comons July 9.

November 27. Atkins tells Commons there is not enough agreement between the parties to allow proposals for devolution to be brought forward.

2. The Prior initiative

April 5 1982 Prior publishes White Paper "Northern Ireland: a framework for devolution." Proposes 78-seat assembly elected by PR to which powers (again broadly those of 1973) could be transferred when members agreed on how they could be exercised ("rolling devolution").

April 28. Commons debate. Molyneaux calls proposals "totally unworkable".

May 10. Second reading of Northern Ireland Bill based on White Paper: voting 291 to 29. Enacted July 23.

October 20. Assembly elections. Result: OUP 26 seats, DUP 21, SDLP 14, APNI 10, PSF 5, Ind Unionist 1, UPUP 1.

November 11. Assembly begins work. Boycotted as "unworkable and unacceptable" by SDLP; also by Provisional Sinn Fein.

December 16. Seamus Mallon (SDLP) unseated by electoral petition because he is member of Irish Senate.

November 21 1983. OUP members boycott Assembly after killings at Darkley. Only DUP and APNI (33 seats) are still there.

May 23 1984. OUP return because they want to debate James Prior's "misrule" of the province.

December 6 1985. APNI join SDP and PSF in boycotting the Assembly in protest against action of OUP and DUP who have suspended normal business to set up grand committee to draw up a report on the Anglo-Irish Agreement.

June 19 1986. House of Commons approves draft Northern Ireland Assembly (Dissolution) Order.

3. The Brooke initiative.

January 9 1990. In speech at Bangor, Brooke says time may have come for new round of talks on devolution.

July 19. Brooke drops plans to make statement to Commons because of disagreements over the staging of the talks and particularly over the point at which the government of the Republic is to become involved.

September. Brooke reported to be considering imposing a timetable for the talks since the parties cannot agree on one.

March 26 1991. Brooke tells Commons talks are to start with meetings under Anglo-Irish Agreement suspended for 10 weeks while they take place. There will be three stages (or "strands"):

(1) Talks between the province's constitutional parties.
(2) N.Ireland parties meet government of Republic.
(3) Meetings on London-Dublin relationship.

April 30. Talks begin at Stormont.

May 6. Talks halted by disagreement over stage at which Dublin is to become involved, where meetings should be held, and who should preside in later stages.

May 15. Unionists, dissatisfied with Brooke, take their case to John Major. SDLP leave Stormont: will return when progress is possible.

May 30. Unionists reject choice of Lord Carrington, former British Foreign secretary, as chairman.

June 17. Talks resume. All sides now agree to accept Sir Ninian Stephen, former Governor-General of Australia, as chairman.

June 21. Unionists threaten to pull out if talks scheduled under Anglo-Irish Agreement proceed as planned on July 16.

July 3. Brooke tells Commons that talks are off, at least for the time being.

September 8. Brooke says he is ready to resume his initiative.

...riends, I am very proud to be speaking to ye...
here today at the grave of Theobald Wolfe Ton...

Gerry Adams
Provisional Sinn Fein

CABINET CHANGES 1979-90

Names in bold are those of new appointments. Those in italics are ministers continuing in their former office.

CABINET CHANGES 1979-83

	4-5.5.79	5.1.81	14.9.81	5-6.4.82	6.1.83
Prime Minister	M.Thatcher	M.Thatcher	M.Thatcher	M.Thatcher	M.Thatcher
Lord Chancellor	Ld Hailsham	Ld Hailsham	Ld Hailsham	Ld Hailsham	Ld Hailsham
Home Secretary	W.Whitelaw	W.Whitelaw	W.Whitelaw	W.Whitelaw	W.Whitelaw
Foreign Secretary	Ld Carrington	Ld Carrington	Ld Carrington	**F.Pym**	F.Pym
Chancellor	Sir G.Howe	Sir G.Howe	Sir G.Howe	Sir G.Howe	Sir G.Howe
Chief Secretary	J.Biffen	**L.Brittan**	L.Brittan	L.Brittan	L.Brittan
Trade	J.Nott	**J.Biffen**	J.Biffen	**Ld Cockfield**	Ld Cockfield
Industry	Sir K.Joseph	Sir K.Joseph	**P.Jenkin**	P.Jenkin	P.Jenkin
Employment	J.Prior	J.Prior	**N.Tebbit**	N.Tebbit	N.Tebbit
Defence	F.Pym	**J.Nott**	J.Nott	J.Nott	**M.Heseltine**
Lord President of the Council	Ld Soames [1,6]	Ld Soames [1,6]	**F.Pym** [3]	**J.Biffen** [3]	J.Biffen [3]
Chancellor of the Duchy of Lancaster	N.St J-Stevas [3]	**F.Pym** [3]	**Lady Young** [1,6]	**C.Parkinson** [5]	C.Parkinson [5]
Lord Privy Seal	Sir I.Gilmour [2]	Sir I.Gilmour [2]	**H.Atkins** [2]	**Lady Young** [1,6]	Lady Young [1,6]
Education	M.Carlisle	M.Carlisle	**Sir K.Joseph**	Sir K.Joseph	Sir K.Joseph
Health & Soc Sec	P.Jenkin	P.Jenkin	**N.Fowler**	N.Fowler	N.Fowler
Environment	**M.Heseltine**	M.Heseltine	M.Heseltine	M.Heseltine	**T.King**
Transport	not in Cabinet	**N.Fowler**	**D.Howell**	D.Howell	D.Howell
Energy	D.Howell	D.Howell	**N.Lawson**	N.Lawson	N.Lawson
Agriculture	P.Walker	P.Walker	P.Walker	P.Walker	P.Walker
Scotland	G.Younger	G.Younger	G.Younger	G.Younger	G.Younger
Wales	N.Edwards	N.Edwards	N.Edwards	N.Edwards	N.Edwards
Northern Ireland	H.Atkins	H.Atkins	**J.Prior**	J.Prior	J.Prior
Paymaster General	A.Maude	[7]	**C.Parkinson**	[7]	[7]

CABINET CHANGES 1983-87

	11-12.6.83	16.10.83	10.9.84	2.9.85	9.1.86	25.1.86	21.5.86
Prime Minister	M.Thatcher	M.Thatcher	M.Thatcher	M.Thatcher	M.Thatcher	M.Thatcher	M.Thatcher
Lord Chancellor	Ld Hailsham	Ld Hailsham	Ld Hailsham	Ld Hailsham	Ld Hailsham	Ld Hailsham	Ld Hailsham
Home Secretary	**L.Brittan**	L.Brittan	L.Brittan	**D.Hurd**	D.Hurd	D.Hurd	D.Hurd
Foreign Secretary	**Sir G.Howe**	Sir G.Howe	Sir G.Howe	Sir G.Howe	Sir G.Howe	Sir G.Howe	Sir G.Howe
Chancellor	**N.Lawson**	N.Lawson	N.Lawson	N.Lawson	N.Lawson	N.Lawson	N.Lawson
Chief Secretary	**P.Rees**	P.Rees	P.Rees	**J.MacGregor**	J.MacGregor	J.MacGregor	J.MacGregor
Trade & Industry	**C.Parkinson**	**N.Tebbit**	N.Tebbit	**L.Brittan**	L.Brittan	**P.Channon**	P.Channon
Employment	N.Tebbit	**T.King**	T.King	**Ld Young**	Ld Young	Ld Young	Ld Young
Defence	M.Heseltine	M.Heseltine	M.Heseltine	M.Heseltine	**G.Younger**	G.Younger	G.Younger
Lord President of the Council	**Ld Whitelaw** [1]	Ld Whitelaw [1]	Ld Whitelaw [1]	Ld Whitelaw [1]	Ld Whitelaw [1]	Ld Whitelaw [1]	Ld Whitelaw [1]
Chancellor of the Duchy of Lancaster	**Ld Cockfield** [9]	Ld Cockfield [9]	**Ld Gowrie** [8]	**N.Tebbit** [5]	N.Tebbit [6]	N.Tebbit [6]	N.Tebbit [6]
Lord Privy Seal	**J.Biffen** [3]	J.Biffen [3]	J.Biffen [3]	J.Biffen [3]	J.Biffen [3]	J.Biffen [3]	J.Biffen [3]
Education	Sir K.Joseph	Sir K.Joseph	Sir K.Joseph	Sir K.Joseph	Sir K.Joseph	Sir K.Joseph	**K.Baker**
Health & Soc Sec	N.Fowler	N.Fowler	N.Fowler	N.Fowler	N.Fowler	N.Fowler	N.Fowler
Environment	**P.Jenkin**	P.Jenkin	P.Jenkin	**K.Baker**	K.Baker	K.Baker	**N.Ridley**
Transport	**T.King**	**N.Ridley**	N.Ridley	N.Ridley	N.Ridley	N.Ridley	**J.Moore**
Energy	**P.Walker**	P.Walker	P.Walker	P.Walker	P.Walker	P.Walker	P.Walker
Agriculture	**M.Jopling**	M.Jopling	M.Jopling	M.Jopling	M.Jopling	M.Jopling	M.Jopling
Scotland	G.Younger	G.Younger	G.Younger	G.Younger	**M.Rifkind**	M.Rifkind	M.Rifkind
Wales	N.Edwards	N.Edwards	N.Edwards	N.Edwards	N.Edwards	N.Edwards	N.Edwards
Northern Ireland	J.Prior	J.Prior	**D.Hurd**	**T.King**	T.King	T.King	T.King
Paymaster General	(no appointment)			**K.Clarke** [10]	K.Clarke [10]	K.Clarke [10]	K.Clarke [10]
Minister without Portfolio	(no appointment)		**Ld Young** [9]	(no appointment)			

CABINET CHANGES 1987-88

	13.6.87	26.10.87	10.1.88	25.7.88
Prime Minister	M.Thatcher	M.Thatcher	M.Thatcher	M.Thatcher
Lord Chancellor	**Ld Havers**	**Ld Mackay**	Ld Mackay	Ld Mackay
Home Secretary	D.Hurd	D.Hurd	D.Hurd	D.Hurd
Foreign Secretary	Sir G.Howe	Sir G.Howe	Sir G.Howe	Sir G.Howe
Chancellor	N.Lawson	N.Lawson	N.Lawson	N.Lawson
Chief Secretary	**J.Major**	J.Major	J.Major	J.Major
Trade & Industry	**Ld Young**	Ld Young	Ld Young	Ld Young
Employment	**N.Fowler**	N.Fowler	N.Fowler	N.Fowler
Defence	G.Younger	G.Younger	G.Younger	G.Younger
Lord President of the Council	Ld Whitelaw	Ld Whitelaw	**J.Wakeham** [3]	J.Wakeham [3]
Chancellor of the Duchy of Lancaster	**K.Clarke** [10]	K.Clarke [10]	K.Clarke [10]	**A.Newton** [10]
Lord Privy Seal	**J.Wakeham** [3]	J.Wakeham [3]	**Ld Belstead** [1]	Ld Belstead [1]
Education	K.Baker	K.Baker	K.Baker	K.Baker
Health	{			**K.Clarke**
Social Security	**J.Moore**	J.Moore	J.Moore	**J.Moore**
Environment	N.Ridley	N.Ridley	N.Ridley	N.Ridley
Transport	**P.Channon**	P.Channon	P.Channon	P.Channon
Energy	**C.Parkinson**	C.Parkinson	C.Parkinson	C.Parkinson
Agriculture	**J.MacGregor**	J.MacGregor	J.MacGregor	J.MacGregor
Scotland	M.Rifkind	M.Rifkind	M.Rifkind	M.Rifkind
Wales	**P.Walker**	P.Walker	P.Walker	P.Walker
Northern Ireland	T.King	T.King	T.King	T.King

CABINET CHANGES 1989-90

	24.7.89	26.10.89	3.1.90	4.5.90	14.7.90	2.11.90	28.11.90
Prime Minister	M.Thatcher	M.Thatcher	M.Thatcher	M.Thatcher	M.Thatcher	M.Thatcher	**J.Major**
Lord Chancellor	Ld Mackay	Ld Mackay	Ld Mackay	Ld Mackay	Ld Mackay	Ld Mackay	Ld Mackay
Home Secretary	D.Hurd	**D.Wadd'ton**	D.Wadd'ton	D.Wadd'ton	D.Wadd'ton	D.Wadd'ton	**K.Baker**
Foreign Secretary	**J.Major**	**D.Hurd**	D.Hurd	D.Hurd	D.Hurd	D.Hurd	D.Hurd
Chancellor	N.Lawson	**J.Major**	J.Major	J.Major	J.Major	J.Major	**N.Lamont**
Chief Secretary	N.Lamont	N.Lamont	N.Lamont	N.Lamont	N.Lamont	N.Lamont	**D.Mellor**
Trade & Industry	N.Ridley	N.Ridley	N.Ridley	N.Ridley	**P.Lilley**	P.Lilley	P.Lilley
Employment	N.Fowler	N.Fowler	**M.Howard**	M.Howard	M.Howard	M.Howard	M.Howard
Defence	**T.King**	T.King	T.King	T.King	T.King	T.King	T.King
Lord President of the Council	Sir G.Howe[3]	Sir G.Howe[3]	Sir G.Howe[3]	Sir G.Howe[3]	Sir G.Howe[3]	**J.MacGregor**[3]	J.MacGregor[3]
Chancellor of the Duchy of Lancaster	**K.Baker**[5]	K.Baker[5]	K.Baker[5]	K.Baker[5]	K.Baker[5]	K.Baker[5]	**C.Patten**[5]
Lord Privy Seal	Ld Belstead[1]	Ld Belstead[1]	Ld Belstead[1]	Ld Belstead[1]	Ld Belstead[1]	Ld Belstead[1]	**Ld Waddington**[1]
Education	**J.MacGregor**	J.MacGregor	J.MacGregor	J.MacGregor	J.MacGregor	**K.Clarke**	K.Clarke
Health	K.Clarke	K.Clarke	K.Clarke	K.Clarke	K.Clarke	**W.Waldegrave**	W.Waldegrave
Social Security	**A.Newton**	A.Newton	A.Newton	A.Newton	A.Newton	A.Newton	A.Newton
Environment	**C.Patten**	C.Patten	C.Patten	C.Patten	C.Patten	C.Patten	**M.Heseltine**
Transport	**C.Parkinson**	C.Parkinson	C.Parkinson	C.Parkinson	C.Parkinson	C.Parkinson	**M.Rifkind**
Energy	**J.Wakeham**	J.Wakeham	J.Wakeham	J.Wakeham	J.Wakeham	J.Wakeham	J.Wakeham
Agriculture	**J.Gummer**	J.Gummer	J.Gummer	J.Gummer	J.Gummer	J.Gummer	J.Gummer
Scotland	M.Rifkind	M.Rifkind	M.Rifkind	M.Rifkind	M.Rifkind	M.Rifkind	**I.Lang**
Wales	P.Walker	P.Walker	P.Walker	**D.Hunt**	D.Hunt	D.Hunt	D.Hunt
Northern Ireland	**P.Brooke**	P.Brooke	P.Brooke	P.Brooke	P.Brooke	P.Brooke	P.Brooke

1 Leader of the House of Lords.
2 Chief FCO spokesman in the Commons.
3 Leader of the Commons; St John Stevas was also Arts minister. Howe was also Deputy Prime Minister.
4 Responsible for government information.
5 Chairman of Conservative Party.
6 Minister for the Civil Service.
7 Office held jointly with that of Chancellor of the Duchy.
8 Responsible for Civil Service and Arts.
9 Responsible for enterprise and job creation.
10 Commons spokesman for Lord Young's departmental responsibilities.

OF THATCHER'S 1979 CABINET:

Still in Cabinet after 1983 election:
Thatcher, Hailsham, Whitelaw, Howe, Biffen, Joseph, Prior, Jenkin, Heseltine, Younger, Edwards
Still in Cabinet after 1987 election:
Thatcher, Whitelaw, Howe, Younger
In John Major's first Cabinet:
Heseltine *(recalled by Major after being out of Cabinet since January 1986)*

OF THATCHER'S 1983 CABINET:

Still in Cabinet after 1987 election:
Thatcher, Howe, Lawson, Parkinson, Whitelaw, Fowler, King, Walker, Younger
In John Major's first Cabinet:
Heseltine *(recalled, see above)*, King

Margaret Thatcher's Cabinet June 1979. Standing, from left: Michael Jopling *(Parliamentary Secretary to the Treasury)*, Norman Fowler, John Biffen, David Howell, Norman St. John-Stevas, Humphrey Atkins, George Younger, Michael Heseltine, Nicholas Edwards, Patrick Jenkin, John Nott, Mark Carlisle, Angus Maude, Sir John Hunt *(Secretary of the Cabinet)*. **Seated from left:** Sir Ian Gilmour, Lord Soames, Sir Keith Joseph, Lord Carrington, William Whitelaw, Mrs. Margaret Thatcher, Lord Hailsham, Sir Geoffrey Howe, Francis Pym, James Prior, Peter Walker.

John Major's Cabinet April 1991. Standing, from left: Richard Ryder *(Parliamentary Secretary to the Treasury and Government Chief Whip)*, Ian Lang, Peter Lilley, Michael Howard, Peter Brooke, Tony Newton, John Wakeham, Chris Patten, John Gummer, David Hunt, William Waldegrave, David Mellor, Sir Robin Butler *(Secretary of the Cabinet and head of the Home Civil Service)*. **Seated from left:** John MacGregor, Tom King, Norman Lamont, Lord Waddington, Lord McKay, John Major, Douglas Hurd, Kenneth Baker, Michael Heseltine, Kenneth Clarke, Malcolm Rifkind

PRINCIPAL FREE VOTES AND REBELLIONS

Sometimes – usually on issues of conscience, like the death penalty – MPs are allowed a free vote. Sometimes they vote as they feel, regardless of whips' instructions – as on the Shops Bill and the Mates amendment on the Poll Tax. Here is the record of some of those votes

1. Second reading of Shops Bill (to liberalise law on Sunday trading), April 14 1986.
The Government was defeated in this vote and the Bill was lost.
/ denotes vote for the Bill, **x** denotes a vote against it

2. Motion to allow televising of Commons proceedings, February 9 1988.
/ denotes in favour of televising, **x** denotes a vote against it. **FREE VOTE**: the motion was carried.

3. Amendment by M.Mates (Con, Hampshire E) to introduce an element of banding into the Community Charge (Poll Tax), April 18 1988.
/ denotes a vote for amendment, **x** denotes a vote against it. The amendment was lost

4. Vote on restoration of death penalty, June 7 1988.
/ denotes a vote for restoration, **x** denotes a vote against it. **FREE VOTE**: restoration was rejected.

5. Vote on the second reading of the War Crimes Bill, allowing prosecution of suspected persons resident in Britain even though the crime occurred abroad, March 19 1990.
/ denotes a vote to allow such prosecutions, **x** denotes a vote against it. **FREE VOTE:** the Bill was given a second reading.

6. Vote during passage of Human Fertilisation and Embryology Bill, on clause permitting research into embryos over 14 day period, March 23, 1990.
/ denotes approval of research, **x** a vote against it. **FREE VOTE:** the House voted to sanction research.

7. Vote on new clause for the same Bill on the night of April 24-25, approving abortions until 24th week (previously 28th week).
/ denotes approval of abortion over 24 week period, **x** denotes vote against. **FREE VOTE:** the clause was approved.

other symbols:
- **n** denotes MP had not yet been elected to Parliament
- **o** denotes MP did not vote. (This does not necessarily mean a deliberate abstention: the MP may have been ill, on other Parliamentary duties, or the Chairman of the committee handling the relevant Bill)
- **(/)** denotes MP was a teller in favour
- **(x)** denotes MP was a teller against
- **s** denotes speaker or deputy
- **!** shown by Hansard as voting both for and against

CONSERVATIVES

Member of Parliament	Constituency	Sunday Trading	Broad-cast	Poll Tax	Capital Punish.	War Crimes	Embryo Research	Abortion
ADLEY R	Christchurch	/	o	/	/	x	o	o
AITKEN J	Thanet S	/	/	/	o	x	x	o
ALEXANDER R	Newark	/	/	x	o	/	x	/
ALISON M	Selby	/	x	x	x	/	x	/
ALLASON R	Torbay	n	x	x	o	/	o	/
AMERY J	Brighton Pav	/	/	x	x	x	o	o
AMESS D	Basildon	x	x	x	/	/	x	x
AMOS A	Hexham	n	/	x	x	o	x	x
ARBUTHNOT J	Wanstead	n	x	x	/	/	/	/
ARNOLD J	Gravesham	n	x	x	/	/	/	x
ARNOLD Sir T	Hazel Grove	/	/	x	/	o	x	/
ASHBY D	Leics NW	/	x	x	(x)	/	x	x
ASPINWALL J	Wansdyke	x	x	x	/	o	x	x
ATKINS R	S Ribble	/	x	x	/	/	x	x
ATKINSON D	Bournemouth E	/	/	x	o	/	x	o
BAKER K	Mole Valley	/	/	x	x	/	/	/
BAKER N	Dorset N	/	x	x	/	o	x	o
BALDRY T	Banbury	/	x	x	x	/	/	o
BANKS R	Harrogate	/	x	x	x	o	/	/
BATISTE S	Elmet	/	x	x	/	/	x	/
BEAUMONT-DARK A	B'mh'm Selly Oak	x	x	/	/	/	x	o
BELLINGHAM H	Norfolk NW	o	/	x	/	x	/	/
BENDALL V	Ilford N	o	x	x	/	/	x	x
BENNETT N	Pembroke	n	x	x	o	x	x	(x)
BENYON W	Milton Keynes	x	x	/	o	o	(x)	x
BEVAN D G	B'mh'm Yardley	x	/	x	/	/	x	x
BIFFEN J	Shropshire N	/	/	/	x	x	x	o
BLACKBURN J	Dudley W	x	x	x	/	o	o	o
BLAKER Sir P	Blackpool S	/	x	x	/	x	/	o
BODY Sir R	Holland with Boston	x	x	x	x	x	x	/
BOSCAWEN R	Somerton	(/)	x	(x)	/	x	/	/
BONSOR Sir N	Upminster	/	x	x	/	o	/	o
BOSWELL T	Daventry	n	/	x	x	/	/	/
BOTTOMLEY P	Eltham	/	/	x	x	o	/	/
BOTTOMLEY Mrs V	Surrey SW	/	/	x	x	o	/	/
BOWDEN A	Brighton K'town	x	x	x	o	/	x	x
BOWDEN G	Dulwich	o	x	x	/	o	/	/
BOWIS J	Battersea	n	/	x	x	o	x	x
BOYSON Sir R	Brent N	/	x	x	/	/	o	o
BRAINE Sir B	Castle Point	x	/	x	/	/	x	x
BRANDON-BRAVO M	Nottingham S	/	/	x	/	/	x	o
BRAZIER J	Canterbury	n	x	x	/	/	x	x
BRIGHT G	Luton S	/	x	x	/	/	x	/
BROOKE P	City of London	/	x	x	x	/	/	o
BROWN M	Brigg	/	o	x	/	/	/	/
BROWNE J	Winchester	/	x	x	/	o	o	/
BRUCE I	Dorset S	n	/	x	(/)	/	/	/
BUCK Sir A	Colchester N	/	/	/	x	o	/	/
BUDGEN N	W'hampton SW	/	x	x	x	x	x	o
BURNS S	Chelmsford	n	x	x	/	/	x	x
BURT A	Bury N	o	x	x	o	o	x	o
BUTCHER J	Coventry SW	/	x	x	/	o	x	x
BUTLER C	Warrington S	n	x	x	/	/	/	/
BUTTERFILL J	Bournemouth W	o	x	x	x	/	/	x
CARLISLE J	Luton N	x	o	x	/	x	/	o
CARLISLE K	Lincoln	/	/	x	x	o	/	/

CONSERVATIVES

Member of Parliament	Constituency	Sunday Trading	Broad-cast	Poll Tax	Capital Punish.	War Crimes	Embryo Research	Abortion
CARRINGTON M	Fulham	n	x	x	/	/	/	/
CARTISS M	Yarmouth	/	x	x	/	o	o	o
CASH W	Stafford	/	x	x	/	o	x	x
CHALKER Mrs L	Wallasey	/	/	x	/	/	o	o
CHANNON P	Southend W	/	x	x	x	o	x	x
CHAPMAN S	Barnet	x	x	x	/	/	/	/
CHOPE C	So'ton Itchen	/	x	x	/	o	o	x
CHURCHILL W	Davyhulme	/	x	x	/	o	o	o
CLARK A	Plymouth Sutton	/	x	x	/	/	x	x
CLARK M	Rochford	x	x	x	o	/	/	/
CLARK Sir W	Croydon S	/	x	x	o	o	x	x
CLARKE K	Rushcliffe	/	/	x	x	/	/	/
COLVIN M	Romsey	/	x	x	/	o	/	/
CONWAY D	Shrewsbury	/	x	x	/	/	x	x
COOMBS A	Wyre Forest	n	x	x	/	/	/	/
COOMBS S	Swindon	/	/	x	/	/	x	x
COPE Sir J	Northavon	/	x	x	x	o	/	/
CORMACK P	Staffs S	x	/	/	o	x	x	o
COUCHMAN J	Gillingham	/	x	x	x	o	(/)	/
CRAN J	Beverley	n	x	x	/	o	/	/
CRITCHLEY J	Aldershot	/	o	/	x	o	o	o
CURRIE Mrs E	Derbyshire S	/	/	x	/	o	/	o
CURRY D	Skipton	n	/	x	x	/	o	o
DAVIES Q	Stamford	n	x	x	/	o	/	/
DAVIS D	Boothferry	n	x	x	/	o	/	x
DAY S	Cheadle	n	x	x	/	/	x	o
DEAN Sir P	Woodspring	s	s	s	s	s	s	s
DEVLIN T	Stockton S	n	/	x	/	o	x	x
DICKENS G	Littleborough	/	x	x	/	o	x	o
DICKS T	Hayes	x	x	x	/	o	x	x
DORRELL S	Loughborough	/	/	x	x	(/)	/	o
D-HAMILTON Lord J	Edinburgh W	/	/	x	x	/	x	/
DOVER D	Chorley	x	/	x	/	o	x	x
DUNN R	Dartford	/	x	x	/	o	x	x
DURANT Sir T	Reading W	/	x	x	/	/	/	/
DYKES H	Harrow E	/	o	/	x	o	/	o
EGGAR T	Enfield N	/	o	x	/	/	/	o
EMERY Sir P	Honiton	/	x	x	/	o	/	/
EVANS D	Welwyn	n	x	x	/	o	/	/
EVENNETT D	Erith	o	/	x	/	o	x	x
FAIRBAIRN Sir N	Perth	/	x	o	o	x	o	o
FALLON M	Darlington	/	x	x	/	o	x	x
FARR Sir J	Harborough	/	x	x	/	o	/	o
FAVELL T	Stockport	/	x	x	/	o	x	o
FENNER Dame P	Medway	/	/	x	o	o	o	o
FIELD B	Isle of Wight	n	/	x	/	/	/	/
FINSBERG Sir G	Hampstead	/	x	o	o	/	o	o
FISHBURN D	Kensington	n	n	n	n	o	o	o
FOOKES Dame J	Plymouth Drake	/	/	x	/	/	x	o
FORMAN N	Carshalton	/	x	x	x	/	/	/
FORSYTH M	Stirling	/	x	x	/	/	x	x
FORTH E	Mid Worcs	/	(x)	x	/	o	o	o
FOWLER Sir N	Sutton Coldfield	/	/	x	/	o	/	o
FOX Sir M	Shipley	/	x	x	/	/	x	/
FRANKS C	Barrow	/	x	x	x	/	o	o
FREEMAN R	Kettering	/	x	x	x	/	x	/

CONSERVATIVES

Member of Parliament	Constituency	Sunday Trading	Broad-cast	Poll Tax	Capital Punish.	War Crimes	Embryo Research	Abortion
FRENCH D	Gloucester	n.	x	x	/	o	x	x
FRY P	Wellingborough	x	x	x	/	o	x	x
GALE R	Thanet N	x	x	x	/	o	/	/
GARDINER Sir G	Reigate	/	o	x	/	o	/	/
GAREL-JONES T	Watford	/	/	(x)	x	/	x	x
GILL C	Ludlow	n	x	x	/	o	/	/
GILMOUR Sir I	Chesham	/	/	/	x	x	/	/
GLYN Sir A	Windsor	/	x	o	o	/	/	/
GOODHART Sir P	Beckenham	x	x	/	/	o	/	/
GOODLAD A	Eddisbury	/	x	x	x	o	/	/
GOODSON-WICKES C	Wimbledon	n	x	x	/	/	/	/
GORMAN Mrs T	Billericay	n	x	x	/	x	/	(/)
GORST J	Hendon N	/	/	/	o	/	o	o
GRANT Sir A	Cambs SW	x	x	x	/	/	o	o
GREENAWAY H	Ealing N	x	x	x	/	o	x	x
GREENAWAY J	Ryedale	n	/	x	(/)	/	/	/
GREGORY C	York	x	x	x	/	o	x	x
GRIFFITHS Sir E	Bury St Edmunds	o	x	x	/	o	/	o
GRIFFITHS P	Portsmouth N	x	x	x	/	x	x	o
GRIST I	Cardiff C	/	x	x	x	/	/	/
GROUND P	Feltham & Heston	/	/	x	x	o	x	/
GRYLLS M	Surrey NW	/	x	x	/	o	o	o
GUMMER J	Suffolk Coastal	/	x	x	x	/	x	x
HAGUE W	Richmond, Yorks	n	n	n	n	/	x	x
HAMILTON A	Epsom	/	x	x	/	o	/	o
HAMILTON N	Tatton	/	o	x	/	(x)	x	x
HAMPSON K	Leeds NW	/	/	/	x	o	/	/
HANLEY J	Richmond, Surrey	/	/	x	/	o	/	/
HANNAM J	Exeter	x	x	x	/	/	/	/
HARGREAVES A	B'mh'm Hall Green	n	x	x	/	o	/	/
HARGREAVES K	Hyndburn	x	/	/	/	/	x	x
HARRIS D	St Ives	x	/	x	x	/	x	/
HASELHURST A	S Walden	/	o	/	x	o	/	/
HAWKINS C	High Peak	x	x	x	x	/	x	/
HAYES J	Harlow	/	/	x	x	/	x	x
HAYHOE Sir B	Brentford	/	/	/	o	x	x	o
HAYWARD R	Kingswood	/	x	x	/	x	x	/
HEATH E	Old Bexley	/	o	/	o	x	o	o
H-AMORY D	Wells	/	/	x	x	o	/	o
HESELTINE M	Henley	/	/	/	x	o	/	o
HICKS Mrs M	W'hampton NE	n	x	x	/	/	x	x
HICKS R	Cornwall SE	/	x	/	/	o	o	/
HIGGINS T	Worthing	x	x	x	x	/	/	o
HILL J	So'ton Test	/	x	x	o	o	x	x
HIND K	Lancs W	x	x	x	/	/	x	x
HOGG D	Grantham	x	/	x	x	o	/	/
HOLT R	Langbaurgh	o	x	x	/	/	x	x
HORDERN Sir P	Horsham	/	/	x	/	x	/	o
HOWARD M	Folkestone	/	/	x	x	/	/	/
HOWARTH A	Stratford	/	/	x	x	o	/	/
HOWARTH G	Cannock	/	x	x	/	o	/	o
HOWE Sir G	Surrey E	/	/	x	o	o	/	/
HOWELL D	Guildford	o	x	x	/	o	o	o
HOWELL R	Norfolk N	o	x	o	/	x	o	o
HUGHES R	Harrow W	n	/	x	x	/	x	x
HUNT D	Wirral W	/	x	x	x	/	o	o

CONSERVATIVES

Member of Parliament	Constituency	Sunday Trading	Broadcast	Poll Tax	Capital Punish.	War Crimes	Embryo Research	Abortion
HUNT Sir J	Ravensbourne	/	x	o	o	o	/	/
HUNTER A	Basingstoke	x	x	x	/	o	x	x
HURD D	Witney	/	/	x	x	o	/	o
IRVINE M	Ipswich	n	/	/	x	x	/	/
IRVING Sir C	Cheltenham	x	x	x	x	o	x	o
JACK M	Fylde	n	x	x	o	/	/	/
JACKSON R	Wantage	/	/	x	/	/	/	o
JANMAN T	Thurrock	n	x	x	/	/	x	x
JESSEL T	Twickenham	x	x	x	o	/	x	x
JOHNSON SMITH Sir G	Wealden	/	/		x	/	o	o
JONES G	Cardiff N	x	x	x	o	/	x	/
JONES R	Herts W	/	x	x	/	/	x	/
JOPLING M	Westmorland	/	o	x	x	o	/	/
K-BOWMAN Dame E	Lancaster	x	x	x	/	/	x	x
KEY R	Salisbury	o	/	x	/	o	/	/
KING R	B'h'm Northfield	/	x	x	/	/	x	x
KING T	Bridgwater	/	x	x	x	o	/	o
KIRKHOPE T	Leeds NE	n	x	x	/	o	x	x
KNAPMAN R	Stroud	n	x	x	/	/	/	x
KNIGHT G	Derby N	/	x	x	/	o	/	/
KNIGHT Dame J	B'h'm Edgbaston	x	x	x	/	o	x	x
KNOWLES M	Nottingham E	/	/	x	/	o	o	o
KNOX D	Staffs Moorlands	/	/	/	x	x	/	/
LAMONT N	Kingston	/	/	x	x	o	/	o
LANG I	Galloway	/	x	x	/	o	/	o
LATHAM M	Rutland	x	/	x	o	/	x	x
LAWRENCE I	Burton	o	x	x	/	o	x	x
LAWSON N	Blaby	/	x	x	x	o	/	o
LEE J	Pendle	/	/	x	/	/	/	/
LEIGH E	Gainsborough	/	x	x	/	/	x	(x)
L-BOYD M	Morecambe	/	x	x	x	/	/	o
LESTER J	Broxtowe	o	/	/	x	o	/	/
LIGHTBOWN D	Staffs SE	/	x	x	/	o	x	x
LILLEY P	St Albans	/	x	x	x	o	x	/
LLOYD Sir I	Havant	o	o	x	x	x	/	o
LLOYD P	Fareham	/	x	x	x	o	x	/
LORD M	Suffolk C	o	x	x	/	o	x	/
LUCE Sir R	Shoreham	/	/	x	o	/	x	/
LYELL Sir N	Mid-Beds	/	/	x	o	/	/	/
McCRINDLE Sir R	Brentwood	/	/	x	/	x	/	o
MACFARLANE Sir N	Sutton	o	x	x	/	/	x	o
MACGREGOR J	Norfolk S	/	/	x	x	/	/	/
MACKAY A	Berkshire E	/	/	x	/	/	/	/
MACLEAN D	Penrith	/	x	x	/	/	/	/
MCLOUGHLIN P	Derbyshire W	o	x	x	/	o	o	x
McNAIR-WILSON Sir M	Newbury	x	x	x	x	o	x	o
McNAIR-WILSON Sir P	New Forest	/	x	x	/	x	/	o
MADEL D	Beds SW	/	x	x	x	o	/	/
MAJOR J	Huntingdon	/	x	x	x	o	/	o
MALINS H	Croydon NW	x	x	o	/	o	/	x
MANS K	Wyre	n	x	x	/	o	x	x
MAPLES J	Lewisham W	/	/	x	x	/	/	o
MARLAND P	Gloucs W	/	x	x	o	o	/	/
MARLOW T	N'hampton N	/	o	x	/	o	x	o
MARSHALL J	Hendon S	o	/	x	/	/	x	x
MARSHALL Sir M	Arundel	o	o	x	x	/	x	x

CONSERVATIVES

Member of Parliament	Constituency	Sunday Trading	Broad-cast	Poll Tax	Capital Punish.	War Crimes	Embryo Research	Abortion
MARTIN D	Portsmouth S	n	x	x	/	x	/	/
MATES M	Hants E	o	o	/	/	x	/	o
MAUDE F	Warwickshire N	/	x	x	/	/	/	x
MAWHINNEY B	Peterborough	o	o	x	/	/	x	/
M-HYSLOP R	Tiverton	x	x	o	/	x	/	o
MAYHEW Sir P	Tunbridge W	/	/	x	x	/	o	o
MELLOR D	Putney	/	o	x	x	/	/	o
MEYER Sir A	Clwyd NW	/	/	/	x	x	/	/
MILLER Sir H	Bromsgrove	/	o	x	/	o	/	o
MILLS I	Meriden	/	x	x	/	x	x	/
MISCAMPBELL N	Blackpool N	/	x	o	x	o	/	/
MITCHELL A	Gedling	n	x	x	/	/	/	/
MITCHELL Sir D	Hants NW	/	x	x	/	o	/	x
MOATE R	Faversham	x	x	x	x	o	x	x
MONRO Sir H	Dumfries	/	x	x	/	o	x	x
MONTGOMERY Sir F	Altrincham	/	x	x	/	o	x	x
MOORE J	Croydon C	/	x	x	/	/	/	o
MORRIS M	Northampton S	x	/	x	o	/	/	/
MORRISON Sir C	Devizes	/	/	/	x	x	/	/
MORRISON Sir P	Chester	/	x	x	/	/	x	x
MOSS M	Cambs NE	n	x	x	/	x	/	/
MOYNIHAN C	Lewisham E	/	o	x	o	/	x	o
MUDD D	Falmouth	x	x	o	/	x	x	o
NEALE Sir G	Cornwall N	/	x	x	/	/	/	/
NEEDHAM R	Wilts N	/	o	x	x	o	/	o
NELSON A	Chichester	/	(/)	x	x	x	/	/
NEUBERT Sir M	Romford	/	x	x	/	/	x	x
NEWTON T	Braintree	/	o	x	x	o	/	/
NICHOLLS P	Teignbridge	/	x	x	/	/	x	x
NICHOLSON D	Taunton	n	/	x	/	/	x	o
NICHOLSON Mrs E	Devon W	n	/	x	x	/	/	/
NORRIS S	Epping Forest	/	n	n	n	/	/	o
ONSLOW C	Woking	/	x	x	x	o	x	o
OPPENHEIM P	Amber Valley	/	o	x	/	/	/	o
PAGE R	Herts SW	/	x	x	o	/	/	/
PAICE J	Cambs SE	n	/	x	/	/	/	/
PARKINSON C	Hertsmere	/	x	x	o	o	/	/
PATNICK I	Sheffield Hallam	n	x	x	/	(/)	/	/
PATTEN C	Bath	/	o	x	o	/	x	x
PATTEN J	Oxford W	/	x	x	x	/	x	x
PATTIE G	Chertsey	/	o	x	/	/	/	/
PAWSEY J	Rugby	x	x	x	/	o	x	x
PEACOCK Mrs E	Batley	x	x	/	/	o	x	o
PORTER B	Wirral S	o	x	x	/	x	o	o
PORTER D	Waveney	n	x	x	/	/	/	x
PORTILLO M	Southgate	/	x	x	/	/	o	o
POWELL W	Corby	/	x	x	x	(x)	o	o
PRICE Sir D	Eastleigh	/	/	x	/	o	x	o
RAFFAN K	Delyn	/	x	x	o	o	/	/
RAISON Sir T	Aylesbury	/	/	/	x	o	/	/
RATHBONE T	Lewes	/	/	/	o	x	/	/
REDWOOD J	Wokingham	n	/	x	/	/	x	o
RENTON T	Mid Sussex	/	/	x	x	/	/	/
RHODES JAMES Sir R	Cambridge	o	/	x	x	/	/	o
RIDDICK G	Colne Valley	n	x	/	/	o	/	/
RIDLEY N	Cirencester	/	x	x	/	/	/	o

The **Election**

CONSERVATIVES

Member of Parliament	Constituency	Sunday Trading	Broad-cast	Poll Tax	Capital Punish.	War Crimes	Embryo Research	Abortion
RIDSDALE Sir J	Harwich	o	x	x	/	o	/	o
RIFKIND M	E'burgh Pentlands	/	/	x	x	o	o	o
ROBERTS Sir W	Conwy	/	/	x	o	/	/	o
ROE Mrs M	Broxbourne	/	x	x	o	/	x	x
ROSSI Sir H	Hornsey	/	/	x	o	/	x	x
ROST P	Erewash	/	/	x	/	o	o	o
ROWE A	Mid Kent	/	/	x	!	o	/	o
RUMBOLD Mrs A	Mitcham	/	x	x	/	/	x	x
RYDER R	Mid Norfolk	/	/	x	x	o	/	/
SACKVILLE T	Bolton W	o	o	x	x	o	/	/
SAINSBURY T	Hove	/	/	x	x	/	o	o
SAYEED J	Bristol E	x	x	x	o	/	/	/
SCOTT N	Chelsea	/	/	x	x	/	/	/
SHAW D	Dover	n	x	x	/	/	/	/
SHAW Sir G	Pudsey	/	x	x	x	x	/	/
SHAW Sir M	Scarborough	/	x	o	o	x	/	/
SHELTON Sir W	Streatham	o	x	x	o	o	x	x
SHEPHARD Mrs G	Norfolk SW	n	/	x	/	/	/	o
SHEPHERD C	Hereford	/	x	x	/	o	/	/
SHEPHERD R	Aldridge	o	/	x	/	o	/	o
SHERSBY M	Uxbridge	x	/	x	/	/	o	o
SIMS R	Chislehurst	/	/	x	/	o	/	/
SKEET Sir T	Beds N	/	x	x	/	x	x	x
SMITH Sir D	Warwick	o	x	x	o	x	x	x
SMITH T	Beaconsfield	/	/	x	x	o	/	/
SOAMES N	Crawley	/	x	x	x	o	/	o
SPEED K	Ashford	/	x	o	o	x	o	x
SPELLER T	Devon N	/	/	x	/	x	x	x
SPICER Sir J	Dorset W	/	x	x	/	o	x	/
SPICER M	Worcs S	/	x	x	x	/	/	o
SQUIRE R	Hornchurch	/	/	(/)	x	o	/	/
STANBROOK I	Orpington	x	x	x	/	x	x	o
STANLEY Sir J	Tonbridge	/	/	x	x	/	/	/
STEEN A	South Hams	/	x	o	/	/	/	/
STERN M	Bristol NW	/	o	x	x	o	/	/
STEVENS L	Nuneaton	x	/	x	/	/	/	x
STEWART A	Sherwood	o	x	x	/	/	/	o
STEWART J A	Eastwood	/	x	x	o	/	x	x
STEWART Sir I	Herts N	/	x	x	/	o	/	o
STOKES Sir J	Halesowen	x	x	x	/	x	o	o
SUMBERG D	Bury S	/	x	x	/	/	x	o
SUMMERSON H	Walthamstow	n	x	x	/	/	x	/
TAPSELL Sir P	Lindsey E	x	x	/	x	x	o	o
TAYLOR I	Esher	n	x	x	x	/	/	/
TAYLOR J M	Solihull	o	x	x	/	o	/	/
TAYLOR Sir T	Southend E	x	x	x	/	/	/	o
TEBBIT N	Chingford	/	x	x	/	o	x	x
T-MORRIS P	Leominster	/	/	/	x	x	/	o
THATCHER Mrs M	Finchley	/	x	x	/	/	/	o
THOMPSON D	Calder Valley	/	x	x	/	/	x	/
THOMPSON P	Norwich N	x	/	x	o	x	x	x
THORNE N	Ilford S	x	o	x	/	x	x	x
THORNTON M	Crosby	o	x	x	/	o	x	x
THURNHAM P	Bolton NE	/	o	x	o	o	/	/
TOWNEND J	Bridlington	/	x	x	/	o	/	/
TOWNSEND C	Bexleyheath	/	/	/	x	x	/	/

CONSERVATIVES

Member of Parliament	Constituency	Sunday Trading	Broad-cast	Poll Tax	Capital Punish.	War Crimes	Embryo Research	Abortion
TRACEY R	Surbiton	/	x	x	/	/	x	/
TREDINNICK D	Bosworth	n	x	x	/	/	/	/
TRIPPIER D	Rossendale	/	x	x	/	/	x	x
TROTTER N	Tynemouth	/	x	x	/	o	/	/
TWINN I	Edmonton	/	x	x	/	/	o	x
VAUGHAN Sir G	Reading E	x	x	x	/	o	x	/
VIGGERS P	Gosport	x	o	x	/	x	/	/
WAKEHAM J	Colchester S	/	x	x	x	o	/	o
WALDEGRAVE W	Bristol W	/	x	x	x	/	/	o
WALDEN G	Buckingham	/	x	x	x	/	x	/
WALKER B	Tayside N	/	x	x	/	/	/	/
WALKER P	Worcester	/	/	x	o	o	x	o
WALLER G	Keighley	/	/	x	x	/	/	x
WALTERS Sir D	Westbury	/	x	o	x	x	o	o
WARD J	Poole	/	x	x	/	o	/	/
WARDLE C	Bexhill	/	x	x	/	o	x	/
WARREN K	Hastings	/	x	x	/	o	x	/
WATTS J	Slough	/	x	x	/	o	x	x
WELLS B	Hertford	o	x	/	/	o	/	/
WHEELER Sir J	Westminster N	/	x	x	x	/	/	/
WHITNEY R	Wycombe	/	/	x	o	x	/	x
WIDDECOMBE Miss A	Maidstone	n	/	x	/	x	x	x
WIGGIN J	Weston	/	x	x	/	x	/	/
WILKINSON J	Ruislip	x	o	x	o	x	/	/
WILSHIRE D	Spelthorne	n	o	x	x	/	/	/
WINTERTON Ms A	Congleton	x	x	x	/	o	x	x
WINTERTON N	Macclesfield	x	x	x	/	o	x	x
WOLFSON M	Sevenoaks	/	x	x	/	/	/	/
WOOD T	Stevenage	/	/	x	/	/	/	/
WOODCOCK M	Ellesmere Port	/	x	x	/	o	o	o
YEO T	Suffolk S	/	/	/	/	o	/	o
YOUNG Sir G	Acton	/	/	(/)	x	/	/	o
YOUNGER G	Ayr	/	x	x	/	/	/	o

*The*Election

LABOUR

Member of Parliament	Constituency	Sunday Trading	Broad-cast	Poll Tax	Capital Punish.	War Crimes	Embryo Research	Abortion
ABBOTT Ms D	Hackney N	n	/	/	x	/	/	/
ADAMS Mrs I	Paisley	n	n	n	n	n	n	n
ALLEN G	Nottingham N	n	/	/	x	/	/	/
ANDERSON D	Swansea W	x	/	/	x	o	o	o
ARCHER P	Warley W	x	/	/	x	/	/	/
ARMSTRONG Ms H	Durham NW	n	/	/	x	/	/	/
ASHLEY J	Stoke S	x	/	/	o	o	/	/
ASHTON J	Bassetlaw	x	x	/	x	o	o	o
BANKS T	Newham NW	x	/	/	x	/	/	/
BARNES H	Derbyshire NE	n	/	/	x	o	o	o
BARRON K	Rother Valley	x	/	/	x	o	/	/
BATTLE J	Leeds W	n	/	/	x	o	x	o
BECKETT Mrs M	Derby S	x	/	/	x	/	/	/
BELL S	Middlesbrough	x	/	/	x	o	x	x
BENN T	Chesterfield	x	/	/	x	/	/	/
BENNETT A	Denton	x	/	/	x	x	/	/
BENTON J	Bootle	n	n	n	n	n	n	n
BERMINGHAM G	St Helens N	x	/	/	x	/	x	/
BIDWELL S	Southall	x	/	/	x	o	o	/
BLAIR A	Sedgefield	x	/	/	x	o	/	/
BLUNKETT D	Sheffield B'Side	n	/	/	x	o	/	/
BOATENG P	Brent S	n	/	/	x	/	/	/
BOOTHROYD Miss B	W Bromwich W	x	s	s	s	s	s	s
BOYES R	Houghton	x	/	/	x	/	/	/
BRADLEY K	M/C Withington	n	/	/	x	o	/	/
BRAY J	Motherwell S	x	/	/	x	/	o	o
BROWN G	Dunfermline E	x	/	/	x	o	/	/
BROWN N	Newcastle E	x	/	/	x	o	/	/
BROWN R	E'burgh Leith	x	/	/	x	o	/	/
BUCKLEY G	Hemsworth	n	/	/	x	o	x	/
CABORN R	Sheffield C	x	/	/	x	/	/	/
CALLAGHAN J	Heywood	x	x	/	x	/	/	/
CAMPBELL R	Blyth Valley	n	/	/	x	o	/	/
C-SAVOURS D	Workington	x	x	/	x	/	o	o
CANAVAN D	Falkirk W	x	/	/	x	o	x	x
CLARK D	S Shields	x	x	/	x	/	/	/
CLARKE T	Monklands W	x	/	/	x	/	x	x
CLAY B	Sunderland N	x	/	/	x	o	/	/
CLELLAND D	Tyne Bridge	x	x	/	x	/	/	/
CLWYD Mrs A	Cynon Valley	x	/	/	x	o	/	/
COHEN H	Leyton	x	/	/	x	/	/	/
COOK F	Stockton N	x	/	/	x	o	/	/
COOK R	Livingston	x	/	/	x	/	/	/
CORBETT R	B'mh'm Erdington	x	/	/	x	/	/	/
CORBYN J	Islington N	x	/	/	x	o	/	/
COUSINS J	Newcastle C	n	/	/	x	/	/	o
COX T	Tooting	o	x	/	x	/	/	/
CROWTHER J	Rotherham	x	/	/	o	/	/	/
CRYER R	Bradford S	n	/	/	x	/	/	/
CUMMINGS J	Easington	n	/	/	x	o	o	x
CUNLIFFE L	Leigh	x	x	/	x	/	x	o
CUNNINGHAM J	Copeland	x	/	/	x	o	/	/
DALYELL T	Linlithgow	x	/	/	x	o	/	/
DARLING A	E'burgh C	n	/	/	x	/	/	/
DAVIES D	Llanelli	x	/	/	x	o	x	/
DAVIES R	Caerphilly	x	/	/	x	/	/	/

LABOUR

Member of Parliament	Constituency	Sunday Trading	Broad-cast	Poll Tax	Capital Punish.	War Crimes	Embryo Research	Abortion
DAVIS T	B'mh'm Hodge Hill	x	x	/	x	o	o	/
DEWAR D	G'sgow Garscadden	x	/	/	x	o	/	/
DIXON D	Jarrow	x	/	/	x	/	x	/
DOBSON F	Holborn	x	/	/	x	/	/	/
DORAN F	Aberdeen S	n	/	/	x	o	/	/
DUFFY Sir P	Sheffield A'cliffe	x	x	/	x	o	(x)	x
DUNNACHIE J	G'gow Pollok	n	/	/	x	o	x	/
DUNWOODY Mrs G	Crewe	x	/	/	o	/	(/)	(/)
EADIE A	Midlothian	x	/	/	o	o	/	/
EASTHAM K	M/c Blackley	x	o	/	x	/	/	/
EDWARDS H	Monmouth	n	n	n	n	n	n	n
EVANS J	St Helens N	x	o	/	x	/	/	/
EWING H	Falkirk E	x	x	o	o	x	o	/
FATCHETT D	Leeds	x	/	/	x	o	/	/
FAULDS A	Warley E	x	x	/	o	o	x	x
FIELD F	Birkenhead	x	x	/	x	/	x	x
FIELDS T	L'pool Broadgreen	x	/	/	x	/	/	/
FISHER M	Stoke C	x	/	/	x	o	o	o
FLANNERY M	Sheffield H'b'gh	x	/	/	o	o	/	/
FLYNN P	Newport W	n	/	/	x	/	/	/
FOOT M	Blaenau Gwent	x	/	/	x	/	/	/
FOSTER D	Bishop Auckland	x	/	/	x	/	/	/
FOULKES G	Carrick	x	/	/	x	o	/	/
FRASER J	Norwood	x	/	/	x	/	/	/
FYFE Mrs M	G'gow Maryhill	n	/	/	x	/	/	/
GALBRAITH S	Strathkelvin	n	/	/	x	o	o	o
GALLOWAY G	G'gow Hillhead	n	o	/	x	o	x	o
GARRETT J	Norwich S	n	/	/	x	o	/	/
GARRETT E	Wallsend	x	x	/	x	o	o	o
GEORGE B	Walsall S	x	/	/	x	o	o	/
GILBERT J	Dudley E	o	o	/	o	o	o	o
GODMAN N	Greenock	x	/	/	x	o	/	/
GOLDING Ms L	Newc'tle-u-Lyme	n	/	/	x	/	/	/
GORDON Mrs M	Bow	n	/	/	x	/	o	/
GOULD B	Dagenham	x	/	/	x	o	o	/
GRAHAM T	Renfrew W	n	/	/	x	o	x	/
GRANT B	Tottenham	n	/	/	o	/	/	/
GRIFFITHS N	Edinburgh S	n	/	/	x	o	/	/
GRIFFITHS W	Bridgend	n	/	/	x	o	/	/
GROCOTT B	Wrekin	n	/	/	(x)	o	/	/
HAIN P	Neath	n	n	n	n	n	n	n
HARDY P	Wentworth	x	/	/	o	/	/	/
HARMAN Ms H	Peckham	x	/	/	x	/	/	/
HATTERSLEY R	B'mh'm Sparkbrook	x	/	/	x	/	o	o
HAYNES F	Ashfield	(x)	/	/	x	/	/	/
HEAL Mrs S	Mid-Staffs	n	n	n	n	n	/	/
HEALEY D	Leeds E	x	/	o	x	o	/	o
HENDERSON D	Newcastle N	n	o	/	x	/	/	/
HINCHCLIFFE D	Wakefield	n	/	/	x	o	/	/
HOEY Miss K	Vauxhall	n	n	n	n	o	/	/
HOGG N	Cumbernauld	x	/	/	x	/	/	/
HOOD J	Clydesdale	n	/	/	x	o	/	/
HOWARTH G	Knowsley N	n	/	/	x	/	o	o
HOWELL D	B'mh'm Small Heath	x	o	o	x	/	o	o
HOWELLS K	Pontypridd	n	n	n	n	/	/	/
HOYLE D	Warrington N	x	o	/	x	o	/	/

LABOUR

Member of Parliament	Constituency	Sunday Trading	Broad-cast	Poll Tax	Capital Punish.	War Crimes	Embryo Research	Abortion
HUGHES J	Coventry NE	n	/	/	x	/	o	o
HUGHES R	Aberdeen N	x	/	/	x	o	/	/
HUGHES R	Newport E	x	x	/	x	o	/	/
ILSLEY E	Barnsley C	n	x	/	x	o	o	/
INGRAM A	E Kilbride	n	/	o	x	/	/	/
JANNER G	Leicester W	x	x	/	x	/	/	o
JONES B	Alyn	x	x	/	x	/	/	/
JONES M	Clwyd SW	n	/	/	x	o	/	o
KAUFMAN G	M/c Gorton	x	/	/	x	o	o	/
KILFOYLE P	L'Pool Walton	n	n	n	n	n	n	n
KINNOCK N	Islwyn	x	/	/	x	/	/	/
LAMBIE D	Cunninghame S	x	/	/	o	o	/	/
LAMOND J	Oldham C	x	/	/	o	o	o	o
LEADBITTER T	Hartlepool	x	/	o	x	/	/	/
LEIGHTON R	Newham NE	x	x	/	x	/	/	/
LESTOR Miss J	Eccles	n	/	/	x	/	/	/
LEWIS T	Worsley	x	/	/	x	o	/	/
LITHERLAND R	M/c Central	x	/	/	o	/	/	/
LIVINGSTONE K	Brent E	n	/	/	x	/	/	/
LLOYD T	Stretford	x	/	/	x	/	/	/
LOFTHOUSE G	Pontefract	x	x	/	x	/	x	x
LOYDEN E	L'pool Garston	x	o	/	x	o	o	o
McALLION J	Dundee E	n	/	/	x	o	/	/
McAVOY T	G'gow Rutherglen	n	/	/	x	o	x	x
McCARTNEY I	Makerfield	n	/	/	x	o	/	/
MACDONALD C	W Isles	n	/	/	o	o	x	x
McFALL J	Dunbarton	n	/	/	x	/	x	x
McKAY A	Barnsley W	x	/	/	x	/	/	/
McKELVEY W	Kilmarnock	x	/	/	x	o	/	/
McLEISH H	Fife C	n	/	/	x	o	/	/
McMASTER G	Paisley S	n	n	n	n	n	n	n
McNAMARA K	Hull N	x	/	/	x	o	x	x
McWILLIAM J	Blaydon	x	o	/	o	/	/	/
MADDEN M	Bradford W	x	/	/	x	/	/	/
MAHON Mrs A	Halifax	n	/	/	x	/	/	/
MAREK J	Wrexham	x	x	/	x	/	/	/
MARSHALL D	G'gow Shettleston	x	/	/	x	o	x	/
MARSHALL J	Leicester S	n	x	/	x	/	/	/
MARTIN M	G'gow Springburn	x	/	/	x	o	x	x
MARTLEW E	Carlisle	n	/	/	x	o	/	/
MAXTON J	G'gow Cathcart	x	/	/	x	o	/	/
MEACHER M	Oldham W	x	/	/	x	o	o	/
MEALE A	Mansfield	n	/	/	x	/	/	/
MICHAEL A	Cardiff S	n	/	/	x	/	/	/
MICHIE B	Sheffield Heeley	x	/	/	x	/	/	/
MITCHELL A	Grimsby	o	(/)	/	x	x	/	/
MOONIE L	Kirkcaldy	n	/	/	x	/	/	/
MORGAN R	Cardiff W	n	/	/	x	/	/	/
MORLEY E	Glanford	n	/	/	x	o	/	/
MORRIS A	M/c Wythenshawe	o	/	o	x	/	/	/
MORRIS J	Aberavon	x	/	/	x	o	x	o
MOWLAM Ms M	Redcar	n	/	/	x	o	/	/
MULLIN C	Sunderland S	n	/	/	x	o	/	/
MURPHY P	Torfaen	n	/	/	o	/	x	x
NELLIST D	Coventry SW	x	/	o	x	o	/	/
OAKES G	Halton	x	x	/	x	o	x	x

LABOUR

Member of Parliament	Constituency	Sunday Trading	Broad-cast	Poll Tax	Capital Punish.	War Crimes	Embryo Research	Abortion
O'BRIEN W	Normanton	x	x	/	x	/	x	o
O'HARA E	Knowsley S	n	n	n	n	n	n	n
O'NEILL M	Clackmannan	x	/	/	x	o	o	/
ORME S	Salford E	x	o	/	x	/	/	/
PARRY R	L'pool Riverside	o	/	/	o	o	x	o
PATCHETT T	Barnsley E	x	x	/	x	/	/	/
PENDRY T	Stalybridge	x	(x)	/	x	o	o	o
PIKE P	Burnley	x	/	/	x	/	/	/
POWELL R	Ogmore	(x)	/	/	x	/	/	/
PRESCOTT J	Hull E	x	/	/	x	/	/	/
PRIMAROLO Ms D	Bristol S	n	/	/	x	o	/	/
QUIN Ms J	Gateshead E	n	/	/	x	o	/	/
RADICE G	Durham N	o	/	/	x	o	/	/
RANDALL S	Hull W	x	o	/	x	/	o	o
REDMOND M	Don Valley	x	/	/	x	o	/	o
REES M	Morley & Leeds S	o	/	/	x	/	/	/
REID J	Motherwell N	n	/	/	x	o	x	o
RICHARDSON Ms J	Barking	x	/	/	x	/	/	/
ROBERTSON G	Hamilton	x	/	/	x	x	x	/
ROBERTSON J H	E Lothian	x	/	/	x	o	/	x
ROBINSON G	Coventry NW	x	/	/	x	o	/	/
ROGERS A	Rhondda	x	/	/	x	o	/	/
ROOKER J	B'mh'm Perry Barr	x	x	/	x	/	/	/
ROONEY T	Bradford N	n	n	n	n	n	n	n
ROSS E	Dundee W	x	x	/	x	o	/	/
ROWLANDS E	Merthyr	x	/	/	x	o	/	x
RUDDOCK Mrs J	Deptford	n	/	/	x	o	/	/
SEDGEMORE B	Hackney S	x	/	/	x	/	/	/
SHEERMAN B	Huddersfield	x	/	/	x	o	/	o
SHELDON R	Ashton	x	/	/	o	/	/	/
SHORE P	Bethnal Green	x	/	/	x	o	o	/
SHORT Ms C	B'mh'm Ladywood	x	/	/	x	o	/	/
SKINNER D	Bolsover	x	/	/	x	/	/	/
SMITH A	Oxford E	n	/	/	x	/	/	/
SMITH C	Islington S	x	/	/	x	o	/	/
SMITH J	Monklands E	x	/	/	x	o	/	/
SMITH J	Vale of Glam	n	n	n	n	o	o	/
SNAPE P	W Bromwich E	o	x	/	x	o	o	/
SOLEY C	Hammersmith	x	/	/	x	o	/	/
SPEARING N	Newham S	o	o	/	x	o	/	o
STEINBERG G	Durham	n	/	/	x	o	/	/
STOTT R	Wigan	x	/	/	o	o	/	/
STRANG G	E'burgh E	x	/	/	x	o	/	/
STRAW J	Blackburn	x	o	/	x	o	/	/
TAYLOR Mrs A	Dewsbury	n	o	/	x	/	o	/
THOMPSON J	Wansbeck	x	x	/	o	/	o	o
TURNER D	W'hampton SE	n	/	/	x	o	/	/
VAZ K	Leicester E	n	/	/	x	o	x	o
WALKER H	Doncaster C	s	s	s	s	s	s	s
WALLEY Ms J	Stoke N	n	/	/	x	/	/	/
WARDELL G	Gower	x	x	/	o	o	/	/
WAREING R	L'pool W Derby	x	/	/	x	/	/	o
WATSON M	Glasgow C	n	n	n	n	/	/	/
WELSH M	Doncaster N	o	/	/	x	o	/	/
WILLIAMS A	Swansea W	x	/	/	x	/	/	/
WILLIAMS A W	Carmarthen	n	/	/	x	o	/	/

LABOUR

Member of Parliament	Constituency	Sunday Trading	Broad-cast	Poll Tax	Capital Punish.	War Crimes	Embryo Research	Abortion
WILSON B	Cunninghame N	n	/	/	x	o	/	/
WINNICK D	Walsall N	x	/	/	x	/	/	/
WISE Mrs A	Preston	n	/	/	x	o	/	/
WORTHINGTON A	Clydebank	n	/	/	x	o	/	/
WRAY J	G'gow Provan	n	/	/	x	o	/	o
YOUNG D	Bolton SE	x	/	/	o	o	/	/

LIBERAL DEMOCRATS

Member of Parliament	Constituency	Sunday Trading	Broad-cast	Poll Tax	Capital Punish.	War Crimes	Embryo Research	Abortion
ALTON D	L'pool Mossley H	x		/	x	/	x	x
ASHDOWN P	Yeovil	x	/	/	x	o	/	x
BEITH A	Berwick	x	/	/	x	/	x	x
BELLOTTI D	Eastbourne	n	n	n	n	n	n	n
BRUCE M	Gordon	o	/	/	x	o	/	/
CAMPBELL M	Fife NE	n	/	/	x	x	/	/
CARLILE A	Montgomery	x	o	/	x	/	/	/
CARR M	Ribble Valley	n	n	n	n	n	n	n
FEARN R	Southport	n	/	/	x	/	x	x
HOWELLS G	Ceredigion	x	/	/	x	o	/	/
HUGHES S	Southwark	x	/	/	x	/	o	x
JOHNSTON Sir R	Inverness	x	o	/	o	o	/	/
KENNEDY C	Ross	x	/	/	x	o	/	x
KIRKWOOD A	Roxburgh	/	/	/	x	o	/	/
LIVSEY R	Brecon	x	/	/	o	/	/	/
MACLENNAN R	Caithness	x	/	/	x	o	/	/
MICHIE Mrs R	Argyll	n	/	/	x	o	/	/
SMITH Sir C	Rochdale	x	o	/	/	o	o	o
STEEL Sir D	Tweedale	x	o	/	x	o	/	/
TAYLOR M	Truro	n	/	/	x	o	/	/
WALLACE J	Orkney	x	/	/	x	o	o	x

NATIONALISTS

Member of Parliament	Constituency	Sunday Trading	Broad-cast	Poll Tax	Capital Punish.	War Crimes	Embryo Research	Abortion
DOUGLAS R	Dunfermline	x	o	/	x	o	x	o
EWING Ms M	Moray	o	/	/	x	o	o	o
JONES I W	Ynys Mon	n	/	/	x	/	/	/
SALMOND A	Banff	n	/	/	x	o	o	/
SILLARS J	G'gow Govan	n	n	n	n	/	x	o
THOMAS D E	Meirionnydd	x	/	/	x	/	/	/
WELSH A	Angus E	n	/	/	/	o		x
WIGLEY D	Caernarfon	x	/	/	x	o	/	/

INDEPENDENT SOCIAL DEOCRATS

Member of Parliament	Constituency	Sunday Trading	Broad-cast	Poll Tax	Capital Punish.	War Crimes	Embryo Research	Abortion
BARNES Mrs R	Greenwich	n	/	/	x	/	/	/
CARTWRIG°HT J	Woolwich	x	o	/	x	o	/	/
OWEN D	Plymouth D'port	x	/	o	x	o	o	o

OTHERS

Member of Parliament	Constituency	Sunday Trading	Broad-cast	Poll Tax	Capital Punish.	War Crimes	Embryo Research	Abortion
ADAMS G (PJF)	Belfast W	o	o	o	o	o	o	o
BEGGS R (UUP)	Antrim E	x	x	/	/	o	x	o
FORSYTHE C (UUP)	Antrim S	x	x	/	/	o	x	o
HUME J (SDLP)	Foyle	o	o	/	o	o	x	x
KILFEDDER J (UPUP)	Down N	x	/	/	o	o	x	x
McCREA Rev R (DUP)	Mid Ulster	x	o	o	/	o	x	o
McGRADY E (SDLP)	Down S	n	o	/	x	o	x	x
MAGINNIS K (UUP)	Fermanagh	x	o	/	o	o	o	o
MALLON S (SDLP)	Newry	o	o	/	x	o	x	x
MOLYNEAUX J (UUP)	Lagan Valley	x	x	/	/	/	x	o
PAISLEY Rev I (DUP)	Antrim N	x	o	/	/	o	x	x
ROBINSON P (DUP)	Belfast E	x	o	/	/	o	x	x
ROSS W (UUP)	Londonderry E	x	x	/	/	/	x	o
SMYTH Rev M (UUP)	Belfast S	x	/	o	/	/	x	o
TAYLOR J D (UUP)	Strangford	x	x	o	o	o	o	/
TRIMBLE D (UUP)	Upper Bann	n	n	n	n	n	n	n
WALKER A C (UUP)	Belfast N	x	o	/	/	o	x	o

[N.B. Although Hansard shows a total vote against in the abortion division of 129, only 128 names are listed.]

THE LABOUR-CONSERVATIVE
BATTLEGROUND

The table which follows shows the swings required for seats to change hands between the Conservatives and Labour at the next election. Subsequent tables show the result of other swings between the competing parties.

"Swing" is a useful shorthand way of measuring how one party is doing compared with another. It is defined as the average of one party's gain and another's loss. If the Conservative vote falls by 3 per cent and the Labour vote rises by 5, that is a swing of 4 per cent (3+5/2=4). If both parties lose ground to a third, the swing is the difference between their losses divided, by two. If the Labour vote is down 7 points and the Conservative vote is down 3 points, there is a swing to the Conservatives, whose loss is the smaller, of 7-3/2=2 per cent. The same rule applies if both parties *increase* their vote, when the swing will be the difference between their gains divided by two.

The shares of the mainland vote at the last election were: Conservative 43, Labour 32, Alliance 23. If an opinion poll today shows Conservative 39, Labour 40, Liberal Democrats 17, the Conservatives are down 4 points and Labour up 8, so the swing between them is 4+8/2=6 per cent.

The figure to the left of the constituency's name in the left-hand column shows the percentage majority won at the last election by the party which took the seat. *The swing needed for the attacking party to displace it will be half that majority.*

To get a Commons majority of 1, Labour needs 326 of the 651 seats being contested at this election (one more than last time, because the Milton Keynes constituency has been divided into two). If the Conservatives lose 51 seats they lose their majority. If Labour gains 97 it becomes the majority party.

The tables show the effect of a straight swing between the parties: eg Conservatives down 1 percentage point and Labour up 1 percentage point, with other parties unchanged, is a 1 per cent swing to Labour.

However even a straight swing between Conservatives and Labour can have consequences for other parties. For instance: at Portsmouth South, the result at the last election was Conservative 43.3, Alliance 42.9, Labour 13.0. A straight 1 per cent swing from Conservative to Labour at the coming election would produce this result: Conservative 42.3, Lib Dems 42.9, Labour 14.0. So the Lib Dems would have won as a byproduct of a swing between the two other parties.

The table of the Conservative/Labour battleground which follows has three columns. The left-hand column shows the seats which would change hands between the party defending and the party attacking. Where the seat is listed in brackets, this shows that the attacking party finished in third place at the last election; the sign (3) means that you will find the same seat listed elsewhere on the charts as a possible gain for another party.

The two other columns show *consequential* changes. The second column shows seats which the attacking party would pick up from parties other than its main opponent. One example is Liverpool Mossley Hill, where the result in 1987 was Conservative 17.5 per cent, Labour 38.8, Alliance 43.7. A 6 per cent swing from Conservative to Labour (Conservative -6, Labour +6), with Liberal Democrat support unchanged, would produce this result: Conservative 11.5, Labour 44.8, Liberal Democrat 43.7. So although the Liberal Democrat vote stayed steady, Labour would take the seat from the Liberal Democrats.

The third column shows additional seats which the defending party would lose on the basis of each percentage level of swing.

The swing between the two main parties needed for a seat on the consequential lists to change hands will be EQUAL to the majority printed alongside it.

To test how the tables work, take this example. Suppose there were to be a straight swing from Conservative to Labour of 3 per cent (Conservative -3, Labour +3) uniformly across the country. Labour would take 35 seats from the Conservatives, but the Conservatives would lose 41 because six more would fall consequentially to the Liberal Democrats (Portsmouth S, Cambridgeshire NE, Edinburgh W, Hereford, Bath and Colne Valley). We do not count Stockton S, shown higher up on the list, as a Liberal gain, since this has now passed to Labour.

You can now use the table to project the shape of the next House of Commons. At the last election the Conservatives won 375 seats, but if the pattern of voting was identical at the coming election they could expect 377,

with additional seats at Croydon NW, now held by the Speaker who is not standing again, and one in Milton Keynes following its division.

So start with the figures Conservatives 377 seats, Labour 229, Lib Dems 19 SDP 3, Others 6. If there is a straight swing of 3 per cent from Conservative to Labour, the scoreboard would look like this:

Conservatives 377 less 35 lost to Labour and 6 lost to Lib Dem = 336.

Labour 229 plus 35 gained from Conservatives = 264

Lib Dems 19 plus 6 gained from Conservative = 25

SDP 3, Nationalists 6 (unchanged) Northern Ireland MPs 17 : total 651.

The Conservatives would have 336 seats: all other parties combined would have 315. So the Conservatives would have an overall majority of 21.●

THE 4-6-8 FORMULA.

So here are Labour's targets for success:

A FOUR PER CENT SWING:

The Conservatives will lose their overall majority if they lose 51 seats. Assuming they win the consequential seats on the list, this would require a swing to Labour of **4** per cent.

A SIX PER CENT SWING

Again assuming they pick up consequential seats and seats where they start third, a swing of **6.1** per cent to Labour would mean that Labour would win more seats than the Conservatives.

AN EIGHT PER CENT SWING

On the same basis, Labour would win an overall majority on a swing of **8** per cent.

CONSERVATIVE SEATS VULNERABLE TO LABOUR

ON A SWING TO LABOUR OF 1 PER CENT

% MAJORITY	STRAIGHT GAINS Con to Lab	CONSEQUENTIAL CHANGES	
		Lib Dem/SD to Lab	Con to Lib Dem
0.24	York		
0.34	Ayr		
0.43	Wolverhampton NE		
0.46	Dulwich		
0.52	Wallasey		
0.97	Nottingham E		*0.38* Portsmouth S
1.20	Stirling		
1.43	Thurrock		
1.66	Ipswich		
1.73	Bolton NE		
1.81	Battersea		

Lab gain 11 from Con
Lib Dem gain 1 from Con
Con lose 12
Result: CON 365 LAB 240 LIB DEM 20

ON A SWING TO LABOUR OF 2 PER CENT

% MAJORITY	STRAIGHT GAINS Con to Lab	CONSEQUENTIAL CHANGES	
		Lib Dem/SD to Lab	Con to Lib Dem
2.23	Lancashire W		
2.31	Batley & Spen		
2.33	Delyn		
3.01	Hornsey & W'd Green		*1.30* Stockton S (3)
3.21	Ellesmere Pt & Neston		
3.35	Langbaurgh		
3.43	Corby		
3.75	(Stockton S) (3)		

Lab gain 19 from Con
Lib Dem gain 1 from Con
Con lose 20
Result: CON 357 LAB 248 LIB DEM 20

ON A SWING TO LABOUR OF 3 PER CENT

% MAJORITY	STRAIGHT GAINS Con to Lab	CONSEQUENTIAL CHANGES	
		Lib Dem/SD to Lab	Con to Lib Dem
4.17	Nottingham S		
4.29	Walthamstow		
4.45	Tynemouth		
4.56	Hyndburn		
4.83	Cardiff C		
4.89	B'ham Selly Oak		
4.90	Hampstead		
4.94	Cannock & Burntwood		
4.99	Darlington		*2.49* Cambridgeshire NE
5.01	Warwickshire N		*2.50* Edinburgh W
5.07	Pendle		
5.16	Bury S		
5.28	Basildon		
5.71	Streatham		*2.70* Hereford
5.88	B'ham Northfield		*2.73* Bath
5.99	B'ham Yardley		*2.98* Colne Valley (3)

Lab gain 35 from Con
Lib Dem gain 6 from Con
Con lose 41
Result: CON 336 LAB 264 LIB DEM 25

ON A SWING TO LABOUR OF 4 PER CENT

% MAJORITY	STRAIGHT GAINS Con to Lab	CONSEQUENTIAL CHANGES	
		Lib Dem/SD to Lab	Con to Lib Dem
6.08	Stockport		
6.10	Warrington S		
6.22	Coventry SW		
7.18	Barrow & Furness		*3.43* Hazel Grove
7.24	Swindon		
7.30	(Colne Valley) (3)		
7.34	Slough		
7.50	Kingswood		
7.69	Sherwood		
7.86	Westminster N		*3.88* Richmond & Barnes

CONSERVATIVES LOSE OVERALL MAJORITY
Lab gain 45 from Con
Lib Dem gain 7 from Con
Con lose 52
Result: CON 322 LAB 274 LIB DEM 26

(3) denotes a three-party marginal which appears in more than one column.
A seat listed in brackets is one where the attacking party finished third in 1987.

ON A SWING TO LABOUR OF 5 PER CENT

% MAJORITY	STRAIGHT GAINS	CONSEQUENTIAL CHANGES	
	Con to Lab	Lib Dem/SD to Lab	Con to Lib Dem
8.20	Bristol E		
8.21	Bolton W		
8.27	Rossendale		
8.30	Edinburgh Pentlands (3)		
8.30	Lewisham W		*4.31* Kincardine
9.10	Feltham & Heston		
9.24	Chester		
9.55	Luton S	*4.72* Woolwich	
9.79	Elmet	*4.85* L'pool Mossley Hill	

Lab gain 54 from Con, 1 from Lib Dem, 1 from SDP
Lib Dem gain 8 from Con, lose 1 to Lab
SDP lose 1 to Lab
Con lose 62
Result: CON 315 LAB 285 LIB DEM 26

ON A SWING TO LABOUR OF 6 PER CENT

% MAJORITY	STRAIGHT GAINS	CONSEQUENTIAL CHANGES	
	Con to Lab	Lib Dem/SD to Lab	Con to Lib Dem
10.02	Pembroke		
10.04	Croydon NW		
10.16	Calder Valley		
10.31	Nuneaton		
10.67	Harlow		
10.73	Keighley		
10.87	Ilford S	*5.42* Rochdale	
10.93	Lewisham E		
11.56	Derby N	*5.59* (Brecon & Radnor)(3)	
11.65	(Cambridge) (3)	*5.74* Greenwich	
11.87	Dover		

Lab gain 65 from Con, 3 from Lib Dem, 2 from SDP
Lib Dem gain 8 from Con, lose 3 to Lab
SDP lose 2 to Lab
Con lose 73
Result: CON 304 LAB 299 LIB DEM 24

ON A SWING TO LABOUR OF 7 PER CENT

% MAJORITY	STRAIGHT GAINS Con to Lab	CONSEQUENTIAL CHANGES	
		Lib Dem/SD to Lab	*Con to Lib Dem*
12.01	Bristol NW		
12.07	Vale of Glamorgan †		
12.18	Southampton Itchen		
LABOUR BECOMES LARGEST PARTY			
12.32	Southampton Test		
12.36	Bury N		
12.84	Lincoln		
12.95	Mitcham & Morden		
13.34	Chorley		
13.38	Leicestershire NW		
13.75	Hayes & Harlington		

Lab gain 75 from Con, 3 from Lib Dem. 2 from SDP
Lib Dem gain 8 from Con, lose 3 to Lab
SDP lose 2 to Lab
Con lose 83
Result: CON 294 LAB 309, LIB DEM 24

ON A SWING TO LABOUR OF 8 PER CENT

% MAJORITY	STRAIGHT GAINS Con to Lab	CONSEQUENTIAL CHANGES	
		Lib Dem/SD to Lab	*Con to Lib Dem*
14.15	S.Ribble		
14.24	Lancaster		
14.26	Kensington		
14.41	Putney		
14.43	(Eastwood) (3)		
14.46	Brentford & Isleworth		
15.05	Fulham		*7.43 Conwy*
15.20	Edmonton		
15.23	Gravesham		
15.53	Eltham		
15.64	Erith & Crayford	*7.72 Southwark*	*7.83 Cheltenham*
15.65	Norwich N		
15.79	Peterborough		
15.84	Dudley W		
15.85	Derbyshire S		*7.92 Plymouth Sutton*
15.95	Blackpool S		*7.97 Plymouth Drake(3)*
LABOUR GAIN OVERALL MAJORITY			

Lab gain 91 from Con, 4 from Lib Dem, 2 from SDP
Lib Dem gain 12 from Con, lose 4 to Lab
SDP lose 2 to Lab
Con lose 103
Result: CON 274 LAB 326, LIB DEM 27

† *indicates that a by-election has taken place in this constituency since the last general election: see page 259*
(3) denotes a three-party marginal which appears in more than one column.
A seat listed in brackets is one where the attacking party finished third in 1987.

ON A SWING TO LABOUR OF 9 PER CENT

% MAJORITY	STRAIGHT GAINS	CONSEQUENTIAL CHANGES	
	Con to Lab	Lib Dem/SD to Lab	Con to Lib Dem
16.17	Davyhulme		8.10 Devon N
16.43	(Conwy) (3)		8.20 Isle of Wight
16.47	Erewash		
16.48	(Stevenage) (3)		
16.69	B'ham Hall Green		
16.70	Dumfries		
16.90	High Peak		
17.00	Blackpool N		
17.06	(Littleborough & Saddleworth) (3)		
17.08	Amber Valley		
17.09	Burton		
17.20	(Plymouth Drake) (3)		
17.91	Northampton N		8.99 Oxford W & Abingdon

Lab gain 104 from Con, 4 from Lib Dem, 2 from SDP
Lib Dem gain 13 from Con, lose 4 to Lab
SDP lose 2 to Lab
Con lose 117
Result: CON 260 LAB 339 LIB DEM 28

ON A SWING TO LABOUR OF 10 PER CENT

% MAJORITY	STRAIGHT GAINS	CONSEQUENTIAL CHANGES	
	Con to Lab	Lib Dem/SD to Lab	Con to Lib Dem
18.32	(Welwyn Hatfield)		
18.36	Waveney		
18.46	Gloucestershire W		
18.58	Cardiff N		9.32 Falmouth & C'borne
19.75	Worcester		9.84 Cornwall N
19.85	Monmouth †		

Lab gain 110 from Con, 4 from Lib Dem, 2 from SDP
Lib Dem gain 15 from Con, lose 4 to Lab
SDP lose 2 to Lab
Con lose 125
Result: CON 252, LAB 345, LIB DEM 30

† indicates that a by-election has taken place in this constituency since the last general election: see page 259
(3) denotes a three-party marginal which appears in more than one column.
A seat listed in brackets is one where the attacking party finished third in 1987.

LABOUR SEATS VULNERABLE TO CONSERVATIVE

ON A SWING TO CONSERVATIVE OF 1 PER CENT

% MAJORITY	STRAIGHT GAINS Lab to Con	CONSEQUENTIAL CHANGES	
		Lib Dem to Con	Lab to Lib Dem/SNP
0.10	Mansfield	*0.13* Brecon	
0.60	Bradford S		
0.64	Norwich S		
0.80	Dewsbury		
0.90	Glanford		
1.89	Crewe		

Con gain 6 from Lab, 1 from LD
CON 384 LAB 223, LD 18

ON A SWING TO CONSERVATIVE OF 2 PER CENT

% MAJORITY	STRAIGHT GAINS Lab to Con	CONSEQUENTIAL CHANGES	
		Lib Dem to Con	Lab to Lib Dem/SNP
2.11	Carlisle		
2.13	Halifax		
2.18	Clwyd SW (3)		
2.21	Walsall S		
2.25	Wrekin		
2.30	W. Bromwich E		
2.41	Leicester W		
2.62	Oxford E		
2.76	Bristol S		
2.84	Aberdeen S		
2.97	Tooting		
3.15	Derby S		
3.29	Nottingham N		
3.30	Bradford N †		
3.32	Leicester S		
3.55	Walsall N		
3.68	Leicester E		*1.85* Blyth Valley (Lib Dem)
3.84	Edinburgh S		*1.95* Islington S (Lib Dem)

Con gain 24 from Lab, 1 from LD. LD gain 2 from Lab. Lab lose 26
CON 402 LAB 203 LD 20

ON A SWING TO CONSERVATIVE OF 3 PER CENT

% MAJORITY	STRAIGHT GAINS Lab to Con	CONSEQUENTIAL CHANGES	
		Lib Dem to Con	Lab to Lib Dem/SNP
4.20	Brent E		
4.26	Copeland		
4.76	Strathkelvin		*2.20* Dundee E (SNP)
5.30	Wakefield		
5.38	Newcastle C		
5.51	Edinburgh C		
5.94	Dagenham		

Con gain 31 from Lab, 1 from LD. LD gain 2 from Lab. SNP gain 1 from Lab. Lab lose 34
CON 409 LAB 195 LD 20 NAT 7

ADDITIONAL LABOUR TARGETS
(CONSERVATIVE-HELD SEATS VULNERABLE TO LABOUR ARE IN THE BATTLEGROUND SECTION)

SEATS VULNERABLE ON A SWING TO LABOUR OF UP TO 3%

% MAJORITY	FROM LIB DEM	FROM NAT	FROM SDP
4.72			Woolwich
4.85	L'pool Mossley Hill		
5.42	Rochdale		
5.59	(Brecon) (3)		
5.74			Greenwich

SEAT VULNERABLE ON A SWING TO LABOUR OF UP TO 4%

% MAJORITY	FROM LIB DEM	FROM NAT	FROM SDP
7.72	Southwark		

SEAT VULNERABLE ON A SWING TO LABOUR OF UP TO 6%

% MAJORITY	FROM LIB DEM	FROM NAT	FROM SDP
11.48	Inverness		

SEAT VULNERABLE ON A SWING TO LABOUR OF UP TO 7%

% MAJORITY	FROM LIB DEM	FROM NAT	FROM SDP
13.81			(Plymouth D'port)

ADDITIONAL CONSERVATIVE TARGETS
(LABOUR-HELD SEATS VULNERABLE TO THE CONSERVATIVES ARE IN THE BATTLEGROUND SECTION)

SEAT VULNERABLE ON A SWING TO CONSERVATIVE OF UP TO 1%

% MAJORITY	FROM LIB DEM	FROM NAT	FROM SDP
0.13	Brecon (3)		

SEATS VULNERABLE ON A SWING TO CONSERVATIVE OF UP TO 2%

% MAJORITY	FROM LIB DEM	FROM NAT	FROM SDP
3.35		Angus E	
3.39	Southport		
3.63	Fife NE		
3.79	Argyll		

SEAT VULNERABLE ON A SWING TO CONSERVATIVE OF UP TO 3%

% MAJORITY	FROM LIB DEM	FROM NAT	FROM SDP
5.55		Banff	

SEATS VULNERABLE ON A SWING TO CONSERVATIVE OF UP TO 4%

% MAJORITY	FROM LIB DEM	FROM NAT	FROM SDP
8.09	Montgomery		
8.16		Moray	
8.21	Truro		
9.73	Ceredigion		
10.00		Ynys Mon	

LIBERAL DEMOCRAT TARGETS

SEATS VULNERABLE ON A SWING TO LIB DEM OF UP TO 1%

% MAJORITY	FROM CONSERVATIVE	FROM LABOUR
0.38	Portsmouth S	
1.30	Stockton S (3)	
1.85		Blyth Valley
1.95		Islington S

SEATS VULNERABLE ON A SWING TO LIB DEM OF UP TO 2%

% MAJORITY	FROM CONSERVATIVE	FROM LABOUR
2.49	Cambridgeshire NE	
2.50	Edinburgh W	
2.70	Hereford	
2.73	Bath	
2.98	Colne Valley (3)	
3.43	Hazel Grove	
3.88	Richmond & Barnes	

SEATS VULNERABLE ON A SWING TO LIB DEM OF UP TO 3%

% MAJORITY	FROM CONSERVATIVE	FROM LABOUR
4.31	Kincardine	
5.52		Sheffield Hillsborough

SEATS VULNERABLE ON A SWING TO LIB DEM OF UP TO 4%

% MAJORITY	FROM CONSERVATIVE	FROM LABOUR
7.43	Conwy (3)	
7.76		Glasgow Hillhead
7.83	Cheltenham	
7.92	Plymouth Sutton	
7.97	Plymouth Drake (3)	

SEATS VULNERABLE ON A SWING TO LIB DEM OF UP TO 5%

% MAJORITY	FROM CONSERVATIVE	FROM LABOUR
8.10	Devon N	
8.17	(Cardiff C)	
8.20	Isle of Wight	
8.99	Oxford W	
9.32	Falmouth	
9.35	Cambridge (3)	
9.54	Stevenage (3)	
9.62		Newcastle Under Lyme
9.64		Leeds W
9.84	Cornwall N	
9.98		Newcastle N

† indicates that a by-election has taken place in this constituency since the last general election: see page 259
(3) denotes a three-party marginal which appears in more than one column.
A seat listed in brackets is one where the attacking party finished third in 1987.

SEATS VULNERABLE ON A SWING TO LIB DEM OF UP TO 6%

% MAJORITY	FROM CONSERVATIVE	FROM LABOUR
10.07	Leeds NW	
10.26	Crosby	
11.03	Devon W	
11.44	Chelmsford	
11.51	Pudsey	
11.57		Leyton
11.77		Durham
11.82	Cornwall SE	

SEATS VULNERABLE ON A SWING TO LIB DEM OF UP TO 7%

% MAJORITY	FROM CONSERVATIVE	FROM LABOUR
12.12	Littleborough (3)	
12.16	Winchester	
12.25	Eastwood (3)	
12.56		(Clywd SW)(3)
12.63	Exeter	
13.16	Wyre Forest	
13.64		Bow & Poplar
13.52	Twickenham	
13.75	(Edinburgh Pentlands)(3)	
13.78	Sheffield Hallam	
13.85	Weston-super-Mare	
14.06	Hastings	
14.20	Bristol W	
14.51	St Ives	
14.52	Congleton	
14.78	Ryedale	
14.91	Pembroke	
15.21	Westbury	
15.47	E. Lindsey	
15.97	Wells	

† *indicates that a by-election has taken place in this constituency since the last general election: see page 259*
(3) denotes a three-party marginal which appears in more than one column.
A seat listed in brackets is one where the attacking party finished third in 1987.

NATIONALIST TARGETS

% MAJORITY	FROM CONSERVATIVE	FROM LABOUR
2.20		Dundee E
8.95	Galloway	
12.02	Perth & Kinross	
12.34		(Carmarthen)
12.43	Tayside N	
14.18		Western Isles

3 WAY MARGINALS

CONSERVATIVE HELD

	CON	LAB	L/SD	OTHER
CAMBRIDGE	40.0	28.3	30.6	Grn 1.1
CARDIFF C	37.1	32.3	29.3	PC 1.3
COLNE VALLEY	36.4	29.1	33.4	Grn 1.1
EASTWOOD	39.5	25.1	27.2	SNP 8.2
EDINBURGH PENTL'DS	38.3	30.0	24.5	SNP 7.2
EDINBURGH W	37.3	22.2	34.9	SNP 5.6
LITTLEBOROUGH	43.1	26.0	30.9	–
PEMBROKE	41.0	31.0	26.1	PC 1.9
PLYMOUTH DRAKE	41.3	24.1	33.3	Grn 1.3
STEVENAGE	42.1	25.4	32.5	–
STOCKTON S	35.0	31.3	33.7	–

LABOUR HELD

	CON	LAB	NAT	OTHER
CARMARTHEN	27.4	35.4	23.0	SDP 13.3 Grn 0.9

	CON	LAB	L/SD	OTHER
CLWYD SW	33.2	35.4	22.9	PC 8.5

LIBERAL DEMOCRAT HELD

	CON	LAB	LIB DEM	OTHER
BRECON	34.7	29.2	34.8	PC 1.3

HELD BY IND SDP

	CON	LAB	SDP	OTHER
PLYMOUTH D'PORT	29.3	28.4	42.3	

† indicates that a by-election has taken place in this constituency since the last general election: see page 259
(3) denotes a three-party marginal which appears in more than one column.
A seat listed in brackets is one where the attacking party finished third in 1987.

THE KEY MARGINALS,
REGION BY REGION

READING THE FOLLOWING TABLES:

The three numbers to the left of each constituency name show who won the seat at the general elections of 1979, 1983 and 1987.

1 indicates a Conservative win
2 indicates a Labour win
3 indicates a Liberal,Liberal Democrat or Social Democrat win
4 indicates a Nationalist win
0 indicates that the boundaries of the constituency have substantially altered since 1979 and so no direct comparison is possible

EXAMPLE:

CONSERVATIVE SEATS VULNERABLE TO LABOUR

Last 3	constituency	Con maj	Con	Lab	Lib/SD	Sitting MP	Since
011	**LEWISHAM E**	10.93	45.1	34.2	20.7 (SDP)	C.Moynihan	83
2*11	**MITCHAM & MORDEN ç ‡**	12.95	48.2	35.2	16.6 (SDP)	Mrs A.Rumbold	82*
211	**HAYES & HARLINGTON ç**	13.75	49.2	35.5	15.3 (SDP)	T.Dicks	83
111*	**KENSINGTON**	14.26	47.5	33.3	17.2 (SDP)		
By-election 14.7.88:		3.44	41.6	38.2	10.8 (LD) 5.0 (SDP)	D.Fishburn	
111	**PUTNEY**	14.41	50.5	36.1	12.4 (Lib) 1	D.Mellor	79
011	**(PLYMOUTH DRAKE) (3)**	17.20	41.3	24.1	33.3 (SDP)	Miss J.Fookes	74¹

The table shows the winning party's *percentage* majority (i.e. at Putney it is 14.41%)

* indicates that there was by-election in the constituency: e.g. if the * follows the first figure it will have taken place between 1979 and 1983.

‡ indicates a seat which changed hands at a by-election between 1979 and 1987: details are given at the end of the region's tables.

The figures far right indicate the year when the incumbent MP first represented all or part of this constituency. If there is an asterisk, the MP came in on a by-election.

§ indicates that the MP had also represented the seat in an earlier period: the details appear at the end of the table.

† indicates the present MP is not standing for re-election.
ç indicates that a Labour MP representing all or part of this seat switched to the SDP between 1979 and 1983.

74¹ indicates the general election of February 1974,

74² indicates the general election of October 1974,

If the seat is in brackets, the attacking party finished 3rd and not 2nd here in 1987

(3) indicates a 3 way marginal

GREATER LONDON

SHARE OF VOTE IN LAST 4 GENERAL ELECTIONS

	Con	Lab	Lib/SD	Swing
1974 [2]	37.4	43.8	17.1	
1979	46.0	39.6	11.9	6.4 to Con
1983	43.9	29.8	24.9	3.9 to Con
1987	45.8	31.5	21.3	0.1 to Con
1974-87	+8.4	-12.3	+4.2	10.4 to Con

THOUGH NATIONAL issues increasingly dictate the pattern of local elections, the process also works the other way round. Disappointing Labour results in Greater London, like the loss of Battersea and Walthamstow in 1987, appeared to reflect the parties' reputations in local government rather than national issues or the defects of the defeated MPs. The loss of Battersea, one of three seats within the London borough of Wandsworth, also reflects the erosion of traditionally working-class territory, increasingly taken over by the affluent middle-class. Alf Dubs, the Labour MP defeated in 1987 by John Bowis, is fighting again, but the seat may be harder to recapture than the tiny Conservative majority suggests. Neighbouring Putney should be safe for Chief Secretary to the Treasury David Mellor and Labour could have difficulty hanging on to Tooting, the third Wandsworth seat, defended by the long-serving and stentorian Tom Cox. There could also be problems for Ken Livingstone in Brent East, where Labour's Town Hall record has many acerbic critics, Livingstone among them. And a swing of only 3 per cent would remove Bryan Gould, who is assured of a front-line job in a Labour Cabinet, from Dagenham.

Despite the so-called Lambeth effect, Labour did well in Streatham in 1987 and has again picked a moderate candidate in Keith Hill, who – like Kate Hoey, who won Vauxhall at the June 1989 by-election – is detached from the controlling group on the Labour council. Labour also has hopes of a better-than-average performance in the seat of the Home Office minister Angela Rumbold at Mitcham and Morden, in a borough where Labour had one of its best results in the 1990 local elections.

North of the river the veteran Conservative member Sir Hugh Rossi is standing down in the highly marginal seat of Hornsey and Wood Green, where he has several times survived against the odds. The seat has one of the highest black/Asian populations of any Conservative-held constituency. But his neighbour in Hampstead and Highgate, Sir Geoffrey Finsberg, is standing down: the new Conservative candidate is Oliver Letwin, a former Thatcher think tank member. The Labour challenger is the actress Glenda Jackson. Having failed to turn the Conservatives out by a mere 815 votes in the July 1988 by-election, Ann Holmes is standing again in Kensington against the Conservative Dudley Fishburn.

If Labour win Brentford and Feltham, that will put into the Commons a husband and wife – Ann Keen at Brentford and Isleworth and her husband Alan at Feltham. Labour also hopes to dislodge two of the three remaining SDP members, Rosie Barnes in Greenwich, where it needs a 2.9 per cent swing for victory, and John Cartwright, who has represented Woolwich first as a Labour MP and then for the SDP, since 1974. Though he would go on a swing of 2.4 per cent, he may prove harder to dislodge than Mrs Barnes.

The Liberal Democrats will again be pursuing Richmond and Barnes and Twickenham, the two constituencies in the London borough of Richmond, where they are in control of the town hall. Local government results give the Liberals a chance in two Labour seats – Newham South, where the swing required is 4.7 per cent, and Bow and Poplar, where they need a swing of 6.9 per cent. But Chris Smith should be safer than the figures suggest in Islington South and Finsbury now that George Cunningham, a Labour MP of fierce independence who switched to the Social Democrats, is not standing.

The fate of the third party vote will matter in other seats, too. In places like Lewisham East, defended by former Minister for Sport Colin Moynihan, and Eltham, where Peter Bottomley faced severe local criticism over roadbuilding plans before he left the Government, there could be scope for substantial tactical voting if the 20 per cent who backed the Alliance in 1987 decided to switch this time. The third party vote is even bigger at Erith and Crayford where the former Labour MP James Wellbeloved switched to the SDP. Wellbeloved is not standing this time and much could hang on the fate of the 25.3 per cent of the vote which went to the Alliance last time. ●

CONSERVATIVE SEATS VULNERABLE TO LABOUR

Last 3	constituency	Con maj	Con	Lab	Lib/SD	Sitting MP	Since
011	DULWICH	0.46	42.4	42.0	14.5 (SDP)	G.Bowden	83
021	BATTERSEA	1.81	44.2	42.4	11.9 (SDP)	J.Bowis	87
011	HORNSEY & WOOD GREEN	3.01	43.0	40.0	15.1 (SDP)	Sir H.Rossi †	66
221	WALTHAMSTOW	4.29	39.0	34.8	25.1 (SDP)	H.Summerson	87
011	HAMPSTEAD	4.90	42.5	37.6	19.3 (SDP)	G.Finsberg †	70
011	STREATHAM	5.71	45.0	39.2	15.8 (Lib)	Sir W.Shelton	70
011	WESTMINSTER N	7.86	47.3	39.5	12.1 (SDP)	Sir J.Wheeler	79
011	LEWISHAM W	8.30	46.2	37.9	15.9 (Lib)	J.Maples	83
211	FELTHAM	9.10	46.5	37.4	16.1 (SDP)	P.Ground	83
011	CROYDON NW ‡	10.04	47.0	37.0	16.0 (Lib)	H.Malins	83
011	ILFORD S	10.87	48.4	37.5	14.1 (Lib)	N.Thorne	79
011	LEWISHAM E	10.93	45.1	34.2	20.7 (SDP)	C.Moynihan	83
2*11	MITCHAM & MORDEN ‡ ⊊	12.95	48.2	35.2	16.6 (SDP)	Mrs A.Rumbold	82*
211	HAYES & HARLINGTON ⊊	13.75	49.2	35.5	15.3 (SDP)	T.Dicks	83
111*	KENSINGTON	14.26	47.5	33.3	17.2 (SDP)		
BY-ELECTION 14.7.88:		3.44	41.6	38.2	10.8 (LD) 5.0 (SDP)	D.Fishburn	
111	PUTNEY	14.41	50.5	36.1	12.4 (Lib)	D.Mellor	79
111	BRENTFORD & ISLEWORTH	14.46	47.7	33.2	17.5 (SDP)	Sir B.Hayhoe †	70
11*1	FULHAM ‡	15.05	51.8	36.7	10.4 (SDP)	M.Carrington	86*
011	EDMONTON	15.20	51.2	36.0	12.8 (SDP)	I.Twinn	83
011	ELTHAM	15.53	47.5	32.0	20.5 (Lib)	P.Bottomley	76*
211	ERITH & CRAYFORD ⊊	15.64	45.2	29.5	25.3 (SDP)	D.Evennett	83

LABOUR SEATS VULNERABLE TO CONSERVATIVE

Last 3	Constituency	Lab maj	Con	Lab	Lib/SD	Sitting MP	Since
022	TOOTING	2.97	41.3	44.2	13.2 (SDP)	T.Cox	70
022	BRENT E	4.20	38.4	42.6	14.5 (SDP)	K.Livingstone	87
022	DAGENHAM	5.94	38.5	44.4	17.1 (SDP)	B.Gould	83
222	NEWHAM S	9.31	34.2	43.6	22.2 (SDP)	N.Spearing	74*

CONSERVATIVE SEATS VULNERABLE TO LIBERAL DEMOCRAT

Last 3	Constituency	Con maj	Con	Lab	Lib/SD	Sitting MP	Since
011	RICHMOND & BARNES	3.88	47.7	7.1	43.9 (Lib)	J.Hanley	83
011	TWICKENHAM	13.52	51.9	8.4	38.3 (Lib)	T.Jessel	70

LABOUR SEATS VULNERABLE TO LIBERAL DEMOCRAT

Last 3	Constituency	Lab maj	Con	Lab	Lib/SD	Sitting MP	Since
022	ISLINGTON S & FINSBURY ç	1.95	20.6	40.1	38.1 (SDP)	C.Smith	83
222	LEYTON ç	11.57	29.1	41.2	29.7 (Lib)	H.Cohen	83
022	BOW & POPLAR	13.64	20.1	46.4	32.7 (Lib)	Mrs M.Gordon	87

LIBERAL DEMOCRAT SEAT VULNERABLE TO LABOUR

Last 3	Constituency	LD maj	Con	Lab	Lib/SD	Sitting MP	Since
0*33	S/THWARK & B/MONDSEY ‡	7.72	12.6	39.7	47.4 (Lib)	S.Hughes	83*

SDP SEATS VULNERABLE TO LABOUR

Last 3	Constituency	SDP maj	Con	Lab	Lib/SD	Sitting MP	since
233	WOOLWICH ç	4.72	21.2	37.0	41.8 (SDP)	J.Cartwright	74[2]
02*3	GREENWICH ‡	5.74	23.3	34.9	40.6 (SDP)	Mrs R.Barnes	87*

‡ CROYDON NW: won by Liberal at by-election of 22.10.81, regained by Conservatives at 1983 election.
MITCHAM & MORDEN. Won by Conservatives at by-election of 3.6.82 from Bruce Douglas-Mann who was elected for Labour but resigned on switching to the SDP.
FULHAM. Won by Labour at by-election of 10.4.86, regained by Conservatives at 1987 election.
GREENWICH. Won by SDP at by-election of 26.2.87.
SOUTHWARK & BERMONDSEY. Won by Liberal at by-election of 24.2.83.

SOUTH EAST

SHARE OF VOTE IN LAST 4 GENERAL ELECTIONS

	Con	Lab	Lib/SD	Swing
1974[2]	45.2	30.7	23.7	
1979	57.2	24.0	17.7	9.4 to Con
1983	54.5	15.8	29.0	7.0 Con to L/SD
1987	55.6	16.8	27.2	1.5 L/SD to Con
1974-87	+10.4	-13.9	+3.5	12.2 Lab to Con

O F THE 104 seats in the South East outside London, Labour won only one – Oxford East – in 1987. Much is made of the Conservative humiliation in Scotland, where they took only 10 of 72 seats, but Labour's predicament in the South is very much worse. The result was even more disastrous because it was linked with a dearth of good second places: only nine of the 103 Conservative-held seats in the region would fall to Labour on a swing of 10 per cent or less. Compare that with 1959 when, as now, the Conservatives had a Commons majority of 100, and you get a telling index of Labour's electoral decline: then, there were more than 30 seats in the region which rated as Conservative-Labour marginals on this test.

To make any sort of showing here in the coming election, Labour needs to win back seats in the heartland of Essex man where an electorate rich in escapees from London's East End deserted the party in droves for Thatcherite Toryism. Places like Thurrock, won by the very right wing Tim Janman in 1987; Basildon, a new-town seat which votes for a Labour council but a Conservative MP; and another new town seat, Harlow. The two Southampton seats, Itchen and Test, in another town which has tended to vote Labour at local level but Conservative in national elections, will be another crucial test of Labour's electoral recovery: the result at Itchen last time closely echoed the national result.

Stevenage is the sort of seat Labour need to take despite starting in third place if they are to have any hope of outright victory. The Liberal Democrats would take it on a swing from the Conservatives of 5 per cent; or Labour could come from behind to win it on a swing of 8.4 per cent.

The list of Liberal Democrat hopefuls is headed by Portsmouth South, the scene of an Alliance by-election triumph in June 1984, to be fought this time by the man who won it then, Mike Hancock – but now as a Liberal Democrat. The Isle of Wight was Liberal until 1987, when a rise in the Labour vote from an astonishing 2.4 per cent in 1983 to 5.9 per cent may have helped the Conservatives to regain it. The most exotic fight could be at Oxford West and Abingdon, the seat of the Home Office minister John Patten, where Sir Wiliam Goodhart, once one of the SDP great and good, is standing for the Liberal Democrats and Bruce Kent, the most famous champion of nuclear disarmament, will be fighting for Labour. The Liberal Democrats hope to benefit from the ructions in the Conservative party at Winchester, where the sitting MP John Browne has been deselcted but plans to run as an independent Conservative against the new Conservative candidate Gerry Malone, once MP for Aberdeen South.

The South East has an extra seat in this election: Milton Keynes, where the sitting Conservative MP William Benyon is retiring, has been split into two: South West and North East. Both look likely Conservative territory, though Labour outpolled the Conservatives in the South West constituency in the 1991 local elections. ●

CONSERVATIVE SEATS VULNERABLE TO LABOUR

Last 3	Constituency	Con maj	Con	Lab	Lib/SD	Sitting MP	Since
021	THURROCK	1.43	42.5	41.0	16.5 (SDP)	T.Janman	87
011	BASILDON	5.28	43.5	38.3	18.2 (Lib)	D.Amess	83
011	SLOUGH	7.34	47.0	39.6	13.4 (SDP)	J.Watts	83
011	LUTON S	9.55	46.2	36.7	17.1 (Lib)	G.Bright	79
211	HARLOW	10.67	47.2	36.6	16.2 (SDP)	J.Hayes	83
011	DOVER	11.87	46.0	34.1	19.9 (SDP)	D.Shaw	87
011	SOUTHAMPTON ITCHEN ç	12.18	44.3	32.1	23.6 (SDP)	C.Chope	83
011	SOUTHAMPTON TEST	12.32	45.6	33.2	21.2 (Lib)	J.Hill §	79
011	GRAVESHAM	15.23	50.1	34.8	15.1 (Lib)	J.Arnold	87
(011	STEVENAGE(3)	16.47	42.1	25.4	32.5 (SDP)	T.Wood	83)
(011	WELWYN HATFIELD	19.26	45.6	26.4	27.3 (SDP)	D.Evans	87)

§ Hill also represented Southampton Test from 70 to October 74

LABOUR SEATS VULNERABLE TO CONSERVATIVE

Last 3	Constituency	Lab maj	Con	Lab	Lib/SD	Sitting MP	Since
012	OXFORD E	2.62	40.4	43.0	15.6 (Lib)	A.Smith	87

CONSERVATIVE SEATS VULNERABLE TO LIBERAL DEMOCRAT

Last 3	Constituency	Con maj	Con	Lab	Lib/SD	Sitting MP	Since
01*1	PORTSMOUTH S ‡	0.38	43.3	13.0	42.9 (SDP)	D.Martin	87
331	ISLE OF WIGHT	8.20	51.2	5.9	42.9 (Lib)	B.Field	87
011	OXFORD WEST & ABINGDON	8.99	46.4	14.9	37.4 (SDP)	J.Patten	79
011	STEVENAGE (3)	9.54	42.1	25.4	32.5 (SDP)	T.Wood	83
011	CHELMSFORD	11.44	51.9	6.9	40.5 (Lib)	S.Burns	87
011	WINCHESTER	12.16	52.3	6.6	40.2 (SDP)	J.Browne	79
011	HASTINGS & RYE	14.06	50.1	13.1	36.0 (Lib)	K.Warren †	70
011	EASTBOURNE	30.19	59.9	8.8	29.7 (Lib)		
BY-ELECTION 18.10.90: LIB DEM GAIN LD maj 9.87			40.9	5.0	50.8 (LD)	D.Bellotti	

‡ PORTSMOUTH S: won by SDP at by-election of 14.6.84, regained by Conservatives at 1987 election.

SOUTH WEST

SHARE OF VOTE IN LAST 4 GENERAL ELECTIONS

	Con	Lab	Lib/SD	Swing
1974[2]	43.1	29.1	27.4	
1979	51.3	24.8	22.7	6.3 to Con
1983	51.4	14.7	33.2	5.2 Con to L/SD
1987	50.6	15.9	33.0	0.3 Con to L/SD
1974-87	+7.5	-13.2	+5.6	10.4 Lab to Con

ANOTHER LABOUR wasteland. As late as 1979 Labour outpolled the Liberals in this region and took five seats to their one. Now they have only one – Bristol South – and there are only four others where they start in second place. Since October 1974, when they last won a general election, Labour have seen their share of the South West vote decline from 29 to 16 per cent.

Their best hopes this time are the cities of Bristol and Plymouth. Of their four target seats, two are in Bristol and a third, Kingswood, takes in a slice of the city. Bristol East was the seat which Tony Benn lost in 1983, putting himself out of the running for the Labour leadership. In Plymouth, in local government terms a Labour city, they start third in all three constituencies, but hope to benefit from the decline and fall of the SDP. Plymouth Drake, held by Janet Fookes (who if she survives will be a contender for Speaker of the Commons) qualifies as a three-way marginal. The Liberal Democrats could take it on a swing of 4 per cent, but Labour nurse hopes of coming from behind and taking it on a swing of 9 per cent. All three parties have hopes of Devonport, where Dr David Owen has decided not to stand again. The Conservatives need a swing of 6.5 to take the seat: Labour could do it on 6.9. The third Plymouth seat, Sutton, held by the maverick Conservative minister Alan Clark, could be more of a straight Conservative-Lib Dem fight.

There are several seats here which look ripe for tactical voting. In Chris Patten's Bath and in Cheltenham – where the Conservative party has been in turmoil over the selection of John Taylor,

a black, non-local candidate – the Labour vote has been so much squeezed already that there may not be much more to give. The same is true of Jeremy Thorpe's old seat of Devon North, Cornwall North and Cornwall South East, based on the old Bodmin seat (though Bodmin itself has moved into Cornwall North), which the Conservative Robert Hicks lost to the Liberal Paul Tyler in February 1974 and regained from him eight months later.

Perhaps the most intriguing contest will be in Falmouth and Camborne. David Mudd, the Conservative MP since 1970 when he won it from Labour's Dr John Dunwoody, became increasingly detached from his party, fighting the 1987 campaign as a kind of Cornish independent and playing down his party affiliation. Now he is standing down. His replacement is Sebastian Coe, a great international athlete, but no Cornishman. The SDP had a fine result in 1987, and the Liberal Democrats should start as the obvious challengers. If tactical voters swing from Labour, which took 20.8 per cent of the vote in 1987, to the Liberal Democrats, Coe could be in trouble. Other seats where there might be room for tactical voting are Exeter, where Labour, who lost the seat to the Conservatives in 1970 (that was *Mrs* Dunwoody), finished third in 1987 with 22.5 per cent; and Bristol West, where the Health Secretary William Waldegrave would lose to the Liberal Democrats on a swing of just over 7 per cent. Much will hang on whether past Labour voters decide on the basis of recent electoral recovery that their party is in with a chance, or whether they look for other means of turning out the Conservatives. ●

CONSERVATIVE SEATS VULNERABLE TO LABOUR

Last 3	Constituency	Con maj	Con	Lab	Lib/SD	Sitting MP	Since
211	SWINDON	7.24	43.8	36.6	19.6 (SDP)	S.Coombes	83
011	KINGSWOOD	7.50	44.9	37.4	17.7 (SDP)	R.Hayward	83
011	BRISTOL E	8.20	43.6	35.4	20.4 (Lib)	J.Sayeed	83
011	BRISTOL NW	12.01	46.6	34.6	18.8 (SDP)	M.Stern	83
(011	PLYMOUTH DRAKE (3)	17.20	41.3	24.1	33.3 (SDP)	Miss J.Fookes	74[1])
111	GLOUCESTERSHIRE W	18.46	46.2	27.8	26.0 (SDP)	P.Marland	79

LABOUR SEATS VULNERABLE TO CONSERVATIVE

Last 3	Constituency	Lab maj	Con	Lab	Lib/SD	Sitting MP	Since
022	BRISTOL S	2.76	38.1	40.9	19.5 (SDP)	Mrs D.Primarolo	87

CONSERVATIVE SEATS VULNERABLE TO LIBERAL DEMOCRAT

Last 3	Constituency	Con maj	Con	Lab	Lib/SD	Sitting MP	Since
111	BATH	2.73	45.4	10.6	42.7 (SDP)	C.Patten	79
011	CHELTENHAM	7.83	50.2	7.5	42.3 (Lib)	Sir C.Irving †	74[2]
011	PLYMOUTH SUTTON	7.92	45.8	16.4	37.8 (Lib)	A.Clark	74[1]
011	PLYMOUTH DRAKE (3)	7.97	41.3	24.1	33.3 (SDP)	Miss J.Fookes	74[1]
011	DEVON NORTH	8.10	50.9	6.3	42.8 (Lib)	A.Spellar	79
011	FALMOUTH & CAMBORNE	9.32	43.9	20.8	34.6 (SDP)	D.Mudd †	70
011	CORNWALL N	9.84	51.7	6.4	41.9 (Lib)	Sir G.Neale	79
011	DEVON WEST & TORRIDGE	11.02	50.3	8.5	39.2 (Lib)	Miss E.Nicholson	87
011	CORNWALL SE	11.82	51.6	8.7	39.7 (Lib)	R.Hicks §	74[2]
111	EXETER	12.62	44.4	22.5	31.8 (SDP)	J.Hannam	70
011	WESTON-SUPER-MARE	13.85	49.4	11.4	35.6 (SDP)	J.Wiggin	69*
011	BRISTOL W	14.19	45.5	20.9	31.3 (Lib)	W.Waldegrave	79
011	ST IVES	14.50	48.4	17.8	33.8 (SDP)	D.Harris	83
011	WESTBURY	15.21	51.6	12.0	36.4 (Lib)	Sir D.Walters †	64
011	WELLS	15.97	53.5	8.7	37.6 (Lib)	D.Heathcoat-Amory	83

§ Hicks represented Bodmin from 70 to February 74. The seat became Cornwall SE after the 1979 election.

LIB DEM SEATS VULNERABLE TO CONSERVATIVE

Last 3	Constituency	LD maj	Con	Lab	Lib/SD	Sitting MP	Since
03*3	TRURO	8.21	40.8	10.2	49.0 (Lib)	M.Taylor	87*

SDP SEAT VULNERABLE TO CONSERVATIVES

Last 3	Constituency	SD maj	Con	Lab	Lib/SD	Sitting MP	Since
033	PLYMOUTH DEVONPORT (3)	12.99	29.3	28.4	42.3 (SDP)	Dr D.Owen †	66

SDP SEAT VULNERABLE TO LABOUR

Last 3	Constituency	SD maj	Con	Lab	Lib/SD	Sitting MP	Since
(033	PLYMOUTH DEVONPORT (3)	13.80	29.3	28.4	42.3 (SDP)	Dr D.Owen †	66)

EAST ANGLIA

SHARE OF VOTE IN LAST 4 GENERAL ELECTIONS

	Con	Lab	Lib/SD	Swing
1974[2]	43.8	35.5	20.6	
1979	50.8	32.6	16.0	5.0 to Con
1983	51.0	20.5	28.2	6.2 to Con
1987	52.1	27.1	25.7	0.05 to Lab
1974-87	+8.3	-8.4	+5.1	8.4 to Con

EAST ANGLIA may only have a few marginal seats in this election, but one of them offers a classic three-way struggle that could well produce one of the most intriguing contests. Cambridge is Labour in local government, but more often than not Conservative at national level. Robert Rhodes James, a historian and biographer who was once an assistant clerk in the Commons, is standing down.

The Alliance came second in 1987 with 30.6 per cent of the vote, and the Liberal Democrats could win on a swing of 5 per cent this time. But the Alliance candidate then was Shirley Williams and now that she has gone, Labour, who could win on a swing of 6 per cent, hope to emerge as the main challengers. Unless there is a crop of constituency polls (which is likely) the mechanism to trigger a tactical vote won't be there. If the two parties once again take a near-equal share of the vote, that may well ensure continuing Conservative tenure.

Clement Freud, a Liberal MP for this area since he won the old Isle of Ely seat in the 1973 by-election, lost Cambridgeshire North East to the Conservative Malcolm Moss in 1987. He is not standing again. Lib Dem chances would be brighter if there were more of a Labour vote to squeeze. The other Cambridgeshire marginal is Peterborough, which like most other new town seats has not been kind to Labour in recent elections. The incumbent Conservative Dr Brian Mawhinney is a minister at the Northern Ireland office.

Labour hope to reunite Norwich North, which they lost in 1983, with Norwich South, which went Conservative in 1983 but returned to Labour in 1987. There is a solid third-party vote in each of these constituencies, and the way it moves could be crucial, particularly in Norwich South. Labour's best chance of all should be Ipswich, though this seat maintains the old East Anglian tradition of refusing to swim with the tide. In February 1974 Ernle Money held it against the swing for the Conservatives. He lost in October to Ken Weetch, who held it for Labour against the swing in 1979 and 1983, only to lose it against the swing to Michael Irvine, son of the former Labour minister Sir Arthur Irvine, in 1987. ●

CONSERVATIVE SEATS VULNERABLE TO LABOUR

Last 3	Constituency	Con maj	Con	Lab	Lib/SD	Sitting MP	Since
021	**IPSWICH**	**1.66**	44.4	42.7	12.6 (SDP)	M.Irvine	87
(011	**CAMBRIDGE (3)**	**11.65**	40.0	28.3	30.6 (SDP)	R.Rhodes James †	76*)
011	**NORWICH N**	**15.65**	45.8	30.2	24.0 (Lib)	P.Thompson	83
011	**PETERBOROUGH**	**15.79**	49.4	33.7	16.1 (Lib)	B.Mawhinney	79
011	**WAVENEY**	**18.35**	48.4	30.0	21.6 (SDP)	D.Porter	87

LABOUR SEAT VULNERABLE TO CONSERVATIVE

Last 3	Constituency	Lab maj	Con	Lab	Lib/SD	Sitting MP	Since
012	**NORWICH S**	**0.64**	37.2	37.9	24.9 (SDP)	J.Garrett §	87

§ Garrett also represented Norwich S from February 1974 – 1983

CONSERVATIVE SEATS VULNERABLE TO LIBERAL DEMOCRAT

Last 3	Constituency	Con maj	Con	Lab	Lib/SD	Sitting MP	since
031	**CAMBRIDGESHIRE NE**	**2.49**	47.0	8.5	44.5 (Lib)	M.Moss	87
011	**CAMBRIDGE (3)**	**9.35**	40.0	28.3	30.6 (SDP)	R.Rhodes James †	76*

EAST MIDLANDS

SHARE OF VOTE IN LAST 4 GENERAL ELECTIONS

	Con	Lab	Lib/SD	Swing
1974[2]	38.2	43.1	17.2	
1979	46.6	39.6	12.8	6.0 to Con
1983	47.2	28.0	24.1	6.1 to Con
1987	48.6	30.0	21.0	0.3 to Lab
1974-87	+10.4	-13.1	+3.8	11.8 to Con

THIS HAS been as grim a region as any for Labour since 1979. They did badly in 1983 and badly again in 1987 when things went better nationally, hurt this time by the backwash of the miners' strike of 1984-85 when the Nottinghamshire coalfield stood out against the NUM national leadership and worked through the strike. That experience seemed to solidify a mood which was already working against Labour when the Conservatives captured seats in mining areas, like Sherwood in 1983. At the 1979 election there were 27 constituencies in Nottinghamshire, Derbyshire and Leicestershire: Labour won 15 and the Conservatives 12. At the 1983 election there were 29 constituencies (following boundary changes) of which Labour won 9 and the Conservatives 20.

In 1987 the Conservatives tightened their grip on these seats and even came close to turning Labour out of Mansfield, where Alan Meale, who backed the NUM, replaced the retiring Labour MP Don Concannon, who had sympathised with the UDM breakaway. But they regained the two seats in Leicester they had lost four years earlier. The three East Midland cities of Derby, Leicester and Nottingham were always rich in marginals and continue that way since the boundary revision which followed the 1979 election. All eight of the main city seats qualify as marginals:

	Maj 79	Maj 83	Maj 87
Derby N	Lab 0.3	Con 6.9*	Con 11.6
Derby S	Lab 11.3	Lab 0.9*	Lab 3.2
Leicester E	Lab 5.6	Con 2.0	Lab 3.7
Leicester S	Lab 3.8	Con 0.0	Lab 3.3
Nottingham N	Lab 5.8	Con 0.7*	Lab 3.3
Nottingham S	Lab 4.4	Con 11.8*	Con 4.2
Nottingham E	Lab 10.6	Con 3.3*	Con 1.0

* denotes a major boundary change

Among the marginal incumbents is Margaret Beckett (Derby South) who is destined for a big government job, probably Chief Secretary to the Treasury, if Labour returns to power. In October 1974, as Margaret Jackson, she took Lincoln from Dick Taverne, whose breakaway from Labour to form his own party was a precursor of the SDP split in 1981. She lost the seat in 1979 and was out of the Commons for four years before returning for Derby South. Among possible Conservative casualties is Edwina Currie (Derbyshire South), the former minister who lost her job after some ill-advised remarks about eggs. Sandy Feather, Labour's candidate at Corby, is the son of Vic Feather, the former TUC general secretary. At High Peak, the Conservative MP, Christopher Hawkins, is standing down for reasons of health. The Liberal Democrats, not strong in this territory, have their eyes on Sir Peter Tapsell's seat, Lindsey East.●

CONSERVATIVE SEATS VULNERABLE TO LABOUR

Last 3	Constituency	Con maj	Con	Lab	Lib/SD	Sitting MP	Since
011	NOTTINGHAM E	0.97	42.9	42.0	14.7 (Lib)	M.Knowles	83
011	CORBY	3.43	44.3	40.9	14.8 (Lib)	W.Powell	83
011	NOTTINGHAM S	4.17	44.7	40.5	14.8 (SDP)	M.Brandon-Bravo	83
011	SHERWOOD	7.69	45.8	38.2	16.0 (SDP)	A.Stewart	83
011	DERBY N	11.56	48.8	37.3	13.4 (Lib)	G.Knight	83
011	LINCOLN	12.84	46.5	33.7	19.4 (SDP)	K.Carlisle	79
011	LEICESTERSHIRE NW	13.38	47.6	34.3	17.1 (Lib)	D.Ashby	83
011	DERBYSHIRE S	15.85	49.1	33.2	17.7 (SDP)	Mrs E.Currie	83
011	EREWASH	16.47	48.6	32.1	19.3 (SDP)	P.Rost †	70
011	HIGH PEAK	16.90	45.7	28.8	25.5 (SDP)	C.Hawkins †	83
011	AMBER VALLEY	17.08	51.4	34.4	14.2 (Lib)	P.Oppenheim	83
011	NORTHAMPTON N	17.91	48.0	30.1	20.7 (Lib)	A.Marlow	79

LABOUR SEATS VULNERABLE TO CONSERVATIVE

Last 3	Constituency	Lab maj	Con	Lab	Lib/SD	Sitting MP	Since
022	MANSFIELD	0.10	37.3	37.5	22.2 (SDP)	A.Meale	87
222	LEICESTER W	2.41	42.0	44.5	13.5 (SDP)	G.Janner	70
022	DERBY S	3.15	40.5	43.7	15.8 (SDP)	Mrs M.Beckett	83
012	NOTTINGHAM N	3.29	41.6	44.9	11.7 (SDP)	G.Allen	87
212	LEICESTER S	3.32	40.8	44.2	13.8 (Lib)	J.Marshall	87§
212	LEICESTER E ç	3.68	42.5	46.1	11.4 (SDP)	K.Vaz	87

§ Marshall was also MP for Leicester S from October 74 to 83

CONSERVATIVE SEAT VULNERABLE TO LIBERAL DEMOCRATS

Last 3	Constituency	Lab maj	Con	Lab	Lib/SD	Sitting MP	Since
011	LINDSEY EAST	15.47	52.16	11.14	36.69 (Lib)	Sir P. Tapsell	66

WEST MIDLANDS

SHARE OF VOTE IN LAST 4 GENERAL ELECTIONS

	Con	Lab	Lib/SD	Swing
1974[2]	37.5	43.9	17.8	
1979	47.1	40.1	11.5	6.7 to Con
1983	45.0	31.2	23.4	3.4 to Con
1987	45.5	33.3	20.8	0.8 to Lab
1974-87	+8.0	-10.6	+3.0	9.3 to Con

THE THATCHER years were sometimes grim for manufacturing England, but the West Midlands, heartland of manufacturing, continued to look like predominantly Conservative territory until the autumn of 1990, when in the high tide of protest over the poll tax and misery over mortgages, the party lost Mid-Staffordshire, one of its safest seats, to Labour on a swing of 21.4 per cent. Opinion polls at that time suggested the seat might revert to the Conservatives in a general election, and given the exceptional size of the swing there is clearly a prospect of that; though the polls said Greenwich would return to Labour after Rosie Barnes won it for the SDP in 1987, and she proved them wrong.

Though the 1987 election produced a modest swing to Labour across the region, its gain at The Wrekin was offset by the loss of Wolverhampton North East to the Conservative Maureen Hicks. This time their target seats include Warwickshire North, defended by the minister Francis Maude; the Birmingham Selly Oak constituency of the voluble Tory populist Anthony Beaumont-Dark; and Birmingham Northfield, which Labour won in a by-election in October 1982 only to lose it at the general election eight months later.

Labour may be in some trouble in Coventry South-East where Dave Nellist, expelled from the party for alleged links with the Militant Tendency, may stand as an independent. His record as a constituency MP has won praise even from some who strongly oppose his views.

This is mostly barren territory for third parties. Hereford looks promising for the Liberal Democrats, but so it has before and the Conservatives have always fought them off. Results in the last two rounds of local elections suggest a Liberal surge in Birmingham Yardley; if they can carry that over to the general election this seat may be more marginal than the figures make it look. Peter Walker, a long-serving cabinet minister of (in the Thatcher years) dissident tendencies, is standing down at Worcester, but the loss of his personal vote seems unlikely to threaten the Tories. Just a small Conservative push would give them both Walsall seats, West Bromwich East, held by the cheerfully combative Peter Snape for Labour, and The Wrekin, which has changed hands pretty regularly throughout this century – though so has the nature of the constituency, which is now based on Telford new town. ●

CONSERVATIVE SEATS VULNERABLE TO LABOUR

Last 3	Constituency	Con maj	Con	Lab	Lib/SD	Sitting MP	Since
021	WOLVERHAMPTON NE	0.43	42.1	41.7	16.2 (Lib)	Mrs M.Hicks	87
011	BIRMINGHAM SELLY OAK	4.89	44.2	39.3	15.4 (Lib)	A.Beaumont-Dark	79
011	CANNOCK & BURNTWOOD	4.94	44.5	39.5	16.0 (Lib)	G.Howarth	83
011	WARWICKSHIRE N	5.01	45.1	40.1	14.8 (SDP)	F.Maude	83
1*11	BIRMINGHAM NORTHFIELD ‡	5.88	45.1	39.3	15.6 (SDP)	R.King	83
011	BIRMINGHAM YARDLEY	5.99	42.6	36.6	20.8 (Lib)	D.Gilroy Bevan	79
011	COVENTRY SW	6.22	43.3	37.0	19.7 (Lib)	J.Butcher	79
011	NUNEATON	10.31	44.9	34.6	19.2 (SDP)	L.Stevens	83
011	DUDLEY W	15.84	49.8	34.0	16.2 (Lib)	J.Blackburn	79
011	BIRMINGHAM HALL GREEN	16.69	44.8	28.2	27.0 (SDP)	A.Hargreaves	87
111	BURTON	17.09	50.7	33.6	15.7 (Lib)	I.Lawrence	74[1]
011	WORCESTER	19.75	48.2	28.4	23.4 (SDP)	P.Walker †	61*
011	STAFFORDSHIRE MID	25.89	50.6	24.7	23.2 (Lib)		
BY-ELECTION	22.3.90: LAB GAIN Lab maj	16.76	32.3	49.1	11.1 (LD) 2.5 (SDP)	Mrs S.Heal	

LABOUR SEATS VULNERABLE TO CONSERVATIVE

Last 3	Constituency	Lab maj	Con	Lab	Lib/SD	Sitting MP	Since
022	WALSALL S	2.21	42.7	44.9	12.4 (Lib)	B.George	74[1]
012	WREKIN	2.25	40.6	42.8	16.6 (SDP)	B.Grocott	87
022	WEST BROMWICH E	2.30	40.2	42.6	17.1 (Lib)	P.Snape	74[1]
022	WALSALL N	3.55	39.0	42.6	18.4 (Lib)	D.Winnick	79

CONSERVATIVE SEATS VULNERABLE TO LIB DEM

Last 3	Constituency	Con maj	Con	Lab	Lib/SD	Sitting MP	Since
111	HEREFORD	2.70	47.5	7.7	44.8 (Lib)	C.Shepherd	74[2]
011	WYRE FOREST	13.15	47.1	18.9	34.0 (Lib)	A.Coombs	87

LABOUR SEAT VULNERABLE TO LIB DEM

Last 3	Constituency	Lab maj	Con	Lab	Lib/SD	Sitting MP	Since
02*2	NEWCASTLE-UNDER-LYME	9.62	27.9	40.5	30.9 (Lib)	Mrs L.Golding	86*

‡ BIRMINGHAM NORTHFIELD: Won by Labour at by-election of 28.10.82, regained by Conservatives at 1983 election.

WALES

SHARE OF VOTE IN LAST 4 GENERAL ELECTIONS

	Con	Lab	Lib/SD	Nat	Swing
1974 [2]	23.9	49.5	15.5	11.1	
1979	32.2	48.6	10.6	8.6	4.6 to Com
1983	31.0	37.5	23.2	7.8	5.0 to Con
1987	29.5	45.1	17.9	7.3	4.6 to Lab
1974-87	+5.6	-4.4	+2.4	-3.8	5.0 to Con

LABOUR DID well here in 1987 and two of its three gains from the Conservatives in by-elections since have come in Wales – Vale of Glamorgan on a swing of 12.4 per cent and Monmouth on a swing of 12.6. Should the Labour trend continue, Labour could hope to take Delyn, where Keith Raffan has decided at the age of 41 not to run again, and Cardiff Central, held by Ian Grist, recently dropped as a Welsh office minister. They will also hope to capture Pembroke, which has not been Labour since Desmond Donnelly, its MP from 1950 became first Independent Labour and then a Democrat in the 1966 parliament.

The problem for the Liberal Democrats is that the seats they fancy are three-party marginals where Labour is also in with a chance. They start second in Conwy, which would go Liberal Democrat on a swing of 4 per cent or Labour on a swing of 8 per cent, but third in Cardiff Central, where Labour needs a 3 per cent swing and the Liberal Democrats a 4 per cent swing. The tightest constituency of all, though, is Brecon and Radnor,

a Liberal gain in the 1985 by-election, where the Conservatives start just 0.1 per cent behind Richard Livsey and Labour could come from third place to win on a swing of 3 per cent. The Liberal Democrats have to worry about Alex Carlile's Montgomery; but it will take a bigger disturbance to dislodge the long-serving Geraint Howells from Ceredigion and Pembroke North.

The Nationalists flourish in pockets – Caernarfon has become one of the safest seats in Britain – but flounder in others. At the Monmouth by-election in May 1991 a joint Plaid Cymru Green Party candidate finished behind Screaming Lord Sutch.

There are no seats easily vulnerable to Nationalist attack, while Ynys Mon (Anglesey) would go back to the Conservatives, who lost it in 1987, on a swing of around 5 per cent. Dafydd Elis Thomas, who has held the seat since 1974, is not defending Meirionydd Nant Conwy, where the Nationalist majority over the Conservatives last time was 11.7 per cent.●

CONSERVATIVE SEATS VULNERABLE TO LABOUR

Last 3	Constituency	Con maj	Con	Lab	Lib/SD	Nat	Sitting MP	Since
011	DELYN	2.33	41.4	39.1	17.0 (Lib)	2.5	K.Raffan †	83
011	CARDIFF C(3)	4.83	37.1	32.3	29.3 (Lib)	1.3	I.Grist	74[1]
011	PEMBROKE	10.02	41.0	31.0	26.1 (Lib)	1.9	N.Bennett	87
011*	VALE OF GLAMORGAN	12.07	46.8	34.7	16.7 (SDP)	1.8		
BY-ELECTION 4.5.89: LAB GAIN Lab maj 12.60			36.3	48.9	4.2 (LD) 2.3 (SDP)	3.5	J.Smith	
(011	CONWY (3)	16.43	38.7	22.3	31.2 (Lib)	7.8	Sir W.Roberts	70)
011	CARDIFF N	18.58	45.3	26.7	26.5 (SDP)	1.5	G.Jones	83
011*	MONMOUTH	19.85	47.5	27.7	24.0 (SDP)	0.8		
BY-ELECTION 16.5.91: LAB GAIN Lab maj 5.33			34.0	39.3	24.8 (SDP)	0.6 @	H.Edwards	

@ denotes joint Plaid Cymru and Green Party candidate

LABOUR SEATS VULNERABLE TO CONSERVATIVE

Last 3	Constituency	Lab maj	Con	Lab	Lib/SD	Nat	Sitting MP	Since
012	CLWYD SW	2.18	33.2	35.4	22.9 (SDP)	8.5	M.Jones	87
022	CARMARTHEN (3)	7.98	27.4	35.4	13.3 (SDP)	23.0	A.Williams	87

CONSERVATIVE SEATS VULNERABLE TO LIBERAL DEMOCRAT

Last 3	Constituency	Con maj	Con	Lab	Lib/SD	Nat	Sitting MP	Since
011	CONWY (3)	7.43	38.7	22.3	31.2 (Lib)	7.8	Sir W.Roberts	70
(011	CARDIFF C (3)	7.74	37.1	32.3	29.3 (Lib)	1.3	I.Grist	74¹)
(011	PEMBROKE (3)	14.91	41.0	31.0	26.1 (Lib)	1.9	N.Bennett	87)

LABOUR SEAT VULNERABLE TO LIBERAL DEMOCRAT

Last 3	Constituency	Lab maj	Con	Lab	Lib/SD	Nat	Sitting MP	Since
(012	CLWYD SW	12.56	33.2	35.4	22.9 (SDP)	8.5	M.Jones	87)

LIBERAL DEMOCRAT SEAT VULNERABLE TO LABOUR

Last 3	Constituency	LD maj	Con	Lab	Lib/SD	Nat	Sitting MP	Since
(11*3	BRECON & RADNOR ‡ (3)	5.59	34.7	29.2	34.8 (Lib)	1.3	R.Livsey	85*)

LIBERAL DEMOCRAT SEATS VULNERABLE TO CONSERVATIVE

Last 3	Constituency	LD maj	Con	Lab	Lib/SD	Nat	Sitting MP	Since
11*3	BRECON & RADNOR ‡ (3)	0.13	34.7	29.2	34.8 (Lib)	1.3	R.Livsey	*85
133	MONTGOMERY	8.09	38.5	10.4	46.6 (Lib)	4.5	A.Carlile	83
033	C'DIGION AND P'BROKE N	9.73	26.9	18.6	36.6 (Lib)	16.2	G.Howells	74¹

NATIONALIST SEATS VULNERABLE TO CONSERVATIVE

Last 3	Constituency	Nat maj	Con	Lab	Lib/SD	Nat	Sitting MP	Since
114	YNYS MON	10.00	33.2	16.9	6.7 (SDP)	43.2	I.Jones	87
044	MEIRIONNYDD N CONWY	11.65	28.3	16.9	14.8 (SDP)	40.0	D.E.Thomas	74¹

LABOUR SEAT VULNERABLE TO NATIONALIST

Last 3	Constituency	Lab maj	Con	Lab	Lib/SD	Nat	Sitting MP	Since
(022	CARMARTHEN (3)	12.34	27.4	35.4	13.3 (SDP)	23.0	A.Williams	87)

‡ Brecon and Radnor. Won by Liberal at by-election of 4.7.85

NORTH WEST

SHARE OF VOTE IN LAST 4 GENERAL ELECTIONS

	Con	Lab	Lib/SD	Swing
1974[2]	37.0	44.6	18.0	
1979	43.7	42.6	13.0	4.4 to Con
1983	40.0	36.0	23.4	1.5 to Con
1987	38.0	41.2	20.6	3.6 to Lab
1974-87	+1.0	-3.4	+2.6	2.2 to Con

I N 1983 Labour took the last Conservative seat in Liverpool; in 1987 it cleared the Conservatives out of Manchester. Elsewhere in the region the story was rather different, with a crop of new young Conservative members elected in 1983 in Bury North and South, Bolton North East and West, Stockport, Hyndburn (based on the former Accrington seat) and Lancashire West (which includes Skelmersdale new town) and holding their seats in 1987 – mostly with reduced majorities, though Kenneth Hargreaves at Hyndburn went from 21 (0.0 per cent) to 2,220 (4.6 per cent) while Alistair Burt at Bury North improved from 2,792 (5.3 per cent) to 6,911 (12.3).

Arithmetically the most vulnerable North West Conservative is the Overseas Development minister, Lynda Chalker, at Wallasey, but local election results suggest that the internal feuding which has riven Merseyside north and south of the river may have blunted Labour's chances. In neighbouring Birkenhead, the Labour MP Frank Field was ousted by his local party but the decision was suspended to allow an internal inquiry. He was later reselected, though in contentious circumstances, leaving the local party bitter and divided. The Labour MP for Liverpool Broadgreen Terry Fields, expelled from the party for alleged links with Militant, is likely to stand as an independent. As the sitting MP, he could fare better than the "Real Labour" candidate who stood against Labour, with Militant support, in the Walton by-election.

The Department of Environment minister David Trippier could be in difficulties in Rossendale and Darwen, one of a string of Pennine seats which tend to vote more Conservative than they look. Peter Morrison, Mrs Thatcher's last parliamentary private secretary, is standing down at Chester where the new Conservative candidate is the entertainer Gyles Brandreth. Pendle, which is largely the old Nelson and Colne constituency, has been the scene of especially bitter opposition to the poll tax: the Conservatives must hope that this has now been dissipated by the Chancellor's cuts and the promise to scrap it. The constituency is a nest of Liberal community politics veterans, but their hopes for second place in 1987 were not realised.

This is one of the North West constituencies where there might be scope for tactical voting – as there also might in former SDP territory like Warrington South and Stockport. But Littleborough and Saddleworth, a name whose decorative portliness does justice to its Conservative MP, Geoffrey Dickens, could prove to be one of those three-way marginals where the two challenging parties slug it out to the benefit of the Conservatives. The Liberal Democrats, starting second, need a swing of just over 6 per cent; Labour, starting third, a swing of about 9 per cent.

Liberal Democrat hopes hang on Ribble Valley, their by-election success of March 1991 won on a swing of 24.8 per cent, which owed quite a lot to the poll tax. Crosby, the scene of a spectacular Alliance gain when Shirley Williams was candidate, may be tougher than it looks; Hazel Grove is a perennial hope which has stubbornly stuck with the Tories.

The Conservatives will be wanting revenge in Southport, an unexpected loss to the Alliance last time. The Liberal Democrats could have trouble in Rochdale, where Sir Cyril Smith really is retiring this time, and in Liverpool Mossley Hill, the only non-Labour seat in the city. ●

CONSERVATIVE SEATS VULNERABLE TO LABOUR

Last 3	Constituency	Con maj	Con	Lab	Lib/SD	Sitting MP	Since
111	WALLASEY	0.52	42.5	41.9	15.6 (SDP)	Mrs L.Chalker	74[1]
011	BOLTON NE	1.73	44.4	42.6	13.0 (SDP)	P.Thurnham	83
011	LANCASHIRE W	2.23	43.7	41.5	14.8 (SDP)	K.Hind	83
011	ELLESMERE PORT & NESTON	3.21	44.4	41.2	14.1 (SDP)	M.Woodcock †	83
011	HYNDBURN	4.56	44.4	39.8	15.2 (SDP)	K.Hargreaves	83
011	PENDLE	5.07	40.4	35.3	24.3 (Lib)	J.Lee	79
011	BURY S	5.16	46.0	40.9	13.1 (SDP)	D.Sumberg	83
011	STOCKPORT	6.08	41.4	35.3	22.1 (SDP)	A.Favell	83
011	WARRINGTON S	6.10	42.0	35.8	22.2 (Lib)	C.Butler	87
011	BOLTON W	8.21	44.3	36.1	19.6 (SDP)	T.Sackville	83
011	ROSSENDALE & DARWEN	8.27	46.6	38.3	15.1 (Lib)	D.Trippier	79
011	CHESTER	9.24	44.9	35.6	19.5 (Lib)	Sir P.Morrison †	74[1]
011	BURY N	12.36	50.1	37.8	12.1 (Lib)	A.Burt	83
011	CHORLEY	13.34	48.0	34.7	16.1 (Lib)	D.Dover	79
011	S.RIBBLE	14.15	47.2	33.1	19.7 (Lib)	R.Atkins	79
011	LANCASTER	14.24	46.7	32.4	19.9 (Lib)	Dame E.K-Bowman	70
111	BLACKPOOL S	15.95	48.0	32.1	19.9 (SDP)	Sir P.Blaker †	64
011	DAVYHULME	16.17	46.6	30.4	23.0 (Lib)	W.Churchill	70
111	BLACKPOOL N	17.00	48.0	31.0	21.0 (Lib)	N.Miscampbell †	62*
(011	LITTLEBRO. & S/DLEWTH (3)	17.06	43.1	26.0	30.9 (Lib)	G.Dickens	83)

LABOUR SEAT VULNERABLE TO CONSERVATIVE

Last 3	Constituency	Lab maj	Con	Lab	Lib/SD	Sitting MP	Since
022	CREWE & NANTWICH	1.89	42.1	44.0	13.9 (SDP)	Mrs G.Dunwoody	74[1]

CONSERVATIVE SEATS VULNERABLE TO LIBERAL DEMOCRAT

Last 3	Constituency	Con maj	Con	Lab	Lib/SD	Sitting MP	Since
011	HAZEL GROVE	3.43	45.5	11.8	42.0 (Lib)	Sir T.Arnold	74[2]
0*11	CROSBY ‡	10.26	46.2	17.9	35.9 (SDP)	M.Thornton	83
011	LTTLBRO. & SDDLWTH (3)	12.12	43.1	26.0	30.9 (Lib)	G.Dickens	83
011	CONGLETON	14.52	48.3	17.9	33.8 (Lib)	Mrs A.Winterton	83
011*	RIBBLE VALLEY	39.43	60.9	17.7	21.4 (SDP)		
BY-ELECTION 7.3.91 LIB DEM GAIN		LD maj 9.97	38.5	9.4	48.5 (LD)	M.Carr	

LIBERAL DEMOCRAT SEAT VULNERABLE TO CONSERVATIVE

Last 3	Constituency	LD maj	Con	Lab	Lib/SD	Sitting MP	Since
113	SOUTHPORT	3.39	44.5	6.4	47.9 (Lib)	R.Fearn	87

LIBERAL DEMOCRAT SEATS VULNERABLE TO LABOUR

Last 3	Constituency	LD maj	Con	Lab	Lib/SD	Sitting MP	Since
033	LIVERPOOL MOSSLEY HILL	4.85	17.5	38.8	43.7 (Lib)	D.Alton	79*
333	ROCHDALE	5.42	18.6	38.0	43.4 (Lib)	Sir C.Smith †	72*

‡ CROSBY: Seat was won by SDP at by-election of 26.11.81, regained by Conservatives at 1983 election.

NORTH

SHARE OF VOTE IN LAST 4 GENERAL ELECTIONS

	Con	Lab	Lib/SD	Swing
1974[2]	31.7	49.9	17.1	
1979	37.7	47.8	13.0	4.1 to Con
1983	34.6	40.2	25.0	2.3 to Con
1987	32.3	46.4	21.0	4.3 to Lab
1974-87	+0.6	-3.5	+3.9	2.1 to Con

THE NORTH, like the North West, swung only modestly to the Conservatives in their three great election years of 1979, 1983 and 1987. The region has 36 seats, only two fewer than Wales, but few marginals, The most intriguing is Stockton South, which the SDP MP Ian Wrigglesworth lost to the Conservative Tim Devlin in 1987 with Labour breathing hotly down the necks of both of them. Wrigglesworth, now Sir Ian, is not standing again. The Liberal Democrats would take it on a swing of 1 per cent, Labour on a swing of 2 per cent. Langbaurgh, which contains much of the old Cleveland constituency, including towns like Guisborough and Saltburn, together with some Middlesbrough suburbs, looks decidedly hopeful for Labour, as does Tynemouth, which has remained a lonely Conservative outpost in largely Labour territory (Newcastle Central, Conservative in 1983, succumbed to Labour in 1987). Langbaurgh's Conservative MP, Richard Holt, died suddenly on September 22, 1991. There was a 6.4 per cent swing to Labour in Tynemouth

in 1987. At Darlington Michael Fallon, the Education Minister, who lost the 1983 by-election to Ossie O'Brien but took the seat three months later at the general election, will put up a sturdy fight. Cecil Franks, at Barrow and Furness, turned out Labour's Albert Booth in 1983 in a contest dominated by doubts about the future of the town's defence industry if Labour won. That is still a sensitive issue, as was seen when Labour tried to dissuade the Campaign for Nuclear Disarmament from holding a rally in the town.

Dr Jack Cunningham, Labour Campaign Co-ordinator, has a campaign of his own to co-ordinate in marginal Copeland – the former Whitehaven: only the name was changed in the last boundary review.

Liberal Democrats will hope to revive the SDP surge which in 1987 came close to taking Blyth Valley. The Liberal Democrats had an astonishing local election success in 1991 in the Wear Valley district, which is partly in Durham North West and partly in Bishop Auckland. ●

CONSERVATIVE SEATS VULNERABLE TO LABOUR

Last 3	Constituency	Con maj	Con	Lab	Lib/SD	Sitting MP	Since
011	LANGBAURGH	3.35	41.7	38.4	19.9 (Lib)	R.Holt **	83
(031	STOCKTON S(3)	3.75	35.0	31.3	33.7 (SDP)	T.Devlin	87)
011	TYNEMOUTH	4.45	43.2	38.8	18.0 (Lib)	N.Trotter	74'
2*11	DARLINGTON ‡	4.99	46.6	41.6	11.8 (Lib)	M.Fallon	83
011	BARROW & FURNESS	7.18	46.5	39.3	14.2 (SDP)	C.Franks	83

LABOUR SEATS VULNERABLE TO CONSERVATIVE

Last 3	Constituency	Lab maj	Con	Lab	Lib/SD	Sitting MP	Since
222	CARLISLE	2.11	40.1	42.2	17.7 (SDP)	E.Martlew	87
222	COPELAND	4.26	43.0	47.2	9.1 (SDP)	J.Cunningham	70
012	NEWCASTLE C	5.38	38.9	44.2	15.8 (SDP)	J.Cousins	87

CONSERVATIVE SEAT VULNERABLE TO LIBERAL DEMOCRAT

Last 3	Constituency	Con maj	Con	Lab	Lib/SD	Sitting MP	Since
031	STOCKTON S (3)	1.30	35.0	31.3	33.7	T.Devlin	87

LABOUR SEATS VULNERABLE TO LIBERAL DEMOCRAT

Last 3	Constituency	Lab maj	Con	Lab	Lib/SD	Sitting MP	Since
022	BLYTH VALLEY	1.85	16.9	42.5	40.6 (SDP)	R.Campbell	87
022	NEWCASTLE N	9.98	24.6	42.7	32.7 (Lib)	D.Henderson	87
022	DURHAM	11.77	21.9	44.9	33.2 (SDP)	G.Steinberg	87

‡ DARLINGTON. Won by Labour at by-election of 24.3.83 but regained by Conservatives at 1983 General Election
** R. Holt died on September 22 1991. Labour gained Langbaurgh at a by-election on November 7.

YORKSHIRE AND HUMBERSIDE

SHARE OF VOTE IN LAST 4 GENERAL ELECTIONS

	Con	Lab	Lib/SD	Swing
1974[2]	31.9	46.9	20.4	
1979	38.8	44.9	15.4	4.5 to Con
1983	38.7	35.3	25.5	4.8 to Con
1987	37.4	40.6	21.7	3.3 to Lab
1974-87	+5.5	-6.3	+1.3	5.9 to Con

A SWING of 5.4 per cent to Labour in Yorkshire and Humberside would give them five gains from the Conservatives, and some should be easy. York, which Labour lost to the Conservative Conal Gregory in 1983, has the smallest Tory majority in Britain and Batley and Spen is not much more substantial.

Colne Valley – much changed by the boundary review which followed the 1979 election – has a turbulent history. The Liberal Richard Wainwright took it off Labour in 1966, the year of a great Labour victory; lost it to Labour in 1970, the year that Labour lost office, and recaptured it in February 1974, when Labour returned to power. He kept it until 1987 when he lost to the Conservative Graham Riddick. Now it's a three-way marginal, which the Conservatives could lose to the Liberal Democrats on a swing of 1.5 per cent or to Labour on a swing of 3.7. Calder Valley was a Liberal hope in 1987 but they were beaten down into third place by resurgent Labour, who now start as the obvious challengers. The Lib Dems may have difficulty persuading old Alliance supporters that they have the better chance of supplanting the Tories.

The Conservatives could gain a clutch of seats on a modest swing, from Bradford South, which would go on a swing of 0.3, to Bradford North, which would fall on a swing of 1.7. But the party was badly beaten at Bradford North in the by-election of November 1990: its share of the vote fell by 22.7 per cent and it slumped to third place behind the Liberal Democrats. A Labour defeat at Dewsbury would cost them a rising front-bench star in Ann Taylor.

Ryedale, which went to the Alliance in the by-election of May 1986, looks safe for the Conservatives now. But the Liberal Democrats will hope to rock the Tories in Richmond, where the SDP took 32.2 per cent of the vote and the Liberal Democrats 22.1 per cent in the by-election of February 1989, which followed Leon Brittan's departure for Brussels. Since the Conservative share of the vote was 37.2 per cent, a single third-party candidate, such as they'll have this time, would probably have won it by a mile. ●

CONSERVATIVE SEATS VULNERABLE TO LABOUR

Last 3	Constituency	Con maj	Con	Lab	LibSD	Sitting MP	Since
211	YORK	0.24	41.6	41.4	16.0 (SDP)	C.Gregory	83
011	BATLEY & SPEN	2.31	43.4	41.1	14.3 (SDP)	Mrs E.Peacock	83
(031	COLNE VALLEY (3)	7.30	36.4	29.1	33.4 (Lib)	G.Riddick	87)
011	ELMET	9.79	46.9	37.1	16.0 (SDP)	S.Batiste	83
011	CALDER VALLEY	10.16	43.5	33.4	23.1 (Lib)	D.Thompson	79
011	KEIGHLEY	10.73	45.8	35.0	19.2 (Lib)	G.Waller	83

LABOUR SEATS VULNERABLE TO CONSERVATIVE

Last 3	Constituency	Lab maj	Con	Lab	Lib/SD	Sitting MP	Since
022	BRADFORD S	0.60	40.8	41.4	17.8 (SDP)	R.Cryer	87
012	DEWSBURY	0.80	41.6	42.4	16.0 (SDP)	Mrs A.Taylor	83
012	GLANFORD & SCUNTHORPE	0.90	42.6	43.5	13.7 (SDP)	E.Morley	87
012	HALIFAX	2.13	41.3	43.4	15.3 (SDP)	Mrs A.Mahon	87
022*	BRADFORD N	3.30	39.5	42.8	17.7 (SDP)		
BY-ELECTION 8.11.90		26.40	16.8	51.7	25.3 (LD)	T.Rooney	
022	WAKEFIELD	5.30	41.3	46.6	12.1 (SDP)	D.Hinchcliffe	87

CONSERVATIVE SEATS VULNERABLE TO LIBERAL DEMOCRAT

Last 3	Constituency	Con maj	Con	Lab	Lib/SD	Sitting MP	Since
031	COLNE VALLEY (3)	2.98	36.4	29.1	33.4 (Lib)	G.Riddick	87
011	LEEDS NW	10.07	43.5	21.7	33.5 (Lib)	K.Hampson	74[1]
011	PUDSEY	11.51	45.5	20.5	34.0 (Lib)	Sir G.Shaw	74[1]
011	SHEFFIELD HALLAM	13.78	46.3	20.4	32.5 (Lib)	I.Patnick	87
01*1	RYEDALE ‡	14.78	53.3	8.1	38.6 (Lib)	J.Greenway	87
011*	RICHMOND	34.25	61.2	11.8	27.0 (Lib)		
BY-ELECTION 23.2.89		5.01	37.2	4.9	22.1 (LD)32.2 (SD)	W.Hague	

LABOUR SEATS VULNERABLE TO LIBERAL DEMOCRAT

Last 3	Constituency	Lab maj	Con	Lab	Lib/SD	Sitting MP	Since
022	SHEFFIELD HILLSBOROUGH	5.52	17.5	44.0	38.5 (Lib)	M.Flannery †	74[1]
032	LEEDS WEST	9.64	23.2	43.2	33.6 (Lib)	J.Battle	87

‡ RYEDALE: this seat was won by Liberal at by-election of 8.5.86, regained by Conservatives at 1987 election.

SCOTLAND

SHARE OF VOTE IN LAST 4 GENERAL ELECTIONS

	Con	Lab	Lib/SD	Nat	Swing
1974[2]	24.7	36.3	8.3	30.7	
1979	31.4	41.5	9.0	18.1	0.8 to Lab
1983	28.4	35.1	24.5	11.8	1.7 to Con
1987	24.0	42.4	19.2	14.0	5.9 to Lab
1974-87	-0.7	+6.1	+10.9	-16.7	3.4 to Lab

SCOTLAND NEVER took to Thatcherism. Though some argued that Scotland, the land of Adam Smith, was in a sense its birthplace, Scotland swung away from the Conservatives during her ascendancy; by 1987 her party had less of the popular vote than it took when Labour won in October 1974, and was left with just 10 seats out of 72.

That leaves Labour with not a lot to attack; but there are still a few seats which would go on swings of under 5 per cent. One is Ayr, which apart from York is the seat with the thinnest Tory majority, and which could be even more precarious now that the much-respected George Younger, former Scottish secretary, is retiring from politics. The new Conservative candidate, Phil Gallie, adheres to Michael Forsyth's what-we-need-is-to-give them-more-Thatcherism tendency. Forsyth, the MP for Stirling, was Scottish secretary Malcolm Rifkind's deputy. As a champion of Thatcherite values he was pushed by that wing of the party as a better man than his boss. Forsyth is a brave and resourceful fighter, but any further swing to the left would probably do for him. Malcolm Rifkind, too, is decidedly vulnerable, though he has confounded reports of his early extinction before: there is a solid centre vote in his constituency whose destination this time could possibly tilt the outcome. Among the Labour seats which the Conservatives hope to win back is Strathkelvin and Bearsden, which hardly looks Labour territory, but was won in 1987 by the formidable Strathclyde neurologist Sam Galbraith, now back on the Labour front bench after a serious illness.

Tactical voting is better developed in Scotland than anywhere else in the Kingdom: see the way, for instance, that voters have clearly picked the Alliance in some constituencies, the Nationalists in others, to topple Government candidates. The Liberal Democrats will be looking this time to add Edinburgh West, held by Scotish office minister Lord James Douglas-Hamilton, and Kincardine and Deeside, to their collection. Alick Buchanan-Smith, the Conservative MP for Kincardine, who died in August 1991, had plainly signalled his detachment from Thatcherite Conservatism and his support for devolution. Even a modest Conservative upsurge, though, will threaten two of the 1987 class of Lib Dem MPs: Menzies Campbell at Fife North East and in Argyll and Bute, Mrs Ray Michie, daughter of John Bannerman, the legendary Liberal campaigner in thinner years than these.

The Nationalists had a mixed election last time, losing Dundee East, the seat of their leader Gordon Wilson, and Western Isles, where their former leader Donald Stewart stood down. But they picked up three new seats – Angus East, Banff and Buchan, won by new party leader Alex Salmond, and Moray – and added another in the Glasgow Govan by-election of November 10 1988, won by Jim Sillars, the former Labour and Scottish Labour MP. It would need a swing of 5.9 per cent since the by-election to restore it to Labour. They have also added the seat at Dunfermline West, where the Labour MP Dick Douglas, discontented with his party particularly for its failure to campaign for non-payment of the poll tax, switched to the SNP: but holding that will be a very tall order – the SNP took only 8.7 per cent of the vote here in 1987 and finished fourth.

The list of Nationalist targets is headed by Galloway and Upper Nithsdale, a revised version of a constituency which they held from October 1974 to 1979. The Conservative incumbent is Ian Lang, John Major's Scottish secretary. Another coveted scalp would be that of Sir Nicholas

CONSERVATIVE SEATS VULNERABLE TO LABOUR

Last 3	Constituency	Con maj	Con	Lab	Lib/SD	Nat	Sitting MP	Since
011	AYR	0.34	39.4	39.1	14.8 (Lib)	6.7	G.Younger †	64
011	STIRLING	1.20	37.8	36.5	14.9 (Lib)	10.8	M.Forsyth	83
011	EDBURGH. PENTLANDS (3)	8.30	38.3	30.0	24.5 (SDP)	7.2	M.Rifkind	74[1]
(011	EASTWOOD (3)	14.43	39.5	25.1	27.2 (SDP)	8.2	A.Stewart	79)
011	DUMFRIES	16.70	41.8	25.2	18.0 (SDP)	14.2	Sir H.Monro	64

LABOUR SEATS VULNERABLE TO CONSERVATIVE

Last 3	Constituency	Lab maj	Con	Lab	Lib/SD	Nat	Sitting MP	Since
012	ABERDEEN S	2.84	34.8	37.7	20.9 (SDP)	6.6	F.Doran	87
012	EDINBURGH S	3.84	33.8	37.7	22.5 (SDP)	5.1	N.Griffiths	87
012	STRATHKELVIN & B/DEN	4.76	33.4	38.1	21.4 (Lib)	7.1	S.Galbraith	87
012	EDINBURGH C	5.51	34.7	40.2	17.9 (Lib)	6.2	A.Darling	83

CONSERVATIVE SEATS VULNERABLE TO LIBERAL DEMOCRAT

Last 3	Constituency	Con maj	Con	Lab	Lib/SD	Nat	Sitting MP	Since
011	EDINBURGH W	2.50	37.3	22.2	34.9 (Lib)	5.6	Lord J.Douglas-Hamilton	74[2]
011	KINCARDINE & DEESIDE	4.31	40.7	15.9	36.3(Lib)	6.5	A.Buchanan-Smith **	64
(011	EDBURGH PENTLANDS (3)	13.75	38.3	30.0	24.5(SDP)	7.2	M. Rifkind	74[1])
011	EASTWOOD (3)	12.25	39.5	25.1	27.2 (SDP)	8.2	A.Stewart	79)

** A. Buchanan-Smith died on August 29 1991. The Liberal Democrats gained the seat on November 7.

LIBERAL DEMOCRAT SEATS VULNERABLE TO CONSERVATIVE

Last 3	Constituency	LD maj	Con	Lab	Lib/SD	Nat	Sitting MP	Since
013	FIFE NE	3.63	41.2	7.4	44.8 (Lib)	6.6	M.Campbell	87
013	ARGYLL & BUTE	3.79	33.5	12.1	37.3 (Lib)	17.1	Mrs R.Michie	87

LABOUR SEAT VULNERABLE TO LIBERAL DEMOCRAT

Last 3	Constituency	Lab maj	Con	Lab	Lib/SD	Nat	Sitting MP	Since
032	GLASGOW HILLHEAD ‡	7.76	14.4	42.9	35.1 (SDP)	6.5	G.Galloway	87

‡ GLASGOW HILLHEAD. won by SDP from Conservatives in by-election of 25.3.82 gained by Labour at 1987 General Election

LIBERAL DEMOCRAT SEAT VULNERABLE TO LABOUR

Last 3	Constituency	Lib maj	Con	Lab	Lib/SD	Nat	Sitting MP	Since
033	I'NESS, NAIRN & L'ABER	11.48	23.0	25.4	36.8 (Lib)	14.8	Sir R.Johnston	64

NATIONALIST SEATS VULNERABLE TO CONSERVATIVE

Last 3	Constituency	Nat maj	Con	Lab	Lib/SD	Nat	Sitting MP	Since
014	ANGUS E	3.35	39.0	10.8	7.8 (SDP)	42.4	A.Welsh §	87
014	BANFF & BUCHAN	5.55	38.7	7.5	9.6 (SDP)	44.2	A.Salmond	87
014	MORAY	8.16	35.0	11.3	10.5 (Lib)	43.2	Mrs M.Ewing	87

§ Welsh was also MP for Angus E from October 1974-79.

CONSERVATIVE SEATS VULNERABLE TO NATIONALIST

Last 3	Constituency	Con maj	Con	Lab	Lib/SD	Nat	Sitting MP	Since
011	G'OWAY & U NITHSDALE	8.95	40.4	12.9	14.6 (Lib)	31.5	I.Lang	79
011	PERTH & KINROSS	12.02	39.6	15.9	16.9 (Lib)	27.6	Sir N.Fairbairn	74[2]
011	TAYSIDE N	12.43	45.4	8.8	12.9 (Lib)	32.9	W.Walker	79

LABOUR SEATS VULNERABLE TO NATIONALIST

Last 3	Constituency	Lab maj	Con	Lab	Lib/SD	Nat	Sitting MP	Since
442	DUNDEE E	2.20	12.9	42.3	4.6 (Lib)	40.1	J.McAllion	87
442	WESTERN ISLES	14.18	8.1	42.7	20.7 (SDP)	28.5	C.MacDonald	87
022*	GLASGOW GOVAN	52.53	11.9	64.8	12.3 (SDP)	10.4		
BY-ELECTION 10.11.88: NAT GAIN Nat maj 11.80			7.3	37.0	7.3 (LD)	48.8	J.Sillars	

LABOUR SEAT DEFENDED BY MP WHO HAS SWITCHED TO NATIONALIST

Last 3	Constituency	Lab maj	Con	Lab	Lib/SD	Nat	Sitting MP	Since
022	DUNFERMLINE W	23.92	23.1	47.1	21.1 (SDP)	8.7	R.Douglas	79

CONTESTS FOR PARTY LEADERSHIPS

LABOUR
November 4 and 10 1980
Party leadership (resignation of J. Callaghan)
Electorate: all Labour MPs (268)

FIRST BALLOT	votes	%
D.Healey	112	42.3
M.Foot	83	31.3
J.Silkin	38	14.3
P.Shore	32	12.1

(Silkin and Shore eliminated)

SECOND BALLOT	votes	%
M.Foot	139	51.9
D.Healey	129	48.1

FOOT elected.

LABOUR
September 27 1981
Deputy leadership (Challenge by T. Benn)
Electorate: electoral college at party conference;
weightings – unions 40 per cent, constituency parties 30 per cent, parliamentary party 30 per cent.

FIRST BALLOT (%)	TUs	CLPs	PLP	ALL
D.Healey	61.74	17.89	51.02	45.37
T.Benn	16.02	78.27	22.44	36.63
J.Silkin	22.23	3.83	26.53	18.00

(Silkin eliminated)

SECOND BALLOT (%)	TUs	CLPs	PLP	ALL
D.Healey	62.48	18.91	65.86	50.43
T.Benn	37.51	81.09	34.13	49.57

HEALEY elected

SOCIAL DEMOCRATS
Postal ballot: result announced July 2 1982
Leadership
Electorate: all party members (62,372)

	votes	%
R.Jenkins	26,246	55.7
D.Owen	20.864	44.3

turnout: 75.6 per cent JENKINS elected

SOCIAL AND LIBERAL DEMOCRATS
Postal ballot: result announced July 28 1988
Leadership
Electorate: all party members

	votes	%
P.Ashdown	41,401	71.9
A.Beith	16,202	28.1

Turnout: 72 per cent
ASHDOWN elected

LABOUR
October 2 1988
Leadership and deputy leadership (challenges by T. Benn and others)
Electorate: electoral college (see above)

Leadership (%):	TUs	CLPs	PLP	ALL
N.Kinnock	99.15	80.42	82.47	88.63
T.Benn	0.85	19.56	17.52	11.37

Deputy leadership (%):	TUs	CLPs	PLP	ALL
R.Hattersley	78.35	60.36	57.92	
J.Prescott	21.64	26.15	23.98	
E.Heffer	0.02	13.49	18.10	

CONSERVATIVES
December 5 1989
Leadership (challenge by Sir A. Meyer)
Electorate: all Conservative MPs (374)

	votes	%
M.Thatcher	314	90.5
Sir A.Meyer	33	9.5

(There were 24 spoiled papers; 3 MPs abstained. Thatcher was supported by 84 per cent of Conservative MPs).

CONSERVATIVES
November 20 and 27 1990
Leadership (challenge to Mrs M. Thatcher)
Electorate: all Conservative MPs (372)

FIRST BALLOT	votes	%
M.Thatcher	204	57.3
M.Heseltine	152	42.7

(Thatcher required a majority of votes cast plus 15 per cent more of all eligible votes than her opponent. She failed by 4 votes to attain this total and declined to stand in the second ballot.)

SECOND BALLOT	votes	%
J.Major	185	49.7
M.Heseltine	131	35.2
D.Hurd	56	15.1

(As Major had less than 50 per cent of the vote, the rules required a third ballot but after Heseltine and Hurd had withdrawn, the requirement was waived.)

GENERAL AND EUROPEAN ELECTIONS SINCE 1945

JULY 5 1945*	VOTES	%	SEATS	
Conservative	9,101,099	36.2	197	
National	133,179	0.5	2	
Nat Liberal	37,732	2.9	11	
Conservative and allies (Total)	9,972,010	39.6	210	
Labour	11,967,746	48.0	393	
Liberal	2,252,430	9.0	12	
Independent Labour Party	46,769	0.2	3	
Communist	102,780	0.4	2	
Common Wealth	110,634	0.5	1	
Others	642,826	2.3	22	
Electorate	33,240,391	72.8		
Swing Conservative to Labour		11.8		
Labour majority			147	

* Because of holiday weeks, some constituencies voted later. The results were also delayed by collection of votes from forces abroad and were not announced until July 26.

FEBRUARY 23 1950	VOTES	%	SEATS	
Conservative	11,507,061	40.0	282	
Nat Lib & Con	985,343	3.4	16	
Conservative and allies (Total)	12,492,404	43.4	298	
Labour	13,266,176	46.1	315	
Liberal	2,621,487	9.1	9	
Communist	91,765	0.3	0	
Others	299,292	1.1	3	
Electorate	34,412,255	83.9		
Swing Labour to Conservative		2.9		
Labour majority			6	

OCTOBER 25 1951	VOTES	%	SEATS
Conservative	12,660,061	44.3	302
Nat Lib & Con	1,058,138	3.7	19
Conservative and allies (Total)	13,718,199	48.0	321
Labour	13,948,883	48.8	295
Liberal	730,546	2.6	6
Communist	21,640	0.1	0
Others	177,326	0.5	3
Electorate	**34,645,573**	**82.5**	
Swing Labour to Conservative		**0.9**	
Conservative majority			**16**

MAY 26 1955	VOTES	%	SEATS
Conservative	12,468,778	46.6	324
Nat Lib & Con	842,113	3.1	21
Conservative and allies (Total)	13,310,891	49.7	345
Labour	12,405,254	46.4	277
Liberal	722,402	2.7	6
Others	321,182	1.2	2
Electorate	**34,858,263**	**76.7**	
Swing Labour to Conservative		**2.0**	
Conservative majority			**59**

OCTOBER 8 1959	VOTES	%	SEATS
Conservative	12,985,081	46.6	345
Nat Lib & Con	765,794	2.8	20
Conservative and allies (Total)	13,750,875	49.4	365
Labour	12,216,172	43.8	258
Liberal	1,640,760	5.9	6
Others	254,845	0.9	1
Electorate	**35,397,080**	**78.8**	
Swing Labour to Conservative		**1.0**	
Conservative majority			**99**

OCTOBER 15 1964	VOTES	%	SEATS
Conservative	11,676,512	42.2	298
Nat Lib & Con	326,130	1.2	6
Conservative and allies (Total)	12,002,642	43.4	304
Labour	12,205,808	44.1	317
Liberal	3,099,283	11.2	9
Others	349,415	1.3	0
Electorate	**35,894,054**	**77.1**	
Swing Conservative to Labour		**3.0**	
Labour majority			**5**

MARCH 31 1966	**VOTES**	**%**	**SEATS**
Conservative	11,268,676	41.3	250
Nat Lib & Con	149,779	0.6	3
Conservative and allies (Total)	11,418,455	41.9	253
Labour	13,096,629	48.0	364
Liberal	2,327,457	8.6	12
Others	422,206	1.5	1
Electorate	**35,957,245**	**75.8**	
Swing Conservative to Labour		2.7	
Labour majority			97

JUNE 18 1970	**VOTES**	**%**	**SEATS**
Conservative	13,145,123	46.4	330
Labour	12,208,758	43.1	288
Liberal	2,117,035	7.5	6
SNP	306,802	1.1	1
Plaid Cymru	175,016	0.6	0
Others	265,224	1.3	5
Electorate	**39,342,013**	**72.0**	
Swing Labour to Conservative		4.7	
Conservative majority			31

FEBRUARY 28 1974	**VOTES**	**%**	**SEATS**
Conservative	11,872,180	37.9	297
Labour	11,645,616	37.2	301
Liberal	6,059,519	19.3	14
SNP	633,180	2.0	7
Plaid Cymru	171,374	0.6	2
Others	958,293	3.0	14
Electorate	**39,753,863**	**78.8**	
Swing Conservative to Labour		1.3	
No overall majority			

OCTOBER 10 1974	**VOTES**	**%**	**SEATS**
Conservative	10,462,565	35.8	277
Labour	11,457,079	39.2	319
Liberal	5,346,704	18.3	13
SNP	839,617	2.9	11
Plaid Cymru	166,321	0.6	3
Others	916,818	3.2	12
Electorate:	**40,072,970**	**72.8**	
Swing Conservative to Labour		2.1	
Labour majority			4

MAY 3 1979	VOTES	%	SEATS
Conservative	13,697,923	43.9	339
Labour	11,532,218	36.9	269
Liberal	4,313,804	13.8	11
SNP	504,259	1.6	2
Plaid Cymru	132,544	0.4	2
Others	1,040,614	3.4	12
Electorate	41,095,649	76.0	
Swing Labour to Conservative		5.2	
Conservative majority			44

JUNE 9 1983	VOTES	%	SEATS
Conservative	13,012,316	42.4	397
Labour	8,456,934	27.6	209
Liberal	4,210,115	13.7	17
SDP	3,570,834	11.7	6
Liberal/SDP Alliance (Total)	7,780,949	25.4	23
SNP	331,975	1.1	2
Plaid Cymru	125,309	0.4	2
Ecology Party	53,848	0.2	0
Others	909,806	2.9	17
Electorate	42,192,999	72.7	
Swing Labour to Conservative		3.9	
Conservative majority			144

JUNE 11 1987	VOTES	%	SEATS
Conservative	13,760,583	42.3	376
Labour	10,029,807	30.8	229
Liberal	4,173,450	12.8	17
SDP	3,168,183	9.7	5
Liberal/SDP Alliance (Total)	7,341,633	22.5	22
SNP	416,473	1.3	3
Plaid Cymru	123,599	0.4	3
Green Party	89,753	0.3	0
Others	767,730	2.4	17
Electorate	43,180,753	75.3	
Swing Conservative to Labour		1.7	
Conservative majority			101

	PROPORTION OF VOTERS				PROPORTION OF ELECTORATE		
	Con	Lab	Lib/All		Con	Lab	Lib/All
1970	46.4	43.1	7.5		33.4	31.0	5.4
1974[1]	37.9	37.2	19.3		29.9	29.3	15.2
1974[2]	35.8	39.2	18.3		26.1	28.6	13.3
1979	43.9	36.9	13.8		33.3	28.1	10.5
1983	42.4	27.6	25.4		30.8	20.0	18.5
1987	42.3	30.8	22.5		31.9	23.2	17.0

EUROPEAN ELECTIONS
ENGLAND, SCOTLAND AND WALES *(FIRST PAST THE POST SYSTEM)*

POLLING DAY	June 7 1979	%	seats	June 14 1984	%	seats	June 15 1989	%	seats
Conservative	6,508,493	50.6	60	5,426,821	40.8	45	5,331,077	34.7	32
Labour	4,253,207	33.0	17	4,865,261	36.5	32	6,153,640	40.1	45
Liberal	1,690,599	13.1	0	986,292	6.2	0			
SDP				75,886	0.5	0			
Lib/SDP							2,591,635	19.5	0
Green							2,292,705	14.9	0
SNP	247,836	1.9	1	230,594	1.7	1	406,686	2.7	1
Plaid Cymru	83,399	0.6	0	103,031	0.8	0	115,062	0.8	0
Others	90,318	0.7	0	95,531	0.7	0	41,295	0.3	0
Electorate	40,529,970	31.8		41,917,313	31.8		42,590,060	35.9	

NORTHERN IRELAND *(STV: FIGURES SHOW % SHARE OF FIRST PREFERENCE VOTE)*

	1979	1984	1989
DUP (I.Paisley)	29.8*	33.6*	29.6*
SDLP (J.Hume)	24.6*	22.1*	25.2*
OUP (J.Taylor)	21.9*	21.5*	(J.Nicholson) 22.0*
PSF (D.Morrison)	13.3	9.1	
Alliance (O.Napier)	6.8	(D.Cook) 5.0	(J.T.Alderdice) 5.2
Workers (S.Lynch)	1.3	1.0	
Ecol/Green (C.McGuigan)	0.3	(M.H.Samuel) 1.2	
Con (A.Kennedy)	4.8		
Lab Regional Govt (M.Langhammer)	0.7		
Lab 87 (B.Caul)	0.2		
Ind UU/UPUP†(J.Kilfedder)	6.7	3.0	
OUP (H.West)	10.0		
Ind (Mrs B.McAliskey)	5.9		
Ind (D.Bleakley)	1.6		
Ind Lab (P.Devlin)	1.1		
UPNI (E.Cummings)	0.6		
Rep (P.Brennan)	0.6		
Rep (F.Donnelly)	0.2		
Lib (J.Murray)	0.2		
Electorate:	1,028,837	1,064,035	1,120,508
Turnout:	55.6	65.4	48.8

*elected. † Ind UU 1979; UPUP 1984   *Source: F.W.S.Craig: British Electoral Facts, Britain Votes, Europe Votes*

BY-ELECTIONS SINCE 1988

1. KENSINGTON
July 14 1988
(death of Sir Brandon Rhys Williams)

			% BE	% GE 1987
D. Fishburn	Con	9,829	41.6	47.5
Mrs A.Holmes	Lab	9,014	38.2	33.3
W. Goodhart	Lib Dem	2,546	10.8	17.2‡
J.Martin	SDP	1,190	5.0	-
P. Hobson	Grn	572	2.4	1.7
Con majority		815	3.4	14.2
Swing Con to Lab			5.4	
Electorate/ turnout		45.830	51.6	64.7

ALSO STOOD: Mrs C.Payne (Rainbow Alliance) 193 (0.8), D.Sutch (Monster Raving) 61 (0.3), J.Duignan (London Class War) 60 (0.3), B.Goodier (Anti Left Fascist) 31 (0.1), B.McDermott (Free Trade Liberal) 31 (0.1), R.Edey (Fair Wealth) 30 (0.1), W.Scola (Leveller) 27 (0.1), J.Crowley (Anti Yuppie) 24 (0.1), J.Connell (Peace) 20 (0.1), Dr K.S.Trivedi (Ind Janata) 5 (0.0)
LOST DEPOSITS: All candidates bar Fishburn, Holmes, Goodhart and Martin.

2. GLASGOW GOVAN
November 10 1988
(B.Millan resigned to become a European Commissioner)
SNP GAIN FROM LAB

			% BE	% GE 1987
J.Sillars	SNP	14,677	48.8	10.4
R.Gillespie	Lab	11,123	37.0	64.8
G.Hamilton	Con	2,207	7.3	11.9
B.Ponsonby	Lib Dem	1,246	4.1	12.2‡
G.Campbell	Grn	345	1.1	—
SNP majority		3,554	11.8	
Lab majority				52.5
Swing Lab to SNP			33.1	
Electorate/ turnout		49,994	60.4	73.4

ALSO STOOD: D.Chalmers (Comm) 281 (0.9), D.Sutch (Monster Raving) 174 (0.6), F.Clark (Rainbow Alliance) 51 (0.2).
LOST DEPOSITS: Ponsonby, Campbell, Chalmers, Sutch, Clark.

‡ denotes candidate of Liberal/SDP Alliance

3. EPPING FOREST
December 15 1988
(death of Sir J.Biggs-Davison)

			% BE	% GE 1987
S.Norris	Con	13,183	39.5	60.9
A.Thompson	Lib Dem	8,679	26.0	-
S.Murray	Lab	6,261	18.7	18.4
M.Pettman	SDP	4,077	12.2	19.4 ‡
A.Sims	Grn	672	2.0	1.3
Con majority		4,504	13.5	41.5
Electorate/turnout		67,991	49.1	76.3

*SDP 19.4

ALSO STOOD: Mrs T.Wingfield (Ind NF) 286 (0.9), D.Sutch (Monster Raving) 208 (0.6), Miss J.Moore (Rainbow Alliance) 33 (0.1), B.Goodier (Vote No Belsen) 16 (0.0)
LOST DEPOSITS: Sims, Wingfield, Sutch, Moore, Goodier.

4. PONTYPRIDD
February 23 1989
(death of B. John)

			% BE	% GE 1987
K.Howells	Lab	20,549	53.4	56.3
S.Morgan	PC	9,755	25.3	5.3
N.Evans	Con	5,212	13.5	19.5
T.Ellis	Lib Dem	1,500	3.9	18.9 ‡
T.Thomas	SDP	1,199	3.1	-
Lab majority		10,794	28.0	36.8
Swing Lab to Pl C			11.5	
Electorate/turnout		61,193	62.2	76.8

ALSO STOOD: D.Richards (Comm) 239 (0.6), D.Black (Ind) 57 (0.2)
LOST DEPOSITS: Ellis, Thomas, Richards, Black

5. RICHMOND (Yorks)
February 23 1989
(L.Brittan resigned to become a European Commissioner)

			% BE	% GE 1987
W.Hague	Con	19,543	37.2	61.2
M.Potter	SDP	16,909	32.2	27.0 ‡
Mrs B.Pearce	Lib Dem	11,589	22.1	
F.Robson	Lab	2,591	4.9	11.8
R.Upshall	Grn	1,473	2.8	—
Con majority		2,634	5.0	34.2
Electorate/turnout		81,568	64.4	72.1

ALSO STOOD: D.Sutch (Monster Raving) 167 (0.3), A.Millns (Keep Theakstons British) 113 (0.2), Ms L. St Claire (Corrective) 106 (0.2), N. Watkins (Official Liberal) 70 (0.1)
LOST DEPOSITS: Robson, Upshall, Sutch, Millns, St Claire, Watkins.

6. VALE OF GLAMORGAN
May 4 1989
(death of Sir R.Gower)
LAB GAIN FROM CON

			% BE	% GE 1987
J.Smith	Lab	23,342	48.9	34.7
R.Richards	Con	17,314	36.3	46.8
F.Leavers	Lib Dem	2,017	4.2	–
J.Dixon	PC	1,672	3.5	1.8
K.Davies	SDP	1,098	2.3	16.7‡
Mrs M.Wakefield	Grn	971	2.0	–
Lab majority		6,028	12.6	
Con majority				12.1
Swing Con to Lab			12.4	
Electorate/turnout		67,549	70.7	79.3

ALSO STOOD: C.Tiarks (Protect NHS) 847 (1.8), D.Sutch (Monster Raving) 266 (0.6), E.Roberts (Welsh Ind Soc & Ecol) 148 (0.3), Ms L. St Claire (Corrective) 39 (0.1) D.Black (Christian Alliance) 32 (0.1)
LOST DEPOSITS: all candidates bar Smith and Richards.

7.GLASGOW CENTRAL
June 15 1989
(death of R.McTaggart)

			% BE	% GE 1987
M.Watson	Lab	14,480	54.6	64.5
A.Neil	SNP	8,018	30.2	9.9
A.Hogarth	Con	2,028	7.6	13.0
Ms I.Brandt	Grn	1,019	3.8	0.9
R.McCreadie	Lib Dem	411	1.5	10.5 ‡
P.Kerr	SDP	253	1.0	
Lab majority		6,462	24.4	51.5
Swing Lab to Nat			15.1	
Electorate/turnout		50,254	52.8	65.6

ALSO STOOD: Ms L.Murdoch (Rev. Comm) 141 (0.5), B.Kidd (Scot Soc) 137 (0.5), D. Lettice (WRP) 48 (0.2)
LOST DEPOSITS: Brandt, McCreadie, Kerr, Murdoch, Kidd, Lettice

8. VAUXHALL
June 15 1989
(S.Holland resigned to take up post overseas)

			% BE	% GE 1987
Ms K.Hoey	Lab	15,191	52.8	50.2
M.Keegan	Con	5,425	18.8	29.0
M.Tuffrey	Lib Dem	5,043	17.5	18.2‡
H.Bewley	Grn	1,767	6.1	1.8
Lab majority		9,766	34.0	21.2
Swing Con to Lab			6.4	
Electorate/turnout		64,905	44.4	64.0

ALSO STOOD: H.Andrew (People`s Candidate) 302 (1.0), D.Allen (The Greens) 264 (0.9), R.Narayan (Civil Liberties) 179 (0.6), D.Milligan (R.C.P.) 177 (0.6), P. Harrington (Official NF) 127 (0.4), D. Sutch (Monster Raving) 106 (0.4), D.Black (Christian Alliance) 86 (0.3), E.Budden (NF) 83 (0.3), G.Rolph (Fellowship) 24 (0.1), W.Scola (Leveller) 21 (0.1)
LOST DEPOSITS: all candidates bar Hoey, Keegan, Tuffrey and Bewley.

9. STAFFORDSHIRE MID
March 22 1990
(death of J.Heddle)
LAB GAIN FROM CON

			% BE	% GE 1987
Mrs S.Heal	Lab	27,649	49.1	24.7
C. Prior	Con	18,200	32.3	50.6
T.Jones	Lib Dem	6,315	11.2	23.2 ‡
I.Wood	SDP	1,422	2.5	–
R.Saunders	Grn	1,215	2.2	–
Lab majority		**9,499**	**16.8**	
Con majority				25.9
Swing Con to Lab			21.4	
Electorate/turnout		72,728	77.5	79.4

ALSO STOOD: J.Bazeley (Anti-Thatcher Con) 547 (1.0), D.Sutch (Monster Raving) 336 (0.6), C.Hill (NF) 311 (0.6), C.Abell (NHS Supporters) 102 (0.2), N.Parker-Jervis (Against Immigration) 71 (0.1), S.Fawlty-Hughes (ind) 59 (0.1), Ms L St Claire Love (Correct Edification) 51 (0.1), B.Mildwater (Save the 2CV) 42 (0.1), D.Black (Christian Patriotic Alliance) 39 (0.1).LOST DEPOSITS: all candidates bar Heal, Prior and Jones

10. UPPER BANN
May 17 1990
(death of H.McCusker)

			% BE	% GE 1987
D.Trimble	UU	20,547	58.0	61.5
Mrs B.Rodgers	SDLP	6,698	18.9	20.5
Ms S.Campbell	SF	2,033	5.7	7.4
H. Ross	Ulster Ind	1,534	4.3	—
T.French	Workers	1,083	3.1	4.7
Mrs C.Jones	Con	1,038	3.0	—
W.Ramsay	Alliance	948	2.7	5.9
P.Doran	Grn	576	1.6	—
UU majority		**13,949**	**39.1**	**41.0**
Swing UU to SDLP			1.0	
Electorate/turnout		66,377	53.4	65.6

ALSO STOOD: G.McMichael (Ulster Dem) 600 (1.7), J.Holmes (Right to Vote Labour) 235 (0.6), A.Dunn (SDP) 154 (0.4)
LOST DEPOSITS: all candidates bar Trimble, Rodgers and Campbell

11. BOOTLE
May 24 1990
(death of A.Roberts)

			% BE	% GE 1987
M.Carr	Lab	26,737	75.4	66.9
J.Clappison	Con	3,220	9.1	20.1
J.Cunningham	Lib Dem	3,179	9.0	–
F Brady	Grn	1,267	3.6	–
J.Holmes	SDP	155	0.4	13.0 ‡
Lab majority		**23,517**	**66.3**	**46.8**
Swing Con to Lab		8.8		
Electorate/turnout		70,178	50.6	72.9

ALSO STOOD: K.White (Lib) 474 (1.3), D.Sutch (Monster Raving) 418 (1.2), T.Schofield (Ind) 27 (0.1)
LOST DEPOSITS: Brady, White, Sutch, Holmes, Schofield

12.KNOWSLEY S
September 27 1990
(death of S.Hughes)

			% BE	% GE 1987
E.O'Hara	Lab	14,581	68.8	64.5
L.Byrom	Con	3,214	15.2	21.6
C.Hancox	Lib Dem	1,809	8.5	13.9 ‡
R.Georgeson	Grn	656	3.1	—
Lab majority		11,367	53.6	42.9
Swing Con to Lab			5.4	
Electorate/turnout		63,433	33.4	74.1

ALSO STOOD: I.Smith (Lib) 628 (3.0), D.Sutch (Monster Raving) 197 (0.9), Lady C.Whiplash (Corrective) 99 (0.5)
LOST DEPOSITS: Georgeson, Smith, Sutch, Whiplash

13. EASTBOURNE
October 18 1990
(death of I.Gow)
LIB DEM GAIN FROM CON

			% BE	% GE 1987
D.Bellotti	Lib Dem	23,415	50.8	29.7 ‡
R.Hickmet	Con	18,865	40.9	59.9
C.Atkins	Lab	2,308	5.0	8.8
D.Aherne	Grn	553	1.2	1.6
Lib Dem majority		4,550	9.9	
Con majority				30.2
Swing Con to Lib Dem			20.1	
Electorate/turnout		75,904	60.7	75.6

ALSO STOOD: M-T.Williamson (Lib) 526 (1.1), Lady C.Whiplash (Corrective) 216 (0.5), J.McAuley (NF) 154 (0.3), E.Page (Retired Police Officer) 35 (0.1)
LOST DEPOSITS: Aherne, Williamson, Whiplash, McAuley, Page.

14.BOOTLE
November 8 1990
(death of M.Carr)

			% BE	% GE 1987	%MAY 90
J.Benton	Lab	22,052	78.4	66.9	75.4
J.Clappison	Con	2,587	9.2	20.1	9.1
J.Cunningham	Lib Dem	2,216	7.9	13.0 ‡	9.0
F.Brady	Grn	557	2.0	—	3.6
Lab majority		19,465	69.2	46.8	66.3
Swing Con to Lab			11.2		
Electorate/turnout		70,881	39.7	72.9	50.6

ALSO STOOD: D.Sutch (Monster Raving) 310 (1.1), K.White (Lib) 291 (1.0), D.Black (Christian Alliance) 132 (0.5)
LOST DEPOSITS: Brady, Sutch, White, Black.

15. BRADFORD N
November 8 1990
(death of P. Wall)

			% BE	% GE 1987
T.Rooney	Lab	18,619	51.7	42.8
D.Ward	Lib Dem	9,105	25.3	17.7 ‡
Miss J.Atkin	Con	6,048	16.8	39.5
D.Pidcock	Islamic	800	2.2	—
M.Knott	Grn	447	1.2	—
Lab majority		9,514	26.4	3.3
Swing Con to Lab			15.8	
Electorate/turnout		67,444	53.5	72.7

ALSO STOOD: R.Tenney (NF) 305 (0.8), J.Floyd (Christian Alliance) 219 (0.6), W.Beckett (Monster Raving) 210 (0.6), N. Nowosielski (Lib) 187 (0.5), M.Wigglesworth (Independent Con) 89 (0.2)
LOST DEPOSITS: all bar Rooney, Ward and Atkin

16. PAISLEY N
November 29 1990
(death of A.Adams)

			% BE	% 1987
Mrs K.Adams	Lab	11.353	44.0	55.5
R.Mullin	SNP	7,583	29.4	12.9
E.Marwick	Con	3,835	14.8	15.8
J.Bannerman	Lib Dem	2,139	8.3	15.8 ‡
D.Mellor	Grn	918	3.6	—
Lab majority		3,770	14.6	39.7
Swing Con to Lib Dem			14.0	
Electorate/turnout		48,063	53.7	73.5

LOST DEPOSIT: Mellor

17. PAISLEY S
November 29 1990
(death of N.Buchan)

			% BE	% GE 1987
G.McMaster	Lab	12,485	46.1	56.2
I.Lawson	SNP	7,455	27.5	14.0
J.Workman	Con	3,627	13.4	14.7
A.Reid	Lib Dem	2,660	9.8	15.1 ‡
Ms E.Collie	Grn	835	3.1	—
Lab majority		5,030	18.6	41.0
Swing Lab to Nat			11.8	
Electorate/turnout		49,199	55.0	75.3

LOST DEPOSIT: Collie

18. RIBBLE VALLEY
March 7 1991
(elevation to Lords of D.Waddington)
LIB DEM GAIN FROM CON

			% BE	% 1987
M.Carr	Lib Dem	22,377	48.5	21.4 ‡
N.Evans	Con	17,776	38.5	60.9
Mrs J.Farrington	Lab	4,356	9.4	17.7
D.A.Brass	Ind Con	611	1.3	—
Ms H.Ingham	Grn	466	1.0	—
Lib Dem majority		4,601	10.0	
Con majority				39.4
Swing Con to Lib Dem			24.8	
Electorate/turnout		64,878	71.2	79.1

ALSO STOOD: D.Sutch (Monster Raving) 278 (0.6), S.Taylor (Lib) 133 (0.3), Ms L.St Clair (Corrective) 72 (0.2), S.Fawlty Hughes (Raving Loony) 60 (0.1)
LOST DEPOSITS: all bar Carr, Evans and Farrington

19. NEATH
April 4 1991
(death of D.Coleman)

			% BE	% GE 1987
P.Hain	Lab	17,962	51.8	63.4
D.Evans	PC	8,132	23.4	6.4
R.Evans	Con	2,995	8.6	16.1
D.Lloyd	Lib Dem	2,000	5.8	14.1 ‡
J.Warman*	SDP	1,826	5.3	
Lab majority		9,830	28.4	47.2
Swing Lab to PC			14.3	
Electorate/turnout		54,482	63.7	78.8

ALSO STOOD: R.Jeffreys (Ind Lab) 1,253 (3.6), D.Sutch (Monster Raving) 263 (0.8), B.Kirk (Captain Beany) 262 (0.8)
LOST DEPOSITS: Jeffreys, Sutch, Kirk
* Warman was candidate for SDP/Alliance at 1987 general election.

20. MONMOUTH
May 16 1991
(death of Sir J.Stradling Thomas)
LAB GAIN FROM CON

			% BE	% GE 1987
H.Edwards	Lab	17,733	39.3	27.7
R.Evans	Con	15,327	34.0	47.5
Mrs F.David	Lib Dem	11,164	24.8	24.0 ‡
Lab majority		2,406	5.3	
Con majority				19.8
Swing Con to Lab			12.6	
Electorate/turnout		59,460	75.8	80.8

ALSO STOOD: D.Sutch (Monster Raving) 314 (0.7), M.Witherden (PC-Grn)* 277 (0.6), P.Carpenter (Unitax) 164 (0.4), L. St C Whiplash (Corrective) 121 (0.3)
LOST DEPOSITS: Sutch, Witherden, Carpenter, Whiplash
* Witherden was the joint candidate of Plaid Cymru and the Green Party. The Plaid Cymru candidate at the 1987 election took 0.8 per cent of the vote.

21. LIVERPOOL WALTON
July 4 1991
(death of E. Heffer)

			%BE	%GE 1987
P. Kilfoyle	Lab	21,317	53.1	64.4
P. Clark	Lib Dem	14,457	36.0	21.2 ‡
Mrs L. Mahmood	Real Lab	2,613	6.5	—
B. Greenwood	Con	1,155	2.9	14.4
Lab Majority		6,860	17.1	43.2
Swing Lab to Lib Dem			13.1	
Electorate/Turnout		70,803	56.7	73.6

ALSO STOOD: D. Sutch (Monster Raving) 546 (1.4), G. Lee-Delisle (Lee -Delisle Party) 63 (0.2)
LOST DEPOSIT: Greenwood, Sutch and Lee-Delisle

22. HEMSWORTH
November 7 1991
(death of G.Buckley)

			%BE	%GE 1987
D.Enright	Lab	15,895	66.3	67.0
Mrs V.Megson	Lib Dem	4,808	20.1	15.8
G.Harrison	Con	2,512	10.5	17.2
Lab majority		11,087	46.3	49.8
Swing Lab to Lib Dem			2.5	
Electorate/turnout		56,247	42.8	75.7

ALSO STOOD: P.Ablett (Ind Lab) 648 (2.7), T.Smith (Corrective) 108 (0.5)
LOST DEPOSITS: Ablett, Smith

23. LANGBAURGH
November 7 1991
(death of R.Holt)
LAB GAIN FROM CON

			%BE	%GE 1987
Dr A.Kumar	Lab	22,442	42.9	38.4
M.Bates	Con	20,467	39.1	41.7
P.Allen	Lib Dem	8,421	16.1	19.9
G.Parr	Grn	456	0.9	—
Lab majority		1,975	3.8	
Con majority				3.3
Swing Con to Lab			3.6	
Electorate/turnout		80,220	65.4	78.8

ALSO STOOD: R.Holt (Yorkshire Party) 216 (0.4), L.St Clair (Corrective) 198 (0.4), N.Downing (Football Supporters) 163 (0.3)
LOST DEPOSITS: Parr, Holt, St Clair, Downing

24. KINCARDINE & DEESIDE
November 7 1991
(death of A.Buchanan-Smith)
LIB DEM GAIN FROM CON

			%BE	%GE 1987
N.Stephen	Lib Dem	20,779	49.0	36.3
M.Humphrey	Con	12,955	30.6	40.6
A.Macartney	SNP	4,705	11.1	6.4
M.Savidge	Lab	3,271	7.7	15.9
S.Campbell	Grn	683	1.6	0.6
Lib Dem majority		7,824	18.5	
Con majority				4.3
Swing Con to Lib Dem			11.4	
Electorate/turnout		64,618	67.0	75.2

LOST DEPOSIT: Campbell

CHANGE IN PARTIES' SHARE OF THE VOTE AT MAINLAND BY-ELECTIONS 1987-9

		Con	Lab	Lib Dem/SDP	Green	Nationalist
14.7.88	Kensington	-5.9	+4.8	(-1.4)	+0.7	–
10.11.88	Glasgow Govan	-4.6	-27.9	(-8.2)	IN 1.2	+38.4
15.12.88	Epping Forest	-21.4	+0.3	(+18.8)	+0.7	–
23.2.89	Pontypridd	-6.0	-2.9	(-11.9)	–	+20.0
23.2.89	Richmond	-24.0	-6.9	(+27.2)	IN 2.8	–
4.4.89	Vale of Glamorgan	-10.5	+14.2	(-10.2)	IN 2.0	+1.7
15.6.89	Glasgow Central	-5.4	-9.9	(-8.0)	+2.9	+20.2
15.6.89	Vauxhall	-10.2	+2.6	(-0.7)	+4.3	–
22.3.90	Mid-Staffs	-18.3	+24.4	(-9.5)	IN 2.2	–
24.5.90	Bootle	-11.0	+8.5	(-3.6)	IN 3.6	–
26.9.90	Knowsley S.	-6.3	+4.3	(-5.4)	IN 3.1	–
18.10.90	Eastbourne	-19.0	-3.8	(+21.1)	-0.3	–
8.11.90	Bootle*	-10.9	+11.5	(-5.1)	IN 2.0	–
8.11.90	Bradford N.	-22.7	+8.9	(+7.6)	IN 1.2	–
29.11.90	Paisley N.	-1.0	-11.5	(-7.5)	IN 3.6	+16.5
29.11.90	Paisley S.	-1.3	-10.1	(-5.3)	IN 3.1	+13.5
7.3.91	Ribble Valley	-22.4	-8.3	(+27.1)	IN 1.0	–
4.4.91	Neath	-7.5	-11.6	(-3.0)	–	+17.0
16.5.91	Monmouth	-13.5	+11.6	+0.8	**	–
4.7.91	Liverpool Walton	-11.5	-11.3	+14.8	–	–
7.11.91	Hemsworth	-6.7	-0.7	+4.2	–	–
7.11.91	Kincardine & Deeside	-10.0	-8.2	+12.7	+1.0	+4.7
7.11.91	Langbaurgh	-2.6	+4.5	-3.8	IN 0.9	–

IN indicates party which did not stand in the previous general election.

Figures in brackets in Lib Dem/SDP column show vote for Lib Dem and/or SDP at by-election compared with Alliance vote at 1987 election. Those with no brackets are Lib Dem only, compared with Alliance, after winding up of SDP.

* changes since the by-election of May 24 were: Con +0.1; Lab +3.0; Lib Dem -1.1; Green -1.6

** Greens and Nationalists fielded a joint candidate who took 0.6 per cent of the vote

OPINION POLLS 1983-91

State of the parties on The Guardian running averages of the
last five polls, end of each month.

1983	Con	Lab	L/SD
January	-	-	-
February	-	-	-
March	-	-	-
April	-	-	-
May	-	-	-
June	-	-	-
July	-	-	-
August	45	28	26
September	45	28	25
October	42	37	20
November	43	35	20
December	42	37	19

1984	Con	Lab	L/SD
January	42	38	19
February	41	38	20
March	40	39	19
April	41	38	20
May	40	38	21
June	38	38	22
July	37	39	23
August	38	39	22
September	40	37	21
October	43	35	21
November	44	34	21
December	42	33	23

1985	Con	Lab	L/SD
January	41	33	25
February	38	36	25
March	37	37	25
April	36	38	25
May	33	36	29
June	32	35	31
July	32	36	30
August	31	36	31
September	31	32	35
October	32	37	29
November	35	36	27
December	35	35	28

1986	Con	Lab	L/SD
January	31	36	31
February	31	36	31
March	32	36	30
April	33	39	26
May	32	39	27
June	33	39	25
July	33	38	26
August	34	37	26
September	35	39	24
October	39	39	19
November	40	38	20
December	40	37	21

1987	Con	Lab	L/SD
January	39	38	21
February	39	36	23
March	39	32	28
April	42	31	24
May	44	34	20
June	42	34	22
July	47	32	19
August	48	33	17
September	48	35	15
October	48	36	13
November	48	36	14
December	48	35	15

1988	Con	Lab	Lib Dem*	SDP
January	47	36	15	-
February	46	38	13	-
March	45	38	9	5
April	44	40	8	5
May	44	39	8	5
June	47	38	8	4
July	45	39	9	5
August	47	36	9	5
September	46	39	9	4
October	46	37	9	5
November	43	39	9	5
December	44	36	9	5

*L/SD for January and February

1989	Con	Lab	Lib Dem	SDP	Grn
January	46	37	9	4	-
February	41	39	9	7	-
March	42	39	8	6	-
April	42	39	9	6	-
May	42	42	7	3	-
June	37	45	6	3	6
July	37	43	5	3	9
August	39	44	6	2	7
September	37	44	6	3	8
October	37	48	6	2	5
November	36	47	6	3	5
December	39	47	5	3	5

1990	Con	Lab	Lib Dem	SDP	Grn
January	36	48	5	3	5
February	34	50	6	3	5
March	30	54	6	3	5
April	31	51	7	3	5
May	35	50	7	2	5
June	37	50	7	-	4
July	36	48	9	-	5
August	37	49	8	-	3
September	37	46	12	-	3
October	34	45	14	-	4
November	46	39	10	-	3
December	44	42	9	-	2

1991	Con	Lab	Lib Dem
January*	45	42	9
February	45	42	9
March	39	40	16
April	42	40	14
May	37	42	16
June	39	41	15
July	38	43	14
August	40	42	13
September	40	40	15

*Since several pollsters were no longer reporting the Green vote separately, the average for the Greens was discontinued at this point.

HOW THE POLLS MOVED IN THE LAST TWO ELECTIONS

GUARDIAN RUNNING AVERAGES, DAILY. DATES SHOW THE NUMBER OF DAYS BEFORE POLLING DAY: i.e. E-30 IS 30 DAYS BEFORE POLLING DAY. THE AVERAGE OF THE POLLS WILL BE REPORTED DAILY IN THE GUARDIAN DURING THE CAMPAIGN.

| | 1983 | | | | 1987 | | | | NOW | | | |
	Con	Lab	L/SD	Other	Con	Lab	L/SD	Other	Con	Lab	Lib Dem	Other
E-31					43	30	25	2				
E-30	47	34	18	1	42	30	25	2				
E-29	47	32	20	1	43	29	25	3				
E-28	47	32	19	1	42	30	26	2				
E-27	47	32	19	1	42	30	26	2				
E-26	47	32	19	1	42	30	26	2				
E-25	47	32	19	1	42	30	26	2				
E-24	47	33	18	2	42	32	24	2				
E-23	46	33	19	2	42	32	24	2				
E-22	47	32	20	2	42	33	24	2				
E-21	47	33	19	2	42	33	23	2				
E-20	46	34	18	2	42	34	22	2				
E-19	46	34	18	2	42	34	22	2				
E-18	46	34	18	2	42	34	22	2				
E-17	47	34	18	1	42	34	22	2				
E-16	49	33	17	1	42	32	22	2				
E-15	48	33	18	2	43	35	20	2				
E-14	48	32	19	1	43	35	20	2				
E-13	49	31	19	1	44	30	20	2				
E-12	49	31	19	1	44	34	20	2				
E-11	49	31	19	1	44	34	20	2				
E-10	47	30	21	2	44	34	20	2				
E-9	46	30	22	2	43	34	21	2				
E-8	46	30	23	2	43	34	21	2				
E-7	46	30	23	1	42	35	21	2				
E-6	46	29	24	1	42	35	21	2				
E-5	46	29	24	1	43	35	21	2				
E-4	46	27	25	2	43	35	21	2				
E-3	46	27	25	2	44	33	21	2				
E-2	46	26	26	2	43	34	22	2				
E-1	46	27	26	2	42	34	22	2				
GE	44	28	26	2	43	32	23	2				

(Totals may not add up to 100 per cent because of rounding)